MACHIAVELLI

MACHIAVELLI

THE CHIEF WORKS AND OTHERS

TRANSLATED BY ALLAN GILBERT

VOLUME ONE

Non in exercitu, nec in robore . . .

Duke University Press   Durham and London   1989

TABLE OF CONTENTS

VOLUME ONE

VOLUME TWO

VOLUME THREE   Page

ILLUSTRATIONS

PREFACE

The Translation

The first duty of a translator is to bring over into his own tongue what his author says. But this statement is deceptively simple. Shall the rendering be free or close? At its worst, free means a hasty paraphrase, often perversion or absolute error. At its best, freedom exacts such familiarity with the language of the text that its lesser shades of meaning appear in English as idiomatic as is the original Italian. Close may be taken to indicate a word-for-word transfer that is no language, obscuring sense and obliterating distinction. Or close may imply such sympathy with the great work that its significance and even its individual qualities come out in the substituted language. The best free version and the best close version have in common a demand for labor such that on a word or a sentence the translator may multiply the time that went into its original setting down. To defend either free or close rendering, not seldom an attempt to justify slight effort, obscures the translator's prime duty: to do the best he can for his author, whether freely or closely.

Desiring to put before a twentieth-century audience precisely what was penned more than four centuries earlier, the worker is now and then obliged to ask: Can this be what Machiavelli wrote? He may curb his doubts, contenting himself with what is printed in an accepted text; or he may allow himself to attempt textual investigation. The ideal translator first edits the best critical text; I regret that I have not carried on such double labor. Yet I have seen enough to conclude that, heavy as is our debt to Mazzoni and Casella for their text of the literary and historical works (1929), their labors are not final. In some cases I have chosen to follow the first printed editions. Now and then—and this has been more often in works not edited by Mazzoni and Casella—I have translated what seems to be the meaning, always with a note of warning.

The hope to naturalize in his own idiom the stylistic qualities and the spirit of a great work is the translator's will-o'-the-wisp. So seldom does it happen, that the man who believes he has accomplished it is likely to be a victim of self-delusion. Yet one is still in duty bound to strive for some shadow of the original effect. But since a translator can attain no more than a shadow, a reader's competence in a foreign language can be set low—

indeed, very low—before he is well advised to read only versions in his own tongue. As commentaries such versions have their place. But we can suppose them equivalent to their prototypes only when we imagine that translators are stylists with the power of the geniuses they interpret, and assume that the English and Italian languages are alike in their resources. To expect from a translation the effect of an original is to demand an English PRINCE written by Machiavelli himself. My English PRINCE and MANDRAGOLA cannot satisfy such a demand.

Machiavelli subtly exploited the possibilities, including the colloquial qualities, of Florentine speech; such is his command of word order that through inversion he can get emphasis without appearing to use resources not at the command of any normal speaker. Some of his effective devices, such as the verb at the beginning of the sentence, can seldom be carried into English; non-idiomatic English hardly renders idiomatic Italian. I hope readers will forgive something to my effort to secure Machiavellian emphasis. Since most translators of THE PRINCE and the other works make little effort—to my ear—to bring over into their own tongue the qualities of Machiavelli's style, an effort to do so deserves some lenience.

If a reader is to grasp the qualities depending on union of language and content, to appreciate the greatness diffused through every part of a great work and supported continually by such details as the word order, he must turn to the original. In a lifetime of translating, I have learned by experience what poor things translations are; yet I have learned also how much—like many humble things—they are needed. If a translator is entitled to a crown, its jewels are readers who by his effort have been persuaded, or driven, to read the great originals in the languages of their conception.

The Works Included

The present edition includes all of the works on which depends the fame of Machiavelli, and a considerable number of the secondary writings. To attempt completeness would be of little value to most readers of translations. For example, the DISCOURSE ABOUT OUR LANGUAGE, even if the translator were convinced that Machiavelli wrote it, is so concerned with the Italian of Florence that it is of slight value to one who does not know the language. Passages of general application that might be assigned to Niccolò are weaker expressions of what appears in other works, such as the suggestions on the nature of comedy, given more fully, clearly, and characteristically in the Address to the Reader preceding CLIZIA. Other pieces sometimes printed in Italian were evidently never brought to a state approved for publication, such as pages for Books Nine and later of the HISTORY OF FLORENCE. Parts of this material are clearly only notes and sketches. There are also notes collected from reading, probably without special intention, such as the SENTENZE DIVERSE or VARIOUS MAXIMS. Other notes depend largely on conversation and observation; they could be shown to government officials in need of briefing, for example the SUMMARY OF THE AFFAIRS OF THE CITY OF LUCCA and ON THE NATURE OF THE GAULS. The latter bears as well on topics in the DISCOURSES. Such writings shade insensibly into the reports and letters Machiavelli wrote as Florentine secretary, in some of which he is hardly more than penman. Among this varied material, I have tried to select what seemed most interesting and most nearly completed by its author.

In making such a selection, and still more in dealing with the best known of his writings, one meets difficulties rising from Machiavelli's slight interest in printing his works. The first DECENNALE, MANDRAGOLA, and THE ART OF WAR were published during his lifetime. Study of the text of MANDRAGOLA suggests that if he read proof at all, he did it carelessly. Of the major writings left unprinted, we must always ask: Did he leave a manuscript that he considered entirely ready for the printer? What changes did his grandson and others concerned in publication make in the manuscript versions? About the text of any work not published by its author, uncertainty is not to be avoided.

Among the pieces seldom or never translated that I offer, I have been generous with those in verse, and with others of literary quality. The world over, Machiavelli has been known as historian and political thinker; indeed, he himself said he had a passion for politics. But he was also a poet, as is proclaimed by MANDRAGOLA, still sometimes passed over in silence even by learned and devoted students of the political writings, though when it is mentioned it is accepted as perhaps the first, certainly one of the greatest, of Italian comedies. Anyone who reads Machiavelli should have at hand the Secretary's literary works, and not merely because they present a side of the man little known, but because they react powerfully on our judgments of his historical and political compositions.

Notes and Index

The notes are not primarily factual, being intended to suggest something about Machiavelli, such as his method of using Livy's HISTORY, or to explain difficulties in reading.

The index has been especially designed to supply cross references, so that all passages in which Machiavelli deals with any topic can easily be brought together. I have omitted factual matters of secondary importance in order to devote more space to the presentation of Machiavelli's thought.

TEXTS USED IN TRANSLATING

TUTTE LE OPERE STORICHE E LETTERARIE DI NICCOLÒ MACHIAVELLI, *a cura di Guido Mazzoni e Mario Casella, Firenze 1929.*

TUTTE LE OPERE *di Niccolò Machiavelli, a cura di Francesco Flora e di Carlo Cordiè, 1959, 1960 (to be completed).*

LE OPERE DI NICCOLÒ MACHIAVELLI, *per cura di P. Fanfani e di L. Passerini e di G. Milanesi, Firenze 1873-77 (incomplete).*

OPERE DI NICCOLÒ MACHIAVELLI, *Italia 1813.*

OPERE MINORI DI NICCOLÒ MACHIAVELLI, *con note di F. L. Polidori, Firenze 1852.*

IL PRINCIPE DI NICCOLÒ MACHIAVELLI, *Firenze (Giunta) 1532.*

IL PRINCIPE DI NICCOLÒ MACHIAVELLI, *Rome (Blado) 1532.*

DISCORSI DI NICCOLÒ MACHIAVELLI, *Firenze (Giunta) 1531.*

LIBRO DELLA ARTE DELLA GUERRA DI NICCOLÒ MACHIAVELLI, *Firenze (Giunta) 1524.*

COMEDIA DI CALLIMACO & DI LUCRETIA, *[Firenze ?] [1524 ?].*

MANDRAGOLA, *a cura di S. Debenedetti, Strasburgo (Bibliotheca Romanica).*

NICCOLÒ MACHIAVELLI, ISTORIE FIORENTINE, *per cura di Plinio Carli, Firenze 1927.*

Niccolò Machiavelli, LETTERE FAMILIARI *pubblicate per cura di Edoardo Lisio, Firenze 1883.*

Niccolò Machiavelli, LETTERE FAMILIARI, *a cura di Gerolamo Lazzeri, Milano 1923.*

Machiavelli, LETTERE, *[a cura di Giuseppe Lesca], Firenze 1929.*

Niccolò Machiavelli, LETTERE, *a cura di Franco Gaeta, Milano 1961.*

Oreste Tommasini, LA VITA E GLI SCRITTI DI NICCOLÒ MACHIAVELLI, *vol. 2, parte 2, Appendice, Roma 1911.*

Pasquale Villari, NICCOLÒ MACHIAVELLI . . . *illustrati con nuovi documenti, Milano 1912-1914.*

VOLUME ONE

A PROVISION FOR INFANTRY

[A selection from the Preamble]

[Dated 6 December 1506.
This document indicates the partial acceptance by Florence of Machiavelli's idea, prominent in THE PRINCE *and* THE ART OF WAR, *that a country should be defended by her own citizens. Though justice is the foundation of Machiavellian theory, he seldom, as here, speaks directly on it.]*

Whereas it has been observed by the Magnificent and Exalted Signors that all republics which in times past have preserved and increased themselves have always had as their chief basis two things, to wit, justice and arms, in order to restrain and to govern their subjects, and in order to defend themselves from their enemies; and whereas they have observed that your republic is well founded on good and holy laws, and organized for the administration of justice, and that she lacks only to be well provided with arms; and since through long experience, indeed with great expense and danger, she has learned how little hope it is possible to place in foreign and hired arms, because when they are numerous and of high repute they are either unendurable or suspected, and if they are few and without reputation, they are of no use, these signors judge it well that she should be armed with her own weapons and with her own men.

THE PRINCE

List of Chapters

[In a letter of 10 December 1513, Machiavelli says that he had written a little work on princedoms, and that he was still enlarging and revising it. This process of improvement may have gone on for years. Yet in 1513 THE PRINCE, or the part he had then written, was so nearly finished that he was showing it to one of his friends and considering the wisdom of presenting it to Giuliano de' Medici. On Machiavelli's death in 1527 it was still unprinted, appearing only in 1532.

The work falls into several sections. Chapters 1–11 deal with various types of princedom, emphasizing the new prince. In Chapters 12–14, the independent but related topic of warfare is treated, with the dominating belief that a wise ruler relies on an army of citizens rather than of mercenaries.

With Chapter 15 Machiavelli abandons his tractate on princedoms to write nine chapters based on a type of book familiar in his age, the treatise of advice to princes, or de regimine principum. This is the section of THE PRINCE that has roused most opposition. The usual work of the sort was highly moral, exhorting the prince to exemplify all the Christian virtues. Paradoxically, Machiavelli, though asserting the reality of those virtues, declares that a prince who blindly attempts to put them into practice, especially in foreign relations, will ruin himself.

With Chapter 24 begins the last section of the work, making practical application to Italy. First the errors of Italian princes are exposed. The twenty-fifth chapter, on Fortune, though having wide and general application, follows a statement in the preceding chapter that Italian princes should not charge their sufferings to Fortune; Machiavelli, though allowing that goddess enormous power, asserts the effectiveness of human industry and capacity; man is not wholly subject to his environment. In the last chapter Niccolò reveals his prime reason for the whole work; however much he delighted in observing politics, the practical value of statesmanship for liberating Italy from foreign tyranny and from domestic bad government seldom left his mind. The only hope for Italian unity he saw in a wise and strong prince. Patriotism led him to find that delivering prince among the Medici and, in the language of Biblical metaphor, to declare that God had opened the way for that Italian courage in which Petrarch expressed his confidence. This delivering prince of necessity possesses all the abilities detailed through the preceding chapters; his figure dominates the little work.

This deliverer, it is true, does not always appear in the first eleven chapters, which bear marks of Machiavelli's attempt to write the scientific treatise his temperament and his hopes could not permit. The eleventh chapter, on the princedoms of the Church, is a vestige of the original plan for surveying princely states of all sorts; it is connected with the deliverer only in that the Medici family held the papacy, that the ecclesiastical state was important in Italy, and that its rulers, like others, had their share in determining Italy's fate. Something of the sort can be said of other topics scattered through the work. On observing these digressions and fresh starts, we can think THE PRINCE badly planned and inconsequent; we may even grant indulgence to the hasty readers who have felt in the concluding chapter a spirit not justified by what precedes. But as we look further, we judge that as THE PRINCE breaks the strict bounds of the treatise, it takes on the qualities of the unfettered, conversation-like or letter-like familiar essay. The topics of sorrow for Italy, desire for her liberation from foreign king and native tyrant, the power of Fortune, the possibility that effort, courage, and wisdom can overcome the vicissitudes of life, the need for adaptation to immediate environment, courage to abandon traditional formulas, the new rather than the securely established prince—all these recur to give, if not unity, relationship between the parts.

Dominant is the figure of the prince perfect in goodness, in active energy, in prudence, ruling for the common good of all the people of Italy. With such qualities, the prince transcends all human sovereigns, though some of them furnished hints from which to derive the qualities of the ideal ruler. Cesare Borgia showed some of the practical capacity essential for the liberation of the peninsula, though he fell short in prudence, even in courage—and much more in desire for universal happiness. Machiavelli's perfect prince is to be found only in the realm of the imagination. He is the Agamemnon of medieval interpreters of the ILIAD, the Emperor of Dante's COMEDY and MONARCHY, the Godfrey of JERUSALEM DELIVERED, Spenser's King Arthur, "perfected in the politic virtues." Niccolò's delivering ruler is the poet's dream of a monarch who masters the world's harsh realities. Had he remained a mere practical man, Machiavelli would have looked with despair on Italian ills as beyond cure. But from exact yet imaginative observing of good and bad, he gained material for the poet's vision. Whatever else THE PRINCE may be, it is first of all a poem, a poem of trust that human goodness, strength and wisdom, personified in an ideal ruler, can afford man such measure of happiness as follows from good government.]

THE PRINCE

Niccolò Machiavelli to the Magnificent
Lorenzo de'Medici

ALMOST ALWAYS THOSE WHO WISH TO GAIN A
prince's favor come into his presence with such of their possessions
as they hold dearest or in which they see him take most pleasure.
Hence many times princes receive as gifts horses, weapons, cloth of
gold, precious stones, and similar ornaments befitting their greatness.[1]
Wishing, then, for my part to come before Your Magnificence with
some proof that I am your loyal subject, I have found among my
treasures nothing I hold dearer or value so high as my understanding
of great men's actions, gained in my lengthy experience with recent
matters and my continual reading on ancient ones. My observations—which with close attention I have for a long time thought over
and considered, and recently have collected in a little volume—I
send to Your Magnificence. And though I judge this work unworthy to come into your presence, yet I fully trust that in your
kindness you will accept it, considering that I cannot make you a
greater gift than to give you the means for learning, in a very short
time, everything that I, in so many years and with so many troubles
and perils, have discerned and comprehended.

This work of mine I have not adorned or loaded down with
swelling phrases or with bombastic and magnificent words or any
kind of meretricious charm or extrinsic ornament, with which many
writers dress up their products, because I desire either that nothing
shall beautify it, or that merely its unusual matter and the weight of
its subject shall make it pleasing.

No one, I hope, will think that a man of low and humble station
is overconfident when he dares to discuss and direct the conduct of
princes, because, just as those who draw maps of countries put themselves low down on the plain to observe the nature of mountains and
of places high above, and to observe that of low places put themselves
high up on mountain tops, so likewise, in order to discern clearly the

1. *In the first sentence, the prince is singular; in this one, plural. Such shifts occur many*
times in this work.

people's nature, the observer must be a prince, and to discern clearly that of princes, he must be one of the populace.

Accept this little gift, then, I beg Your Magnificence, in the spirit in which I send it; for if you consider it and read it with attention, you will discern in it my surpassing desire that you come to that greatness which Fortune and all of your own abilities promise you. And if from the summit of your lofty station, Your Magnificence ever turns your eyes to these low places, you will perceive how long I continue without desert to bear the burden of Fortune's great and steady malice.

CHAPTER 1. THE VARIOUS TYPES OF PRINCE-DOM AND HOW THEY ARE GAINED

All the states, all the dominions that have had or now have authority over men have been and now are either republics or prince-doms. Princedoms are either hereditary, where the family of their ruler have for a long time been princes, or they are new ones. The new ones are either wholly new, as was Milan for Francesco Sforza, or they are like members joined to the hereditary state of the prince who conquers them, as is the Kingdom of Naples for the King of Spain. Dominions gained in this way are either accustomed to living under a prince or are used to being free. And they are gained either with other men's armies or with one's own, either through Fortune or through strength and wisdom.[1]

1. Strength and wisdom *render the single word* virtù, *which is not equivalent to the English* virtue, *as now generally understood. Commonly Machiavelli uses the word as did his contemporaries and predecessors as far back as Dante. If he is in any way exceptional, it is that now and then he gives it more suggestion of moral excellence than was usual. For the most part, the word has little ethical suggestion, or none at all. I have varied the translation according to the author's meaning.*

CHAPTER 2. HEREDITARY PRINCEDOMS

I shall omit discussing republics because elsewhere I have dis-cussed them at length.[1] I shall concern myself with the princedom only, shall proceed by weaving together the threads mentioned

1. *Perhaps in the* DISCOURSES, *which, however, are not limited to republics,* vs THE PRINCE *is not confined to princedoms.*

above, and shall consider how these princedoms can be governed and preserved.

[Hereditary Rulers Can Avoid Offensive Changes]

I say, then, that hereditary states accustomed to the family of their prince are preserved with many fewer difficulties than are new states; the prince needs only to refrain from going beyond the customs of his forefathers, for otherwise he can let time take care of what happens. Thus, if such a prince uses ordinary care, he always retains his position unless some unusual and excessive force deprives him of it; and if he is deprived of it, he gets it back whenever bad luck strikes the usurper. In Italy the Duke of Ferrara is an example; he repelled the Venetian attacks in 1484 and those of Pope Julius in 1510 for no reason except his long tenure of that lordship. A prince by birth has fewer reasons and less need for giving offence than does a new ruler. Hence an established prince will certainly be better loved, and if excessive vices do not make him hated, it is reasonable that his people naturally will wish him well. The remote origin and long continuance of such sovereignty cover with oblivion recollections of radical changes and their causes, because one change always leaves some projecting bricks for the building-on of the next one.

CHAPTER 3. MIXED PRINCEDOMS

[New Princedoms Difficult]

In the new princedom difficulties appear. First I discuss the princedom not wholly new but a sort of member of an older state, so that the entire dominion can almost be called mixed. The variations in such a member originate chiefly in a natural difficulty evident in all new princedoms. That is, men gladly change their ruler, believing that they will better themselves. This belief makes them take up arms against him, but in so doing they deceive themselves, for later they learn through experience that they have become worse off. This situation results from another natural and normal necessity, namely that a new prince is always obliged to damage his recently gained subjects with soldiers and to oppress them in countless ways necessitated by his recent conquest. Hence you have as enemies all those you have damaged in taking possession of that princedom,[1] and you cannot retain as friends those who put you there, since you cannot give them such satisfaction as they looked forward to, and since you cannot use strong medicines against them because you are indebted to them. Always, even though a new prince is very strong in armies, he must have the inhabitants' favor when moving into a new province. For these reasons Louis XII, King of France, captured Milan quickly and quickly lost her. To take her from him the first time Lodovico's forces alone were enough because the people who opened the city-gates to Louis, finding themselves deceived in their judgment and in the benefit they had looked forward to, could not endure the vexatious actions of the new prince.

[A Second Conquest]

Yet it is true that when a new ruler acquires for the second time districts that have rebelled, he loses them with greater difficulty because, using the rebellion as an opportunity, he is less hesitant to secure himself by punishing the guilty, by learning the truth about those he suspects, and by taking precautions in the weakest places. Thus to cause the French king to lose Milan the first time, it was enough that a mere Duke Lodovico should make a disturbance on the borders,[2] but the second time all the world had to be against him, and his armies had to be destroyed or driven from Italy; this was brought about by the causes mentioned above. Nevertheless, both the first time and the second, Milan was taken from him.

[Securing Conquests]

The general causes for the first loss have been considered. It now remains to tell those of the second, and to see what resources he had against it, and what anybody in his situation might have, to enable him to sustain himself in his acquisition better than did the King of France. I say, then, that those states which, after they are acquired, are united to an old state belonging to him who gains them, are either in the same region and of the same language or they are not. When they are, it is very easy to retain them, especially when they are unused to living in freedom; to hold them securely, the conqueror

1. *Machiavelli often makes such shifts as here, from the impersonal* one *to* you, *as though directly addressing his prince.*
2. *That is, a slight disturbance by a man as weak as Duke Lodovico was enough.*

needs only to wipe out the line of the prince who was ruling them, because as to other things, if their old conditions are preserved and their customs are not diverse, men continue to live quietly. This is true of Burgundy, Brittany, Gascony and Normandy, which have been for a long time with France; and though in language they differ somewhat from her, nevertheless their customs are the same, so they get on easily with one another. So the ruler who acquires such states, if he is determined to keep them, observes two cautions: first, he wipes out the family of their long-established prince; second, he does not change either their laws or their taxes. If he so acts, in a very short time they unite with his old princedom in a single body.[3]

[Conquered States Unlike an Original Dominion]

But when new states are conquered in a province different in language, customs and institutions, then difficulties arise; then a ruler must have great good fortune and great skill if he is to keep them. The chief and most effective means is for the conqueror of such states to go in person to dwell in them. This makes his conquest more lasting and more secure, as it has done for the Turk in Greece. Notwithstanding all the other methods he has practiced for holding her, if he had not gone to Greece to dwell, he could not possibly have held her. When you are on the spot, you see maladies originate and quickly you can cure them; not being there, you learn about them when they are serious and no longer curable. None of your officials, moreover, can plunder the state where you reside; your subjects are pleased with such direct access to their prince: therefore they have more reason to love you if they are disposed to be good, and if disposed to be otherwise, to fear you. Any foreigner who would like to attack such a state feels greater hesitation. Altogether, if a prince dwells in a state, he has a hard time losing it.[4]

[Colonies]

The next best expedient is to send colonies into one or two places to be like fetters for that state, because a prince must either do this or keep there many men-at-arms and infantry. On colonies a prince does not spend much, so without expense to him or with but little

3. In the original of this clause, new states *is referred to by a singular verb and* prince *by a plural pronoun.*

4. *How stupid can princes be? Cf. chap. 24.*

he sends them and keeps them there. He damages only those inhabitants (and they are unimportant in that state) whose fields and
houses he confiscates to make provision for the colonists. Moreover,
those damaged, being scattered and poor, never can harm him: all
the rest on the one hand are undamaged (hence are likely to be quiet)
and on the other hand are in terror of making some mistake, and
therefore of faring like those whose property has been confiscated.
I conclude that such colonies are not expensive, are more loyal than
a garrison and cause less damage. Those who are damaged, being
poor and scattered, as I have said, cannot harm their ruler.

[*No Half-Way Measures*]

In this connection we observe that men should be either treated
generously or destroyed, because they take revenge for slight injuries—
for heavy ones they cannot; hence an injury done to a man should be
such that it does not fear revenge.[5]

[*Garrisons Injurious and Costly*]

If instead of colonies a new prince keeps soldiers in a conquered
province, he spends more by far, since he uses up the income from
that state in holding it; thus his gain becomes a loss. With soldiers
he does much greater damage because he harms the entire state by
changing the quarters of his army. Of this vexation everybody feels
some part, so everybody becomes his enemy; and they are enemies
who can hurt him, since, though oppressed, they remain in their old
homes.[6] In every way, then, to hold a province with soldiers is
unprofitable while to do so with colonies is profitable.

[*How to Treat Lesser Powers*]

It is prudent for a prince who conquers a state in a province
different from his old dominion in the way I have spoken of,[7] to
make himself the head and defender of the lesser potentates in the
vicinity, to strive to weaken the potentates of the province itself, and
to keep on the watch lest in some unexpected way a foreigner as
strong as himself come in. Always such a strong foreigner is brought

5. *This condensed expression means: An injury done to a man should be so nearly total that
the doer need not fear that the injured man will ever become strong enough to take revenge.*
6. *They still have their wealth and their local connections.*
7. *Different in customs and language.*

in by natives who are discontented, either through too much ambition or through fear, as long ago the Romans were brought into
Greece by the Aetolians; indeed into every province that the Romans
subdued they were brought by its inhabitants. The order of things
is that as soon as a strong foreigner enters a province all its inhabitants who are not very strong join him, moved by their envy of other
inhabitants who have been stronger than themselves; hence with
respect to these lesser potentates an intruder has no trouble in winning
them over, because at once they all willingly unite with the state he
has conquered to form a single body. He has only to take care that
they do not get too large forces and too great influence; with his own
forces and their aid, he easily can put down such as are strong, so
that he becomes entirely master of that province. A new ruler who
does not manage this matter well loses very soon what he has acquired
and, while he holds it, suffers countless difficulties and vexations.

[*Roman Procedure*]

The Romans, in the regions they conquered, attended well to
these matters, for they sent colonies, showed favor to those not very
powerful without increasing their power, humbled the powerful, and
did not allow influence there to be grasped by powerful foreigners.
I am sure Greece alone is example enough: there the Romans
showed favor to the Achaians and the Aetolians, humbled the
Macedonian kingdom, and drove out Antiochus; never did the
deserts of the Achaians or the Aetolians gain them permission to
build up a state, nor did Philip's persuasions ever induce the Romans
to be his friends without humbling him; Antiochus' strength could
not make them consent to his holding any territory in that region.

[*Foresight; Putting Off War*]

In these instances the Romans did what all wise princes do: these
take thought not merely for present discords but also for future ones,
and the latter they forestall with every sort of ingenuity; when foreseen
far ahead, discords easily can be remedied, but when you wait until
they are upon you, the medicine is not in time; they have grown
incurable. It is the same as with the hectic fever; the physicians say
that when the disease begins it is easy to cure but hard to recognize,
but in the course of time, when not recognized and treated at the

beginning, it becomes easy to recognize and hard to cure. So it is in things of state; on early recognition (which is granted only to a prudent man), the maladies that spring up in a state can be healed speedily; but when, not being recognized, they are allowed to increase in such a way that everybody recognizes them, they can no longer be remedied. Hence the Romans, seeing their troubles far ahead, always provided against them, and never let them continue in order to avoid a war, because they knew that such a war is not averted but is deferred to the other side's advantage. Hence they chose to wage war against Philip and Antiochus in Greece in order not to have to wage it against them in Italy; yet they could just then have avoided both—something they did not choose to do. Nor did they ever approve what all day is in the mouths of the wise men of our age: to profit from the help of time; but they did profit from that of their own vigor and prudence.[8] Time indeed drives all things onward and can take with him good as well as bad, bad as well as good.

[*The Early Success of King Louis in Italy*]

But let us come back to the King of France, and find out if he did any of the things mentioned. And I shall speak of Louis, and not of Charles, as one whose procedure we can better see, since he longer held control in Italy. You will observe that he did the opposite of what should be done in order to hold a new possession in a province differing from his old dominion.[9] King Louis was brought into Italy by the ambition of the Venetians, who planned to gain control of half Lombardy through his coming. I do not mean to condemn this decision made by the King because, in order to set foot in Italy, and having no allies in that land—on the contrary, as the result of King Charles's policies, all gates were shut against him— he was forced to accept such alliances as he could, and the decision he took would have turned out well, if in his other dealings he had made no mistakes. By occupying Lombardy, then, the King at once regained for the French crown the high reputation Charles had lost it; Genoa yielded, the Florentines became his friends; the Marquis of Mantua, the Duke of Ferrara, the Bentivogli, the Lady of

8. *They were contented to enjoy the profit offered by their own vigor and prudence.*
9. *Different in customs and language, as indicated above.*

Forlì, the Lords of Faenza, of Pesaro, of Rimini, of Camerino, of Piombino, the Lucchese, the Pisans, the Sienese—all these came to greet him and to become his allies. And then the Venetians could see the rashness of their decision; to gain two towns in Lombardy, they made the King master over a third of Italy.

[*What the King Should Have Done*]

Consider now, anyone, with how little trouble the King could have retained his ascendancy in Italy if he had observed the rules given above and kept all his friends secure and protected; for they, being in large numbers and weak and afraid—one of the Church, another of the Venetians—were always obliged to stand by him; and by means of them, he could easily secure himself against anyone there who continued to be strong. But no sooner was he in Milan than he did the opposite, giving aid to Pope Alexander so that he could conquer the Romagna. Nor did he understand that by this policy he was making himself weak—by getting rid of his friends and those who had thrown themselves into his arms—and the Church strong, by adding to the spiritual power which gives her such great influence, so much temporal power. Yet having made his first mistake, he was forced to go on until, to put an end to Alexander's ambition and keep him from becoming ruler of Tuscany, the King was forced to come into Italy. Nor was it enough for him to make the Church strong and to get rid of his own friends, but in his desire for the Kingdom of Naples he divided it with the King of Spain; whereas at first he was master of Italy, he gave himself an equal there, so that the ambitious men of this country and those dissatisfied with him had somewhere to turn; and whereas he could have left in that kingdom a king who would pay him tribute, he took him out of it, in order to put there one who could drive out even himself.[10]

[*Do Not Attempt What Is Beyond Your Own Unaided Power*]

Truly it is very natural and normal to wish to conquer, and when men do it who can, they always will be praised, or not blamed. But when they cannot and try to do so all the same, herein lies their error and their blame. If the French king, then, could with his own forces have attacked Naples, he should have done so; if he could not attack

10. *Instead of leaving in the Kingdom of Naples a weak ruler of that territory only, he put there the King of Spain, strong because of his other dominions.*

with his own forces, he should not have divided the Kingdom. If his partition of Lombardy with the Venetians deserved excuse, since by means of it he set foot in Italy, the other partition deserved reproach, not being excused by such necessity.

[King Louis' Six Mistakes]

So far, then, Louis had made these five mistakes: he had destroyed the lesser powers, had increased in Italy the might of one already powerful, had brought into the country a foreigner of great strength, had not come there to live, and had not brought in colonies. Even these mistakes, during his lifetime,[11] might not have injured him if he had not made a sixth mistake, that of taking their dominion from the Venetians. If he had not made the Church strong and had not brought Spain into Italy, to humble Venice would have been reason/ able and necessary, but having made his earlier decisions, he should never have agreed to her ruin. As long as she was powerful, she would have kept Spain and the Church far from any enterprise in Lombardy,[12] both because she would not have agreed to such an enterprise without becoming mistress of the province herself and because Spain and the Pope would not have tried to take Lombardy from France to give their conquest to Venice; for attacking both France and Venice the other two would not have had courage.[13] If anybody says: 'King Louis granted the Romagna to Alexander and the Kingdom to Spain in order to avoid a war,' I answer, with the reasons given above, that an evil never should be allowed to continue for the sake of escaping war, because you do not escape it but put it off to your disadvantage. And if some others allege the King's promise to the Pope to carry on that affair for him in return for the dissolution of his marriage and Rouen's hat,[14] I answer with what I say below on princes' agreements and how they ought to be kept.[15] King Louis has lost Lombardy, then, through not keeping any of those rules kept by others who have taken provinces which they intended to hold. And this is no miracle, but very normal and reasonable.

11. *Is it possible that Machiavelli wrote this passage after the death of Louis XII in 1515?*
12. *If the Venetians had been strong, the Pope and the King of Spain would not have put in northern Italy the army that fought the French at Ravenna.*
13. *The Pope and the Spanish would not have attacked an alliance of France and the Venetians.*
14. *The Bishop of Rouen was made cardinal by Pope Alexander VI.*
15. *Chap. 18.*

[Machiavelli's Reply to Rouen]

On this subject I talked with Rouen at Nantes, when Valentino (for that was the popular name for Cesare Borgia, Pope Alexander's son) was taking over the Romagna. For the reasons I have given, when the Cardinal of Rouen said to me that the Italians know nothing of war, I answered that the French know nothing of politics, because if they knew anything, they would not let the Church attain such strength. And experience shows that her strength in Italy, and that of Spain, have been caused by the King of France, and his ruin caused by them.

[Powerful Helpers Feared]

From this we get a general rule that never or seldom deceives us: namely, he who is the reason for another's growing powerful falls; because he creates that power either with ingenuity or with force, and both of these are feared by the one who has grown powerful.

CHAPTER 4. WHY DARIUS' KINGDOM THAT ALEXANDER CONQUERED DID NOT RE/ VOLT FROM HIS SUCCESSORS AFTER HIS DEATH

[Two Types of State]

Considering the difficulties in holding a state newly gained, we must wonder about the empire of Alexander the Great. He became lord of Asia in a few years and died when he had scarcely conquered it; so it would seem reasonable that the entire state should have re/ belled; nevertheless Alexander's successors retained it, and they had no trouble in holding it except what developed among themselves, through their own ambition. To explain this, I say that the prince/ doms of which we have any record are governed in two different ways: in one there is a prince, and all the others are as servants who, through his favor and appointment, assist as agents in governing the kingdom. In the other, there is a prince, with barons who hold their rank not through the ruler's favor but through their ancient blood. Such barons as these have states and subjects of their own, who acknowledge them as their lords and have for them a natural affection. States governed by a prince and his servants think their prince more powerful, because in all his territory they receive no superior except him; and if they obey some other man, they consider him an agent and official, and feel for him no personal love.

[*Turkey and France as Examples*]

Examples of these two different methods of governing in our times are the Turk and the King of France. The whole monarchy of the Turk is governed by one ruler; the others are his servants; dividing his kingdom into sanjaks, he sends them various adminis-trators, and changes and varies these as he likes. But the King of France is placed amidst a long-established multitude of lords' ac-knowledged by their own subjects and loved by them; such lords have their vested rights; these the king cannot take from them without danger to himself. On considering, then, both of these countries, you see that there will be difficulty in gaining the Turk's country but, when it is conquered, great ease in holding it. So, on the contrary, you see that in some respects the country of France can be more easily occupied but that it can be held only with great difficulty.

[*Turkey Hard to Conquer, Easy to Hold*]

The cause of difficulty in gaining possession of the Turk's king-dom is that an invader cannot be called in by the nobles of that kingdom, or hope through the rebellion of those around the Turk to make the undertaking easier. This follows from the reasons given above because, all the officials being slaves and bound to him, they are harder to bribe; and if indeed they are bribed, little profit can be expected from them, since they cannot lead the people after them, for the reasons given. Hence, anyone who assails the Turk must reckon on finding a united country and must depend more on his own forces than on revolt by others. But when once the Turk is conquered and so completely defeated in battle that he cannot remake his armies, there is nothing more to dread, except the prince's family. When this is wiped out, not a person is left whom the conqueror needs to fear, since none of the others has influence with the people; and as before his victory the invader could rest no hope on them, so after it he need not fear them.

1. *Various modern texts have here the words* in that state, *found in manuscripts but not in the editions of 1532.*

[*France Easy to Conquer, Hard to Hold*]

The opposite is true in kingdoms organized like that of France, because you easily can enter them if you win over some of the barons of the kingdom, for you always find malcontents and those who wish for revolution. These, for the reasons aforesaid, can open your road into that country and help you toward an easy victory. This situation, then, if you try to maintain yourself, brings in its train countless difficulties, both with those who have aided you and with those you have overcome. It is not enough to wipe out the family of the prince, because there still remain those lords who will become the leaders of new rebellions; and since you can neither satisfy them nor wipe them out, you lose that state whenever their opportunity comes.

[*A Parallel in Roman History*]

Now if you consider the nature of Darius' government, you find it like the Turk's kingdom; therefore Alexander's first necessity was to overthrow him wholly and to deprive him of the open country.[2] After this victory, Darius being dead, that state was secure to Alexander, for the reasons discussed above. And his successors, if they had been united, could have enjoyed it at their ease, nor did any rebellions arise in that kingdom except what they themselves stirred up. But countries organized like that of the French king cannot be occupied in such great quiet. This was the cause of the numerous revolts of Spain, of Gaul, and of Greece against the Romans, resulting from the numerous princedoms in those lands; for as long as there continued any tradition of them, always because of it the Romans were uncertain in their possession; but when that tradition was wiped out by the power and permanence of the Empire, they became secure possessors there. And when later the Romans were fighting among themselves, each one of them could lead after him part of those provinces, according to the authority he had gained in them; and the provinces, since the families of their ancient lords had been wiped out, accepted as rulers none but the Romans.

2. *The country as distinguished from walled cities. Darius could no longer keep an army in the field. Cf.* PRINCE *10.*

[*Different Countries, Different Problems*]

Considering then, all these things, no one should be astonished at the ease with which Alexander retained control in Asia, and at the difficulties others have had in keeping what they have gained, such as Pyrrhus and many besides. This does not result from the great or little ability of the conqueror but from diversity in their subject matter.

CHAPTER 5. HOW STATES OR PRINCIPALITIES ARE TO BE MANAGED THAT, BEFORE THEY WERE CONQUERED, LIVED UNDER THEIR OWN LAWS

[*Three Methods*]

When those states that are conquered in the way aforesaid[1] are accustomed to living under their own laws and in liberty, you can hold them in three ways. The first: lay them waste. The second: go to dwell there in person. The third: let them live under their own laws, taking tribute from them and setting up within them a government by a small number who keep them constantly your friends;[2] because such a government, having been brought into being by the new prince, knows that it cannot stand without his friendship and power and must do everything to support him; for by means of her own citizens a conqueror more easily holds a city accustomed to freedom than in any other way, if he decides to preserve her. As examples there are the Spartans and the Romans. The Spartans held Athens and Thebes by setting up in them a government by a small number; yet they lost them. The Romans, in order to hold Capua, Carthage, and Numantia, destroyed them, and did not lose them. They tried to hold Greece almost as the Spartans did, making her free and allowing her to keep her own laws, but they did not succeed. Hence they were forced to destroy many cities of that province in order to hold her; because in truth there is no certain way for holding such states except destruction.

1. *As an addition to a state already possessed (chap. 3).*
2. *A government by a small number of citizens of the conquered states who will keep those states loyal to the conquerors.*

[*The Spirit of Liberty*]

And he who becomes master of a city used to being free and does not destroy her can expect to be destroyed by her, because always she has as a pretext in rebellion the name of liberty and her old customs, which never through either length of time or benefits are forgotten. And in spite of anything that can be done or foreseen, unless citizens are disunited or dispersed, they do not forget that name and those institutions, and in any emergency instantly they run back to them, as Pisa did a hundred years after she had been reduced to servitude by the Florentines. But cities or provinces used to living under a prince, when his family is wiped out—since on one side they are used to obeying and on the other do not have their old prince—do not agree to set up as prince one of their fellow citizens. Live as free men they cannot. Hence, they are slower to take up arms, and with more ease a prince can gain their support and make himself sure of them. But in republics there is more life, more hate, greater longing for revenge; they are not permitted to rest—nor can they be—by the recollection of their ancient liberty; so the surest way is to wipe them out or to live among them.

CHAPTER 6. NEW PRINCEDOMS GAINED THROUGH A MAN'S OWN ARMIES AND ABILITY

[*Imitation of Great Men*]

No one should be astonished if in the following discussion of completely new princedoms[1] and of the prince and of government, I bring up the noblest examples. Because, since men almost always walk in the paths beaten by others and carry on their affairs by imitating—even though it is not possible to keep wholly in the paths of others or to attain the ability of those you imitate—a prudent man will always choose to take paths beaten by great men and to imitate those who have been especially admirable, in order that if his ability does not reach theirs, at least it may offer some suggestion of it; and he will act like prudent archers, who, seeing that the mark they plan

1. *The princedom wholly new is the second class mentioned at the beginning of chap. 3. Chaps. 3, 4, and 5 deal with states added by their conqueror, whether prince or republic, to an established dominion.*

to hit is too far away and knowing what space can be covered by the power of their bows, take an aim much higher than their mark, not in order to reach with their arrows so great a height, but to be able, with the aid of so high an aim, to attain their purpose.

[*Ability versus Fortune*]

I say then, that in princedoms wholly new, where the prince is new, there is more or less difficulty in keeping them, according as the prince who acquires them is more or less able. And because transformation from private person into prince takes for granted either ability or Fortune, either of these two evidently in part diminishes many difficulties; nevertheless, he who depends least on Fortune sustains himself longest. Greater facility is also developed by such a prince when, not having other states, he is constrained to come in person to dwell in his new possession.

[*Examples of Ability*]

But coming to those who through their own ability and not through Fortune have been transformed into princes, I say that the most admirable are Moses, Cyrus, Romulus, Theseus, and the like. And though Moses should not be discussed, since he was a mere executor of things laid down for him by God, nevertheless he ought to be exalted, if only for the grace that made him worthy to speak with God. But let us look at Cyrus and the others who gained or founded kingdoms. You will find them all amazing; and if you look at their actions and their individual methods, they seem not different from those of Moses, who had so great a teacher. And on inspecting their actions and their lives, we see that they had from Fortune nothing more than opportunity, which gave them matter into which they could introduce whatever form they chose; and without opportunity, their strength of will would have been wasted, and without such strength the opportunity would have been useless. It was, then, necessary for Moses that the people of Israel be in Egypt, enslaved and downtrodden by the Egyptians, so that to escape from bondage they would prepare their minds for following him. It was essential that Romulus should not live in Alba and should be exposed at birth, if he was going to be king of Rome and the founder of that city as his home. It was needful for Cyrus that the Persians be disgusted with the rule of the Medes, and the Medes made soft and effeminate through long peace. It would have been impossible for Theseus to show his ability if the Athenians had not been scattered. Their opportunities, then, made these men prosper, since their surpassing abilities enabled them to recognize their opportunities. As a result, their countries were exalted and became very prosperous. Those who become princes through exacting courses, like these men, gain the princedom with difficulty but hold it with ease.

[*Introducing New Institutions*]

Their difficulties in gaining the princedom partly result from the new institutions and customs they are forced to introduce, in order to establish their rule and their safety. So they should observe that there is nothing more difficult to plan or more uncertain of success or more dangerous to carry out than an attempt to introduce new institutions, because the introducer has as his enemies all those who profit from the old institutions, and has as lukewarm defenders all those who will profit from the new institutions. This lukewarmness results partly from fear of their opponents, who have the laws on their side, partly from the incredulity of men, who do not actually believe new things unless they see them yielding solid proof. Hence whenever those who are enemies have occasion to attack, they do it like partisans, and the others resist lukewarmly; thus lukewarm subjects and innovating prince are both in danger.

[*The Unarmed Prophet; Savonarola*]

It is necessary, then, in order to give a good account of this matter, to investigate whether these innovators stand by their own strength or whether they depend on others, that is, if in carrying on their work they need to entreat or if they are strong enough to compel. In the first case, they always have a hard time and accomplish nothing, but when they depend on their own resources and are strong enough to compel, then they are seldom in danger. This is the reason why all armed prophets win, and unarmed ones fall. Because, in addition to what has been said, the people are by nature variable; to convince them of a thing is easy; to hold them to that conviction is hard. Therefore a prophet must be ready, when they no longer believe, to make them believe by force. Moses, Cyrus, Theseus, and Romulus could not have gained long-continued observance for their constitutions if they had been unarmed. In our times Fra Girolamo Savonarola was unarmed; hence he was destroyed amid his institutions when they were still new, as soon as the multitude ceased to believe him, because he had no way to keep firm those who had once believed or to make the unbelieving believe.

[*The Success of Able Men*]

Therefore such able men as I have mentioned have great difficulty as they go forward, for all their dangers are along the road and by their own might they must overcome them. But after they have overcome them and when they are revered, having wiped out those who envy them their lofty position, they are powerful, firm, honored, prosperous.

[*Hiero of Syracuse*]

To such exalted instances I am going to add a lesser instance, yet he has some relation to them, so I intend him to do duty for all of this kind; he is Hiero of Syracuse. This man, though merely a citizen, became prince of Syracuse, yet he owed nothing at all to Fortune except opportunity. The Syracusans when in distress chose him as their general, and in that position he showed himself worthy to be made their prince. Indeed he showed such great ability, even in a private station, that he who writes of him says that "he lacked nothing needed for being a king except the kingdom." He did away with the old army; he organized a new one; he abandoned long-standing alliances; he gained new ones; and when he had alliances and soldiers that were his own, he could on such a foundation build any and every building. So he underwent much labor in gaining and little in keeping.

CHAPTER 7. NEW PRINCEDOMS GAINED WITH OTHER MEN'S FORCES AND THROUGH FORTUNE

[*The Difficulties of an Inexperienced Ruler*]

Those who—though only citizens—become princes simply through Fortune, with little effort become so, but with much effort sustain themselves, for they have no difficulties along the road, because they fly over it, but all the difficulties appear when they are settled. Princes are of this sort when a state is granted to anybody either for money or as a favor from him who grants it, as happened to many in Greece in the cities of Ionia and the Hellespont, where they were made princes by Darius so they would hold those cities for his security and glory. So were set up also those emperors who, though mere citizens, through bribery of the soldiers attained the imperial throne. Such rulers depend solely on a king-maker's will and Fortune—two things most uncertain and unstable; they do not know how to and cannot hold the rank bestowed on them. They do not know how because, if a man is not of great intelligence and vigor, it is not reasonable, when he has always lived in a private station, that he should know how to command; they cannot, because they do not have forces that are sure to be friendly and faithful. Besides, these states that come of a sudden, like all things in nature that spring up and grow quickly, cannot have roots and other related parts. Hence the first unfavorable weather destroys them. Such men as I have spoken of, who so swiftly have become princes, can survive only if they are of such capacity that what Fortune has put into their laps they can straightway take measures for keeping, and those foundations that other princes laid before gaining their positions[1] they can lay afterward. On both these ways that have been mentioned (that is, on becoming prince either through strength and wisdom or through Fortune) I intend to bring forward two instances within the days of our recollection: Francesco Sforza and Cesare Borgia.

[Francesco Sforza]

Francesco, by the necessary methods and by means of his great ability, though born to a private station, became Duke of Milan; and what with a thousand exertions he gained, with little effort he kept.

[Cesare Borgia]

On the other side, Cesare Borgia, called by the people Duke Valentino, gained his position through his father's Fortune and through her lost it,[2] notwithstanding that he made use of every means

1. The others are the princes of chap. 6.
2. In spite of the praise of Valentino that follows, this clause cannot be ignored; Cesare did

and action possible to a prudent and vigorous man for putting down his roots in those states that another man's arms and Fortune bestowed on him. As I say above, he who does not lay his foundations beforehand can perhaps through great wisdom and energy lay them afterward, though he does so with trouble for the architect and danger to the building. So on examining all the steps taken by the Duke, we see that he himself laid mighty foundations for future power. To discuss these steps is not superfluous; indeed I for my part do not see what better precepts I can give a new prince than the example of Duke Valentino's actions. If his arrangements did not bring him success, the fault was not his, because his failure resulted from an unusual and utterly malicious stroke of Fortune.[3]

[Pope Alexander VI Attempts to Make Cesare a Prince]

Alexander VI,[4] in his attempt to give high position to the Duke his son, had before him many difficulties, present and future. First, he saw no way in which he could make him lord of any state that was not a state of the Church, yet if the Pope tried to take such a state from the Church, he knew that the Duke of Milan and the Venetians would not allow it because both Faenza and Rimini were already under Venetian protection. He saw, besides, that the weapons of Italy, especially those of which he could make use, were in the hands of men who had reason to fear the Pope's greatness; therefore he could not rely on them, since they were all among the Orsini and the Colonnesi and their allies. He therefore was under the necessity of disturbing the situation and embroiling the states of Italy so that he could safely master part of them.[5] This he found easy since, luckily for him, the Venetians, influenced by other reasons, had set out to get the French to come again into Italy. He not merely did not oppose their coming; he made it easier by dissolving the early marriage of King Louis. The King then marched into Italy with the Venetians' aid and Alexander's consent; and he was no sooner in Milan than the Pope got soldiers from him for an

---

not in getting his state make a great display of his own ability, as did Francesco Sforza, just mentioned. *Cf.* WORDS TO BE SPOKEN ON PROVIDING MONEY.

3. Namely that, as is said later in this chapter, he was, when his father died, himself very sick.
4. Roderigo Borgia, Alexander VI, Pope from 1492 to 1503.
5. Here I follow the Giunta edition, Florence, 1532.

attempt on Romagna; these the King granted for the sake of his own reputation.[6]

[*Borgia Determines to Depend on Himself*]

Having taken Romagna, then, and suppressed the Colonnesi, the Duke, in attempting to keep the province and to go further, was hindered by two things: one, his own forces, which he thought disloyal; the other, France's intention.[7] That is, he feared that the Orsini forces which he had been using would fail him and not merely would hinder his gaining but would take from him what he had gained, and that the King would treat him in the same way. With the Orsini, he had experience of this when after the capture of Faenza he attacked Bologna, for he saw that they turned cold over that attack. And as to the King's purpose, the Duke learned it when, after taking the dukedom of Urbino, he invaded Tuscany— an expedition that the King made him abandon. As a result, he determined not to depend further on another man's armies and Fortune.

[*The Duke Destroys His Disloyal Generals*]

The Duke's first act to that end was to weaken the Orsini and Colonnesi parties in Rome by winning over to himself all their adherents who were men of rank, making them his own men of rank and giving them large subsidies; and he honored them, according to their stations, with military and civil offices, so that within a few months their hearts were emptied of all affection for the Roman parties, and it was wholly transferred to the Duke. After this, he waited for a good chance to wipe out the Orsini leaders, having scattered those of the Colonna family; such a chance came to him well and he used it better. When the Orsini found out, though late, that the Duke's and the Church's greatness was their ruin, they held a meeting at Magione, in Perugian territory. From that resulted the rebellion of Urbino, the insurrections in Romagna, and countless dangers for the Duke, all of which he overcame with the aid of the French. Thus having got back his reputation, but not trusting France or other outside forces, in order not to have to put them to a test, he turned to trickery. And he knew so well how

6. *Depending on his agreement with the Pope, mentioned near the end of chap. 3.*
7. *The King of France.*

to falsify his purpose that the Orsini themselves, by means of Lord Paulo, were reconciled with him (as to Paulo the Duke did not omit any sort of gracious act to assure him, giving him money, clothing and horses) so completely that their folly took them to Sinigaglia into his hands. Having wiped out these leaders, then, and changed their partisans into his friends, the Duke had laid very good foundations for his power, holding all the Romagna along with the dukedom of Urbino, especially since he believed he had made the Romagna his friend and gained the support of all those people, through their getting a taste of well-being.[8]

[Peace in Romagna; Remirro de Orco]

Because this matter is worthy of notice and of being copied by others, I shall not omit it. After the Duke had seized the Romagna and found it controlled by weak lords who had plundered their subjects rather than governed them, and had given them reason for disunion, not for union, so that the whole province was full of thefts, brawls, and every sort of excess, he judged that if he intended to make it peaceful and obedient to the ruler's arm, he must of necessity give it good government. Hence he put in charge there Messer Remirro de Orco, a man cruel and ready, to whom he gave the most complete authority. This man in a short time rendered the province peaceful and united, gaining enormous prestige. Then the Duke decided there was no further need for such boundless power, because he feared it would become a cause for hatred; so he set up a civil court in the midst of the province, with a distinguished presiding judge, where every city had its lawyer. And because he knew that past severities had made some men hate him, he determined to purge such men's minds and win them over entirely by showing that any cruelty which had gone on did not originate with himself but with the harsh nature of his agent. So getting an opportunity for it, one morning at Cesena he had Messer Remirro laid in two pieces in the public square with a block of wood and a bloody sword near him. The ferocity of this spectacle left those people at the same time gratified and awe-struck.[9]

8. *Guicciardini agrees with Machiavelli in his accounts of good government in the Romagna and of the devotion of the people to Valentino (*HISTORY OF FLORENCE, *chap. 24, p. 266, Bari 1931;* HISTORY OF ITALY, *bk. 6, p. 163, Venice 1592).*

9. *Remirro was executed when Machiavelli was in Cesena as Florentine agent at Cesare's*

[*Cesare Borgia and the King of France*]

But let us turn back to where we left off. When the Duke had become very powerful and in part secure against present perils, since he was armed as he wished and had in great part destroyed those forces that, as neighbors, could harm him, he still, if he intended to continue his course, had before him the problem of the King of France, because he knew that the King, who too late had become aware of his own mistake, would not tolerate further conquest. For this reason the Duke was looking for new alliances and wavering in his dealings with France, as when the French moved upon the Kingdom of Naples against the Spaniards who were besieging Gaeta. And his intention was to make himself secure against them; in this he would quickly have succeeded if Alexander had lived. So these were his ways of acting as to present things.

[*The Duke Looks Ahead*]

But as to future ones, he had to fear, first of all, that the next man in control of the Church would not be friendly to him but would try to take from him what Alexander had given. Against this he planned to secure himself by four methods: first, to wipe out all the families of those lords he had dispossessed, in order to take away from the Pope that opportunity; second, to win to his side all the men of rank in Rome, as I have said, so that by means of them he could keep the Pope in check; third, to render the College as much his own as he could;[10] fourth, to conquer so large an empire, before the Pope died, that he could by himself resist a first attack. Of these four things, on Alexander's death he had completed three; the fourth was almost as good as complete: of the dispossessed rulers he had killed as many as he could reach, and very few escaped; the Roman men of rank he had won over; and in the College he had a very large party; and as to further conquest, he had planned to become ruler of Tuscany, he already possessed Perugia and Piombino, and Pisa he had taken under his protection. And as soon as he no longer needed to defer to the King of France (and he would not

---

court. *In his report to the government at home he first tells of Remirro's imprisonment and of popular feeling against him (*LEGATION *11. 81, Letter of 23 Dec. 1502), and then of the execution (11. 82, Letter of 26 Dec. 1502). Evidently Machiavelli thought the execution not undeserved.*

10. *The body of cardinals, which elects the pope.*

need to do so much longer, since already the French were deprived of the Kingdom by the Spaniards, in such a way that each of them would have to buy his friendship), he would jump into Pisa.[11] After this, Lucca and Siena would yield at once, partly through envy of the Florentines, partly through fear. The Florentines would have no recourse. If he had carried out these plans (and he would have carried them out the very year when Alexander died), he would have gained such forces and such reputation that he could stand by his own strength and would no longer rely on other men's Fortune and forces, but on his own vigor and ability.

[*The Duke Foresaw Much, but Not Everything*]

But Alexander died five years after the Duke first drew his sword. He left Cesare with the province of Romagna alone secure, with all the others in the air, between two very powerful hostile armies, and sick unto death. Yet there was in the Duke so much courage and so much ability, and so well he understood how men can be gained or lost, and so strong were the foundations which in so short a time he had laid that, though alone, if those armies had not been upon him or if he had been in health, he would have mastered every difficulty. And that his foundations were good, we see; for Romagna continued waiting for him more than a month; in Rome, though but half alive, he was secure; and though the Baglioni, Vitelli, and Orsini came into Rome, they did not proceed further against him; if he could not set up as pope the one he wanted, at least he could make sure it would not be someone he did not want. If on Alexander's death he had been in health, everything would have been easy for him. And he said to me himself, on Julius II's accession-day, that he had imagined what could happen when his father died, and for everything he had found a solution, except he had never imagined that at the time of that death he too would be close to dying.

[*The Duke as a Model for a New Prince*]

Having observed, then, all the Duke's actions, I for my part cannot censure him. On the contrary, I think I am right in bringing him forward in this way as worthy of imitation by all those who through Fortune and by means of another's forces attain a ruler's

11. *Jump into Pisa. This figure for a rapid invasion is used by Ariosto in* THE FIVE CANTOS *1. 108.*

position. Since his courage was great and his purpose high, he could not conduct himself otherwise; and his plans were opposed only by the shortness of Alexander's life and his own sickness. Anyone, therefore, who thinks it necessary in his princedom newly won to secure himself against his enemies, to win friends, to conquer by force or by fraud, to make himself loved and feared by the people, followed and respected by the soldiers, to destroy those who can or are likely to injure you,[12] to replace ancient customs with new ways, to be severe and agreeable, magnanimous and liberal, to destroy disloyal armies, to raise new ones, to keep the friendship of kings and of princes in such a way that they are compelled either to aid you with a good grace or to harm you with reluctance, cannot find more recent instances than this man's actions.

[Do Not Trust Men You Have Harmed. Cesare's Blunder]

The single thing for which we can blame him is the election of Julius as pope. In this he made a bad choice because, as I have said, if he could not set up a pope to suit himself, he could exclude from the papacy whomever he wished. He should never have let the papacy go to any cardinal whom he had injured or who, on be coming pope, would need to fear him, because men do injury through either fear or hate. Those whom Cesare had injured were, among others, San Piero ad Vincula, Colonna, San Giorgio, and Ascanio. Any of the others on becoming pope would need to fear him, except Rouen and the Spaniards; the latter were made secure by their alliance and indebtedness, the former by his power, since he was closely connected with the kingdom of France. Therefore the Duke should by all means have chosen a Spaniard as pope,[13] and if he could not, should have agreed to Rouen not to San Piero ad Vincula. To believe that new benefits make men of high rank forget old injuries is to deceive oneself. In this choice, then, the Duke blundered, and it caused his final ruin.

12. *An unusually striking instance of Machiavelli's habit of changing from the impersonal to direct address to his reader, the prince.*

13. *This condensed expression means* tried to bring about the appointment as pope. *Cesare had no direct power. By allowing him greater influence than do some recent historians, Machiavelli makes Cesare's mistake so much the more serious. See* LEGATION 13. 10 *and* 18, *below.*

CHAPTER 8. MEN WHO GAIN A PRINCEDOM THROUGH WICKED DEEDS

[*Two Ways for Rising from a Private Station*]

Because a man born in a private station may make himself prince in two other ways which cannot be attributed entirely to Fortune or to strength and prudence, I do not wish to omit them, though I might discuss one of them more at length where I deal with republics.[1] The two are these: either in some wicked and abominable way a man rises to the princedom, or a private citizen with the aid of his fellow-citizens becomes prince of his native city. Taking up the first way, I shall explain it through two examples, one old, the other recent, without entering otherwise into the merits of this method, because I judge the two[2] enough for imitation by one forced to use it.

[*Agathocles' Success*]

Agathocles the Sicilian, not merely of private but of low and abject station, became king of Syracuse. A potter's son, in every stage of his career he lived a wicked life. Yet while acting wickedly he displayed such strength of mind and body that, entering the army, he rose through its grades to be praetor of Syracuse. Being settled in that rank and determined to become prince and to keep by force and without indebtedness to anyone what would have been granted him by consent,[3] and having made an agreement about this plan of his with Hamilcar, the Carthaginian, who with his armies was campaigning in Sicily, one morning he assembled the people and the Senate of Syracuse as if he were going to consider things relating to the state; and at a given sign he had his soldiers kill all the senators and the richest of the people. These dead, he grasped and held the rule of that city without any opposition from the citizens. And though the Carthaginians twice defeated and finally besieged him, he not merely defended his city but, leaving part of his soldiers for defense against the siege, with the others he attacked

---

1. *Annotators indicate that this is done in the* DISCOURSES, *though none of the chapters they specify are strikingly applicable, and the* DISCOURSES *are not limited to republics (e.g., 2. 24). Did Machiavelli write (or at least plan) a work called* THE REPUBLIC, *which has disappeared?*

2. *Here again I follow the editions of 1532 which give a plural.*

3. *He could have become prince with the consent of the senate and the people but preferred to incur no indebtedness to them.*

Africa; thus in a short time he freed Syracuse from siege and brought the Carthaginians to extreme destitution; they were obliged to make peace with him, to be satisfied with the possession of Africa, and to abandon Sicily to Agathocles.

[*Wickedness Does Not Bring True Glory*]

He who considers, then, the actions and the life of this man, will see nothing or but little that he can ascribe to Fortune, since, as was said above, not through anybody's help but through the grades of the army, which he won with a thousand hardships and dangers, he attained the princedom, and then with many spirited and dan-gerous actions kept it. It cannot, however, be called virtue to kill one's fellow-citizens, to betray friends, to be without fidelity, without mercy, without religion; such proceedings enable one to gain sover-eignty, but not fame. If we consider Agathocles' ability in entering into and getting out of dangers,[4] and his greatness of mind in enduring and overcoming adversities, we cannot see why he must be judged inferior to any of the most excellent generals. Never-theless, his outrageous cruelty and inhumanity together with his countless wicked acts do not permit him to be honored among the noblest men. We cannot, then, attribute to Fortune or to virtue what he accomplished without the one or the other.

[*Liverotto's Treachery at Fermo*]

In our times, when Alexander VI was reigning, Liverotto of Fermo—who many years before had been left when little without a father—was brought up by his maternal uncle, named Giovanni Fogliani, and in the early years of his youth was placed to serve as a soldier under Paulo Vitelli, in order that, well versed in that pro-fession, he might attain some excellent position in an army. Paulo afterward dying, he served under Vitellozzo his brother; in a very short time, being quickwitted and vigorous in body and mind, he became the first man in his army. But since he thought it servile to be a subordinate, he determined, with the aid of some citizens of Fermo who preferred slavery rather than freedom for their native city, and with the help of the Vitelleschi, to capture Fermo. So he wrote to Giovanni Fogliani that, having been many years away from

---

4. *In this clause,* virtue (virtù) *is courage and prudence. In the sentence immediately preceding and that following, moral excellence is also included.*

home, he wished to come to visit him and his native city and also to inspect his inheritance; and—because he had not striven for anything except to gain honor—in order that his fellow citizens might see that he had not spent his time without results, he wished to come with honor escorted by a hundred horsemen from among his friends and servants; and he begged his uncle to be so kind as to arrange that the people of Fermo would receive him honorably. This would bring honor not merely to him but to Giovanni, whose foster child he was. In no way, thereupon, did Giovanni fall short in any duty he owed his nephew, and he had the people of Fermo receive him honorably. Liverotto then took up his lodging in his own mansion. There, having spent some days and carefully made the secret arrange-ments that his future wickedness required, he gave a splendid banquet, to which he invited Giovanni Fogliani and all the leading men of Fermo. When the meal was finished and all the other matters customary at such banquets, Liverotto, according to plan, started certain serious discourses, talking of Pope Alexander's greatness and of Cesare his son and of their enterprises. After Giovanni and the others had replied to these discourses, he at once rose up, saying these were things to speak of in a place more secret; and he withdrew to a chamber to which Giovanni and all the other citizens followed. No sooner were they seated than, from secret places in the room, out came soldiers who killed Giovanni and all the others. After this slaughter, Liverotto mounted his horse and overran the city and besieged in the Palace the chief magistrates, so that for fear they were compelled to obey him and to confirm a government of which he made himself prince.

[*Liverotto's Success*]

When all those were dead who, if they had been discontented, could have injured him, he strengthened himself with new dispo-sitions both civil and military in such a way that for a year, during which he held the princedom, not merely was he safe in the city of Fermo, but he had become an object of fear to all his neighbors. His overthrow, indeed, would have been as difficult as that of Agathocles if he had not let Cesare Borgia deceive him at Sinigaglia when, as I said above, the Duke captured the Orsini and Vitelli. There Liverotto too was taken, a year after the parricide he committed, and along with Vitellozzo, who had been his instructor in good and evil, he was strangled.

[Cruelty Prudently Used]

Some may wonder how it came about that Agathocles and others like him, after countless betrayals and cruelties, could for a long time live safely in their native places and defend themselves from foreign enemies, and the citizens never plotted against them; yet many others, even in peaceful times, could not by means of cruelty carry on their governments—and so much the less in the uncertain times of war. I believe this comes from cruelties badly used or well used. *Well used* we call those (if of what is bad we can use the word *well*) that a conqueror carries out at a single stroke, as a result of his need to secure himself, and then does not persist in, but transmutes into the greatest possible benefits to his subjects. *Badly used* are those which, though few in the beginning, rather increase with time than disappear. Princes who follow the first method can, before God and before men, make some improvement in their position, as Agathocles could; the others cannot possibly sustain themselves.

[Injuries All at Once; Benefits Gradually]

We can learn from this that on seizing a state a prudent[5] conqueror makes a list of all the harmful deeds he must do, and does them all at once, so that he need not repeat them every day, because, not repeating them, he makes men feel secure, and gains their support by treating them well. He who acts otherwise, through either timidity or bad advice, is obliged always to hold his sword in his hand; he can never rely on his subjects, and they, because of fresh and continual injuries, cannot feel secure. Injuries are to be done all together, so that, being savored less, they will anger less; benefits are to be conferred little by little, so they will be savored more.

5. *For the word* prudent, *as for* wise *at the beginning of the next paragraph, there is no equivalent in the Italian; Machiavelli uses the verb* debbe. *If this be rendered* ought *or* must, *the implication is* if he hopes to succeed as conqueror or prince. *Dovere (*debbe) *is used with the sense (recognized by dictionary-makers) of logical necessity. The full reasoning is,* The prince is wise; therefore he must act as Machiavelli says. *Six times Machiavelli gives the idea in full, using an adjective for* wise *as well as* dovere (*chaps. 3, 9, 17, 18, 20, 23); he also specifies the prince as* wise *or* prudent *without* dovere (*chaps. 3, 10 [twice], 13, 19). These indicate how other passages are to be understood. Frequently, then, the seemingly added adjective* wise *can be defended as an exact rendering. Moreover, since Machiavelli is showing what the wise prince is, the use of the adjective is in harmony with the spirit of the work.*

[*In Quiet Times Prepare for Adversity*]

And above all, a wise prince lives with his subjects in such a way that no unforeseen event, either for bad or for good, makes him change;[6] because when, in adverse times, emergencies arise, you are too late for harshness, and the good you do does not help you, because it is considered forced and you get for it no thanks whatever.[7]

6. *That is, to attempt abruptly a policy of doing the injuries just mentioned, or of conferring benefits.*

7 *See chap. 7, n. 12, for the shift in person.*

CHAPTER 9. THE "CIVIL PRINCEDOM"

[*The Rise of the Citizen Prince*]

But let us come to the second case, when a private citizen becomes prince of his native city not through crime or any sort of unjust force but with the aid of his fellow-citizens. This I call a civil princedom. To attain it does not require either ability altogether or Fortune altogether but rather a fortunate shrewdness. To such a princedom a man rises with the aid either of the people or of the rich, for in every city these two opposing parties exist. The civil princedom originates thus: the people desire not to be bossed and oppressed by the rich; the rich desire to boss and oppress the people. As a result of these two opposed desires, one of three effects appears in the city: princely rule or liberty or license.

[*Either the People or the Wealthy May Set Up a Prince*]

Princely rule is produced either by the people or by the rich, according as one or the other of these parties has a motive for it. When the rich see that they cannot resist the people, they give their support to one of themselves and make him prince so that, under his shadow, they can satisfy their desires. The people also, seeing that they cannot resist the rich, give their support to one man and make him prince, so that with his power he will protect them. He who comes to the princedom with the aid of the rich maintains himself with more difficulty than he who gets there with the people's aid, because as prince he is surrounded by many who think themselves his equals, and for this reason he cannot command them or manage them at his will. But a prince who attains his position through popular favor stands there solitary and has around him either nobody or very few who are not prepared to obey. Besides this, a ruler cannot creditably and without injury to others satisfy the rich, but certainly he can satisfy the people, because the people's object is more creditable than that of the rich: the latter wish to oppress and the former not to be oppressed. Besides, against a hostile people a prince can never make himself safe because they are too many; against the rich he can make himself safe because they are few. The worst that a prince can expect from a hostile populace is that it will abandon him; from the hostile rich he must fear that they will not merely abandon him but will also act against him. Since the rich have more perception and more shrewdness than the populace, always they provide time for saving themselves, and they seek favor with any man they expect will win. Further, it is necessary for the prince to live always with the same populace; but he can do without the same rich men, being able to make and unmake them every day, and to take away and give back their reputation as he likes.

[How a Prince Should Regard the Wealthy]

To explain this case better, I say that the rich are to be considered in two ways chiefly: either they so manage their conduct that they commit themselves wholly to your Fortune, or not. Those who so commit themselves and are not rapacious are to be honored and loved; those who do not commit themselves are to be tested in two ways. They act as they do either through timorousness and natural lack of spirit[1] (then you make use of those especially who can offer good advice, because in prosperity you gain honor from them, and in adversity you do not need to fear them). But when by design and for reasons of ambition they do not commit themselves to you, it is a sign that they think more of themselves than of you. From these the prince protects himself, and fears them as though they were open enemies, because always in adverse times they help to ruin him.

[All Princes Need Popular Support]

Therefore a prudent man who becomes prince with the aid of the people keeps their friendship, which is easy, since they ask

1. *The* or *clause to be expected after this is put in a differing form, namely, "But when,"* etc., *below.*

nothing except not to be oppressed. But if, in opposition to the people, he becomes prince with the aid of the rich, before everything else he tries to win the people's support, which is easy if he assumes their protection. And because when men get help where they expect to get harm, they commit themselves the more to their benefactor, the people quickly become better disposed toward such a prince than if he came to authority with their aid. So a wise[2] prince wins their favor in many ways for which, as they vary with the matter to be worked on, no certain rules can be laid down; so I pass over them. I conclude by saying only that the people's friendship is essential to a prince. Otherwise, in adverse times he has no resource.

[*Nabis of Sparta*]

Nabis, Prince of the Spartans, withstood a siege by all Greece and by a Roman army flushed with victory, and against them defended his city and his own position; and when that danger came upon him he needed to do no more than secure himself against a few disloyal citizens, though if his people had been hostile, that would not have been enough.

[*A Strong and Wise Prince Can Rely on the People*]

Let no one oppose this belief of mine with that well-worn proverb: "He who builds on the people builds on mud"; it is indeed true when a private citizen lays his foundation on the people and allows himself to suppose that they will free him when he is beset by his enemies or by public officials. In this case he often does find himself deceived, as in Rome the Gracchi, and in Florence Messer Giorgio Scali. But when he who builds on them is a prince who can command, is a stout-hearted man who does not waver in adverse times, does not lack other preparations, and through his courage and his management keeps up the spirits of the masses, he never is deceived by them, but receives assurance that he has made his foundations strong.

[*The Wise Prince Secures Loyalty in Time of Danger*]

Usually these civil princedoms are in danger when they are in the process of shifting from republic to tyranny, because these princes

2. *See chap. 8, n. 6.*

either give orders themselves or do so by means of public officials. In the latter case, their position is weaker and more perilous, because they depend entirely on the will of those citizens who are holding the public offices; these, especially in adverse times, with great ease can take away the prince's position, either by acting against him or by not obeying him. In time of danger the prince is too late for seizure of absolute authority, because citizens and subjects, in the habit of getting their orders from the public officials, are in these emergencies not disposed to obey his orders; so always in threatening weather he lacks men he can trust. Such a prince cannot rely on what he sees in calm weather, when the citizens have need of the government, because then everybody runs, everybody promises, and each man is willing to die for him, since death is far off; but when-ever the weather is unfavorable, and the government has need of the citizens, then its supporters are but few. And so much the more is this test dangerous in that a ruler can make it but once. Therefore a wise prince takes care to devise methods that force his citizens, always and in every sort of weather, to need the government and himself; and always then they will be loyal.

CHAPTER 10. HOW THE MILITARY POW-ER OF ANY PRINCEDOM IS TO BE ESTI-MATED

[The Self-sustained Prince]

While examining the qualities of these various princedoms, we shall discuss another topic: that is, whether a prince has so much power that by his own strength alone he can repel attack, if necessary, or whether he always needs protection from other rulers. To explain this matter more clearly, I say that I judge a prince able to repel attack by his own strength when, through large resources in men or in money, he can get together an army sufficient to fight a battle with whoever comes to attack him. And by the same principle I judge that a prince always needs help from other princes when he cannot appear against an enemy in the field but is forced to take refuge behind walls and defend them. Of the first case I have spoken and in the future shall say about it what occurs to me. On the second case I cannot say anything further than to encourage such a weak prince to fortify and provision his city and to make no account of the territory lying outside it. Any ruler who fortifies his city well and manages his relations with his subjects in the way explained above and to be dealt with below is attacked only with great hesitation, because men are always enemies of undertakings in which they see difficulties, and they see nothing easy about attacking a prince whose city is powerfully fortified and who is not hated by his people.

[The German Free Cities]

The cities of Germany are wholly free, have little farm land, and obey the Emperor when they feel like it; they do not fear him or any other potentate near them because they are so fortified that everybody reckons their capture as sure to be tedious and difficult. They all have adequate ditches and walls; they have plenty of artillery; and they always reserve in the public storehouses enough to drink and to eat and to burn for a year. Besides that, in order to keep the people fed without using up the public funds, they always have in store everything needed to provide work for a year at those trades that are the strength and the life of the city and of the industries by which the people earn their bread. They also hold military exercises in high repute and moreover have many regulations for maintaining them.[1]

[How a Wise Prince Sustains a Siege]

A prince, then, who has a strong city and does not make himself hated is not attacked. An enemy who is so foolish as to attack him is sure to withdraw in disgrace because the affairs of this world are so shifting that an invader finds it almost impossible to hold his army idle for an entire year in order to besiege such a prince If anyone replies to me: 'When the people have property outside the city and see it burned, they lose patience, and the long siege and their self-love make them forget the prince,' I answer that a powerful and spirited prince always overcomes all such difficulties, giving his subjects sometimes hope that the evil will not be long-continued, sometimes fear of the enemy's cruelty, sometimes securing himself with cleverness against those whom he thinks too presumptuous.

1. *Machiavelli here virtually repeats what he says in his* REPORT ON GERMAN MATTERS, *1508.*

Besides this, the enemy presumably burns and wastes the surrounding country on his arrival, at a time when the citizens' spirits are still hot and determined upon defense; for that reason so much the less the prince needs to hesitate, because after some days, when their spirits have grown cold, the harm is already done, the ills have been suffered and can no longer be remedied. So much the more the people then come forward to unite with their prince, since it appears that he is under obligation to them; for their houses have been burned and their property destroyed in his defense. It is the nature of men to feel as much obligated for benefits they confer as for those they receive. Hence, if everything is well considered, a prudent prince can without difficulty, early and late, keep the spirits of his subjects firm throughout a siege, if he does not lack food and means of defense.

CHAPTER 11. ECCLESIASTICAL PRINCEDOMS

[*The Security of the Clerical Prince*]

Only ecclesiastical princedoms are now left to discuss. For these, all the difficulties come before they are acquired; they are gained either by ability or by Fortune, and without either of these they are maintained, because they are supported by customs grown old in church history, which are now so powerful and of such a sort that they keep their prince in his position, however he acts and lives. The pope alone has states and does not defend them, subjects and does not keep them in order; yet his states, through being undefended, never are snatched away; and his subjects, through not being kept in order, never feel any concern, and do not imagine being alienated from him and cannot be. These princedoms only, then, are secure and prosperous. But since they are protected by superior causes, to which the human mind does not reach, I omit speaking about them because, since they are set on high and maintained by God, to discuss them would be the act of a man presumptuous and rash.

[*The Growth of the Temporal Power*]

Nevertheless, if anybody asks me why the Church, in temporal affairs, has now attained such strength, although prior to Alexander the Italian powers (and not merely those who are called powers but every baron and lord, even the very weakest) in temporal affairs respected her little, but now a king of France trembles before her, and she has shoved him out of Italy and ruined the Venetians—though this situation is well known, I believe I am not superfluous in bringing it back to memory in some detail.

[*The Weakness of the Church before the Reign of Pope Alexander VI*]

Before King Charles of France came into Italy, this land was ruled by the Pope, the Venetians, the King of Naples, the Duke of Milan, and the Florentines. These powers needed to guard against two things: one, the invasion of Italy by a foreign army; two, conquest of more territory by one of the Italian states. Those whom they most needed to watch were the Pope and the Venetians. To hold back the Venetians, all the others needed to form a union, such as that for the defense of Ferrara. To keep the Pope down they made use of the Roman barons, for these, being divided into the two factions of the Orsini and Colonnesi, always had cause for discord; standing with their weapons in their hands before the very face of the pontiff, they kept the papacy weak and unwarlike. And even though a courageous pope such as Sixtus sometimes reigned, yet neither Fortune nor prudence ever released him from this annoyance. The brevity of a pope's reign was the reason for this, because in his tenure of ten years, on the average, he might with difficulty put down one of the factions. For instance, one pope might almost destroy the Colonnesi; then another might come to the throne who was hostile to the Orsini and would let the Colonnesi grow powerful again, yet he would not have time to destroy the Orsini. As a result, the temporal forces of the pope were little respected in Italy.

[*The Temporal Power of Pope Alexander VI*]

Then Alexander VI took office, who beyond all the pontiffs who ever reigned showed how mighty a pope could be in both money and arms. Using as his instrument Duke Valentino and as his opportunity the French invasion, he did all the things I have already set forth among the Duke's actions. And though Alexander's purpose was to strengthen not the Church but the Duke, nonetheless what he did resulted in strength for the Church, which after his death and after the Duke's ruin was the heir of his labors.

[*Julius II Strengthens the Church*]

Then came Pope Julius. He found the Church strong, for she held the entire Romagna, the Roman barons were wiped out and, by Alexander's blows, their conflicts ended. He also found the way prepared for heaping up money by a method never used until Alexander's time. These policies Julius not merely carried on but augmented, for he resolved on taking Bologna and ruining the Venetians and driving the French from Italy. All these enterprises came out well and with so much the more credit to him inasmuch as he did it all to exalt the Church and not any individual. He also kept the Orsini and Colonnesi parties in the situation where he found them, and though they might still have some tendencies toward rebellion, yet two things kept them quiet: one, the might of the Church, which terrifies them; the second, their not having their cardinals, who are the source of the quarrels between them. For these factions never keep quiet at any time when they have cardinals because, in Rome and outside, the latter foster parties, and those barons are compelled to defend them; so from the ambitions of the prelates result quarrels and disturbances among the barons.

[*Good Wishes for Pope Leo X*]

His Holiness Pope Leo, then, found this pontificate very power' ful; and for him we hope that, if his predecessors made it great with arms, he, with his kindness and countless other virtues, will make it very great and respected.[1]

1. Leo X, *Giovanni de' Medici, ascended the papal throne 11 March 1513.*

CHAPTER 12. VARIOUS KINDS OF ARMY; MERCENARY SOLDIERS

[*Good Laws and Good Soldiers*]

Having discussed in detail all the qualities of those princedoms which in the beginning I set out to discuss, and observed in various respects the causes of their well'being and their ill'being, and shown the methods with which many have tried to gain and to hold them, it remains for me now to discuss in general the kinds of attack and defense possible for each of these. We have said above that a prince must have good foundations; otherwise, of necessity he falls. The principal foundations of all states, the new as well as the old and the mixed, are good laws and good armies. And because there cannot be good laws where armies are not good, and where there are good armies, there must be good laws,[1] I shall omit talking of laws and shall speak of armies.

[*The Worthlessness of Mercenaries*]

I say, then, that the armies with which a prince defends his state are either his own, or they are mercenary or auxiliary or mixed. The mercenary and the auxiliary are useless and dangerous; if a prince continues to base his government on mercenary armies, he will never be either stable or safe; they are disunited, ambitious, without discipline, disloyal; valiant among friends, among enemies cowardly; they have no fear of God, no loyalty to men. Your ruin is postponed only as long as attack on you is postponed; in peace you are plundered by them, in war by your enemies. The reason for this is that they have no love for you nor any cause that can keep them in the field other than a little pay, which is not enough to make them risk death for you. They are eager indeed to be your soldiers as long as you are not carrying on war, but when war comes, eager to run away or to leave. This thing is not hard to demonstrate, because the present ruin of Italy is the result of nothing else than her reliance upon mercenaries for a stretch of many years. For some princes they gained real advantages, and they seemed valiant against each other; but when the foreigner came, they showed what they were, so that Charles the king of France was allowed to take Italy with chalk.[2]

1. *Machiavelli's epigrammatic statements, such as "Where there are good armies, there must be good laws," are always to be interpreted in the light of his belief that all subjects are to be debated (*Discourses 1. 18*). He never expects human affairs to yield an absolute truth; he does hope to discover and present such truth as there is. So he sees much, though not perfect, reciprocity between good civil and good military organization. More especially he is thinking of an Italian princedom or republic; bad governments depend upon licentious and avaricious mercenaries; well-governed states are defended by their own citizens, who value the blessings secured for them by good and wise rulers.*

If Machiavelli were reasoning on arms and laws in the present day of huge conscript armies, he would adapt his epigram to conditions, perhaps applying Fabrizio's assertion in The Art of War, *bk. 1, that professional soldiers are dangerous to a state.*

For variations see the Index, s.v. warfare, soldiers, and laws. For laws and morals, see Discourses 1. 18.

2. *According to Philip de Commynes (*Memoires, *bk. 7, chap. 14) Pope Alexander VI said the French came with spurs of wood and with chalk in the hands of their quartermasters to*

And he who used to say that the cause of it was our sins told the truth,[3] but they were not at all such as he supposed they were, but these I have mentioned; and because they were princes' sins, the princes have suffered punishment for them.

[The Prince Must Be His Own General; the Republic Must Have Citizen Generals]

I am going to explain better the wretchedness of such armies. Mercenary generals are men either skilful in warfare or not. If they are, you cannot trust them, because they always are trying to gain power for themselves, either by harassing you who are their master or by harassing others against your intention. But if the general is not competent, he normally ruins you. If somebody replies that whoever has the soldiers under his control will do this, whether or not he is a mercenary, I answer that soldiers have to be managed either by a prince or by a republic. The wise prince goes in person and himself performs the duties of a general. The well-ordered republic commissions a citizen; if it sends one who does not turn out an efficient leader, it replaces him; when he is efficient, it restrains him with laws, so that he does not go out of bounds. From experience we see that princes acting for themselves and armed republics make very great advances, but mercenary forces never do anything but harm. A citizen finds the subjugation of his own city harder when she is a republic armed with her own weapons than when she is armed with foreign weapons.

[Historical Examples of Mercenary Treachery]

Rome and Sparta for many centuries were armed and free. The Swiss are heavily armed and wholly free. Of mercenary forces in antiquity the Carthaginians furnish an example, for they were close to being overcome by their own mercenary soldiers at the end of their first war against the Romans, even though the Carthaginians had as leaders their own citizens. Philip of Macedon was put in

---

indicate their quarters on the doors of the houses in the cities they entered, and needed no other weapons.

3. Savonarola attributed the misfortunes of Italy to moral wickedness, though he was also interested in practical politics and wrote on government. Machiavelli attributed the misfortunes of Italy to such sins as the abandonment of military training that made Florence unable to defend herself.

command of their troops by the Thebans when Epaminondas died; after victory he deprived them of their liberty. The Milanese, after Duke Philip died, employed Francesco Sforza against the Venetians; having defeated the enemy at Caravaggio, he joined with them to crush the Milanese his employers. Sforza his father, having been hired as her general by Queen Joanna of Naples, of a sudden left her weaponless; hence, in order not to lose her kingdom, she was forced to throw herself into the King of Aragon's arms.

[*Florentine Experience*]

And even if the Venetians and the Florentines have in the past increased their empires by means of these soldiers, and yet their generals have not made themselves princes over them but have defended them, I answer that the Florentines in this matter have been favored by chance because, among their competent generals, whom they would have had reason to fear, some have not conquered, some have had opposition, others have turned their ambition else-where. The one who did not conquer was John Hawkwood, whose loyalty—not conquering—we cannot know; but everyone must admit that—conquering—he would have had the Florentines in his power. Sforza always had the Bracceschi opposed to him, so that they watched one another. Francesco turned his ambition on Lombardy, Braccio against the Church and the kingdom of Naples. But let us come to what happened not long ago. Then the Florentines made Paulo Vitelli their general, a man very prudent and one who, rising from a private station, had gained a very high reputation. If he had taken Pisa, no one can deny that the Florentines must have become his servants, because if he had been employed as general by their enemies, they would have had no defense, and if they had kept him, they would have had to obey him.

[*Venetian Troubles with Mercenaries*]

As to the Venetians, if we consider their advances, we shall see that they moved securely and gloriously while they carried on war themselves (before they directed their enterprises to the land), for with their gentlemen and their armed populace they moved with the utmost vigor. But when they undertook fighting on the land, they laid aside this vigor and followed the customs of the Italian wars.

And in the beginning of their expansion on land, since they did not have much territory there and were of lofty reputation, they did not have much to fear from their generals. But when they expanded, which they did under Carmignuola, they got a taste of this mistake. Finding him very able (for under his leadership they defeated the Duke of Milan), and knowing on the other side that he had grown cold in the war, they judged that with him they could conquer no more, because he did not wish to, yet that they could not dismiss him, for fear of losing again what they had won. Hence necessity drove them to kill him in order to secure themselves against him. Later they had for their generals Bartolommeo da Bergamo, Ruberto da San Severino, the Count of Pitigliano, and the like, with whom they had to fear loss, not gain, as finally was evident at Vailà, where in one battle they lost what in eight hundred years they had won with so much effort. From these soldiers, then, come only slow, late, and slender winnings, but sudden and astonishing losses.

[*The History of Mercenaries in Italy*]

And because with these examples I have come into Italy, which for many years has been ruled by mercenary generals, I am going to review them from an earlier time, thinking that when their origin and course are seen they can be better controlled. You must, then, understand that as soon as in modern times the Empire was driven out of Italy, and in temporal matters the pope got more power there, Italy became divided into numerous states, because many of the large cities took arms against their nobles who, with the Emperor's aid, had earlier kept them in subjection; the Church also aided the cities in order to give herself influence in temporal affairs; in many others, citizens became princes. Hence Italy was almost wholly in the hands of the Church and of various republics. Since the priests and the citizens who governed were habituated not to bear arms, they began to hire foreigners. The first who gave reputation to this soldiery was Alberigo da Conio, a Romagnole. From this man's school emerged, among others, Braccio and Sforza, who in their days were masters of Italy. After them came all the others who up to our day have commanded these mercenary soldiers. The result of their efficiency is that Italy has been overrun by Charles, plundered by Louis, violated by Ferdinand, and insulted by the Swiss.

[*War as an Easy Business*]

This is the method they used: First, in order to give reputation to their own forces, they took away the reputation of the infantry. They did this because, being without territory and dependent on their employment, a few infantry did not give them reputation, and for a large number they were unable to provide pay. Hence they turned to cavalry, which, with manageable numbers, brought them income and honor. And things came to such a state that in an army of twenty thousand soldiers there were not two thousand footmen. Besides this, they used every effort to rid themselves and their soldiers from hardship and fear, not killing one another in their combats but taking one another prisoner, without asking ransom. They did not fire on cities at night, and the mercenaries in the cities did not fire on tents; around their camps they did not provide either stockades or ditches; they did not campaign in the winter. And all these things that they allowed among their military customs, they are said to have devised in order to escape hardship and dangers—with the result that they conducted Italy to slavery and infamy.[4]

4. *Machiavelli has been censured for making an unusual use of the word* condotta *("led"), translated* conducted. *Perhaps he is playing with its military sense, even though he does not use in the chapter cognate words, such as* condottiere *("military leader"), which occurs in the following chapter.*

CHAPTER 13. AUXILIARY AND MIXED ARMIES; SUBJECTS AND CITIZENS AS SOLDIERS

[*Recent Instances of Danger from Auxiliary Troops*]

An army is auxiliary (this is the other kind of profitless army)[1] when you summon a powerful man to bring his forces to aid and defend you. So in recent times Pope Julius did, for seeing in his expedition against Ferrara the poor showing of his mercenary soldiers, he turned to auxiliary ones and made an agreement with Ferdinand, King of Spain, who was to aid him with military forces. Such troops can be useful and good in themselves, but for him who invites them are almost always harmful; losing, you are done for; winning, you are their prisoner. Even though ancient histories are full of such

1. *Referring to the second paragraph of the preceding chapter.*

instances, none the less I am not going to abandon this fresh instance of Pope Julius II, whose decision could not have been more ill-advised; in order to get Ferrara, he threw himself entirely into the hands of a foreigner. But his good fortune made a third thing come about, so that he did not gather the fruit of his bad choice: when his auxiliaries were defeated at Ravenna, the Swiss rose up and chased off the winners—against all expectation, both his own and that of others. Hence he was not left as the prisoner of his enemies, who had run away, nor of his auxiliaries, since he had conquered with other weapons than theirs. The Florentines, when wholly unarmed, brought ten thousand French to Pisa to besiege her; through this plan they were in more danger than at any other period of their struggles. The emperor of Constantinople, in order to resist his neighbors, put ten thousand Turks in Greece; when the war was over they would not leave; this began Greek servitude under the infidels.

[No True Victory with Auxiliary Soldiers]

He, then, who plans not to conquer should employ these soldiers: they are much more dangerous than mercenaries, because with auxiliaries ruin is sure; they are all united, all under the command of another. But mercenaries, if after they conquer they are to injure you, need more time and better opportunity, since they are not united, and they are enlisted and paid by you; a third person whom you make their commander cannot at once get power enough to injure you. In short, from mercenaries the greater danger is laziness, from auxiliaries efficiency. Wise princes, therefore, always reject these armies and turn to their own; they choose rather to lose with their own soldiers than to win with the others, judging that not a true victory which they gain with foreign armies.

[Cesare Borgia's Experience with Mercenaries and Auxiliaries]

I shall never hesitate to use as an example Cesare Borgia and his actions. That Duke went into Romagna with auxiliary forces—leading there French soldiers entirely—and with them he took Imola and Forlì. But afterwards, not thinking such forces reliable, he turned to mercenaries, expecting from them less risk—and he hired the Orsini and Vitelli. In employing them, he found them uncertain and unfaithful and risky, so he destroyed them and turned to soldiers of his own. We easily see the difference between one of these armies and the other if we consider the Duke's reputation when he had the French only or when later he had the Orsini and Vitelli, and then observe how different it was when finally he stood alone with his own soldiers; we find that his reputation steadily grew greater; yet never was he estimated high until everybody saw that he was sole master of his own troops.

[*Hiero of Syracuse Rejected Mercenaries*]

I had not intended to depart from fresh Italian instances, yet I am not going to omit Hiero of Syracuse, one of those named above. When the Syracusans made him head of their armies, as I said, he at once saw that their mercenary force was useless, being composed of hirelings like ours now in Italy;[2] so deciding that he could neither keep them nor dismiss them, he cut them entirely to pieces; then he led to war his own soldiers, not foreigners.

[*King David*]

I am going to remind you of an Old Testament figure bearing on this theme. David offered himself to Saul to fight with Goliath the Philistian challenger; then Saul, to give him courage, armed him with the king's own armor. But when David tried it on, he refused it, saying that it did not permit him to make good use of his strength; therefore he preferred to encounter the enemy with his sling and his knife.[3] In short, the armor of another man either falls off your back or weighs you down or binds you.

[*French Folly in Using Auxiliaries*]

After Charles VII, King Louis XI's father, had with his fortune and his ability delivered France from the English, he recognized such a need for arming himself with his own weapons, and set up in his realm the ordinance about men-at-arms and infantry. Then King Louis, his son, abolished that of the infantry and took to hiring

2. *In this clause Machiavelli seems to apply the word* condottieri, *usually meaning* leaders *(often mercenaries), to the whole body of troops. I have therefore rendered it* hirelings.

3. *The Biblical account (1 Samuel 17:50) mentions not a knife but a staff. Since it says that David had no sword,* coltello *is hardly to be translated* sword, *as often in sixteenth-century Italian. David is, however, often represented with Goliath's sword, which he took after striking the giant down with a stone from his sling.*

Swiss. Practical experience now shows that this mistake, followed by others, is one cause of that kingdom's perils: by giving prestige to the Swiss, the King discredited all his own soldiers, because his own infantry he wholly abolished and his men-at-arms he made dependent on the soldiers of another country; being accustomed to fight in company with the Swiss, the French cavalry believe they cannot conquer without them. The result is that French against Swiss are not adequate, and without Swiss they do not risk themselves against others. Thus the French king's army is mixed, partly mercenary and partly his own. Such a force is on the whole much better than one purely auxiliary or purely mercenary, though much inferior to an army entirely his own. The instance just given is enough, because the French kingdom would be unconquerable if Charles's method had been developed or retained.

[Danger from Mercenaries to Be Foreseen]

But men in their imprudence often enter upon some policy which at the moment pleases them without envisaging the poison underneath it, as I said above of the hectic fever. So a prince who does not recognize the ills in his state when they spring up is not truly wise; but this power is given to very few. On considering the chief cause for the fall of the Roman Empire, we find it was solely that she took to hiring Gothic mercenaries. After that beginning, the Empire's forces steadily failed, for she stripped away all her own vigor to give it to the Goths.

[No Prince Safe without His Own Soldiers]

I conclude, then, that without her own armies no princedom is secure; on the contrary, she is entirely dependent on Fortune, not having strength that in adversity loyally defends her. Wise men have always said and believed that "nothing is so weak or shaky as the reputation of a power that does not rely on its own strength."[4] Armies of your own are those made up of your subjects or of citizens of your state or of dependents; all the others are either mercenary or auxiliary. The way to organize armies of your own is easy to find if you peruse the methods of the four I have named above and observe how Philip, Alexander the Great's father, and

4. Tacitus, ANNALS 13. 19. *I have translated the standard text, not that commonly printed in* THE PRINCE.

many other princes and various republics have organized their armies. On such methods as theirs I wholly rely.

CHAPTER 14. A PRINCE'S DUTY ABOUT MILITARY AFFAIRS

[*War Is the Prince's Profession*]

A wise prince, then, has no other object and no other interest and takes as his profession nothing else than war and its laws and discipline; that is the only profession fitting one who commands, and it is of such effectiveness that it not merely sustains in their rank men who are born princes but many times enables men born in a private station to rise to princely stations. On the contrary, when princes are more interested in luxuries than in arms they lose their positions. The chief cause that makes you lose your princedom is neglect of this profession, and the cause that makes you gain it is expertness in this profession. Francesco Sforza, though a private person, by devoting himself to arms became Duke of Milan. His sons, though born dukes, by fleeing from the discomforts of arms, made themselves private persons.

[*The Unmilitary Prince Is Despised*]

The first reason why being unarmed brings you trouble is that it makes you despised; this is one of the stigmas from which the wise prince guards himself, as I explain below.[1] Between an armed and an unarmed man there is no reciprocity, and for an armed man gladly to obey one who is unarmed is unreasonable. An unarmed prince cannot be without fear among armed servants, because when the servant feels contempt and the master feels distrust, by no possibility can the two work well together. Therefore, besides the bad effects already mentioned, a prince unskilled in warfare cannot be esteemed by his soldiers or rely on them.

[*Hunting as Training for War*]

A wise prince, then, never withdraws his thought from training for war; in peace he trains himself for it more than in time of war. He does this in two ways, the first with his actions, the second with

1. *Chap. 19.*

his mind. As to his actions, besides keeping his subjects well organized and trained, he himself continually goes hunting in order to accustom his body to hardships. A further purpose in hunting is to learn the nature of military sites, to observe how the mountains rise, how the valleys are hollowed out, how the plains lie, and to inform himself on the nature of rivers and swamps; to these acquire-ments he gives the utmost attention. Such information is useful in two ways: first, he thoroughly learns his own country and can better understand its defenses; second, by means of his knowledge and experience of such military sites, easily he comprehends the qualities of any other site which he needs to examine for the first time. The hills, the valleys, the plains, the rivers, the swamps of Tuscany, for instance, have a certain likeness to those of other regions; hence from his understanding of the lay of the land in one region he can easily attain understanding of other regions. The prince who lacks ex-pertness in topography lacks the first quality needed by a general, because it teaches how to find the enemy, to choose encampments, to lead armies, to plan battles, and to besiege towns with advantage.

[*Philopoemen's Constant Training for War*]

As to Philopoemen, Prince of the Achaians—the chief thing for which historians praise him is that in times of peace he never interested himself in anything except the methods of war, and when he was in the country with his friends, often he stopped and talked with them: "If the enemy were on that hill and we were here with our army, which of us would have the advantage? How, keeping our formation, could we attack them? If we should wish to retire, how could we do it? If they should retire, how could we follow them?" And he would set before them, as they walked along, all the accidents that can happen in an army; he would learn their opinions, tell his own, back it up with reasons; so that on account of this continual attention, when he was leading an army nothing unexpected could happen for which he did not have the remedy.

[*Imitation of the Great Men of the Past*]

But as to the training of his mind, the prudent prince reads histories and observes in them the actions of excellent men, sees how they have conducted themselves in wars, observes the causes for their victories and defeats, in order to escape the latter and imitate the former; above all, he does as some excellent men have done in the past; they selected for imitation some man earlier than themselves who was praised and honored, and his actions and heroic deeds they always kept before them, as it is said Alexander the Great imitated Achilles; Caesar, Alexander; Scipio, Cyrus. And who- ever reads the life of Cyrus written by Xenophon recognizes afterward in Scipio's life how much that imitation was to his glory and how completely in chastity, affability, courtesy, and liberality Scipio shaped himself by what Xenophon wrote about Cyrus.

[Diligence Can Thwart Fortune]

Such methods as these are always practiced by a wise prince, and never in times of peace is he lazy, but of such times he diligently makes capital on which he can draw in periods of distress, so that when Fortune changes he is ready to withstand her.

CHAPTER 15. THOSE THINGS FOR WHICH MEN AND ESPECIALLY PRINCES ARE PRAIS- ED OR CENSURED

[Ethical Fancies and Stern Reality]

Now it remains to examine the wise[1] prince's methods and conduct in dealing with subjects or with allies. And because I know that many have written about this, I fear that, when I too write about it, I shall be thought conceited, since in discussing this material I depart very far from the methods of the others.[2] But since my purpose is to write something useful to him who comprehends it, I have decided that I must concern myself with the truth of the matter as facts show it rather than with any fanciful notion. Yet many have fancied for themselves republics and principalities that have never been seen or known to exist in reality. For there is such a difference between how men live and how they ought to live that he who abandons what is done for what ought to be done learns his

1. *See chap. 8, n. 5.*
2. *With this chapter begins the part of* THE PRINCE *most akin to the medieval and ren- aissance books giving advice to princes (*DE REGIMINE PRINCIPUM*). See Allan H. Gilbert,* MACHIAVELLI'S "PRINCE" AND ITS FORERUNNERS, *Duke Univ. Press, 1938.*

destruction rather than his preservation,[3] because any man who under all conditions insists on making it his business to be good will surely be destroyed among so many who are not good. Hence a prince, in order to hold his position, must acquire the power to be not good, and understand when to use it and when not to use it, in accord with necessity.

[*Virtues and Vices Deserving Praise and Blame*]

Omitting, then, those things about a prince that are fancied, and discussing those that are true, I say that all men, when people speak of them, and especially princes, who are placed so high, are labeled with some of the following qualities that bring them either blame or praise. To wit, one is considered liberal, one stingy (I use a Tuscan word, for the *avaricious* man in our dialect is still one who tries to get property through violence; *stingy* we call him who holds back too much from using his own goods); one is considered a giver, one grasping; one cruel, one merciful; one a promise-breaker, the other truthful; one effeminate and cowardly, the other bold and spirited; one kindly, the other proud; one lascivious, the other chaste; one reliable, the other tricky;[4] one hard, the other tolerant; one serious, the other light-minded; one religious, the other unbelieving; and the like.

[*Apparent Virtues Not Always Real Ones*]

I am aware that everyone will admit that it would be most praiseworthy for a prince to exhibit such of the above-mentioned qualities as are considered good. But because no ruler can possess or fully practice them, on account of human conditions that do not permit it, he needs to be so prudent that he escapes ill repute for such vices as might take his position away from him, and that he protects himself from such as will not take it away if he can; if he cannot, with little concern he passes over the latter vices. He does not even worry about incurring reproach for those vices without which he can hardly maintain his position, because when we carefully examine

3. *That is, he who abandons a teacher who can instruct him in what is done (the world as it is) for one who teaches only what the teacher thinks it right to do (mere theory) will gain learning which, if he acts on it, will ruin him. Machiavelli is interested in "what ought to be done" in the complex world of affairs rather than in the simpler one of dogma.*

4. *Or astute. Dante writes: "Nobody would say that he is wise who proceeds by means of underhand devices and cheating tricks, but he can be called astute" (*CONVIVIO *4. 27. 48). According to Castiglione, astuteness is prudence unaccompanied by goodness (*COURTIER *4. 32).*

the whole matter, we find some qualities that look like virtues, yet—if the prince practices them—they will be his destruction, and other qualities that look like vices, yet—if he practices them—they will bring him safety and well-being.

CHAPTER 16. LIBERALITY AND STINGINESS

[*The Dangers of Seeking a Reputation for Liberality*]

Beginning then with the first qualities mentioned above, I say that to be considered liberal is good. Nevertheless, liberality, when so practiced that you get a reputation for it, damages you, because if you exercise that quality wisely and rightfully, it is not recognized, and you do not avoid the reproach of practicing its opposite. Therefore, in order to keep up among men the name of a liberal man, you cannot neglect any kind of lavishness. Hence, invariably a prince of that sort uses up in lavish actions all his resources, and is forced in the end, if he wishes to keep up the name of a liberal man, to burden his people excessively and to be a tax-shark and to do everything he can to get money. This makes him hateful to his subjects and not much esteemed by anybody, as one who is growing poor. Hence, with such liberality having injured the many and rewarded the few, he is early affected by all troubles and is ruined early in any danger. Seeing this and trying to pull back from it, he rapidly incurs reproach as stingy.

[*Frugality Is True Liberality*]

Since, then, a prince cannot, without harming himself, make use of this virtue of liberality in such a way that it will be recognized, he does not worry, if he is prudent, about being called stingy; because in the course of time he will be thought more and more liberal, since his economy makes his income adequate; he can defend himself against anyone who makes war on him; he can carry through enterprises without burdening his people. Hence, in the end, he practices liberality toward all from whom he takes nothing, who are countless, and stinginess toward all to whom he gives nothing, who are few. In our times we have not seen great things done except by those reputed stingy; the others are wiped out. Pope Julius II, although he made use of the name of a liberal man in order to gain the papacy, afterward paid no attention to keeping it up, in order to be able to make war. The present King of France carries on so many wars, without laying an excessive tax on his people, solely because his long stinginess helps pay his enormous expenses.[1] The present King of Spain, if he were reputed liberal,[2] would not engage in or complete so many undertakings.

[Be Lavish Only with Other People's Money]

Therefore, in order not to rob his subjects, in order to defend himself, in order not to grow poor and contemptible, in order not to be forced to become extortionate, a wise prince judges it of little importance to incur the name of a stingy man,[3] for this is one of those vices that make him reign. And if somebody says: 'Caesar through his liberality attained supreme power, and many others through being and being reputed liberal have come to the highest positions,' I answer: 'Either you are already prince or you are on the road to gaining that position. In the first case, the kind of liberality I mean is damaging; in the second, it is very necessary to be thought liberal. Now Caesar was one of those who were trying to attain sovereignty over Rome. But if, when he had got there, he had lived on and on and had not restrained himself from such expenses, he would have destroyed his supremacy.' If somebody replies: 'Many have been princes and with their armies have done great things, who have been reputed exceedingly liberal,' I answer you: 'The prince spends either his own money and that of his subjects, or that of others. In the first case the wise prince is economical; in the second he does not omit any sort of liberality. For that prince who goes out with his armies, who lives on plunder, on booty, and on ransom, has his hands on the property of others; for him this liberality is necessary; otherwise he would not be followed by his soldiers. Of wealth that is not yours or your subjects', you can be a very lavish giver, as were Cyrus, Caesar, and Alexander, because to spend what belongs to

1. *Louis XII was publicly ridiculed for his economy, but reduced taxes.*

2. *If he had been extravagant enough to get a reputation for liberality.*

3. *In this clause I have rendered* principe debbe *by "wise prince"; this is in harmony with the word "prudent" in the preceding paragraph, and with the context. Sometimes I have left "prince" unqualified; it is to be understood that in this and the following chapters Machiavelli is presenting the conduct of the wise ruler.*

others does not lessen your reputation but adds to it. Nothing hurts you except to spend your own money.'[4]

[Liberality Destroys Itself]

Moreover, nothing uses itself up as fast as does liberality; as you practice it, you lose the power to practice it, and grow either poor and despised or, to escape poverty, grasping and hated. Yet the most important danger a wise prince guards himself against is being despised and hated; and liberality brings you to both of them. So it is wiser to accept the name of a niggard, which produces reproach without hatred, than by trying for the name of free-spender to incur the name of extortioner, which produces reproach with hatred.

4. *Commenting on the difficulties of the Emperor Maximilian as he observed them, Francesco Vettori writes: "It is not certain that he can hold his soldiers together, because, holding them only by means of money, and lacking it for himself, unless he is provided with it by others (which cannot be known), and, on the other hand, being too liberal, he joins difficulty with difficulty. And though being liberal is a virtue in a prince, nonetheless it is not enough to please a thousand men when one needs twenty thousand, and liberality is of no value where it does not reach" (*LEGATION TO THE EMPEROR, *letter of 8 Feb. 1507. Though signed by Vettori, it was written by Machiavelli).*

CHAPTER 17. CRUELTY AND MERCY: IS IT BETTER TO BE LOVED THAN FEARED, OR THE REVERSE?

[Wise Cruelty Is True Mercy]

Passing on to the second of the above-mentioned qualities,[1] I say that every sensible prince wishes to be considered merciful and not cruel. Nevertheless, he takes care not to make a bad use of such mercy. Cesare Borgia was thought cruel; nevertheless that well-known cruelty of his re-organized the Romagna, united it, brought it to peace and loyalty. If we look at this closely, we see that he was much more merciful than the Florentine people, who, to escape being called cruel, allowed the ruin of Pistoia. A wise prince, then, is not troubled about a reproach for cruelty by which he keeps his subjects united and loyal because, giving a very few examples of cruelty, he is more merciful than those who, through too much mercy, let evils continue, from which result murders or plunder, because the latter commonly harm a whole group, but those execu-

1. *The second pair in the list in chap. 15.*

tions that come from the prince harm individuals only. The new prince—above all other princes—cannot escape being called cruel, since new governments abound in dangers. As Virgil says by the mouth of Dido, "My hard condition and the newness of my sovereignty force me to do such things, and to set guards over my boundaries far and wide."[2]

[Severity Moderated]

Nevertheless, he is judicious in believing and in acting, and does not concoct fear for himself, and proceeds in such a way, moderated by prudence and kindness, that too much trust does not make him reckless and too much distrust does not make him unbearable.

[It Is Safer to Be Feared than Loved]

This leads to a debate: Is it better to be loved than feared, or the reverse? The answer is that it is desirable to be both, but because it is difficult to join them together, it is much safer for a prince to be feared than loved, if he is to fail in one of the two. Because we can say this about men in general: they are ungrateful, changeable, simulators and dissimulators, runaways in danger, eager for gain; while you do well by them they are all yours; they offer you their blood, their property, their lives, their children, as was said above,[3] when need is far off; but when it comes near you, they turn about. A prince who bases himself entirely on their words, if he is lacking in other preparations, falls; because friendships gained with money, not with greatness and nobility of spirit, are purchased but not possessed, and at the right times cannot be turned to account. Men have less hesitation in injuring one who makes himself loved than one who makes himself feared, for love is held by a chain of duty which, since men are bad, they break at every chance for their own profit; but fear is held by a dread of punishment that never fails you.

[How to Avoid Hatred]

Nevertheless, the wise prince makes himself feared in such a way that, if he does not gain love, he escapes hatred; because to be feared and not to be hated can well be combined; this he will always achieve if he refrains from the property of his citizens and his subjects

2. AENEID 1. 563–564.
3. *Chap. 9.*

and from their women. And if he does need to take anyone's life, he does so when there is proper justification and a clear case. But above all, he refrains from the property of others, because men forget more quickly the death of a father than the loss of a father's estate.[4] Besides, reasons for seizing property never fail, for he who is living on plunder continually finds chances for appropriating other men's goods; but on the contrary, reasons for taking life are rarer and cease sooner.

[Generals Must Be Cruel]

But when the prince is with his armies and has in his charge a multitude of soldiers, then it is altogether essential not to worry about being called cruel, for without such a reputation he never keeps an army united or fit for any action. Among the most striking of Hannibal's achievements is reckoned this: though he had a very large army, a mixture of countless sorts of men, led to service in foreign lands, no discord ever appeared in it, either among themselves or with their chief, whether in bad or in good fortune. This could not have resulted from anything else than his well-known inhuman cruelty, which, together with his numberless abilities, made him always respected and terrible in the soldiers' eyes; without it, his other abilities would not have been enough to get him that result. Yet historians, in this matter not very discerning, on one side admire this achievement of his and on the other condemn its main cause.

[Scipio Too Merciful]

And that it is true that Hannibal's other abilities would not have been enough, can be inferred from Scipio (a man unusual indeed not merely in his own days but in all the record of known events) against whom his armies in Spain rebelled—an action that resulted from nothing else than his too great mercy, which gave his soldiers more freedom than befits military discipline. For this, he was rebuked in the Senate by Fabius Maximus, who called him the destroyer of the

4. *Machiavelli wrote to Giovanni de'Medici soon after the return of the family in 1512, pointing out the danger of an attempt to recover property lost in 1494 and later: "Men feel more sorrow for a farm taken away from them than for a brother or a father put to death, because sometimes death is forgotten, but property never. The reason is close to the surface, for everyone knows that a brother cannot rise up again because of a change in government, but there is a possibility of getting back a farm. If this applies to anybody, it applies to the Florentines, because they are commonly more avaricious than generous" (quoted by Tommasini, MACHIAVELLI, I, 601).*

Roman soldiery. The Locrians, who had been ruined by a legate of his, Scipio did not avenge nor did he punish the legate's arrogance— all a result of his tolerant nature. Hence, someone who tried to apologize for him in the Senate said there were many men who knew better how not to err than how to punish errors. This tolerant nature would in time have damaged Scipio's fame and glory, if, having it, he had kept on in supreme command; but since he lived under the Senate's control, this harmful trait of his not merely was concealed but brought him fame.

[*The Prince Should Rely on What Is in His Own Power*]

I conclude, then, reverting to being feared and loved, that since men love at their own choice and fear at the prince's choice, a wise prince takes care to base himself on what is his own,⁵ not on what is another's; he strives only to avoid hatred, as I have said.

5. *In this sentence Machiavelli attaches to the prince the adjective* wise; *usually he leaves it to be inferred.*

CHAPTER 18. HOW PRINCES SHOULD KEEP THEIR PROMISES

[*Craft Conquers Truth*]

How praiseworthy a prince is who keeps his promises and lives with sincerity and not with trickery, everybody realizes. Neverthe-less, experience in our time shows that those princes have done great things who have valued their promises little, and who have under-stood how to addle the brains of men with trickery; and in the end they have vanquished those who have stood upon their honesty.

[*The Prince Must Fight as Both Animal and Man*]

You need to know, then, that there are two ways of fighting: one according to the laws, the other with force. The first is suited to man, the second to the animals; but because the first is often not sufficient, a prince must resort to the second. Therefore he needs to know well how to put to use the traits of animal and of man. This conduct is taught to princes in allegory by ancient authors, who write that Achilles and many other well-known ancient princes were given for upbringing to Chiron the Centaur, who was to guard and educate them. This does not mean anything else (this having as teacher one who is half animal and half man) than that a prince needs to know how to adopt the nature of either animal or man, for one without the other does not secure him permanence.

[*The Fox and the Lion*]

Since, then, a prince is necessitated to play the animal well, he chooses among the beasts the fox and the lion, because the lion does not protect himself from traps; the fox does not protect himself from the wolves. The prince must be a fox, therefore, to recognize the traps and a lion to frighten the wolves. Those who rely on the lion alone are not perceptive. By no means can a prudent ruler keep his word—and he does not—when to keep it works against himself and when the reasons that made him promise are annulled. If all men were good, this maxim would not be good, but because they are bad and do not keep their promises to you, you likewise do not have to keep yours to them. Never has a shrewd prince lacked justifying reasons to make his promise-breaking appear honorable. Of this I can give countless modern examples, showing how many treaties of peace and how many promises have been made null and empty through the dishonesty of princes. The one who knows best how to play the fox comes out best,[1] but he must understand well how to disguise the animal's nature and must be a great simulator and dissimulator. So simple-minded are men and so controlled by immediate necessities that a prince who deceives always finds men who let themselves be deceived.

[*Alexander VI a False-Swearer*]

I am not willing, among fresh instances, to keep silent about one of them. Alexander VI never did anything else and never dreamed of anything else than deceiving men, yet he always found a subject to work on. Never was there a man more effective in swearing and who with stronger oaths confirmed a promise, but yet honored it less. Nonetheless, his deceptions always prospered as he hoped, because he understood well this aspect of the world.

1. *The clause assumes two princes engaged in a war of wits.*

[The Prince Ready, in Necessity, to Abandon Conventional Ethics]

For a prince, then, it is not necessary actually to have all the above-mentioned qualities,[2] but it is very necessary to appear to have them. Further, I shall be so bold as to say this: that if he has them and always practices them, they are harmful; and if he appears to have them, they are useful; for example, to appear merciful, trust-worthy, humane, blameless, religious—and to be so—yet to be in such measure prepared in mind that if you need to be not so, you can and do change to the contrary. And it is essential to realize this: that a prince, and above all a prince who is new, cannot practice all those things for which men are considered good, being often forced, in order to keep his position, to act contrary to truth, contrary to charity, contrary to humanity, contrary to religion. Therefore he must have a mind ready to turn in any direction as Fortune's winds and the variability of affairs require, yet, as I said above,[3] he holds to what is right when he can but knows how to do wrong when he must.[4]

[The Majority Judge by Appearances]

A wise prince,[5] then, is very careful never to let out of his mouth a single word not weighty with the above-mentioned five qualities; he appears to those who see him and hear him talk, all mercy, all faith, all integrity, all humanity, all religion. No quality does a prince more need to possess—in appearance—than this last one, because in general men judge more with their eyes than with their

2. *Machiavelli here assumes the qualification in chap. 15: such qualities "as are considered good."*

3. *Chap. 15, par. 1.*

4. *Machiavelli writes that ambassadors from Bologna urged upon Pope Julius II that he was bound by certain formal agreements the Bolognese had made with preceding popes. Julius replied that "as to the formal agreements he did not care what other popes had done or what he had done himself, because the other popes and himself had not been able to do anything else, and necessity and not desire had made them agree. But when the time came that he could correct them, he believed that if he did not do so he could not make any excuse before God, and for this reason he had acted, and his purpose was to bring it about that Bologna should live properly, as they say [that is, govern herself], and therefore he intended to come to that city in person, and if her way of governing herself should please him, he would ratify it; if it did not please him he would change it. And to be able to do so with arms, if other methods were not enough, he was preparing forces of a sort to make Italy tremble, not merely Bologna" (*LEGATION 20. 44, letter of 3 Oct. 1506*).*

5. *For this and other instances of wise modifying prince, see chap. 8, n. 5.*

hands,[6] since everybody can see but few can perceive. Everybody sees what you appear to be; few perceive what you are, and those few dare not contradict the belief of the many, who have the majesty of the government to support them. As to the actions of all men and especially those of princes, against whom charges cannot be brought in court, everybody looks at their result. So if a prince succeeds in conquering and holding his state, his means are always judged honorable and everywhere praised, because the mob is always fascinated by appearances and by the outcome of an affair; and in the world the mob is everything;[7] the few find no room there when the many crowd together. A certain prince of the present time,[8] whom I refrain from naming, never preaches anything except peace and truth, and to both of them he is utterly opposed. Either one, if he had practiced it, would many times have taken from him either his reputation or his power.[9]

6. *This suggests the expression "to touch with the hand," as in* MANDRAGOLA *V. 2, meaning "to know with certainty."*

7. *Machiavelli is here contrasting not the people and the upper classes, but the wise and the foolish.*

8. *Ferdinand of Spain, who died 23 Jan. 1516. For other passages on him, see the Index.*

9. *That is, there were in his career many occasions, on which, if he had been honest, he would have lost his power.*

CHAPTER 19. A PRINCE MUST AVOID BEING DESPISED AND HATED

[What Produces Hatred]

But because, as to the qualities mentioned above,[1] I have spoken of the most important, I wish to run through the others briefly under this generality: that the wise prince is careful, as is partly explained above,[2] to avoid everything that makes him hated and despised, and any prince who avoids that does what is needed, and in the other kinds of bad repute encounters no danger. It makes him hated above all, as I have said,[3] to be rapacious and to seize upon the property and the women of his subjects; from this he refrains. So long as the great majority of men are not deprived of either property or honor, they are satisfied; thus the prince finds nothing to contend

1. *In chap. 15, par. 2.*   2. *In chaps. 15, 16, 17.*
3. *In chap. 17.*

with except the ambition of the few, which in many ways and easily can be controlled. It makes him despised to be considered change- able, light, effeminate, faint-hearted, irresolute—from which a wise prince guards himself as from a shoal. He strives to make everyone recognize in his actions greatness, spirit, dignity, and strength; in the private business of his subjects, he lays down decisions not to be changed. And he so sustains such opinion about himself that no one imagines he can trick or confuse him.

[*Reputation Brings Safety*]

The prince who gains this opinion about himself has reputation enough. And against one who has reputation, conspiracy is difficult; attack on him is difficult, if only he is thought to be of great merit and revered by his people. Because a prince must have two fears: one within his state, with regard to his subjects; one outside, with regard to foreign powers. From the latter he defends himself with good soldiers and good allies; and always when he has good soldiers he has good allies; and always conditions are firm inside when they are firm outside, if indeed they are not upset by a conspiracy. If those outside do shift, the prince who rules and lives as I direct, if he does not himself lose heart, always repels every assault, as I said Nabis the Spartan did. But as to his subjects, when things outside do not shift, he watches lest they conspire in secret; from this the prince makes himself secure enough if he avoids being hated and despised, and keeps the people contented with him—which he needs to attain, as I said above at length.[4]

[*The Favor of the People a Security against Plots*]

And the prince's strongest resource against conspiracies is not to be hated by the masses, because always a conspirator believes that by the death of the prince he will please the people. But when he believes he will anger them, he does not gather courage to undertake such a plan, because the difficulties on the side of the plotters are countless. From experience we learn that conspiracies have been many but few have had a successful outcome; because he who plots cannot be alone, and he can get no companions except among those he believes dissatisfied. And as soon as you uncover your purpose to a dissatisfied man, you give him a chance to become satisfied, be-

4. Chaps. 9 and 17.

cause obviously he can then expect every sort of advantage.[5] Indeed, when he sees that profit is certain on this side, and on the other is uncertain and full of danger, he must be an uncommon friend or an utterly unyielding enemy to the prince if he is to keep your secret. And to bring the matter into small compass, I say that on the part of the plotter there is nothing but fear, anxiety, dread of punishment—which unnerve him. But on the part of the prince, there are the majesty of his princely rank, the laws, the defensive measures of his friends and of the state—which protect him. Hence, if to all these things is added the people's good will, it is impossible for anyone to be rash enough to conspire. Because, while ordinarily a plotter needs to be afraid before he carries out his evil deed, in this case he must fear also (having as his enemy the people) after the crime is committed, since he cannot by its means hope for any way of escape.[6]

[*The Example of the Bentivogli*]

On this subject I can give countless examples, but I am going to be satisfied with only one, occurring within the memory of our fathers. Messer Annibale Bentivogli, prince in Bologna, the present Messer Annibale's grandfather, being murdered by the Canneschi, who had plotted against him, left no heir except Messer Giovanni, who was in swaddling-clothes. After his murder instantly the people rose up and killed all the Canneschi. This resulted from the popular good will that the Bentivogli family enjoyed in those days; it was so strong that, when after Annibale's death there was no one of that family in Bologna who could rule the city, the Bolognese, getting word that in Florence there was a man of Bentivogli blood, until then supposed the son of a blacksmith, came to Florence for him, and gave over to him the government of their city; this he ruled until Messer Giovanni reached an age fitted for government. I conclude, therefore, that a wise prince gives conspiracies little heed when his people are well-disposed; but when they are hostile and regard him with hatred, he fears everything and everybody.

5. *The man who reveals a plot to a prince can expect great rewards.*
6. *The assassination of an unpopular prince would destroy the power of his personal followers for revenge. That of a popular ruler would not keep the people from punishing his murderers.*

[*The French Constitution Protects All Classes*]

And well-ordered states and wise princes with the utmost attention take care not to make the rich desperate, and to satisfy the people
and keep them contented; this matter is very important for a prince.
The kingdom best organized and governed, in our times, is France;
in it there are numberless good institutions on which depend the
king's liberty and security. Among these, the first is the Parliament
and its authority. The organizer of that kingdom, knowing the
ambition of the powerful and their arrogance, judged a bit in their
mouths necessary for controlling them; and, on the other side, he
knew the hatred of the masses for the rich, founded on fear; yet
when planning to give both classes security, he did not permit their
safety to be the king's special duty, in order to free him from the
hatred he would incur from the rich for favoring the people, and
from the people for favoring the rich. Therefore he set up a third
body as judge,[7] who, without any blame for the king, was to beat
down the rich and favor the humble.[8] Nothing could be better or
more prudent than this law, or a greater cause of security to the
king and the kingdom.

[*The Prince Should Do Favors Himself, Depute Punishments*]

From this we learn something else worthy of note: wise princes
have affairs that bring hatred attended to by others, but those that
bring thanks they attend to themselves. I conclude anew that a
prudent prince shows esteem for the rich, but does not make himself
hated by the people.

[*Roman Emperors as Examples*]

Perhaps many will believe, in view of the lives and deaths of
various Roman emperors, that they are instances opposed to this
belief of mine, since some of these emperors always lived excellently
and showed great vigor of spirit, and yet lost their sovereignty or
were killed by their subjects, who plotted against them. Wishing,
then, to answer these objections, I shall run through the qualities of
some emperors, showing the causes of their destruction—not out of
harmony with what I have put forward; and in so doing I shall

7. *That is, the Parliament.*
8. *In view of what precedes and follows, we expect here a statement that the Parliament made
the rich secure against the masses. Perhaps Machiavelli thought it would be taken for granted.*

bring to attention the things worth noting by one who reads what was done in those times. I think it enough to take all the emperors who succeeded to the throne from Marcus the Philosopher to Max- iminus; they were Marcus, Commodus his son, Pertinax, Julian, Severus, Antoninus Caracalla his son, Macrinus, Heliogabalus, Alexander, and Maximinus.

[Roman Emperors Forced to Win the Soldiers' Favor]

First I observe that while in other princedoms a ruler struggles only against the ambition of the rich and the arrogance of the people, the Roman emperors had a third difficulty: to deal with the cruelty and greed of the soldiers. This difficulty was so great that it caused the ruin of many emperors, since they could not satisfy both soldiers and people. The people loved quiet and therefore loved the modest princes; the soldiers loved a prince of military spirit who was ar- rogant, cruel, and grasping; these qualities they wished him to practice on the people so the troops could have double pay and give vent to their greed and cruelty. As a result of this condition, those emperors who did not have by nature[9] or acquirement so great a reputation that through it they could hold both parties in check, always fell. Most of them, especially those who came to the throne as upstarts, recognizing the problem of these two opposing factions, attempted to please the soldiers, without hesitating to damage the people. This decision was necessary; since princes cannot escape being hated by someone, they should seek first not to be hated by any large groups, and if they cannot attain this, they should make every effort to escape the hatred of the most powerful groups. Therefore those emperors who as new rulers required unusual support, attached themselves to the soldiers rather than to the people. This resulted, nevertheless, to their advantage or not, according as such princes managed to keep up their reputation in the armies.

[Marcus and Pertinax]

For the various reasons mentioned above, Marcus, Pertinax, and Alexander, all being of modest life, lovers of justice, enemies of cruelty, humane, and kindly, all came—Marcus excepted—to un- happy ends. Marcus alone lived and died in the greatest honor,

9. Nature *here seems to mean* birth *or* family. *Cf. what is said below on Marcus and* Commodus.

because he succeeded to the empire by right of birth, and did not have to acknowledge obligation for it to either soldiers or people. Then, since he was supported by many virtues that made him revered, he always, as long as he lived, kept both classes within their limits, and was never hated or despised. But Pertinax was made emperor against the wish of the soldiers, who, being used to living without restraint under Commodus, could not endure the upright life to which Pertinax wished to bring them back; therefore, having made himself hated (and to this hatred was joined contempt because he was old), he fell when he had hardly taken control.

[*A Prince May Be Hated for His Good Deeds*]

From this we learn that hate is incurred as much by means of good deeds as of bad. Therefore, as I said above, if a prince wishes to keep his position, he is often forced to be not good, because when that group—whether the masses, the soldiers, or the rich—which you decide you need to sustain yourself, is corrupt, you have to adapt yourself to its nature in order to please it. Then good works are your enemies.

[*The Good Emperor Alexander Was Murdered*]

But let us come to Alexander, who was of such great goodness that the highest praise assigned to him is this, that in the fourteen years while he held the sovereignty never did he put anyone to death untried. Nonetheless, since he was considered effeminate and a man who let himself be controlled by his mother, and therefore became despised, the army plotted against him and murdered him.

[*The Cruel Severus Was Respected*]

Considering now, on the other side, the qualities of Commodus, Severus, Antoninus Caracalla, and Maximinus, you will find them very cruel and grasping. In order to satisfy the soldiers, they did not refrain from any sort of damage they could do to the people. And all of them, except Severus, came to an unhappy end. He had so much ability that by retaining the soldiers as his friends, even though he oppressed the people, he could always reign successfully; his various abilities made him in the sight of both the soldiers and the people so remarkable that the latter continued to be, as it were, awe-struck and stupefied, and the former respectful and contented.

[*Severus as Fox and as Lion*]

Because the actions of this man were great and noteworthy in a new prince, I wish to show briefly how well he knew how to play the parts of the fox and the lion, whose natures I say above must be imitated by a prince. As soon as Severus realized the Emperor Julian's worthlessness, he convinced the army of which he was general in Slavonia that it was right for them to go to Rome to avenge the death of Pertinax, whom the Pretorian soldiers had killed. Under this pretense, without disclosing his ambition for the empire, he moved his army on Rome; and he was already in Italy before anyone knew he had started. When he arrived in Rome, the Senate, in fear, voted him Emperor, and Julian was killed. After this beginning, there remained for Severus two obstacles to his mastery of the entire domain: one in Asia, where Pescennius Niger, commander of the Asiatic armies, had had himself named Emperor; the other in the West, where Albinus was ruling, who was another aspirant to the Empire. And because he judged it perilous to reveal himself as an enemy to both of them, he determined to attack Niger and to delude Albinus. To the latter he wrote that, being chosen Emperor by the Senate, he wished to share that dignity with him; so he sent him the title of Caesar and, by decree of the Senate, made him his colleague; these things Albinus accepted as genuine. But after Severus had defeated and killed Niger and quieted Eastern affairs, on returning to Rome he complained in the Senate that Albinus, ungrateful for the benefits received from him, had treacherously sought to kill him, and for this reason he was compelled to punish his ingratitude. Then Severus attacked Albinus in France and took from him position and life. On carefully examining this man's deeds, then, we find him a very savage lion and a very tricky fox and see him feared and respected by everybody and not hated by his armies; hence we do not marvel that he, an upstart, could hold so great an empire, because his enormous reputation protected him always from the hatred which his acts of pillage produced in the people.

[*The Cruel Antoninus Caracalla Was Murdered*]

But as to Antoninus, his son, he too was a man who had abilities of the highest quality, and such as made him admirable in the people's view and pleasing to the troops, because he was a soldierly man, fully inured to every sort of hardship, despising all delicate food and every other luxury, which made him loved by all the armies. Nevertheless, his fierceness and cruelty were so great and so unheard of—since, after the slaughter of countless individuals, he killed a great part of the Roman populace and all that of Alex-andria—that he became most hateful to all the world. And he roused the fears even of those attending him; so he was murdered by a centurion in the midst of his army.

[*Precautions against Assassination*]

From Antoninus we learn that such deaths, resulting from the decision of one determined mind, princes cannot avoid, because any man not afraid to die can harm them; but princes need to fear such deaths less in that they are very rare. They need only avoid doing serious injury to any of those who serve them and whom they have around them for the duties of their princedoms. Such injury An-toninus did, for he killed with scornful insolence a brother of that centurion, and every day threatened the man himself, yet kept him in his bodyguard. This was a foolhardy decision and enough to ruin him, just as it did.

[*Commodus Excited Contempt*]

But let us come to Commodus, who could very easily have kept the sovereignty, since he held it by hereditary right, being Marcus' son; he needed only to walk in his father's footsteps, and he would have satisfied soldiers and people. Being of a cruel and savage spirit, in order to practice his greed on the people, he set out to please the armies and make them lawless. On the other hand, not keeping his dignity, going often into the theaters to fight with gladiators, and doing other degrading things unworthy of the im-perial majesty, he became contemptible in the sight of the soldiers. And being hated on one hand and despised on the other, he was plotted against and killed.

[*Maximinus Was Scorned*]

I still need to present Maximinus' qualities. He was a very warlike man, and since the army was disgusted by Alexander's softness, mentioned above, after his murder they gave the empire to

Maximinus. He did not hold it very long, because two things made him hated and despised: one that he was of the lowest rank, for he had once tended sheep in Thrace (a fact well known everywhere, which caused him great loss of dignity in the eyes of everybody); the other was that at the outset of his reign he put off going to Rome to take possession of the imperial throne; thus he gained the reputation of being very cruel, because, through his prefects in Rome and in various places in the empire, he had committed many cruelties.[10] As a result, all the world was moved by contempt for his ignoble blood and by hatred in fear of his savagery, so that first Africa rebelled, then the Senate with all the people of Rome; and all Italy plotted against him. Even his own army took their part, for while he was besieging Aquileia and finding difficulty in her capture, the soldiers, sickened by his cruelty and fearing him less because they saw how many enemies he had, murdered him. I do not intend to discuss Heliogabalus or Macrinus or Julian, who, being generally despised, were quickly disposed of, but I shall come to the end of this discourse.[11]

[Pleasing the Soldiers in Modern Times]

And I say that the princes of our times do not have this difficulty of conducting themselves in a way to give the soldiers unmeasured satisfaction; though they do have to take some thought for the soldiers, yet they can decide that matter quickly, since these modern princes do not have standing armies that have grown old along with the governments and administration of their territories, as had the armies of the Roman empire. Therefore, if then a ruler was forced to please the soldiers rather than the people, because the soldiers were stronger than the people, now all princes, except the Turk and the Soldan, are forced to please the people rather than the soldiers, because the people are the stronger. From this I except the Turk, who always keeps around him twelve thousand infantry and fifteen thousand cavalry, on whom depend the security and strength of his kingdom; hence, setting aside all other considerations, that lord must

10. *Cruelties committed by his agent were charged to him. Cf. Cesare Borgia's precautions against this as to Remirro (chap. 7), and Machiavelli's advice that a ruler's presence prevents misconduct by his officials (chap. 3).*

11. *Verbally, this clause suggests that the preceding material was originally part of the* Discourses on Livy, *transferred without changing the word* discorso, *as perhaps also in the last paragraph of the present chapter. Cf. the formula at the end of* Discourses 1. 29.

maintain the friendship of these troops. Likewise, since the Soldan's realm is entirely in the soldiers' hands,[12] he too must maintain their friendship without regard for the people.

[*Soldan and Pope neither Old nor New Princes*]

You should note that the Soldan's government is different in form from all other princedoms; it is like the Christian papacy, which cannot be called either a hereditary princedom or a new princedom, because the descendants of the old prince are not his heirs and do not rule by inheritance; the new prince is chosen by lawful electors. Since this system was established long ago, it is subject to none of the troubles of new governments; although the prince himself is new, the institutions of the state are old and are designed to receive him as if he were its hereditary lord.

[*A New Prince, Imitating Roman Emperors, Must Choose with Prudence*]

But let us return to our subject. I say that whoever will consider the preceding discourse will see that hate or contempt was the reason for the fall of the emperors named; you will also understand why, when part of them proceeded in one way and part in the opposite, in each group one emperor had a happy and the others an unhappy end. Because for Pertinax and Alexander, since they were new princes, it would have been useless and harmful to try to copy Marcus, who was in the ruler's place by right of descent. And likewise for Caracalla, Commodus, and Maximinus, it would have been dangerous to copy Severus, because they did not have ability enough to follow his footsteps. Hence a new prince in a new princedom cannot copy the actions of Marcus, and yet he does not need to follow those of Severus; but he will take from Severus those methods essential for founding his government, and from Marcus those suitable and splendid for preserving a government long established and firm.

12. *The Mamelukes controlled Egypt.*

CHAPTER 20. WHETHER FORTRESSES AND MANY THINGS THAT PRINCES DO EVERY DAY ARE USEFUL OR HARMFUL

[*Various Policies Followed by Princes*]

Some princes, to hold their states securely, have disarmed their subjects; others have kept the cities under their control divided; some have fostered enmities against themselves; others have tried to gain the support of those they feared at the beginning of their rule; some have built fortresses; some have ruined and destroyed them. Though on all these things I cannot give a final judgment without knowing details about those states where princes must make such decisions, nevertheless I shall speak in that general way which the material itself allows.

[*A New Prince Allows His Subjects Weapons*]

Never has a new prince, then, disarmed his subjects; on the contrary, when he has found them unarmed, invariably he has armed them; because when they are armed those arms become yours; those whom you fear become loyal; and those already loyal continue to be so and instead of mere subjects become your partisans. Because all your subjects cannot be armed, if those you do arm feel that they are favored, with the others you can deal more securely, and that distinction in policy toward those who bear arms, which they recognize, binds them to you; the others excuse you, judging it necessary that those have more reward who undergo more danger and a stronger bond of duty. But when you disarm them, at once you anger them; you show that you distrust them as either cowardly or disloyal; both of these opinions generate hatred against you. And because you cannot remain unarmed, you have to turn to mercenary troops, who have the character explained above;[1] even if they are good, they cannot be strong enough to defend you from mighty foes and from dangerous subjects. Therefore, as I have said, a new prince in a new princedom has always organized armies there; of instances of this, the histories are full.

1. *Chap. 12.*

[*Subjects in an Annexed Province to Be Disarmed*]

But when a prince gains a new state that like a member is joined to his old one, then it is necessary to disarm that state, except those who have been your partisans in its conquest; and them as well, with time and opportunity, you must make soft and effeminate, and you must so arrange matters that the weapons of your entire state are in the hands of your own soldiers—mentioned above[2]—who live close by you in your old state.

[*Do Not Foster Divisions in Subject Cities*]

It was the habit of our forefathers—those who were looked upon as wise—to say that Pistoia had to be held with parties and Pisa with fortresses; and for this reason, they kept fostering quarrels in some of their subject cities, in order to hold them more easily. This plan, in those days when Italy was in a certain way balanced, may have been a good one; but I do not believe that today it can be considered wise advice, because I do not believe that divisions ever do any good; on the contrary, when the enemy approaches, divided cities inevitably are lost at once; because always the weaker party takes the side of the foreign troops, and the other cannot resist. The Venetians, moved by the reasons given above, I believe, commonly fostered in their subject cities the Guelf and Ghibelline factions; and though they never let these factions come to bloodshed, still they fostered such differences of opinion among the citizens, so that, busy over those disputes, they would not unite against Venice. This, as we have seen, did not afterwards turn out to their advantage, because after they were defeated at Vailà, at once some of those cities took courage and deprived them of all their territories. The inference, therefore, from such methods is weakness in the prince, because in a vigorous princedom such divisions are never permitted, for they bring profit only in time of peace, since by their means it is easier to manage subjects; on the coming of war, a plan of that sort shows its fallacy.

[*Enemies Overcome Add to Strength*]

Without doubt princes become strong when they overcome the difficulties and the opposition raised against them; and therefore

2. *Chap. 13.*

Fortune, especially when she wishes to strengthen a new prince, who has more need for gaining reputation than has one of long descent, creates enemies for him and has them move against him, in order that he may have opportunity to conquer them and, with the very ladder that his enemies themselves bring him, may climb still higher. Therefore many hold that a wise prince, when he gets a chance, craftily fosters some enmity against himself, that by crushing it he may make his power greater.

[*Loyalty from Former Enemies*]

Sometimes princes, and especially those who are new, find more loyalty and more assistance in those men who in the beginning of their rule were considered dangerous than in those who in the beginning were trusted. Pandolfo Petrucci, Prince of Siena, controlled his state with the aid of those whom he had feared rather than with the aid of the others. But on this matter I cannot generalize, because the decision varies with the case. Only this I shall say, that those men who in the beginning of a reign were enemies but who need to be supported by the prince if they are to keep their positions, the new ruler always very easily wins over; and they are the more compelled to serve him loyally, in proportion as they realize that they must cancel with their deeds his damaging opinion of them. So the prince always gets from them more profit than from those who, serving him with too much feeling of security, neglect his affairs.

[*Those Dissatisfied with an Old Government Will Be Dissatisfied with a New One*]

Moreover, since the subject demands it, I must not fail to remind any prince who conquers a new state by means of internal aid to consider well what cause moves those who aid him to do so. And if it is not natural affection for the prince, but merely that such supporters were not satisfied with the preceding government, only with labor and great difficulty will he keep them as his friends, because to satisfy them is impossible. On considering carefully the cause for this, with the aid of examples from both ancient and recent affairs, he will see that he can more easily gain as friends men who were satisfied with the preceding government—and hence were his enemies—than he can keep the friendship of those who, through discontent with it, became his allies and aided him in conquering it.

[*Fortresses Are Useful or Not According to Circumstances*]

Princes have been accustomed, in order to hold their states more securely, to build fortresses as bit and bridle for any of their subjects disposed to act against them, and as sure refuges against sudden attacks. I praise this method because it has been used for centuries. Nonetheless, in our day Messer Niccolò Vitelli demolished two for-tresses in Città di Castello in order to hold that city. Guido Ubaldo, Duke of Urbino, on getting back into his lordship from which Cesare Borgia had driven him out, destroyed down to the ground all the fortresses of the province, judging that without them he would find it harder to lose his dukedom again. The Bentivogli, on getting back to Bologna, used like measures. Clearly, then, fortresses are useful or not according to the times; if they do you good in one way, they injure you in another.

[*A Prince's Best Fortress Is That His Subjects Do Not Hate Him*]

The conclusion, then, can be stated thus: a wise prince who is more afraid of his own people than of foreigners builds fortresses; he who is more afraid of foreigners than of his own people rejects them. The Sforza family has been and will be more damaged by the castle of Milan, which Francesco Sforza built, than by any other bad policy in that state. In any case, your best possible fortress is that your subjects do not hate you. Even though you have a fortress, if the people hate you, it does not protect you, because the people when they take up arms never lack foreigners to aid them. In our days, fortresses have not profited any ruler except the Countess of Forlì, after her husband Count Girolamo was killed; her castle did enable her to escape the popular attack, to wait for aid that was coming from Milan, and to regain her position, partly because just then the times were such that no foreigner could aid her subjects. But later even she found her fortress ineffective when Cesare Borgia attacked her, and her hostile people joined with the foreigner. There-fore, then and earlier, she would have been safer not to be hated by the people than to possess a fortress. Considering all these things, then, I praise one prince who builds fortresses and another who does not build them; I blame any prince who, trusting in them, considers the hatred of his people unimportant.

CHAPTER 21. HOW A PRINCE CON, DUCTS HIMSELF IN ORDER TO GAIN A HIGH REPUTATION

[*Reputation from Great Undertakings; Ferdinand of Spain*]

Nothing makes a prince so highly esteemed as do great under, takings and unusual actions. An example in our times is Ferdinand of Aragon, the present king of Spain. He can be called almost a new prince because through fame and glory he has transformed himself from a petty ruler to the foremost king among the Christians. If you consider his actions, you find them all very great and some of them extraordinary. In the early part of his reign he attacked Granada; this undertaking was the foundation of his power. First, he acted when he was otherwise unengaged and had no fear of being hindered; by invading Granada he kept employed the minds of the unruly barons of Castile, who when thinking about war did not think about rebellion. In the meantime he also gained a high reputation and sovereignty over his nobles without their realizing it. With money from the Church and from the people he maintained armies, and in that long war laid a foundation for his military organization, which since has done him honor. Besides this, for the sake of engaging in greater enterprises, he continually availed him, self of religion, for he turned to a pious cruelty, hunting down and clearing out of his kingdom the Marranos; no memorable act could be more pitiable than this or more extraordinary. Under this same cloak of religion, he invaded Africa; he then undertook his expedi, tion to Italy; recently he attacked France; and so always he performed and planned great actions, which kept the minds of his subjects always in suspense and wonder, watching for the outcome. These actions have in such a way grown one from another that between one and the next never has he given people any interval of leisure for working against him.

[Reputation from Spectacular Deeds]

It also helps a prince enormously to give striking displays of ability in dealing with internal affairs (like the actions reported about Messer Bernabo of Milan);[1] hence whenever a citizen offers him an opportunity by doing something unusual, either for good or bad, in the life of the city, he finds a way for rewarding or punishing that citizen that is sure to be much talked about. Above all, a prince strives to gain from all his acts notoriety as a strong man of superior ability.

[Neutrality Makes Enemies]

Further, a prince is respected when he is a true friend and a true enemy, that is, when without reservation he takes his stand as an ally of one prince against another. Such a course is always more advantageous than remaining neutral, because if two potentates among your neighbors come to blows, either they are so strong that if one of them conquers you need to fear the conqueror, or they are not. In either of these two conditions you will always profit most by making open and genuine war. In the first case, if you do not make open war, you are always the prey of the victor, to the delight and gratification of the vanquished, and you can show no reason why anyone should protect you, and no one gives you refuge because the conqueror does not wish allies who are untrustworthy and do not aid him in adversity; the loser does not give you refuge because you have not been willing, with weapons in your hands, to share his fortune.

[The Achaians Were Advised against Neutrality]

Antiochus once came into Greece, brought there by the Aeto-lians to drive out the Romans. He sent ambassadors to the Achaians,

---

1. *Bernabo Visconti, Duke of Milan, 1354–1385. His extraordinary acts are related by story-tellers and chroniclers. For example, the Duke saw some countrymen digging a grave. Asking about it, he was told that a pilgrim had died leaving no property. The priest and sexton refused to have anything to do with his body because they would not be paid. Summoning them, Bernabo asked: "Are these men telling the truth?" The priest and the sexton shouted together: "Signore, we ought to have what is due us." The Duke answered: "And who can give it to you? Can the dead man who does not have it?" But they replied: "We ought to have our due, no matter who pays it." Then said Bernabo: "And I will give it to you; death is your due. Where is the dead man? Bring him here. Put him in the grave. Seize the priest: throw him in. Where is the sexton? Throw him in. Shovel in the earth." And so he had the priest and the sexton*

who were friends of the Romans, to encourage them to take a neutral position. On the other hand, the Romans were urging the Achaians to take up arms for them. The subject came up for dis‑ cussion in the Achaian assembly, where the envoy from Antiochus urged them to stand neutral. The Roman envoy said in opposition: "As to what these men say about your not entering the war, nothing is more remote from your interests; without friendship, without dignity, you will be the victor's booty."[2]

[*Active Alliance Wins Friendship*]

So always he who is not your friend asks you for neutrality, and he who is your friend asks you to come out openly with your weapons. Yet irresolute princes, attempting to escape present danger, most of the time follow the neutral road and most of the time fall. When you as a prince appear as a vigorous supporter of one side, and your ally wins, he is then powerful and you are left at his dis‑ posal, yet he still has a duty to you and has developed love for you; and men are never so dishonorable that with a striking display of ingratitude they will crush a faithful adherent. Moreover, victories are never so unmixed that the victor can be wholly free from scruples, especially as to justice. Even if the ruler whom you support loses, you take refuge with him; as he can, he aids you and you are the ally of a Fortune that can rise again.

[*Alliance with a Weak Prince May Be Profitable*]

In the second situation, when those who are fighting are both so weak that you do not need to fear the victor, you are so much the more prudent in taking his side because you go to the overthrow of one prince with the aid of another who, if he were prudent, would defend him; if the second wins, he is at your disposal, and with your aid he must win.

[*Never Make a Voluntary Alliance with a Stronger Power*]

From this we learn that a wise prince sees to it that never, in order to attack someone, does he become the ally of a prince more

---

buried with the dead pilgrim, and went on his way. See Vito Vitale, "Bernabo Visconti nella novella e nella cronaca contemporanea," in ARCHIVIO STORICO LOMBARDO, ser. 3, XV (1901), 261–285; and Dorothy Muir, MILAN UNDER THE VISCONTI, pp. 70–72.

2. *Livy* 35. 49. *The Latin is inexact.*

powerful than himself, except when necessity forces him, as I said above. If you win, you are the powerful king's prisoner, and wise princes avoid as much as they can being in other men's power. The Venetians allied themselves with France against the Duke of Milan, though they could have avoided that alliance, from which resulted their downfall. But when a prince cannot avoid an alliance (as the Florentines could not when the Pope and Spain attacked Lombardy with their armies) then he joins in, for the reasons given above.[3]

[*Take the Lesser Evil as Good*]

Never should any government believe it can always choose safe courses;[4] on the contrary, it should suppose it can take doubtful ones only, because this is in the order of things, namely, that never do we try to avoid one disadvantage without running into another. So prudence consists in being able to recognize the seriousness of various disadvantages, and in choosing the least bad as good.

[*The Encouragement of Industry and Commerce; Festivals*]

A wise prince also shows himself a lover of the arts and sciences by patronizing accomplished men and honoring those who are excellent in any occupation. Besides, he encourages his citizens in thinking that they can tranquilly carry on their businesses, both in commerce and in agriculture and in every other business of men; he so governs that one man is not afraid to increase his possessions because of dread that they will be taken away, and another to open a trade for fear of the taxes; still further, he prepares rewards for those who try to do these things, and for anyone who plans in any way to enlarge the city or furnish the prince with greater resources. In addition to this, at proper times of the year he engages the people's attention with festivals and shows. And because every city is divided into guilds or into groups, he recognizes those bodies, meets with them sometimes, and makes himself an example of courtesy and princely generosity—always holding fast, nevertheless, the dignity of his high position, because this he never at any time forgets.

3. *In the present chapter.*
4. *On the difficulties of Florentine policy during the campaign of Charles of Bourbon, Machiavelli writes: "The heavens, when they intend to conceal their intentions, bring men into a position where they cannot make any sure plan"* (EXPEDITION II *to Guicciardini, letter of 27 March 1527).*

CHAPTER 22. A PRINCE'S CONFIDEN- TIAL OFFICERS

[*A Prince's Wisdom Appears in His Choice of Officials*]

Of no little importance to a prince is his choice of ministers, who are good or bad according to the prince's intelligence. In forming an opinion about a ruler's brains, the first thing is to look at the men he has around him, for when they are adequate and loyal he can be considered prudent, because he recognizes those who are competent and keeps them loyal. When they are otherwise, the prince is always to be estimated low, because the first error he makes, he makes in choosing advisers. Not a person who knew Messer Antonio da Venafro as the minister of Pandolfo Petrucci, prince of Siena, did not think Pandolfo a very able man, having Messer Antonio as his minister.[1] For brains are of three types: the first comprehends for itself; the second comprehends when another explains; the third does not comprehend either for itself or by means of another's explana- tion.[2] The first is exceedingly good, the second good, the third useless. It must certainly have been true, therefore, that if Pandolfo's brain was not in the first class, it was in the second, because any prince having the judgment to recognize the good or the ill that a man does or says, even though he has no original power of his own, recognizes his minister's deeds as bad or good; he rewards the latter and punishes the others; thus the minister cannot hope to trick him, and is always good.

[*The Minister's Ethics; the Prince's Gratitude*]

But as to how a prince can find out about any minister, there is this way that never fails: when you see that a minister is thinking more about himself than about you, and that in the course of all his actions he is seeking his own profit, such a man as this never is a good minister; never can you rely on him; because he who has your

1. *In one of his last writings Machiavelli quoted Antonio da Venafro with approval: "I remember in the Pisan war that the Pisans, worn out by its length, began to talk among themselves of coming to an agreement with you. When this became known to Pandolfo Petrucci, he sent Messer Antonio da Venafro to exhort them to the opposite. Addressing them publicly, at last Messer Antonio said that they had crossed a sea most tempestuous, and now they were going to drown in a mudhole" (*EXPEDITION II to Guicciardini, letter of 2 April 1527*).
2. *I follow the Florentine and Roman editions of 1532.*

existence in his hands should never think of himself but of his prince,[3] and never bring before him anything not of concern to him. And on the other side the wise prince, in order to keep the minister good, always has him in mind, honors him, makes him rich, puts him under obligation, gives him his share of honors and offices, so that the minister sees he cannot stand without the prince, and so that his many honors make him wish no more honors, his many riches make him wish no more riches, and his many offices make him fear changes. When, finally, the ministers and the princes in relation to the ministers are of such a sort, they can have faith in each other; and when it is otherwise, always the outcome is harmful either to the one or to the other.

3. *"A trustworthy counsellor who puts the good of his master ahead of his own life" (Dolce,* MEDEA, *Prolog).*

CHAPTER 23. HOW FLATTERERS CAN BE AVOIDED

[*To a Prudent Prince, Men Tell the Truth*]

I do not wish to omit an important matter in which princes with difficulty protect themselves from mistake, if they are not very prudent or if they do not make good choices. This is danger from flatterers, of whom courts are full. For men are so well satisfied with themselves and their doings and so deceive themselves about them, that with difficulty they protect themselves against this pest of flattery; and in trying to protect themselves, princes run the risk of becoming despised. There is no other way for securing yourself against flatteries except that men understand that they do not offend you by telling you the truth; but when everybody can tell you the truth, you fail to get respect. Hence a prudent prince uses a third method, choosing for his government wise men and to them alone giving free power to tell him the truth, but on such things only as he asks about, and on nothing else. But he asks them about everything and listens to their opinions; and then he decides for himself, at his own pleasure, on the basis of their advice;[1] and with each of them he so bears himself that every adviser realizes that the more freely he speaks, the better he is received. Except these ad-

1. *I follow the Florentine and Roman editions of 1532.*

visers, the prince listens to no one; he follows up the thing decided on and is firm in his decisions. He who does otherwise either is ruined by flatterers or changes often as the result of varying opinions. As a result, he is not respected.

[*The Emperor Maximilian Does Not Seek Advice*]

In this connection I bring up a modern example. Pre' Luca, agent for Maximilian, the present Emperor, speaking of His Majesty, says that he gets advice from nobody and that he never in anything acts as he wishes to.[2] This results from using a method opposite to that mentioned above, because the Emperor is a secretive man, does not impart his plans to a soul, does not get any opinion on them. But when as they are put into effect they become generally known, they are at once opposed by those around him, and he, being pliable, is pulled away from them. Consequently, what he does one day he destroys the next; no one ever knows what he wishes or intends to do, and on his decisions it is impossible to rely.

[*A Wise Prince Seeks Advice*]

A wise prince,[3] then, seeks advice continually, but when it suits him and not when it suits somebody else; moreover, he deprives everyone of courage to advise him on anything if he does not ask it. But nonetheless he is a big asker and then, on the things asked about, a patient listener to the truth. Further, if he learns that anybody for any reason does not tell him the truth, he is angry.

[*Only a Wise Prince Follows a Wise Policy*]

Because many judge that some princes who are reputed prudent are so considered not on account of their own natures but on account of the good advisers they have around them, I must explain that without doubt they are deceiving themselves. This is a general rule that never fails: a prince who is not wise himself cannot be advised well, unless indeed by chance he turns himself over to a single person—a very prudent man—who entirely controls him. In this case he really could get good advice, but not for long, because that tutor in a short time would take his position away from him. But if

2. *Machiavelli here draws on what he had written in his* REPORT ON GERMAN MATTERS *in 1508.*

3. *On this and other instances of the* wise *prince see chap. 8, n. 5.*

he gets advice from more than one, a prince who is not wise never gets his advice unified, and does not himself know how to unify it; of the advisers, each thinks of his own interests; the prince cannot control or understand them. And they cannot be otherwise; because men always turn out bad for you unless some necessity makes them good. Therefore it is to be concluded that good advice, from whomsoever it comes, must originate in the prince's discretion, and not the prince's discretion in the good advice.

CHAPTER 24. WHY THE PRINCES OF ITALY HAVE LOST THEIR STATES

[*The Advantages of the New Prince*]

The things written above,' carried out prudently, make a new prince seem an old one, and make him quickly safer and firmer in his position than if he were in it by right of descent. Because the actions of a new prince are more closely watched than are those of a hereditary prince; and when these reveal strength and wisdom, they lay hold on men and bind them to him more firmly than does ancient blood. Because men are more affected by present things than by past ones; and if in present conditions they prosper, they rejoice and ask nothing more; in fact, they will in every way defend a new prince, if in other things he does not fail himself. Thus he will gain double glory, for he will both begin a new princedom and will ennoble and strengthen it with good laws, good arms, and good examples. On the other hand a man born a prince who through imprudence loses his princedom will incur double shame.

[*The Wise Ruler Secures Popular Support and Keeps Up His Army*]

And if we consider those rulers who in Italy have lost their positions in our times, as the King of Naples, the Duke of Milan, and others, we find on their part, first, a common failure in their armies, for the reasons that we have discussed above at length.' Then we see that some of them either suffered hostility from the people or, if the people were friendly to them, did not know how to secure themselves against the rich. Without these defects, princes do

1. *In the entire work preceding.*
2. *Chaps. 12, 13, 14.*

not lose their states if they are strong enough to keep an army in the field.[3] Philip of Macedon, not Alexander's father but the one who was conquered by Titus Quintius, did not have much power in comparison with the greatness of the Romans and of Greece, who attacked him. Nonetheless, being a soldierly man and one who knew how to get on with the people and to secure himself against the rich, for many years he kept up the war against the invaders, and if at the end he lost the control of some cities, nevertheless he still retained his kingdom.

[*The Prince Must Rely on His Own Abilities*]

Therefore these princes of ours, who have been many years in their princedoms, and then have lost them, should not blame Fortune, but their own laziness. Never in good weather having imagined there could be a change (it is a common defect in men not to reckon, during a calm, on a storm), when at last bad weather came, they thought only of running away and not of defending themselves; and they hoped that the people, sickened by the conquerors' arrogance, would call them back. This plan, when there are no others, is good; but all the same it is very bad to abandon other expedients for this one, because you should never be content to fall, trusting that someone will come along to pick you up. Either that does not happen, or, if it happens, it brings you no security, because such a resource is abject, and does not depend upon yourself. And those defenses alone are good, are certain, are durable, that depend on yourself and your own abilities.

3. *Cf. chap. 10.*

CHAPTER 25. FORTUNE'S POWER IN HUMAN AFFAIRS AND HOW SHE CAN BE FORESTALLED

[*Fortune Controls More Than Half Our Actions*]

As I am well aware, many have believed and now believe human affairs so controlled by Fortune and by God that men with their prudence cannot manage them—yes, more, that men have no recourse against the world's variations. Such believers therefore decide that they need not sweat much over man's activities but can let

Chance govern them. This belief has been the more firmly held in our times by reason of the great variations in affairs that we have seen in the past and now see every day beyond all human prediction. Thinking on these variations, I myself now and then incline in some respects to their belief. Nonetheless, in order not to annul our free will, I judge it true that Fortune may be mistress of one half our actions but that even she leaves the other half, or almost, under our control.

[*The Floods of Fortune Can Be Controlled*]

I compare Fortune with one of our destructive rivers which, when it is angry, turns the plains into lakes, throws down the trees and the buildings, takes earth from one spot, puts it in another; everyone flees before the flood; everyone yields to its fury and nowhere can repel it. Yet though such it is, we need not therefore conclude that when the weather is quiet, men cannot take precautions with both embankments and dykes, so that when the waters rise, either they go off by a canal or their fury is neither so wild nor so damaging. The same things happen about Fortune. She shows her power where strength and wisdom do not prepare to resist her, and directs her fury where she knows that no dykes or embankments are ready to hold her. If you consider Italy—the scene of these variations and their first mover—you see that she is a plain without dykes and without any embankment; but if she were embanked with adequate strength and wisdom, like Germany, Spain, and France, this flood either would not make the great variations it does or would not come upon us. I think this is all I need to say in general on resisting Fortune.

[*Men Are Fortunate Who Adapt Their Procedure to the Times*]

Limiting myself more to particulars, I say that such princes as I have described live happily today and tomorrow fall without changing their natures or any of their traits. This I believe results, first, from the causes lengthily discussed in the preceding pages,[1] namely, that any prince who relies exclusively on Fortune falls when she varies. I believe also that a prince succeeds who adapts his way of proceeding to the nature of the times, and conversely one does not succeed whose procedure is out of harmony with the times.

1. For example, chaps. 7, 24.

In the things that lead them to the end they seek, that is, glory and riches, men act in different ways: one with caution, another im, petuously; one by force, the other with skill; one by patience, the other with its contrary; and all of them with these differing methods attain their ends. We find also that of two cautious men, one carries out his purpose, the other does not. Likewise, we find two men with two differing temperaments equally successful, one being cau, tious and the other impetuous. This results from nothing else than the nature of the times, which is harmonious or not with their procedure. From that results what I have said: that two men, working differently, secure the same outcome; and of two working in the same way, one attains his end, and the other does not. On this depend variations in success: if, for one whose policy is caution and patience, times and affairs circle about in such a way that his policy is good, he continues to succeed; if times and affairs change, he falls, because he does not change his way of proceeding. Nor is any man living so prudent that he knows how to accommodate himself to this condition, both because he cannot deviate from that to which nature disposes him, and also because, always having prospered while walking in one road, he cannot be induced to leave it. Therefore the cautious man, when it is time to adopt impetuosity, does not know how. Hence he falls; yet if he could change his nature with times and affairs, Fortune would not change.

[*Fortune Favored Pope Julius II*]

Pope Julius II proceeded impetuously in all his affairs; and he found the times and their circumstances so in harmony with his own way of proceeding that he was always successful. Consider the first expedition he attempted against Bologna, while Messer Giovanni Bentivogli was still alive. The Venetians did not approve it, neither did the King of Spain; with France, Julius was negotiating about such an expedition; nonetheless, in his energy and impetuosity he started in person on that campaign. This move made Spain and the Venetians stand uncertain and motionless, the latter through fear, and the other through his wish to regain the whole Kingdom of Naples. And on the other side the Pope dragged after him the King of France, because that King, seeing that Julius had already moved, and wishing to make him a friend in order to humble the Venetians, judged himself unable to deny the Pope soldiers without harming him quite evidently. Julius, then, accomplished with his impetuous movement what no other pontiff, with the utmost human prudence, would ever have accomplished; if he had waited until he could leave Rome with his terms fixed and all things in order, as any other pontiff would have done, he would never have succeeded, because the King of France would have had a thousand excuses and the Venetians would have roused in him a thousand fears.[2] I shall omit his other actions, which were all of the same sort, and for him all came out well. And the shortness of his life did not allow him to get any taste of the opposite; because if times had come when he needed to proceed with caution, they would have brought about his downfall; for never would he have turned away from those methods to which his nature inclined him.

[*"Fortune Friends the Bold"*]

I conclude then (with Fortune varying and men remaining stubborn in their ways) that men are successful while they are in close harmony with Fortune, and when they are out of harmony, they are unsuccessful. As for me, I believe this: it is better to be impetuous than cautious, because Fortune is a woman and it is necessary, in order to keep her under, to cuff and maul her. She more often lets herself be overcome by men using such methods than by those who proceed coldly; therefore always, like a woman, she is the friend of young men, because they are less cautious, more spirited, and with more boldness master her.

2. *I follow the editions of 1532.*

CHAPTER 26. AN EXHORTATION TO GRASP ITALY AND SET HER FREE FROM THE BARBARIANS

[*Italy Ready for a Hero to Unite and Deliver Her*]

Having taken account, then, of everything discussed above,[1] and meditating whether at present in Italy conditions so unite as to offer a new prince glory, and whether the matter to be found here assures to a prudent and able ruler a chance to introduce a form that will

1. *Throughout* THE PRINCE.

bring him glory and her people general happiness,[2] I believe so many things now join together for the advantage of a new prince that I do not know what time could ever be more fit for such a prince to act. If, as I have said,[3] to show Moses' ability the people of Israel needed to be enslaved in Egypt, and to reveal Cyrus' greatness of spirit the Persians had to be oppressed by the Medes, and to exhibit Theseus' excellence the Athenians had to be scattered, so to reveal an Italian spirit's ability Italy needed to be brought to her present condition, to be more slave than the Hebrews, more servant than the Persians, more scattered than the Athenians, without head, without order, beaten, despoiled, lacerated, devastated, subject to every sort of ruination.

[*Who Will the Leader Be?*]

And though up to now various gleams have appeared in some Italians from which we might judge them ordained by God for her redemption, nevertheless we have seen later that, in the highest course of their actions, they have been disapproved by Fortune.[4] Hence, as though without life, she awaits whoever he may be who can heal her wounds and put an end to the devastation and plunder of Lombardy, to the robbery and ransom of the Kingdom and Tus-cany,[5] and cure her of those sores already long since festered. She is now praying God to send someone to redeem her from such bar-barous cruelty and arrogance; she is now also ready and willing to follow a banner, if only there be one who will raise it.

[*The Medici Family Divinely Chosen to Unite Italy*]

There is not, at present, anyone in whom she can have more hope than in your glorious family, which, through its fortune and its wisdom and strength, favored by God and by the Church—of which it is now head—can make itself the leader of this redemption. That will not be very hard if you bring before you the actions and

2. *The clearest statement in* THE PRINCE *of the ruler's function. The philosophical con-cept of form and matter suggests almost creative power in the prince.*

3. *Chap. 6.*

4. *Easily applied to Cesare Borgia (cf. chap. 7, above), but probably including "the Italians mentioned above" of the fourth paragraph of this chapter. Machiavelli's praise of Cesare, though hearty, is limited; nowhere, unless here, does he suggest redemptive qualities in Borgia.*

5. *I follow the editions of 1532.*

the lives of those named above.[6] And though these men were exceptional and marvelous, nevertheless they were men; and every one
of them had a poorer chance than the present one, because their
undertaking was not more just than this, nor easier, nor was God
more friendly to them than to you. Here justice is great, "for a war
is just for those to whom it is necessary, and arms are sacred when
there is no hope except in arms."[7] Now your opportunity is very
great,[8] and when there is great opportunity, there cannot be great
difficulty, if only your family will use the methods of those whom
I have set up as your aim. Besides this, now we see marvelous,
unexampled signs that God is directing you: the sea is divided; a
cloud shows you the road; the rock pours out water; manna rains
down;[9] everything unites for your greatness. The rest you must do
yourself. God does not do everything, so as not to take from us free
will and part of the glory that pertains to us.

[Italy Needs Only Leaders]

It is not astonishing if none of the Italians mentioned above[10] has
been able to do what we hope your illustrious family will do, and if,
in so many convulsions in this land and in so much warfare, Italy's
military vigor always seems extinct. The cause is that her old
institutions were not good, and no one has been wise enough to
devise new ones; and nothing does so much honor to a man newly
risen to power as do the new laws and new institutions he devises.
These things, when they are well based and have greatness in them,
win a new ruler reverence and awe. And in Italy there is no lack of
matter on which to impose any form; there is great power in the
limbs, if only it were not wanting in the heads. Observe in duels
and in combats by small numbers how superior the Italians are in
strength, in skill, in intelligence; but when they are in armies, they
make no showing. And it all results from the weakness of the heads;
because those who are wise are not obeyed—and each one thinks he
is wise—since up to now no one has risen so high, in both ability

6. Moses, Cyrus, Theseus.
7. Livy, HISTORY 9. 1. 10.
8. Everything tends to favor the delivering prince.
9. Exodus 14:17. Note the reference to Moses early in the chapter.
10. Those mentioned above are thought to be Francesco Sforza and Cesare Borgia (chap. 7).
Perhaps Pope Julius II should also be included (chap. 11).

and Fortune, that to him the others yield."[11] This is the reason why for so long a time, in the many wars fought in the past twenty years, whenever there has been an army wholly Italian, it has always failed when tested.   To this the chief witness is the Taro, then Alessandria, Capua, Genoa, Vailà, Bologna, Mestri.

[*The Ruler of Italy Needs an Army of Loyal Subjects*]

If then, your glorious family resolves to follow the excellent men I have named who redeemed their countries, she must before all other things, as the true foundation of every undertaking, provide herself with her own armies, because there cannot be more faithful or truer or better soldiers. And though each one of them is good, they will become better if united, when they see themselves com-manded by their own prince and by him honored and maintained. It is necessary, therefore, for her to prepare such armies in order with Italian might to defend herself against foreigners.

[*New and Superior Tactics*]

And though the Swiss and the Spanish infantry are considered formidable, nonetheless in both there is a defect, by reason of which a third type could not merely withstand them but could feel certain of defeating them, because the Spanish cannot repel cavalry, and the Swiss need to dread infantry when they meet in combat any as stubborn as themselves. Hence experience has shown and will show that the Spanish cannot repel French cavalry, and the Swiss are destroyed by Spanish infantry. And though of this last there has been no complete demonstration, yet one was suggested at the battle of Ravenna, where the Spanish infantry were face to face with the German battalions, which use the same battle array as the Swiss; there the Spanish, with the agility of their bodies and the help of their bucklers, got within the pikes, underneath them,[12] and were safe in attacking the Germans, without the latter having any defense; had the Spaniards not been charged by the cavalry, they would have destroyed all the Germans. A prince who recognizes the defects of

11. *For Machiavelli's later observations of such leaders, see* FAMILIAR LETTERS *219B (Nov. 1526).*

12. *The point of the seventeen-foot pike was some thirteen feet in front of the pikeman. The Spanish soldiers, by ducking, got "within the pikes," that is, nearer the pikeman than the point of his spear.*

both these types of infantry, then, can organize a new one that will repel cavalry and not be afraid of infantry. This will be effected by the nature of their weapons and by change in their tactics.[13] And these are among the things that, as new institutions, give reputation and greatness to a new prince.

[*Final Exhortation to Uniting Italy*]

By no means, then, should this opportunity be neglected, in order that Italy, after so long a time, may see her redeemer come. I cannot express with what love he will be received in all the provinces that have suffered from these alien floods, with what thirst for vengeance, with what firm loyalty, with what gratitude, with what tears! What gates will be shut against him? What peoples will refuse him obedience? What envy will oppose him? What Italian will refuse him homage? For everyone this barbarian tyranny stinks. Let your glorious family, then, undertake this charge with that spirit and that hope with which men undertake just labors, in order that beneath her ensign this native land of ours may be ennobled and, with her guidance, we may realize the truth of Petrarch's words:

> Valor against wild rage
> Will take up arms, and the combat will be short,
> Because ancestral courage
> In our Italian hearts is not yet dead.[14]

13. *See Machiavelli's* ART OF WAR, *especially bks. 2 and 3.*
14. *Petrarch,* CANZONE *16. 13–16.*

A PASTORAL: THE IDEAL RULER

[*Perhaps written as early as 1513; at the latest, it is before the death of Lorenzo de' Medici in 1519.*

In the sixteenth century the pastoral was one of the most esteemed forms of literature, practiced by the most famous poets. The climate for its appreciation has during the last century been so poor that such compositions have received scant attention. To this undervaluation, the great exception in English literature has been the seventeenth-century LYCIDAS, *a typical pastoral both in following the convention of the shepherd life and in devoting higher strains to the public affairs of the age. A writing man like Machiavelli could hardly avoid the pastoral; a man with a passion for politics would not keep politics out of his shepherd poetry. Machiavelli perhaps realized that he was not especially gifted as a pastoral poet; at least he did not publish these verses.*

As a pastoral counterpart to THE PRINCE, *this poem sets before us a ruler whose abilities are suited to the highest tasks. Wisdom, self-control, justice, popularity, eloquence—all are his. These qualities of the ideal prince, Machiavelli, with the allowable exaggeration of pastoral eulogy, found in the Medici prince Lorenzo. And Machiavelli was not the only one who based on that young man great hopes for Florence.*]

1 NOW THAT IN THE SHADE UNDER THIS LAUREL I SEE
   my flock grazing around me, I am resolved to begin a loftier
   work.

4 If ever, sweet flute, your harmony set the rocks in motion,
   made the trees move onward, the rivers stand still, and the
   wind grow quiet,

7 show now your powers united, and so strong that the earth
   may wonder and rejoice, and the sky exult in our songs;

10 yet you may desire another voice and another style, because
   full praise for such beauty requires that loftier genius be
   aroused;

l. 1 For Lorenzo de' Medici as the laurel (lauro), see Ariosto's capitolo NELLA STAGION.
l. 3 Loftier than the normal pastoral, as dealing with a higher subject.

13 since a youth celestial and not earthly, of habits exalted, of godlike qualities, is fittingly praised by a godlike man.

16 Bestow upon me then, O Phoebus, your light; if ever you listen to mortal prayer, now illumine my dark mind.

19 I see your face shining beyond its wont with living glory, nor does wind or cloud afflict this day.

22 Aided by your great might, O sacred Apollo, and by your powers, I resolve to spend it in doing your Hyacinth honor.

25 Hyacinth, your name I am wont to celebrate; and as a re-minder for all now alive, I write it on every tree, on every rock,

28 and with it your beauties great and godlike, and your deeds that are enough to make famous any man who speaks or writes of you.

31 Heaven was striving to show its virtue when it gave us a man so surpassing, to make us partake its beauties.

34 Hence every light before this one grows dim, as soon as we behold those looks deserving every crown and every diadem.

37 Then from the splendor that reigns in that face, and from every part examined for itself, we learn how great is the force of nature.

40 See then the rest in harmony with her; hear, then, the sound of his pleasing words, such as to make a marble-stone, a rock show life.

43 So that earth smiles where you set foot, and the air grows happy wherever the welcome sounds of your voice are heard.

46 When you depart, the little plant that was flowering withers and is left in misery, and the air deprived of you shows grief.

49 And by no means as something less excellent appears your natural desire for gaining fame that will make your glory evident.

52 Hence it is my prayer that I, even I, O Jove divine, among so many trumpets exalting him, may be permitted to make my rude horn resound.

55 All the shepherds who live in this forest, without regarding your youth, have submitted to you their quarrels.

l. 13 *Lorenzo de'Medici the Younger was in 1514 about twenty-two years old. Cf. also line 57.*

l. 31 *The delivering prince of* PRINCE *26 is ordained by God.*

l. 49 *The honor and renown of the ruler is emphasized in* PRINCE *26.*

l. 57 *The pastoral mode of speaking of a good lawgiver (*PRINCE *24).*

58 You with your accomplished and lordly genius, with varied ways and diverse inventions make them return to their fold in happiness.

61 Full of pity you are; if you see a shepherd wretched through adverse fortune or through love, with your pleasing speech you gladden him.

64 Not merely are you the glory of every shepherd; as all can see, you enrich the forests like every god who inhabits them.

67 No longer is it a grief to you, O forests! that Diana lives in Heaven, nor do you long for Phoebus to return to tend Admetus' herds,

70 nor do you any more call for Hecuba's son, nor Cephalus, nor Atlanta, because with this youth you are more happy, more glad.

73 In you I see all the virtues brought together; nor does it seem a marvel, because in shaping you not one god only took part in so great a work.

76 When at the beginning Jove resolved to create you, the first charge he gave to Vulcan, in order more fair, more lively or joyous to make you.

79 Now when Jove sees you created, he shows himself so happy, so joyous in countenance that Ganymede is jealous for his office,

82 for in that earth mingled with water such a spirit Minerva put as time or labor never produces.

85 Your head Venus then surrounded with her immortal graces, and "To shepherds you will always be pleasant and gracious," she said.

88 The white Hours gladly after that plucked violets and fresh flowers and with their juices sprinkled you well, and with various odors.

91 Fierce Mars, that you might shine the more, within your noble breast enclosed a heart like that of Caesar the general, like those of all the generals.

94 A shrewd discernment Mercury instilled, whereby you display or keep hidden your happy fortune and your afflictions and hardships.

l. 91 *The military leader* (PRINCE 14).
l. 94 *The prince can adapt himself to all circumstances* (PRINCE 25).

97 Juno put in citizen's clothing a soul fit to rule empire and kingdoms, and Saturn gave to you Nestor's years.

100 O gift of so many gods, condescend to accept me among your faithful subjects, if to have such a servant you do not scorn.

103 And if I see that my song will delight you, these valleys and these little hills will echo in your praise verses splendid and measureless;

106 for my thoughts are so strained to please you that my desire is only that I shall think of obeying, you of commanding.

109 And though I have been reared in the throng of these rough shepherds, when I speak of you, much higher than my wont I fly.

113 Yet still higher up you will see me mounting if I know that you accept my gift when I recite your praises.

115 Other than this, what I have I give you; yours is the flock you see; even these poor sheep as well are yours.

118 But because the hour has almost come when the animals go to rest, and only the bat is seen at large,

121 I shall keep concealed the love I cherish, and home I shall go with my herd, hoping one day to return more famous

124 to sing your praises, and more happy.

l. 97 *Apparently a reference to the Medici as citizens.*
l. 115 *Cf. the dedication of* The Prince.

A DISCOURSE ON REMODEL-
ING THE GOVERNMENT OF
FLORENCE

[Written on the request of Pope Leo X, Giovanni de'Medici]

[Written about 1520, after the death of Lorenzo de'Medici, Duke of Urbino, and before that of Pope Leo X.

This work is valuable chiefly as showing the flexibility and yet the firmness of Machiavelli's conceptions. On the one hand he realizes, as THE PRINCE *had already indicated, that conditions exist in which absolutism cannot be avoided; on the other, he is sure that for Florence the best form of government is the republican. Even his belief in such a possibility—some-times called an illusion—is not doctrinaire; Florence can be prepared for it by a process of education that admits the fallibility of human material. Though Machiavelli abhorred Medici tyranny, he could accept it when no better possibility was offered; though he estimated Savonarola as dangerously am-bitious and as inadequate in practical affairs, yet he could accept parts of his theory, notably the approval of a Great Council, as fundamental to Floren-tine government.]*

THE REASON WHY FLORENCE THROUGHOUT HER history has frequently varied her methods of government is that she has never been either a republic or a princedom having the qualities each requires, because we cannot call that republic well-established in which things are done according to the will of one man yet are decided with the approval of many;[1] nor can we believe a republic fitted to last, in which there is no content for those elements that must be contented if republics are not to fall. And that this is the truth, we can learn from the governments Florence has had from 1393 until now.

Beginning with the alteration made at that date by Messer Maso degli Albizzi, we see that then the lawmakers intended to give her

1. *A description of the government of Cosimo and Lorenzo de'Medici, in which the real authority had to get the consent of the nominal authority.*

the form of a republic governed by aristocrats, but their form had so many defects that it did not last longer than forty years; and it would have been less permanent if the Visconti wars had not ensued, which kept it united. Its defects were, among others, that it prepared the list of those eligible to office far ahead of time; because of this, fraud was easy, and the choice could be not good; for, since men change easily and turn from good to bad and, on the other hand, places were given to citizens much ahead of time, it could easily happen that the choice was good and the drawing bad.[2] Besides this, nothing was established to cause fear in great men, so that they would not set up factions, which are the ruin of a government. The Signoria,[3] moreover, had slight prestige and too much power, being able to dispose without appeal of the life and property of the citizens, and being able to call the populace to a parliament. Hence it came to be not the defender of the state but a means for causing its ruin, whenʹ ever an influential citizen could either control or befuddle it. On the other hand, as has been said, it had little prestige, because, since often it included men of low station, young men, and had a short term, and did not carry on important business, it could not have prestige.

That constitution also suffered from a failing not of slight imʹ portance: that men in private station took part in deliberations on public business. This kept up the prestige of the men in private stations and took it away from those in official ones, and it had the effect of taking away power and prestige from the magistrates—a thing opposed to every sort of wellʹordered government. To these failings of that constitution was added another, which amounted to as much as all the rest: the people did not have their share. These conditions, altogether, caused countless injustices, and if, as I have said, external wars had not kept that government solid, it would have fallen sooner than it did.

Next, after this, Cosimo's government was established, tending more toward the princedom than toward the republic. If yet it lasted longer than the other, the cause lay in two things: one, that it was established with the people's aid; the other, that it was controlled

2. *A citizen might be fit for an office when his name was put in the pouch containing the names of those eligible, but might be unfit when, much later, on the drawing out of his name, he assumed office.*

3. *The head of the Florentine government, consisting of the Gonfalonier and (usually) eight Priors.*

by the prudence of two such men as Cosimo and Lorenzo his grandson. Nevertheless, such weakness resulted from its having to decide through a large number what Cosimo planned to carry out,[4] that many times he risked the failure of a plan. From this came the frequent parliaments and the frequent exiles that took place during his control, and then at last, at the critical time of King Charles's expedition, the Medici government fell.

After that, the city decided to resume the form of a republic, but did not apply herself to adopting it in a form that would be lasting, because the ordinances then made did not satisfy all the parties among the citizens; and on the other hand, the government could not inflict punishment. And it was so defective and remote from a true republic that a Gonfalonier for life, if he was intelligent and wicked, easily could make himself prince; if he was good and weak,[5] he could easily be driven out, with the ruin of the whole government. Since it would be a long matter to set forth all the reasons, I will tell just one: the Gonfalonier did not have those around him who could protect him, if he were good; nor anyone who, if he were bad, could restrain him or set him right.

The reason why all these governments have been defective is that the alterations in them have been made not for the fulfilment of the common good, but for the strengthening and security of the party.[6] Such security has not yet been attained, because there has always been in the city a party that was discontented, which has been a very powerful tool for anybody who wished to make a change.

The only government now left to consider is that from 1512 to the present, and what its weaknesses and strong qualities have been, but because it is a recent affair and everybody knows it, I shall not speak of it. To be sure, the Duke's death has brought things to a point where new types of government must be considered.[7] So I believe that, to show my loyalty to Your Holiness, I cannot err in saying what occurs to me. First I shall give the opinions of many others as I have heard them stated, next adding my own opinion; if I err, Your Holiness must excuse me as more loving than wise.

I say, then, that some judge no government can be established

4. *His plans became law only through republican channels.*
5. *Virtually a reference to Piero Soderini, such a Gonfalonier for life, driven out in 1512.*
6. *The party making them.*
7. *Lorenzo de' Medici, Duke of Urbino, was in charge of Florence until his death in 1519.*

firmer than that existing in the times of Cosimo and of Lorenzo. Some others wish one more inclusive.[8] They say, indeed—those who would like a government like Cosimo's—that things easily go back to what is natural. For this reason, since naturally Florentine citizens honor your house, enjoy those favors that come from it, and love what it loves, and since they have followed this habit for sixty years, nothing else can happen but that when they see the same ways,[9] the same frame of mind will return to them. Moreover they believe few could continue in an opposing frame of mind—and those few would do so through a habit of opposition, easily got rid of. To these reasons they add necessity, showing that Florence cannot continue without a director; and since she has to have one, it is much better that he be of the house the people are accustomed to bow down to than that either, not having a director, they should live in confusion or, having one, should get him elsewhere—which would bring less prestige and less satisfaction to everybody.

Against this opinion we answer that a government of that sort is risky if for no other reason than that it is weak. If the government of Cosimo had in those times so many weaknesses as are adduced above, in these times such a government would redouble them, because the city, the citizens, the times are different from what they were then, so that by no possibility can anyone devise a government in Florence that can last and be like that one. In the first place, Cosimo's government had the approval of the people generally, and the present one has their disapproval. The citizens of Cosimo's time had never experienced in Florence a government that gave greater power to the people; the present citizens have experienced one that they think more just and that pleases them better. In Italy at that time there was neither army nor power that the Florentines, even though standing alone, could not with their armies resist; but now, since Spain and France are here, the Florentines must ally themselves with one of the two; yet if the ally they select loses, at once they are left as the booty of the victor—a thing that in Cosimo's day would not have happened. Formerly, the citizens were accustomed to paying many taxes; now, through either inability or change in custom, they are out of the habit; and to try to get them back into it is a matter hateful and dangerous. The Medici who were governing

8. *Taking in a larger number of citizens.*
9. *The ways they had been accustomed to under Medici rule.*

then, since they had been educated and brought up among the citizens, conducted themselves with such friendliness that they gained favor. Now, they have grown so great that, since they have gone beyond all the habits of citizens, there cannot be such intimacy and consequently such favor. Hence, considering this unlikeness in times and in men, there cannot be a greater deception than to believe that upon such differently shaped matter one can stamp the same form. And if in that day, as I said above,[10] every ten years the Medici were in danger of losing control, now they would actually lose it. Nor should anyone believe that men easily return to a way of life that is old and habitual, because in truth they do so when the old way of living is more pleasing than the new one, but when it pleases less, they do not return to the old way unless forced to, and they live in it only as long as that force lasts.

Besides this, though it is true that Florence cannot exist without a director, and that if she should have to decide between one un-official director and another, she would like better a director from the house of Medici than one from any other house, nevertheless, if it is a decision between an official and an unofficial director,[11] the official director would always be more pleasing—no matter where taken from—than the unofficial director.

Some hold the opinion that you cannot lose control of the govern-ment without an attack from outside, and believe you will always have time enough to make a friendly arrangement with any invader. In this they deceive themselves seriously, because, usually, alliance is not made with the strongest power but with the power which just then has the best opportunity for injuring you or which your spirit and your fancy most dispose you to love. Your ally may chance to be defeated (and if defeated he is left in the power of the victor) and his conqueror may not decide on a treaty with you, either because you are too late in asking for it or because he has grown to hate you as a result of your connection with his enemies. For example, Lodovico the Duke of Milan would, if he could, have made a treaty with King Louis XII of France. King Frederick would have made

10. P. *103, "the frequent parliaments."* Cf. DISCOURSES *3. 1;* HISTORY OF FLOR-ENCE *6. 7; 7. 1 end.*

11. *An official director would be one constitutionally chosen, as opposed to Cosimo de' Medici as a prince without legal recognition.*

a treaty with the same ruler if he could have secured one.[12] Both of
these princes lost their states through not being able to make treaties;
at such times a thousand accidents spring up to hold you back.
Hence, everything considered, we cannot call a government modeled
on Cosimo's either safe or firm, since it has so many causes for lack
of firmness. Therefore, it should not be acceptable to Your Holiness
and your friends.

As to those who prefer a government more inclusive than
Cosimo's, I say that unless it is inclusive in such a way that it will
become a well-ordered republic, its inclusiveness is likely to make it
fall more rapidly. And if they will explicitly tell how they would
like it organized, I shall give an explicit answer, but since they
continue in generalities, I am not able to answer other than generally.
I believe the following answer alone is enough; so to confute the
government of Cosimo, I say this: No firm government can be
devised if it is not either a true princedom or a true republic, because
all the constitutions between these two are defective. The reason is
entirely evident, because the princedom has just one path to dissolution, that is, to descend toward the republic. And similarly the
republic has just one path toward being dissolved, that is, to rise
toward the princedom. Governments of a middle sort have two
ways: they can rise toward the princedom and descend toward the
republic. From this comes their lack of firmness. It is therefore not
possible, Your Holiness, if you wish to give Florence a firm government for your own glory and the security of your friends, to set up
there other than a true princedom or a republic having its distinctive
parts. Any other form would be useless and very short-lived.

Now as to the princedom, I shall not discuss it in detail, both
because of the difficulty of establishing one here and because there
are no facilities for doing it. Moreover Your Holiness needs to
understand that in all cities where the citizens are accustomed to
equality, a princedom cannot be set up except with the utmost
difficulty, and in those cities where the citizens are accustomed to
inequality, a republic cannot be set up except with the utmost
difficulty. In order to form a republic in Milan, where inequality
among the citizens is great, necessarily all the nobility must be
destroyed and brought to an equality with the others, because among

12. *King Frederick of the Kingdom of Southern Italy.*

them are men so above all rules that the laws are not enough to hold them down, but there must be a living voice and a kingly power to hold them down. On the contrary, in order to have a princedom in Florence, where equality is great, the establishment of inequality would be necessary; noble lords of walled towns and boroughs would have to be set up, who in support of the prince would with their arms and their followers stifle the city and the whole province. A prince alone, lacking a nobility, cannot support the weight of a princedom; for that reason it is necessary that between him and the generality of the people there should be a middle group that will help him support it. This can be seen in all the states with a prince, and especially in the kingdom of France, where the gentlemen rule the people, the princes the gentlemen, and the king the princes.

But because to form a princedom where a republic would go well is a difficult thing and, through being difficult, inhumane and unworthy of whoever hopes to be considered merciful and good, I shall pass over any further treatment of the princedom and speak of the republic, both because Florence is a subject very suitable for taking this form and because I know that Your Holiness is much inclined toward one; and I believe that you defer establishing it because you hope to find an arrangement by which your power in Florence may continue great and your friends may live in security. Since I believe I have discovered one, I hope Your Highness will give attention to my discovery, so that if there is anything good in it, you can make use of it and also learn from it how great is my wish to serve you. And you will see that in this republic of mine your power is not only preserved but is increased, your friends continue to be honored and safe, and the whole body of citizens has evident reasons for being satisfied. With the utmost respect, I beg Your Holiness not to condemn and not to praise this discourse of mine without first reading it through. And likewise I beg you not to be disturbed by some changes in the magistrates, because when things are not well organized, the less there is left of the old, the less there is left of the bad.

Those who organize a republic ought to provide for the three different sorts of men who exist in all cities, namely, the most im⁄portant, those in the middle, and the lowest. And though in Florence the citizens possess the equality mentioned above, nonethe⁄less some of her citizens have ambitious spirits and think they deserve to outrank the others; these must be satisfied in organizing a republic; the last government, indeed, fell for no other cause than that such a group was not satisfied. To men of this sort it is not possible to give satisfaction unless dignity is given to the highest offices in the republic—which dignity is to be maintained in their persons.

By no possibility can this dignity be given to the highest offices in the government of Florence if the Signoria and the members of the College remain in the same condition as in the past. On account of the way in which these groups are chosen—since important and influential men now sit in them only rarely—either this governmental dignity must be lowered and be put in unsuitable places (which is contrary to all political order), or must be abandoned to private individuals.[13] Therefore this method is necessarily to be corrected, and in its correction the loftiest ambition in the city is to be satisfied. This is the way to correct it. Abolish the Signoria, the Eight of *Pratica*, and the Twelve Good Men;[14] and in exchange for them, in order to give dignity to the government, ordain sixtyfive citizens of fortyfive years and more, fiftythree for the major guilds and twelve for the minor guilds, who should remain for life in the government, in the following manner: Choose from the said number a Gonfalonier of Justice for two or three years, if it should not seem proper to set him up for life; the sixtyfour citizens who are left are to be divided into two groups, thirtytwo for each. One group is to govern along with the Gonfalonier for one year, the other group the next year; and so in succession they are to exchange, keeping the arrangement indicated below. All together are to be called the Signoria.

The thirtytwo are to be divided into four groups, eight to a group; and each group is to reside with the Gonfalonier three months in the Palace, and to assume the magistracy with the ceremonies that are customary, and to carry on all the business that the Signoria alone carries on today. And after that, with its other companions of the thirtytwo, it should have all the authority and carry on all the business that today the Signoria, the Eight of *Pratica*, and the

13. *To allow the government to be controlled by political bosses, not in office, as in Cosimo's time.*

14. *The Eight of* Pratica *dealt with foreign and military affairs; the Twelve Good Men with finance and trade.*

members of the College carry on; these are abolished above. So this, as I have said, would be the chief head and chief arm of the govern-ment. This arrangement, if it is carefully considered, will be recognized as giving dignity and influence to the head of the govern-ment, for, evidently, weighty men, who have prestige, will always occupy the highest places. It will not be necessary to consult private individuals—which I said above is pernicious in a republic—because the thirty-two who are not that year in the magistracy can serve for advice and consultation. It will also be possible for your Holiness to put in this first selection, as I shall explain below, all your friends and trusted followers. But let us come to the second rank in the government.

I believe it is necessary, since there are three sorts of men, as I said above, that there be also three ranks in a republic, and not more. Therefore I believe it good to get rid of the jumble of councils that have existed for some time in your city. These have been formed not because they were necessary to good government but to feed through them the vanity of more of the citizens, and to feed it with a thing that in truth is of no consequence for the well-being of the city, because all of these councils can by means of parties be demoralized.

If I am trying, then, to design a republic with three components, it seems to me necessary to abolish the Seventy, the Hundred, and the Council of the People and of the Community; and in exchange for all these to set up a Council of Two Hundred, composed of men at least forty years old, forty of them chosen from the minor guilds and a hundred and sixty from the major guilds; not one of them would be permitted to belong to the Sixty-five. They should hold office for life and be called the Council of the Selected. This Coun-cil, along with the Sixty-five named, should do all the things and have all the power that today is held by the above mentioned councils abolished to make way for it. And this would be the second rank in the government; all of its members would be chosen by Your Holiness. In order to make these changes and to support and regulate the above-mentioned groups and those that will be described below, and for greater security to Your Holiness' authority and friends, Your Holiness and the Most Honorable Cardinal of the Medici must have, by means of the *Balía*,[15] as much authority during

15. Balía *means, in general, power. Specifically, here and usually in Machiavelli, it is a committee with arbitrary power to remodel the Florentine government.*

the lives of both as is held by the entire people of Florence. The magistracy of the Eight of Defence and *Balìa* is to be appointed by the authority of Your Holiness, from time to time. Also, for greater security of the government and of Your Holiness' friends, the levy of infantry is to be divided into two brigades, to which Your Holiness, on your own authority, should provide annually two commissioners, one commissioner for each brigade.

We see that by the things mentioned above we satisfy two sorts of men, and give firmness to your authority in the city and to that of your friends, since you have the military and criminal justice in your hand, the laws in your bosom, and all the heads of the government as your supporters.

It is now left to satisfy the third and final class of men, which is the whole general body of citizens, who will never be satisfied (and he who believes differently is not wise) if their power is not restored or if they do not have a promise that it will be restored. And because to restore it all at one time would not be for the security of your friends, nor for the upholding of the power of Your Holiness, it is necessary in part to restore it and in part to promise to restore it in such a way that they will be altogether certain of having it again. And therefore I judge that you are under the necessity of reopening the Hall of the Council of One Thousand, or at least of the Six Hundred Citizens, who would allot, just as they formerly did, all the offices and magistracies except the aforenamed Sixtyfive, the Two Hundred, and the Eight of *Balìa*; all of these during the life of Your Holiness and of the Cardinal you would appoint. Moreover, in order that your friends may be certain, when there is a choice in the Council, that they have been put in the pouches, Your Holiness is to select eight couplers, who, remaining in secrecy, can declare elected whom they wish, and can deny election to anybody.[16] And in order that the citizens generally may believe that the names of those elected were taken from the pouches,[17] the Council must be permitted to send in security two citizens chosen by it to witness the pouching.

Without satisfying the generality of the citizens, to set up a stable government is always impossible. Never will the generality of the

16. *Texts read: "will not be able to deny election," but considering that the function of the couplers was to see that the right men held office, I assume that the negative should be omitted.*
17. *The word for* be elected, gain the office, *is singular but its meaning seems plural.*

Florentine citizens be satisfied if the Hall is not reopened.[18] There,
fore, if one is to set up a republic in Florence, this Hall must be
reopened and this allotment made to the generality of the citizens.
Your Holiness should realize that whoever plans to take the govern,
ment from you will plan before everything else on reopening it;
therefore it is a good scheme to open it with conditions and methods
that are secure, and to take away from anybody who may be your
enemy opportunity for reopening it to your indignation and with the
destruction and ruin of your friends. If once the government were so
arranged, it would not be necessary, if Your Holiness and the Most
Reverend Monsignor[19] were going to live forever, to provide for
anything else, but you must cease to be, and you wish to leave behind
a perfect republic made strong with all needed parts, which every,
body will see and realize needs to be just as it is. Therefore, in order
that the generality of the people (both because of what is given to
them and of what is promised to them) may be contented, it is nec,
essary, in addition, to arrange as follows: The sixteen Gonfaloniers
of the Companies of the People are to be chosen in the way and for
the time for which they have been chosen up to now; they may be
appointed on the authority of Your Holiness or chosen by the
Council, as you please; you would merely make a second term less
usual, so that the office will be distributed more widely through the
city; and it should be specified that none of them could be taken
from the Sixty,five. When they have been selected, four Provosts
should be among them by lot, to hold office a month; hence at the
end of their term all will have been Provosts. Among these four, one
should be chosen, to reside a week in the Palace with the nine
Signors in residence, so that at the end of the month all four of them
will have been in residence. The said Signors resident in the Palace
are not to do anything in a Provost's absence; he would not have to
give his vote, but merely be a witness of their proceedings. He
could indeed veto their decision in a case,[20] and appeal it to all the
Thirty,two in a body. So in the same way the Thirty,two could not
decide anything without the presence of two of the said Provosts; yet

18. *The Hall of the Grand Council, now called the Hall of the Five Hundred, in the Palace
of the Signory (Palazzo Vecchio). The Grand Council was part of Savonarola's governmen
formed in 1495.*
19. *Cardinal Giuliano de'Medici, later Pope Clement VII.*
20. *What follows makes this evident as the meaning, though the text does not warrant it.*

the two would not have there other authority than to delay a decision considered among the Thirty-two and appeal it to the Council of the Selected. Neither could the Council of the Two Hundred decide anything, if there were not present at least six of the sixteen with two Provosts; yet the latter could not do anything other than take a case away from that Council and appeal it to the Grand Council, when three of them were in agreement to do it. It would not be possible to assemble the Great Council without twelve of the said Gonfaloniers, among them at least three Provosts; there they would be allowed to give a vote like the other citizens.

The establishment of such colleges is necessary after the lifetime of Your Holiness and of the Most Reverend Monsignor for two reasons. One is that if the Signoria or one of the councils[21] does not decide a matter as the result of discord, or does things opposed to the common good through wickedness, somebody may be at hand to take from them that power and appeal their decision to another body, because it is not good that one kind of magistrate or council should be able to retard public business without someone's being there who can arrange for action. It is also not good that office-holders should not have somebody to observe them and make them abstain from actions that are not good. The other reason is that on taking from the generality of the citizens (by removing the present Signoria) the possibility of becoming a Signor, it is necessary to restore to them an office resembling that taken away, and this pro-vostship is greater, more useful to the republic, and more honorable than the earlier office. For the present, it would be well to choose these Gonfaloniers, in order to get the city into proper procedures, but not to allow them to exercise their powers without the permission of Your Holiness; and you might make use of them to get a review of the actions of those groups with respect to your authority and your government.

Besides this, in order to give perfection to the republic after the lifetime of Your Holiness and of the Most Reverend Monsignor, in order that it may not want any part, it is necessary to arrange for a Court of Appeal from the Eight of Defence and *Balìa*, made up of thirty citizens, to be taken from the pouches of the Two Hundred and of the Sixty together. This Court of Appeal would be able to

21. *This meaning is required by what follows but is not derived from either of the usual readings.*

summon the accuser and the accused within a certain time. This appeal, during your lifetime, you would not allow to be used without your permission. This appeal is essential in a republic because a few citizens do not have the courage to punish important men, and therefore it is necessary that for such a result many citizens should join, that their judgment may be secret, and since it is secret, each man may excuse himself. Such an appeal will also be useful during your lifetime in causing the Eight to expedite cases and do justice, because, for fear lest you permit the appeal, they will judge more justly. To keep everything from being appealed, appeal can be forbidden in cases of fraud that do not involve at least fifty ducats, and in cases of violence in which there has been neither breaking of bones nor shedding of blood, unless the damage rises to the sum of fifty ducats.

I believe, considering all this organization as a republic, and without your authority, that it lacks nothing necessary to a free government according to what is above debated and presented at length. But if it is considered while Your Holiness and the Most Reverend Monsignor are still living, it is a monarchy, because you have authority over the armed forces, you have authority over the criminal judges, you keep the laws in your bosom. I do not know anything more to be wished for in a city. Also there is nothing that your friends, such as are good men and intend to live on their own property, need to fear, since Your Holiness has so much power and they sit in the highest seats of the government. We do not see also how the generality of the citizens can be other than satisfied, seeing that part of the allotments have already been made and the others seem as though little by little they would fall into their hands. Because Your Holiness could now and then let the Council choose one of the Sixty-five who is lacking, and also one of the Two Hundred; and some of them you yourself would choose according to the times. And I am certain that in a short time, by means of the power of Your Holiness, who will steer everything, this present government will change in such a way into the other one, and the other into this, that they will become one and the same, and all one body, with peace for the city and everlasting fame for Your Holiness, because always your power can take care of such defects as arise.

I believe the greatest honor possible for men to have is that willingly given them by their native cities; I believe the greatest good to be done and the most pleasing to God is that which one does to one's native city. Besides this, no man is so much exalted by any act of his as are those men who have with laws and with institutions remodeled republics and kingdoms; these are, after those who have been gods, the first to be praised. And because they have been few who have had opportunity to do it, and very few those who have understood how to do it, small is the number who have done it. And so much has this glory been esteemed by men seeking for nothing other than glory that when unable to form a republic in reality, they have done it in writing, as Aristotle, Plato, and many others, who have wished to show the world that if they have not founded a free government, as did Solon and Lycurgus, they have failed not through their ignorance but through their impotence for putting it into practice.

No greater gift, then, does Heaven give to a man, nor can Heaven show him a more glorious road than this. So of all the many blessings God has given to your house and to Your Holiness in person, this is the greatest: that of giving you power and material for making yourself immortal, and for surpassing by far in this way your father's and your grandfather's glory.[22] Consider, then, Your Holiness, first of all, that by holding the city of Florence under these present conditions you risk, on the coming of accidents, a thousand dangers; and before they come, Your Holiness has to endure a thousand vexations unbearable by any man. (Of these vexations you will be assured by the Most Reverend Lord Cardinal, since he has been for these past months in Florence.) They come partly from many citizens who in asking are arrogant and unbearable; partly from many who—since they believe that at present they do not live in security—do nothing else than declare that order should be brought into the government; one says it should be extended and one that it should be retracted, and nobody comes to particulars about the way for retracting or extending, because they are all confused. Though they suspect they are not secure in their present way of life, they do not know how they would like to adjust it; any man who might know how, they do not trust. Thus with their confusion they are enough to upset the most orderly brain.

If you wish, then, to escape these vexations, there are but two ways: either be more sparing with audiences and do not give the

22. *Including Pope Leo's great-grandfather, Cosimo.*

people courage to ask, even in an ordinary way, or to speak when they are not asked, as did the Duke of illustrious memory; or organize the government in such a way that it will administer itself and that Your Holiness will need only to keep half an eye turned on it. Of these methods, this last frees you from dangers and from vexations; the first frees you from vexations only.

But to return to the dangers you run if affairs remain as they are, I wish to make a prediction. I say that if an emergency comes when the city is not at all reorganized, one of two things will be done, or both of them at once: either in riot and haste a head will be set up who with arms and violence will defend the government; or one party will run to open the Hall of the Council and plunder the other party. And whichever of these two things comes about (which God forbid), Your Holiness can imagine how many deaths, how many exiles, how many acts of extortion will result, enough to make the cruelest man—much more Your Holiness, who is most merciful—die of sorrow. There is no other way for escaping these ills than to give the city institutions that can by themselves stand firm. And they will always stand firm when everybody has a hand in them, and when everybody knows what he needs to do and in whom he can trust, and no class of citizen, either through fear for itself or through ambition, will need to desire revolution.

ADVICE TO RAFFAELLO GIRO-LAMI WHEN HE WENT AS AM-BASSADOR TO THE EMPEROR

[*October 1522.*

This letter is in reality autobiographical, showing what Machiavelli himself attempted to do as Florentine agent abroad (the rank of ambassador he never held). Any page of his letters to Florentine authorities exemplifies parts of his advice, as do his REPORT ON THE AFFAIRS OF GERMANY *and his* SUMMARY OF THE GOVERNMENT OF THE CITY OF LUCCA.]

HONORABLE RAFFAELLO: TO BE AN AMBASSADOR is one of those civic functions which bring honor to a citizen; he cannot be called fit for government who is not fit to hold this rank. You are going as official representative into Spain, a country different in her ways and customs from Italy and unknown to you. Further-more, it is your first commission. Hence if you make a good showing in this office, as everybody hopes and believes, you will gain high honor; and so much the higher, the greater the difficulties. Having had some experience in such affairs, I shall tell you, not in presumption but in affection, what I have learned about them.

How to carry out a commission faithfully is known to everybody who is good, but to carry it out adequately is the difficulty. He carries it out adequately who knows well the nature of the prince and of those who control him, and knows how to adapt himself to what makes easiest and clearest the way to a hearing, inasmuch as any difficult business, if one has the ear of the prince, becomes easy. And above all, a representative must strive to get reputation, which he does by striking actions which show him an able man and by being thought liberal and honest, not stingy and two-faced, and by not appearing to believe one thing and say another. This matter is very important; I know men who, through being clever and two-faced, have so completely lost the trust of a prince that they have never afterward been able to negotiate with him. And if, to be sure, sometimes you need to conceal a fact with words, do it in such a way that it does not become known or, if it does become known, that you have a ready and quick defense. Alessandro Nasi gained great honor in France because he was thought a man of integrity; being thought the opposite brought great shame upon a certain other man. This behavior I believe will be easy for you because your nature commands you to act thus.

Great honor also comes to an ambassador from the reports he writes to those who send him. These reports are of three kinds: about things being negotiated; about things decided and finished; about things to be done; he must attempt to predict well the outcome of the last. Of these three, two are hard and one very easy; as to knowing things that have been done, most of the time they can easily be known—unless indeed two princes, for the injury of a third, make a league that must be kept secret until the right time for revealing it comes. This happened when France, the Pope, the Emperor and Spain formed the league of Cambrai, by which the Venetians were overthrown. Such decisions as this are very hard to learn about, and you have to use judgment and inference. To know well the dealings that are going on and to infer their outcome is also hard, because you can be helped merely with inference and judgment.

Because courts always include different kinds of busybodies, alert to find out what is going on, you will profit by making all of them your friends, so that from each one you can learn something. The friendship of such men can be gained by pleasing them with banquets and entertainments; I have seen entertainments given in the houses of very serious men, who thus offer such fellows a reason for visiting them, so that they can talk with them, because what one of them doesn't know another does, and much of the time they all together know everything.

A man who wants others to tell him what they know must tell them what he knows, because the best means for getting information is to give it. Hence a city which wants her ambassador to be honored can do nothing better than to provide him abundantly with reports, because men who see that they can get something are eager to tell him what they know. Hence I urge you to urge the Eight, the Arch-bishop and the secretaries to keep you informed on events in Italy even the slightest; if at Bologna, Siena or Perugia something strange happens, they are to inform you about it; and so much the more about the Pope, Rome, Lombardy or the Kingdom. To know these things, though they are remote from your business, is necessary and useful, for the reason I have given. Hence you should learn in this way the dealings that are going on. But since some of the things you pick up may be true and some false but probable, you need to weigh them in your judgment; from those that have most likeness to the truth you can profit, and the others you can neglect.

These things, then, well learned and better examined, will enable you to examine and consider the outcome of anything and to give your judgment on it as you write about it. And because to put your judgment in your own mouth would be offensive, you can use in such letters this method: first, tell about the affairs that are going on, the men who manage them, and the feelings by which they are moved; then use such words as these: 'Considering, then, everything about which I have written, prudent men here judge that the out- come will be such and such.'¹ This method, well handled, has in my days brought great honor to many ambassadors; also, badly handled, it has dishonored many. And I have seen some who, in order to make their letters richer in information, keep a daily record of what they learn; after eight or ten days they form it into a letter, selecting from the whole mass the part that seems most reasonable.

I have seen also men prudent and experienced in embassies using this method: they put, at least once every two months, before the eyes of him who sends them the exact condition and situation of the city or the kingdom where they are representatives. When well handled, this device brings great honor to the writers and is of great value to the man receiving their letters, because he can more easily make plans when understanding matters in detail than when not under- standing them.

And that you may understand this matter exactly, I shall explain it better. You arrive in Spain, show your commission, your business; you write at once giving early notice of your arrival and of what you have laid before the Emperor and of his answer; you put off until later detailed letters on the affairs of the kingdom and the qualities of the prince, waiting until, after being there for some days, you have fuller knowledge of them. Further, you observe with great care the affairs of the Emperor and of the kingdom of Spain, and give a full account of them. Coming to details, I say that you are to observe

1. *For Machiavelli's own use of this method, many years before, see* LEGATIONS 11. 40 *below.*

the nature of the man: whether he rules for himself or lets himself be ruled; whether he is stingy or liberal; whether he loves war or peace; whether fame or any other passion influences him; whether the people love him; whether he prefers to live in Spain or Flanders; what men he has about him who advise him and their leanings (that is, if they are inclined to get him into new enterprises or if they seek to enjoy the fortune of the present time) and how much control they have over him; whether he changes them or keeps them fixed; whether the King of France has friends among them; whether they can be bribed.

Then, too, it is well to consider the lords and barons who are most with him. How powerful are they? How well satisfied with him are they? If they should grow dissatisfied, how could they injure him if France bribed some of them? Learn also about his brother:[2] How does the Emperor treat him? Is he popular there? Is he satisfied? Could he cause any dissension in that kingdom or in the Emperor's other states? After that, learn the nature of the people, and whether that league which took up arms is entirely quieted or whether there is fear that it may rise up again, and whether France could build a fire under it. You should consider also the Emperor's purpose: how well he understands Italian affairs; whether he covets the territory of Lombardy or intends to let the Sforzas enjoy it; whether he wants to come to Rome and when; how he feels about the Church; how much he trusts the Pope; how satisfied he is with him; if he comes into Italy, what good or what ill the Florentines can hope or fear.

All these things, well considered and well written up, will bring you very great honor; but it is necessary to write about them not once only; every two or three months you must present them afresh with such skill (adding the latest events) that it may seem prudence and necessity, not presumption.

2. *Ferdinand, who succeeded Charles V as Emperor.*

THE LEGATIONS

or

Official Missions for the Florentine Government

[Parts of dispatches dealing with Cesare Borgia]

[*The dispatches that Machiavelli wrote to his superiors at home when representing Florence abroad are greater in bulk than the* HISTORY OF FLORENCE *and the* DISCOURSES *together; they can hardly appear except in an exhaustive edition of his writings; moreover, they should be combined with the official letters from Florence to him and with other state papers of the age. Their value here is in showing the Secretary in the practical work that gave a basis to much in* THE PRINCE, *the* DISCOURSES, *and the* HISTORY OF FLORENCE. *But since those writings were produced after most of his public work had been done, they give what Milton calls its "efficacy and extraction." Hence the official letters do not add to our knowledge of Machiavellian thought, though they reinforce it by supplying background. For example, Machiavelli's acceptance of artillery as important in an army— evident in the* DISCOURSES *and* THE ART OF WAR—*is emphasized by references to cannon in his official dispatches. Readers of Niccolò the thinker and dramatist should not forget Machiavelli the servitor and secretary of the Florentine state, representing her before dukes and princes.*

I have selected, from two of the LEGATIONS, *matter on Cesare Borgia. None of the dispatches is complete. Especially in the Roman letters, numerous other topics appear, such as reports on the news from the disastrous French campaign on the Garigliano in the winter of 1503-1504. There is much of interest also in the reports on his missions to France and to the Emperor, as well as in those written near the end of Machiavelli's life, when under the Medici he again took up his old pursuits. Quotations from some of these, in the notes to other writings, can be found through the index.*

The dispatches are numbered as in the edition by Passerini and Milanesi, 1875; there are, therefore, many gaps in numbering.]

LEGATION 11. AN OFFICIAL MISSION TO DUKE VALENTINO [*CESARE BORGIA*] IN ROMAGNA

[*All the dispatches are directed to the Ten of Liberty and* Balía]

11.5

7 October 1502 [*8 Oct.*] 10 a.m.,[1] from Imola.

... His Excellency Cesare Borgia said he had always wished alliance with Your Lordships, and that he had not attained it more through the malice of others than through cause of his own, saying that he was going to tell me in detail what he never had told anybody about his coming with his army to Florence. And he said that having taken Faenza and made an attempt on Bologna, the Orsini and Vitelli were at him, urging him to decide to return to Rome by way of Florence. This he refused because the Pope, by a Brief, instructed him otherwise. Vitellozzo,[2] weeping, threw himself at his feet to beg him to take that road, promising him that he would not do any violence to the country or to the city. When he would not consent to this, they nevertheless kept at him with similar prayers, so that he yielded as to the coming, but under the condition that the country should not be injured and that the Medici should not be considered.

But still wishing to get some profit from his approach to Florence, he determined within himself to try to make an alliance with Your Lordships, and to avail himself of that opportunity. This is proved by his saying little or nothing of the Medici in any of the parleys that were held—as the commissioners who dealt with him know— and by his never allowing Piero to come into his camp. And many times, when he was at Campi, the Orsini and the Vitelli asked him for permission to attack either Florence or Pistoia, showing him possibilities for success. But he never consented; on the contrary, with a thousand declarations he made them understand that he would oppose them. After the truce was made, the Orsini and Vitelli felt that he had gained his own wish and not theirs, and that their march had been to his profit and their loss. As a result, they

1. *I put in brackets information given in the dispatch on the date and hour of sending.*
2. *One of the Vitelli.*

set about destroying the truce with lies and did all that damage in
order to vex Your Lordships and upset the agreement. And never
has he been able to make atonement to you, both because he cannot
be everywhere and because Your Lordships have not made him the
loan which had been arranged, or rather indicated. So the affair
stood still up to last June, the time of the rebellion of Arezzo; about
that he said he had never earlier heard anything, as he once told the
Bishop of Volterra . . . . But he would have been glad if he had,
because he would have thought it a good opportunity for winning
your gratitude. At that time also nothing was done, either through
the bad luck of both, or because your city was not in a position to
treat and to decide on what would be for the good of each. This he
said gave him much distress.[3] Yet being inclined to benefit you,
since he knew the King's desire, he wrote and sent men speedily to
Vitellozzo, so that he would withdraw from Arezzo. And not
content with that, he went toward Città di Castello with his soldiers;
and he could have taken Vitellozzo's territory away from him, because the chief men of the city came to offer themselves to him.
From this, he says, came the first anger of Vitellozzo and his re-
sentment. About the Orsini, he said he did not know the origin
of their indignation . . . .

He added then that it was now time, if Your Lordships wished
to be his allies, to make pledges, because without regard to the
Orsini he could make alliance with you . . . . He does not see how
Your Lordships can turn away from a plan on which there is
agreement by His Majesty the King and His Holiness Our Lord
the Pope. He added that it would greatly please him, if Vitellozzo
or any other should move toward his states, for you to have your
soldiers appear near Borgo or on those frontiers, in order to give
repute to his affairs . . . .

Although His Excellency, as you see, appears to wish that a
treaty between you and him should be made quickly, he nonetheless,
notwithstanding that I so dealt with him as to get from him some
particulars, always kept his distance, and I never could get from
him more than I have written.

Having heard on my arrival that in the territory of Urbino there
had been some attempt at revolt, and His Excellency in the course of

3. *I have omitted a negative that seems contrary to the meaning.*

his talk having said that he was not worrying over the rebellion of that dukedom against him, I thought it a good thing in replying to ask him how those things were going. To which His Excellency answered: "My having been lenient and having paid little attention to those affairs has done me harm. As you know, in three days I conquered that dukedom, without pulling a hair from anybody's head, except Messer Dolce and two others, who had acted against His Holiness Our Lord the Pope. On the contrary, what is more, I had many of those chief men put in high positions in that state. One of them received authority over certain walls I was having built in the castle of San Leo. Yet two days ago, under cover of bringing up a beam,[4] he plotted a conspiracy with certain farmers of the country. Thus he has taken the castle and it is lost. Some say that in it they shout 'Marco,'[5] some 'Vitelli,' some 'Orsini,' though as yet none of these has revealed himself. Still I count that dukedom lost, being a state flabby and weak, and those men are discontented, since I have vexed them greatly with the soldiers; but I expect to provide for everything. And you can write to your Signors that they should consider their affairs carefully, and inform us quickly, because if the Duke of Urbino returns, and comes from Venice, it is not to their advantage, and less to ours; which means that we can have more faith in each other." . . .

II.6

9 October 1502 [*10 Oct.*] 4 p.m., from Imola.
. . . His Excellency the Duke sent for me . . . and showed me a letter from Monseigneur d'Arles, the Pope's ambassador in France . . . in which he wrote how much the King and Rouen incline to please him; and as soon as they understood his wish to have soldiers for the expedition against Bologna, they ordered Monsieur de Chau' mont at Milano to send the Duke, without making any objection, Monsieur de Lanques with three hundred lances, and if he were asked by the Duke, to go in person toward Parma with three hundred more lances . . . . And His Excellency had me look at Arles's signature . . . which I recognized on account of my experi' ence in France and in Florence . . . . And His Excellency said:

4. *For a fuller account, see* A DESCRIPTION OF THE METHOD USED BY DUKE VALENTINO.
5. *That is, Saint Mark, as supporters of Venice against Duke Valentino.*

"Now you see, Secretary, that this letter is written in answer to the question I asked about attacking Bologna, and you see how vigorous it is; imagine what I can get to defend myself from those men, the greater part of whom His Majesty the King believes are his violent enemies, because they have always tried to move chessmen in Italy for his injury. Believe me that this thing is to my advantage, and the Vitelli cannot reveal themselves at an hour when it will damage me less, nor can I, to strengthen my states, wish for a thing that will be more useful to me; because I shall know this time against whom I have to protect myself, and I shall recognize my friends. And if the Venetians reveal themselves in this matter, which I do not expect, I shall be the better pleased; nor could the King of France be more eager for it. I tell you this, and shall tell it to you on the day when it happens, so that you can write it to those Signors of yours, and they can see that I am not about to give up or to be without friends, among whom I wish to number Their Lordships, if they let me know soon; but if they do not do it now, I shall put them aside; if the water were up to my neck, I should not talk any more about friendship, even though it would always pain me to have a neighbor and not be able to do him good and receive it from him." . . . And again he reminded me when I left him to remind Your Lordships that, if you remain neutral, you will lose under any conditions, but if you join with him you can win.

I cannot express with pen with how much show of love for you he spoke, and with how much justification of things past . . . .

Five days ago he reviewed six thousand infantry selected from his cities, which in two days he can get together . . . . He has as much artillery, and in good order, as almost all the rest of Italy . . . . On the other side, we see his enemies armed and in a position to make a sudden conflagration, and these people are still all Romagnoles, and have not been very well treated because this lord has always shown more favor to his soldiers than to them . . . .

11.9

12 October 1502, from Imola.

. . . When I came into the presence of His Excellency, he said to me: "From all sides we have good news." And he related to me how much had been offered him by the Venetians, . . . saying happily that this year there is a planet hostile to anyone who rebels . . . .

II.IO

13 October 1502, 10 p.m., from Imola.

I have postponed sending my letters until this evening . . . in order better to satisfy Your Lordships about things here, and especially about the wish you express to know where this Lord is with his purpose, and what he is planning about you; but I have not been able to get out of His Excellency more than I have written . . . .

Valentino's secretary says that he does not know what agreements can be made at present with Your Lordships, since this Lord is highly reputed, very fortunate, and accustomed to winning, and his prestige has increased since his employment as general,[1] and yours has decreased; hence it is reasonable that the honor and position you give him should increase rather than decrease. And talking about his good fortune, he came, after his successive undertakings, to this last event, saying that His Excellency could not desire anything more to his advantage than that these movements should occur; the Orsini probably hoped that they could make every man rise up against His Excellency, but every man has changed and revealed that he is on the Duke's side: Your Lordships have sent him an embassy, the Venetians have written to him, His Majesty the King has sent him soldiers. He added that a fortune as green as this was still worth reckoning on. . . . I got nothing else out of him except the knowledge that this Lord has his eyes turned on that employment as general.

I do not wish to neglect telling Your Lordships that that secretary from Ferrara already mentioned, discussing with me the reason that makes the Duke go slowly, says he believes he has written about it to the Pope, and wishes in this matter to go forward in step with him. And I imagine that there can be two other reasons: either that he in no way wishes, until things are cleared up here, to cancel this engagement as general, and therefore he wishes to delay; or that he wishes to wait, before things go farther, until the future Gonfalonier is in the Palace—a law which has given so high a reputation to our city that nobody would believe it.[2]

I cannot and should not, Magnificent Signors, judge these things further; I shall merely continue to give you notice of them

---

1. *By Florence.*

2. *Piero Soderini was elected Gonfalonier for life on 20 Sept. 1502, and was to take office on 1 Nov. 1502.*

from time to time, as they come about; and up to now, from the fourth day of the month, they have made this change that you know of; and the longer fair weather lasts, the harder it will be to work this ground . . . .

11.13

15 October 1502, from Imola.

. . . As to the postscript that Your Lordships write to me about temporizing, not committing you, and seeking to learn his purpose, I believe that up to now I have done the first two things, and on the third I have used my wits. About that, in mine of the thirteenth I wrote in full; not having got anything further since then, it seems to me useless to take the business up again. I do believe, however, that in addition to the other reasons that can make His Excellency stand waiting, there can be one other, and that is his wish to have you directed in this matter by France, since you appear to be waiting for that King's approval . . . .

11.14

16 October 1502, from Imola.

. . . His Excellency this Lord, on receiving a letter . . . which reported the movement of the artillery and the soldiers of Vitellozzo, said to me, if I remember correctly: "Your Signors have had two reasons for hesitating about having those soldiers of theirs approach the frontiers of Vitellozzo: one is that they have awaited the decision of the King on their procedure about movements on this side of Tuscany; the other, the few soldiers they have and the many places they have to garrison. And because I greatly desire that time be saved and that those Signors of yours show me some favor, I am dealing in this way with their two reasons for hesitating. First, about the King, you can be sure that I am more certain than I am of death that His Majesty would like the whole Florentine populace to come in person to aid my cause; and about that they will see very soon a definite reply. As to the other, that they have few soldiers, write to those Signors of yours that if it would cause any inconvenience to take away some of those soldiers from where they are, I am ready to move in person to their assistance and to bear all the weight of the war. I do not ask that they do more than send to those places nearest Città di Castello fifty or sixty cavalry and three or four hundred conscripts, have two pieces of artillery taken there, and conscript in that region a man from each house, and have them reviewed, and so on.[1] And about this I charge you to ask it from them with all the efficacy you can."

These were almost his exact words, and I did not fail to show His Excellency the small number of our soldiers and your fears in taking them away. But he nevertheless has insisted that I write to you and ask. I had to promise, and I have done it apart from the ordinary letter, in order that without making this request by the Duke public, if you decide you can well comply, you can do so more cautiously, and send some conscripts toward Borgo and Anghiari, order some assemblies of soldiers, and other things that he asks, in whole or in part, under the pretext of being suspicious; and on the other side you can give him satisfaction here; indeed, for two you can say four, since this Lord cannot get sure information on it. I beg that Your Lordships will not impute this to me for advice or for presumption,[2] but put it down to a natural affection that every man ought to have for his country . . . .

II.19

20 October 1502, from Imola.

. . . In this court, things to be kept silent are never mentioned to us, and are carried on with wonderful secrecy . . . .

II.22

21 October 1502, from Imola.

. . . Nothing new has happened here except that yesterday evening there came Antonio da Venafro, the agent of Pandolfo Petrucci, and sent by the Orsini; and then he left today. I do not know what was discussed. I shall try to learn . . . .

II.24

23 October 1502 [24 Oct.], from Imola.

. . . His Excellency . . . said to me: "I have told you many times and this evening I tell you again that here we shall be in no need of aid. The French lances will be here soon, and likewise the northern

---

1. *This display would impress Vitellozzo, making him think the Florentines were in alliance with the Duke.*

2. *Of trying to act as adviser without holding a suitable position.*

infantry that I spoke of some days ago, and you see that I hire soldiers of my own every day, and likewise the Pope does not lack money for me, nor the King soldiers. I do not intend to be menacing in deeds or in words, except that perchance my enemies will have to repent of their treachery." And beginning to talk of the Orsini, he said: "They have finally displayed against me the greatest treachery that ever was." . . .

Your Lordships know the words that this Lord uses; . . . consider now the person who is speaking, and judge of them with your usual prudence. As to the state of things here, the government of this Lord since I have been here has rested only on his good fortune— the cause of which has been the firm opinion commonly held that the King of France would aid him with soldiers, and the Pope with money; then there is another thing that has worked for him no less than this one, namely, the sluggishness of his enemies in pressing him. . . .

11.27

27 October 1502, from Imola.

. . . Anybody who examines the qualities of one side and the other recognizes this Lord as a man courageous, fortunate, and full of hope, favored by a pope and by a king, and injured by the other side [*i.e., the Vitelli, etc.*], not merely in a state that he hoped to conquer, but in one that he had conquered. Those others are suspicious about their states; they were fearful of his greatness before they injured him, and now they are much more so, having done him this injury. And it does not appear how he can forgive the injury and those can abandon their fear, nor as a result how they can yield one to the other in the expedition against Bologna and in the Dukedom of Urbino. It is reasonable that they can agree only if they can act in union against a third, in such a way that neither the Duke nor the confederates will have to decrease their forces, but rather each of the parties will grow in reputation and profit. And if this should happen, they can turn nowhere except against Your Lordships or against the Venetians. An expedition against Your Lordships is judged easier as to you, but harder as to the King; that against the Venetians easier as to the King, but harder as to them. The first would be more acceptable to this Duke, and the second more pleasing to the confederates. Nevertheless neither one nor the other is believed in, but they are talked of as things possible. And so I do not meet a person competent to decide on the method of agreement between the parties. And anybody who does decide believes that this Duke will detach from the group some one of these confederates, and when he has defeated the others he will no longer need to fear them and can carry out his designs. I rather believe this, having heard something brief said on it by some of his chief ministers . . . . Now Your Lordships, knowing what is said here, can decide about it best, as much more prudent and of greater experience. I think it good to write you all I hear. . . .

11.36

3 November 1502, from Imola.

. . . I have not tried to speak with the Duke, not having any-thing to tell him that is new, and the same things would bore him. You must recall that nobody speaks with him except three or four of his ministers and some foreigners who have to deal with him about matters of importance, and he does not come out of an antechamber except at eleven or twelve at night or later; for this reason there is no opportunity to speak with him ever, except through an audience appointed; and when he knows that a man brings him nothing but words, he never gives him an audience. This I have said that Your Lordships may not wonder at this decision of mine not to speak with him, and also may not wonder if in the future I write to you about not getting an audience.

11.39

8 November 1502, from Imola [*first letter*].

. . . His Excellency said . . . : "What employment as general will those Signors give me?" To this I answered that I did not know the intention of Your Lordships, but that up to now I was persuaded that His Excellency was turned rather to the idea of employing others. He answered: "What honor will your Signors give me, who make a profession of being a soldier, and am a friend of that government, and do not get employment from it? I do not believe that I deceive myself in this, when I believe I could serve it as well as any other." Then he asked me how many men-at-arms Your Lordships reck-oned on keeping. I said I did not know your intention, but I believed you would expect to keep five hundred of them at least.

He asked me how many of them the Marquis had, and how many we had. I gave him the facts, and he on these words rose up, saying: "Then there is no place for me." . . .

11.40

8 November 1502, from Imola [*second letter*].

It occurs to me . . . to report to Your Lordships a conversation I had with that friend who in past days, as I wrote, said to me that it was not a good thing that Your Lordships should have only a vague relation with this Duke, especially when you could arrange to form closer ties easily, since both of you had wishes and enemies. This same man last evening arranged to speak with me and said: "Secretary, at other times I have suggested to you that for your Signors to have only a vague relation with this Duke brings little profit to him and less to them, for this reason: the Duke, seeing himself left in the air by your Signors, will get a footing with others; and I wish to enlarge on this with you this evening, though I speak only for myself, yet not altogether without foundation.

"This Lord knows very well that the Pope can die any day, and that he needs to think before his death of laying for himself some other foundation, if he intends to preserve the states he now has. His first foundation he is laying on the King of France; his second, on his own armies; and you see that already he has prepared nearly five hundred men-at-arms and the same number of light cavalry, which in a few days will be ready. And because he judges that in time these two foundations may not suffice him, he is planning to make friends of his neighbors and of those who will be forced by necessity to defend him in order to defend themselves; these are the Florentines, the Bolognese, Mantua, and Ferrara.

"And beginning with the last, you see what friendship he has formed with Ferrara, because, besides the marriage of his sister with so large a dower, he has benefited, and is benefiting every day, her cardinal.[1] As to Mantua, he is attempting to do two things: one, to make the brother of the Marquis a cardinal; two, to give the Duke of Ferrara's daughter to the son of the Marquis; for the sake of the hat,[2] the Marquis and his brother are to deposit forty thousand ducats, which then are to serve as the dower of the Duke's daughter; these

1. *Cardinal Ippolito d'Este.*
2. *The Cardinal's hat.*

things will bring results in all cases, and these are ties of nature that will preserve friendship. As to Bologna, he is carrying on some negotiations separate from the allies, which I see prospering; because the Duke of Ferrara urges him; this Duke himself wishes it, and it is for the advantage of the Bentivogli. And indeed this lord was never so eager to possess Bologna as he was to make himself secure as to that state; and whenever this last comes about, he is going to be quiet. And so these four states, if they are united, because they are adjacent to each other and are armed, must be respected, and the King of France is inclined to strengthen them, being able to lay foundations on them.

"As to your Florentine Signors, three days ago I heard the Duke saying about them that he wished they would use his land freely and that he might use theirs, since they are allies of France as he is, and that he is never inclined to act against them in anything, even though not definitely agreed. But if there were a pledge, they would see what difference there is between his friendship and that of others. And to return to our topic, I tell you that keeping your relations vague causes more difficulty to your Signors than to this Duke, because, the Duke having on his side the King and those named earlier, and you having nobody but the King, your Signors will come to have more need for the Duke than the Duke for them. I do not say that for this reason the Duke will not be inclined to do them favors; yet if need comes upon them and he is not pledged, he will be able to do it or not to do it, as seems best to him.

"Now if you say to me, 'What is to be done? Let us move on a bit to something specific,' I shall answer that for your part you have two wounds, which, if you do not cure them, will make you grow sick and perhaps die. One is Pisa, the other is Vitellozzo. And if you retake the first and destroy the second, wouldn't it greatly benefit you? And on the Duke's part I tell you that for His Excellency it would be enough to be honored by you in his old engagement as general; this he values more than money and than anything else; and when you find a way for this, everything will be settled. And if you say, about Vitellozzo, that the Duke has made a bargain with the Orsini and with him, I answer you that their acceptance has not yet come, and the Duke would give the best city he has for it not to come, or for the truce never again to be discussed. Yet when the acceptance does come, where there are men there is a way, and it is better to hear it and speak it than to write it. And in order that you may understand, this Duke must save part of the Orsini because, when the Pope dies, he will still need to have some friends in Rome. But of Vitellozzo he cannot hear any talk, on account of his being a poisonous serpent and the fire of Tuscany and of Italy; and about this agreement that the Orsini are going to make, he has done every⁄ thing and is doing everything to upset it.

"I hope then that you will write to the Gonfalonier or to the Ten all that I have said, as well as another thing that I remind them of: namely, that it easily can happen that the King of France will order your Signors to carry out their agreement to make this Duke their general, and put their soldiers under his command, and they will be forced to do so, and with little good will. And therefore remind Their Lordships that the favor that has to be done, a man had better do of himself and with good will rather than without." And he begged me that about speaking against Vitellozzo and other im⁄ portant things, I should manage this affair secretly. The presentation of this friend was long and of the nature that Your Excellencies understand.[3]

I replied briefly and only to those parts that were of importance. I said first that this Lord acted prudently in arming himself and in finding allies. Second, I confessed to him that we greatly desired both to recover Pisa and to make sure of Vitellozzo, though we were not much concerned about him. Third, as to this Duke's employment as general, I said to him, speaking always for myself only, that His Excellency was not to be judged as are some of the other rulers, who have only the carriage,[4] in comparison with the state he holds; but one should discuss him as a new potentate in Italy, with whom it is more proper to make a league or an alliance than an agreement as general. And because alliances between rulers are maintained with arms, and those alone are what keep them in force, I said that Your Lordships would not believe that you could be secure when three⁄quarters or three⁄fifths of your arms were in the hands of the Duke. I did not say this because I did not judge the Duke to be a man of his word, but because I knew Your Lordships

---

3. *For the function of this obviously fictitious friend, see* ADVICE TO RAFFAELLO GIROLAMI, *above.*

4. *Seemingly proverbial for the trappings of rule without much beneath them.*

were prudent and I realized that Signors should be cautious and never do anything in which they could be deceived.

As to the idea that the King of France could command Your Lordships, I said that there was no doubt that His Majesty could dispose of your city as of his own property; yet neither he nor any other could make you do what for you would be impossible . . . .

II.44

13 November 1502, from Imola.

. . . Your Lordships . . . should remember that I am dealing with a prince who manages things for himself; and if one is not going to write phantasies and dreams, one must verify things, and verifying them takes time; and I am trying to spend it and not to throw it away . . . .

He who waits for time when he has it is hunting for better bread than is made of wheat, and one doesn't always find an opportunity prepared . . . .

Knowing the qualities of the Duke and the qualities of the others [*the Orsini and Vitelli*], I cannot believe that there can be any agreement between them, but I can believe that the Duke may be able to detach some of them. And now things seem to be going along this road, because the Protonotary Bentivoglio is here, as I wrote before, and is negotiating an individual agreement with this Duke, and is about to conclude it; the Bentivogli can excuse themselves for this with the Allies on the ground that the latter have left them in a dangerous position; it will be their security that the King of France pledges to observe such an agreement. And this evening, when I was speaking with the Protonotary, he told me that if Your Lordships would guarantee this agreement for both sides, after the King of France has guaranteed it, Your Lordships would be in condition to go anywhere. The terms of that agreement I do not tell you, not having heard them so put as to satisfy me. If anybody answers that the Duke will find it hard not to fulfil his desire for Bologna, I reply, as I have written before, that he has learned he had better make a lasting alliance than take a city he cannot hold.

Moreover, the Orsini and Vitelli have made a gesture that is enough to make him wise even if he were not, and have shown him that he needs to try to keep what he has conquered rather than to conquer more. And the way to keep it is to continue to be armed

with his own arms, to gain his subjects' favor, and to make allies of
his neighbors. That is his intention. . . .

As to the articles of agreement with the confederates, who have
sent their ratification, as I wrote, this Lord has dispatched one of his
men to the Orsini to see about bringing in the party of Messer
Giovanni Bentivoglio; in this way he keeps them waiting. They are
in the region of Fano and do not advance or retreat. So this part of
the universal peace continues to be ambiguous, and he will come out
ahead who knows best how to get support from the others, and he
will get support who is strongest in men and in allies . . . .

The preparations that are being made here . . . are always continued and are hurried up, though they are slower than one might
suppose they would need to be. And that Your Lordships may
have fuller knowledge of the men on foot and on horseback that are
here and that are expected, I am sending a list; but I send it according
to what I have learned from many persons; since I cannot speak of
what I have seen, I must have recourse to others.

The Duke is here and is not going to leave if Swiss do not come,
who were expected this week, together with other French lances;
they are expected every day. This Lord welcomes, as I have many
times said, all the enemies of Pandolfo Petrucci, Gianpaulo Baglioni,
Vitellozzo, and the Orsini. . . .

11.48

16 November 1502, from Imola.

. . . Wheat sells here at the rate of forty soldi per *staio* by our
measure, and a Messer Jacopo dal Borgo, Lieutenant in this city,
tells me that an inventory has been made of the wheat in this Lord's
territory, and the findings are that all these cities are short, some by
one month's supply, others by two, and that, with the addition of
these foreign soldiers, there will be none too good living in this
country, notwithstanding that this Lord may get supplies from elsewhere. I give Your Lordships notice of this in order that you may
see that nothing comes here from your territory.

A Messer Gabriello da Bergamo is now here; he brought money
from Venice, and does a great deal of business. He showed me last
evening a letter from Venice saying that they have news there of the
return to Portugal from Calicut of four caravels laden with spices.

This news had caused a great drop in the price of their spices, which was a very serious loss to that city. . . .

11.50

20 November 1502, 2 p.m., from Imola.

. . . Last evening I had a long talk with His Excellency . . . . In all my speech I was cautious in two ways: one, not to depart in the least from your instructions; the other, to use words that would not offend him . . . . I said to him that vague alliances carry no obligations and that times change; bad fortune and good fortune do not always find lodging in just one place; every day alliances are made where there is no question of employment as general; durable alliances are those that advantage both sides . . . . Finally . . . he said that if Your Lordships were satisfied with this vague alliance, he is satisfied, speaking here many loving words, etc. "If you wished to make the alliance closer, you knew his disposition." I could not by any words that I used get out anything further. . . .

Of Vitellozzo and Gianpaolo he spoke very damagingly. And I said I had always thought of himself as the winner, and if the first day I had written down what I thought, and now he should read it, it would seem to him a prophecy. I brought up, among the various reasons influencing me, that he was one only and had to do with many, and it was easy to break such chains. He replied that he had broken them in actual fact and had already detached more than four.

And speaking of Gianpaolo, he said to me that he bragged of being much in your favor. I answered that he was once our friend through having been our soldier and being a brave man, but that he had in this last business done us a bad turn. He said then: "I am going to tell you what your Signors do not know. Before he left Perugia and went to meet Vitellozzo in Arezzo, he wrote me a letter saying: 'You know that I am opposed to Vitellozzo, and yet I should like to be with him in putting those Medici back in Florence, but I should not like to give the appearance of doing it for love of Vitellozzo. Therefore I beg you to write me a letter commanding me to enter upon this undertaking.' I wrote it. Now I do not know if it will be made a pretext for blaming me." . . .

11.52

22 November 1502, from Imola.

. . . I have not sought to have any audiences further with the Lord to speak to him again about the reasons that influenced Your Lordships not to discuss his employment as general because, since I think I am acquainted at close quarters with his nature, I do not want to annoy him about what he thinks he understands; which would be rather to put him off than to soften him. And therefore I shall wait until I am addressed about such a thing; and that will be according as time shall control things, which every day are of more import here rather than otherwise. I do not yet know that I can get audience easily, because here they live only to attend to their own profit and to what they think best, without showing any confidence in anybody else. Hence I shall not test the chain, if I am not obliged to, and after I have done it once or twice, I shall not test further, notwithstanding that as yet I have nothing to complain of; yet I should not like to have to do so. Hence, reckoning everything, I strongly wish to have from Your Lordships permission to leave because, beyond seeing that I can do nothing of use to our city, I am getting into bad physical condition; two days ago I had a good deal of fever, and all the time I feel pretty much upset . . . .

11.53

26 November 1502, from Imola.

. . . Two days ago a man came here from Urbino . . . . He reports that certainly there is great terror among the people there— even though they are very determined—and that this truce between the Orsini and Duke Valentino has troubled them greatly. And he tells that two days before he left, the Duke of Urbino assembled first the citizens and then the soldiers (and he says there are no soldiers there except Giovanni di Rossetto and two other captains, and they have some four hundred infantry). And he spoke (though to the groups separately) to quite the same effect to both, announcing that the agreement made between the Orsini and Duke Valentino was sure, and that one between the said Duke and Vitellozzo was far along, and he feared that it would be concluded; and on this matter he asked advice. The citizens replied that they intended to die with him. The soldiers, first having considered what force the Duke of

San Leo in 1957. (*Marchini photograph*)

Urbino could assemble, said that they could protect Urbino and San Leo for him all winter, if the whole world were against them. And so it was proclaimed that all the towns and cities of the state should be evacuated into these two places. And Giovanni di Rossetto sent into San Leo a brother of his with his wife and children. That man also reported how willingly at the beginning the Vitelleschi came to do damage to Duke Valentino, and how much harm they would have done if Lord Paolo Orsini had not held them back; and that six hundred only of Vitellozzo's infantry defeated the Duke's entire army at Fossombrone, where the Duke had one hundred men-at-arms and two hundred light cavalry, who all fled without putting a lance in rest; and in the whole time that they have been in the field there hasn't been a penny in circulation. Yet this Lord from the calends of October to now has spent better than sixty thousand ducats, as Messer Alessandro his Treasurer declared and asserted to me less than two days ago. I have hastened to write this to Your Lordships, to let you see that when someone else is in an uncomfortable position he does not spend less than you do, and is not better served by his soldiers than you are, and on the other hand, he who is armed well, and with his own arms, gets the same effects wherever he turns . . . .

11.56

28 November 1502, noon, from Imola.

. . . Two days ago there came here the President of the Circuit Court that Duke Valentino has set up in this state, who is Messer Antonio da Monte San Savino, a very learned man and of excellent character, and he resides at Cesena. . . .

11.59

2 December 1502, from Imola [*first letter of this date*].

. . . This evening articles of agreement have been solemnly confirmed and established between His Excellency this Prince and Messer Giovanni Bentivoglio. This news, because I think Your Lordships wish it, I send you by special messenger. In addition to the other benefits that our city can hope for from it, I perceive this one, not of low value, namely, that this Duke is now teaching himself to restrain his desires, and perceives that Fortune does not grant

him all of them. This will make him more receptive to any proposi-
tion that Your Lordships may wish to present . . . .

II.62

6 December 1502, from Imola.

. . . Since I had been ten days without going in to speak with
this Lord, and since these articles had been confirmed between His
Excellency and the Bentivogli, I decided yesterday that it would not
be unfitting to get an opportunity to speak with him; audience was
granted me at once. Before I said anything, His Excellency said to
me: "I have had a fancy for speaking with you for the last four or six
days, because Lord Paolo Orsini, the last time he was here, told me
that your Signors sent to him at Urbino two men with the message
that if he or his son wished to make an agreement as general, they
would give him a contract, if he would do something in your behalf
in the affairs of Pisa." Lord Paolo said he had not accepted because
Your Lordships had not refrained from requiring him to act even
against his Excellency.

I asked him if the Lord Paolo had told him the names of those
two men, and if he had shown him their letters of appointment, or
if the Lord Paolo in the past had ever told him any lies.

He replied that he had not shown him any letters, and still less
that he had not said who the men were, and that as to lies, he
certainly had told him many. And so he ended the affair laughing,
notwithstanding that in the beginning he had spoken of it with agi-
tation, seeming to believe it, and being pained by it . . . .

He said that for the present he would not dismiss any French, but
that, when he had settled his affairs, he would not keep more than
two hundred or two hundred and fifty lances, because the men were
unendurable and destroyers of provinces, adding that whereas he
planned to have four hundred and fifty French lances, he had more
than six hundred of them, since all those who were with Monsieur de
Chaumont at Parma had come a few at a time, having heard that
here they could live for the love of God . . . .[1]

1. *The beggar's formula.*

II.72

14 December 1502, from Cesena.

. . . His Excellency the Duke, as I have said, is here with all the French army and his own, except those men who have been all this year at Pesaro, who have not moved from there; the army is quartered in this city and around it, and they live at their discretion—which means in their own way, and not in that of him who lodges them. Your Lordships can imagine how things are going, and how they have gone at Imola (where the Court has been for three months, and for two this entire army), which they have devoured to the stones. Truly that city, and all this country besides, has given proof of its fertility and of what it can bear. I say this to Your Lordships so that you may realize that the French, and all the other soldiers, are not different in Romagna from what they have been in Tuscany; and that there is neither better discipline nor less confusion here than there has been in other places where they have gone . . . .

There is no advantage in my staying here longer; and—speaking to Your Lordships with the fidelity with which I have always served you—it would be much more beneficial for the agreement that has to be made with this Duke to send a man of high standing here instead of to Rome. The reason is this: in the agreement that will have to be made, you will have to satisfy the man here, and not the Pope; and therefore the things that are decided upon by the Pope may well be revoked by him; but the things that are decided upon by him will in no way be revoked by the Pope, unless he sees in it some advantage for himself, as happened in the affairs of Bologna. Moreover, since to negotiate the same thing in two places is dangerous, and therefore it has to be negotiated in one place, it would be better to negotiate it here rather than in Rome. Because for this I would not be and am not sufficient, on account of the need for a man with more discretion, more reputation than I have, and who understands the world better, I have all the time believed it would be a good thing to send here an ambassador—which would have gained as much from this Lord in all the things that needed to be dealt with as any other means that could have been used; everybody here thinks the same as I do. It is true that it would be necessary for him to come not lacking in plans, but decided in several matters; and so without doubt things would be settled, and soon.

In this matter I have earlier paid my debt, and I have not now wished to fail in it, because if the time that has gone by is long, it is not yet lost entirely; and Your Lordships will receive these words as I write them; and again I humbly beg you to furnish me with money and with my release . . . .

11.77

20 December 1502, 10 p.m., from Cesena.

. . . Being this evening at court, I saw all the French officers in a body come to the Duke; and before they went in, they talked together, and as I observed their gestures and actions, they seemed to me angry; and thinking that there might be something new of importance, as soon as they came out, in order to clarify my mind, I went to the house of the Baron di Bierra, with the appearance of visiting him on behalf of Your Lordships, saying that I had just had instructions from you to do so. After greeting me, he took me aside and said: "In two days we are going to leave here and return into the state of Milan; for so we have today had letters to do." When I asked him the cause, he said he did not know, but that all the French were at the same time to leave and go back, and that day after tomorrow they would go away without fail . . . . He said that I could write it for certain to Your Lordships and in addition inform you that money has come to Milan for paying fifteen thousand infantry, who in a month will be assembled.

This thing so unexpected, as I have been able to see by their gestures, has turned the brains of this court upside down; and when it is made public I can write to you more fully how things go. Not being able to understand the cause of such a thing or its basis, I cannot judge it . . . .

Monsieur di Bierra, in his talk with me, said that he and the other officers had decided never to march any more anywhere without having with them men on foot, because with their present method they are not at all safe. And this he said because, as they think, they have received some injuries from the country people here, and have not been able to get from them the services they wanted. I have wished not to fail to write this, since it seems to me they are words worth noting.

The artillery has all been brought here, though before this news its dispatch to Fano had been ordered. I do not now know what will follow, because it seems reasonable on this unexpected event to make new plans . . . .

11.81

23 December 1502, from Cesena.

. . . This departure of the French, as it has been sudden and unforeseen, has given and gives everybody something to say, and every man makes his castles in the air. From a reliable source nothing can be obtained that seems to anybody reasonable; yet I have not failed, in order to get the truth of it, in that diligence that is my duty . . . . I have been talking with Montison. He told me they were going because they had pity on that country and on the Duke, since he had no further need and the country was growing hostile to him, being burdened with so many soldiers.

I have talked with men important here. They have all told me that the Duke could no longer support them, and that if he kept them, he would be more distressed by the arms of his friends than by those of his enemies, and that without them the Duke had left enough soldiers for doing everything. . . .

What at present this Lord wishes or is able to do is unknown, but he is not abandoning any plan made up to now. The artillery has gone ahead, and yesterday six hundred infantry came from Val di Lamona, and a thousand Swiss are at Faenza of those who so long have been expected; and fifteen hundred, including Swiss, Germans, and Gascons, he had already. It is said that the Duke is leaving when these holidays are over in the direction of Pesaro, as was said earlier. On the other hand, he has lost more than half of his forces and two-thirds of his reputation, and it is believed that he will not be able to do many things that he gave signs of earlier and that were thought possible; and San Leo is in the hands of Duke Guidobaldo, and the other fortresses of that state of Urbino are destroyed . . . .

Messer Rimirro,[1] who was the chief man of this Lord, returning yesterday from Pesaro, has been put by this Lord in a dungeon. There are guesses that he will sacrifice him to the people here, who have a very strong desire for it . . . .

1. *Rimirro (or Remirro) de Orco. See* PRINCE 7.

11.82

26 December 1502, 4 p.m., from Cesena.

. . . As I have many times written to Your Lordships, this Lord is very secretive, and I do not believe that what he is going to do is known to anybody but himself. And his chief secretaries have many times asserted to me that he does not tell anything except when he orders it, and he orders it when necessity compels and when it is to be done, and not otherwise. Hence I beg that Your Lordships will excuse me and not impute it to my negligence if I do not satisfy Your Lordships with information, because most of the time I do not satisfy even myself . . . .

Messer Rimirro this morning was found in two pieces on the public square, where he still is; and all the people have been able to see him. Nobody feels sure of the cause of his death, except that so it has pleased the Prince, who shows that he can make and unmake men as he likes, according to their deserts.

[*For Duke Valentino's most striking action between the date of the preceding and of the following letter, see* THE DESCRIPTION OF THE METHOD USED BY DUKE VALENTINO IN KILLING VITELLOZZO VITELLI, *etc.*]

11.95

8 January 1502 [*1503*], from Assisi.

Duke Valentino exhibits a fortune unheard of, a courage and a confidence more than human that he can attain all his desires . . . .

LEGATION 13. AN OFFICIAL MISSION TO THE COURT OF ROME [*THE PAPAL COURT*]

[*All the letters are directed to the Ten of Liberty and* Balía.]

13.10

30 October 1503, 9 p.m., from Rome.

. . . The Cardinals . . . go tomorrow into conclave; . . . and the belief that it must be San Piero in Vincula[1] has so much increased that there are those who give odds of sixty to a hundred on him; and certainly he has much support among the cardinals, and he knows

1. *The cardinal named after that church, later Pope Julius II.*

how to gain them with the methods that are used. Yet Duke Valentino is much sought after by those who wish to be Pope, because of the Spanish cardinals who belong to his faction; hence many cardinals have gone to speak with him every day in the Castle. It is believed, therefore, that the Pope who is to be will be pledged to him, and he lives with this expectation that the new Pontiff will be of his faction.

Rouen has worked hard, and the cardinals who come into the palace are for the most part on his side. It is not clearly understood whether he goes in the direction of Vincula; if it should be so, the situation would need no debate . . . .

13.18

4 November 1503, from Rome.

. . . This Pontiff [*Julius II*] has been elected with very great good will, because, with the exception of three or four cardinals who themselves aspired to the papacy, all the others agreed on him, and Rouen has supported him without any reservation. It is said, as it has been said at other times, that the cause of this support has been that he has promised what has been asked of him; and therefore it is thought that in the fulfilment will lie the difficulty. To Duke Valentino, of whom he has made more use than of any other, it is said that he has promised to restore all the territory of Romagna, and has granted him Ostia for his safety, where Mottino is under arms for him with two ships. The Duke is living in a palace in a place called Stanze Nuove, where he has with him about forty of his chief retainers. It is not known whether he is going to leave or to stay; it is said that he will take the road to Genoa, where he has the larger part of his money, and from there he will go to Lombardy, and raise soldiers, and will take the road to Romagna. And it seems that he may do so, since he still has in money two hundred thousand ducats or more, which are for the most part in the hands of Genoese merchants. Others say he is not intending to leave Rome but to wait for the coronation of the Pope, who will make him Gonfalonier of Holy Church, according to the promises; with the reputation gained from that he can get back his territory. Others, not less prudent, think that this Pontiff, having for his election had need of the Duke, to whom he made big promises, can do nothing else than keep him expectant in this way; yet they fear, if the Duke does not adopt some

other plan than remaining in Rome, that he will be deceived, because they know the natural hatred which His Holiness has always
had for him; the Pope cannot so soon have forgotten the exile in
which he spent ten years. Yet the Duke lets himself be carried away
by that rash confidence of his, and believes that the words of another
man are going to be surer than his own have been. He trusts that
the pledge given in his marriage alliances is going to be kept, because they say that the marriage between Fabio Orsini and Borgia's
sister has been confirmed, and that the Duke's daughter is going to
marry the son of the Prefect.[1] I cannot say anything else about his
affairs nor make up my mind about their necessary end. We must
wait for Time, who is the father of Truth.

I omit telling Your Lordships about the other truces that have
been made and the promises to barons and cardinals, because they
all have fitted the desire of the asker. And Romolino has had the
Segnatura of Justice, and Borgia the Penitenzieria, but it is not yet
known whether they will take possession of them. Moreover, as
has been said above, it seems that the Pope will as yet have to keep
everybody waiting; but he cannot delay very long without making
things plain, and showing to whom he must be and intends to
be a friend . . . .

1. *Francesco Maria della Rovere, Pope Julius' nephew.*

13.22

6 November 1503, from Rome.

. . . Because your [*the Ten at Florence*] letters contained the fall of
Romagna and the purpose of the Venetians, and the state of affairs in
that region, it seemed wise to the Monsignor of Volterra[1] that I should
go at once to the Pope and make known to him your advices; and so it
seemed to the Cardinal of Rouen, who had heard them. I went to
His Holiness and read him your letter. He said he believed that
Dionigio di Naldo would favor Duke Valentino and not the
Venetians, that the Duke of Urbino would be acting according
to his own ideas and not according to those of the Venetians, that
these affairs would take another form as soon as his election to the
Papacy was known, that affairs are going as they are because it is not
yet known, and that he would talk about them with the Cardinal of

1. *Francesco Soderini, Cardinal of Volterra. Machiavelli uses the word* Monsignor *to
indicate a cardinal.*

Rouen. I left His Holiness and talked with Monsignor Ascanio, with San Giorgio and with San Severino, reminding them that now it is not a matter of the liberty of Tuscany, but of the liberty of the Church, and that the Pope would become the chaplain of the Venetians whenever they became greater than they now are, and that it was their duty to provide against it, because they would have to inherit it. We for our part were bringing it before them in time and offering what little we could. These cardinals seemed to wake up and promised to do everything.

I spoke also with the Duke and communicated to him these advices, since it seemed the thing to do, in order to see better his position and what is to be feared or hoped from him. In short, when he heard the news about the castellan of Imola and the attack of the Venetians near Faenza, he was agitated excessively, and complained bitterly of Your Lordships. He said that you had always been his enemies and that he must complain of you and not of the Venetians—because you with a hundred men could have secured those states and you have not been willing to do it—and that he will try to make you the first to repent of it. Since Imola is lost, he does not intend further to assemble soldiers or to lose the rest in order to get back what he has lost. Moreover he does not intend to let you fool him any longer, but will abandon everything there which now is in the hands of the Venetians. He believes you soon will see your state ruined, and he is going to laugh over it. He said also that the French either will lose in the Kingdom or will be kept so busy that they cannot help you. And here he went on at length with words full of poison and anger.

I did not lack matter for an answer, nor would I have lacked words. Yet I used the method of trying to calm him down, and as skilfully as I could got away from him—which seemed to take a thousand years—and went to the Monsignors of Volterra and of Rouen, who were at table; because they were waiting for me with the answer, I told them everything in detail. Rouen was angry at the words he used and said: "God has not up to now left any sin unpunished, and he won't leave so those of that fellow." . . .

It seems, since the Duke keeps on raising soldiers—and those of his ministers whom I know tell me so—that he plans to go to Romagna in any event with as many men as he can. Now that the fortress of Imola has been lost, and this anger of his has resulted from it, I do not know whether he will change his intention. At any rate, as to him, I cannot write anything further to Your Lord-ships. And about the affairs of Romagna, the Monsignor of Rouen and these other cardinals who attend to Italian affairs are intent on deciding one of two things, namely that the said cities of Romagna shall go or be put into the hands either of the Pope or of the King. If they will succeed, I do not know, but I believe they will make every effort in every way, and I do not see that they plan other measures.

13.23

7 November 1503, from Rome.

. . . After I spoke yesterday with the Duke, and left him in that anger that I wrote about to Your Excellencies, he sent for the Most Reverend Cardinal of Volterra, and today again sent for him, and on these two occasions when he spoke to him, and especially this last one, he said, in addition to many expected complaints, that he has letters of the fourth saying that the castellan of Imola was not killed but captured, and that the fortress and the town are held for him, and that Lord Ottaviano Fregoso had come against Imola with many people and had been repulsed. He said that Dionigi di Naldo was on his side and that the Venetians did not have soldiers of much account. It seemed to the Monsignor of Volterra that from such news he had gained a little hope of regaining these states. He complains about the French and about everybody; yet he expects the Pope to make him general of Holy Church, and believes that it will be announced at the Congregation in the morning. The Most Rev-erend Monsignor reminded him that to despair is useless; desperation comes back, generally, on the head of him who despairs. On the other side he encouraged his hope, and made good promises about Your Lordships. Now we must wait to see what will be done tomorrow by the Congregation, and if the Duke will succeed in getting that staff of office; and if he doesn't succeed, what plans he will make. And about everything Your Lordships will be informed, and I should be glad to know how in all conditions I am to conduct myself with the said Duke, and if he is to be kept hoping, and how.

13.26

10 November 1503, from Rome.

In my last letters . . . I told the condition of the Duke's affairs, and that he was hoping to be announced as general of Holy Church in the first Congregation. A Congregation was held yesterday, at which, as I find out, nothing was said about his business . . . . So this is the Duke's position, and wise men make the unfavorable guess that at the end he will come out badly, even though this Pontiff has always been considered a man of great fidelity. The said Duke is busy getting together men-at-arms; and according to what has been said to me by some of his men, he has sent somebody into Lombardy to enlist infantry, so that with the people hired here, with those infantry, and with the reputation of being Gonfalonier and general of Holy Church, he could go to retake his territories. Since he did not succeed in being made Gonfalonier in this first Congregation, as he hoped, I do not know whether he will change his plan or will rely further on the belief that he will be chosen at last. I should be very glad to have from Your Lordships directions on how I am to conduct myself with the said Duke, because to bring him to that region by assuring him so that he will come seems here the proper thing; I do not know whether Your Lordships are of such an opinion.

Recently the Monsignor of Volterra, together with many other cardinals, spoke to His Holiness the Pope about the affairs of Romagna, and he says that he found in His Holiness a strong determination that they should not fall into the hands of the Venetians. He also says that, after many propositions and replies, His Sanctity said: "I have always been a friend to the Venetians, and I still am when they do not claim more than is proper; but when they try to take what belongs to the Church, I am going to use the utmost of my power to keep them from succeeding; and I shall stir up all the Christian princes against them." Hence the said Most Reverend Monsignor feels certain that, in whatever concerns His Holiness, affairs will not go farther . . . .

13.28

10 November 1503, from Rome.

   . . . The Duke of Romagna is getting people ready to leave, and he has obtained letters from the Most Reverend Cardinal of Volterra, from Rouen and from the Pope in his behalf and directed to Your Lordships. The said Duke has thought it a good thing that I too should write informing you that he is sending one of his own men to you to get a safe-conduct, in the form that Your Lordships will see in the attached example. I have been asked to recommend this to Your Lordships and to beg you to use great haste. The man who spoke to me for him declares that the Duke feels confident that, if Your Lordships do not entirely give up, he will soon get those cities from the hands of the Venetians and block their intentions—so large is the sum of money that he still possesses.

13.30

11 November 1503, from Rome.

   . . . He who considers things in Rome sees that here are trans-acted the most important of all the affairs now going on. The first, and the most important, is the matter of France and Spain; the second, the affairs of Romagna; then there are the quarrels between the barons and Duke Valentino. Among all these factions the Pope is placed. Though he has been elected with high favor and high reputation, nevertheless, through having been in his position a short time and not yet having soldiers or money, and through having made everybody promises to gain his election, and everybody's having willingly agreed to it, he can by no means shoulder any big under-taking. On the contrary, he sees that he must take middle ground until time and the fluctuation of affairs force him to declare himself, after he is so well settled in his seat that he can join parties and under-take actions as he pleases . . . . As to the affairs of Romagna, on one side the Venetians are pushing them; on the other you cry out; hence reason demands that they should afflict His Holiness, who is a man of courage and who wants the Church to expand and not to grow less in his time. Nevertheless, Your Lordships will understand from the above how he conducts himself, and you see that on one side he accepts the excuse of the Venetians, appearing to believe that they are moved by their hatred for the Duke and not by their intention to act against the Church . . . .

There remains Valentino. Everybody believes that His Holiness does not naturally wish him any good. Nevertheless he continues to deal with him, for two reasons. First, he wishes to keep his own word, about which he is said to be very careful, and he has obligations to Duke Valentino, having to a great extent to thank him for the papacy. Second, His Holiness thinks that since he himself is without forces, this Duke is more able to resist the Venetians than anybody else. For that reason the Pope has urged the Duke to leave, and has written Briefs to Your Excellencies for passage and safe-conduct, and given other assistance in his affairs . . . . I believe I have needed to say this in detail at present—since I feel the seriousness of what the mind of the Pope may plan, and what he may wish or be able to do, and what he may want you to do—to enable Your Lordships to understand him, and not to have other hope here. But it is necessary for you to think about other methods, such as supporting the Duke or making some other decision when he is there. And you can lay down this presupposition: the Pope is forced to be satisfied, in this situation and for the present, with whatever results in the affairs of Romagna, if only they do not get out of the power of the Church and her vicars.

The Duke sent for me today, and I found him otherwise disposed than I did on my other visit, which I reported in my letters of the sixth and seventh. He said many things which, being reduced into one, show that he wishes to stay here: he will not think on the past but merely about the common good; he will act to keep the Venetians from becoming masters of Romagna; the Pope is ready to aid him. He told me of the Briefs that had been written, and that Your Lordships needed to think on the matter too and give him some support; as to him you could rely on everything. I replied in general, and indicated that he could trust in Your Lordships.

I afterward spoke at length with Messer Alessandro Spannocchi of France, who said to me that perhaps tonight somebody would be sent to you with the Pope's Brief and with the letters they have had written by the Cardinal and myself in the matter of the safe-conduct, and that they had no doubt about getting it. He said that the Duke was uncertain what to do, for he did not know whether he should go by land with his people, who are about four hundred cavalry and the same number of infantry, or whether he should send his people by land and himself go by water to Livorno, and then join his people in your dominion, where he could speak with some citizens and settle his affairs with you; but he is unwilling to waste time, and would hope to find the documents drawn with discretion, and would not like to have to do anything other than sign them. He asks to be advised at Livorno that he would be received, if he should take that road. I answered that I would write to Your Lordships and encouraged him. So Your Lordships can think about it all and make up your minds, and take counsel and prepare to deal with him. Messer Alessandro told me that the Duke, in order to arrange and write a draft of the agreement he is to make with you, would have sent somebody, but he did not like to send a man of small reputation, and one of high reputation he cannot send with security; but when he is in a position to do it, he will send someone . . . .

13.33

13 November 1503, 7 p.m., from Rome.
. . . From my last letters you have learned the plans of the Duke, who is constantly busy raising soldiers both infantry and cavalry, in order to take the road to Romagna; I believe that to quite an extent he is waiting for your decision, and we here cannot treat or carry on any business, not knowing the purpose or the wish of Your Lord⁄ships in this matter; I have many times asked for your judgment on it, but having had no reply, I am left hanging . . . .

13.35

14 November 1503, from Rome.
. . . The Cardinal of Volterra does not know whether the Duke will leave Rome, because he has found him inconstant, irresolute, and timid, and not standing firm in any decision—whether he is so by nature or because these blows from Fortune have stunned him, and, since he is unaccustomed to receive them, his mind is con⁄fused . . . .

Two evenings ago, when I was in the rooms where Duke Val⁄entino lodges, the Bolognese ambassadors came in, and among them was the Protonotary Bentivoglio; and they all went in to speak with the Duke and remained for more than an hour. So thinking that they might have made some agreement, I went today to see the

Protonotary Bentivoglio, with the pretext of visiting him. After some talk, having come to the affairs of the Duke, he told me they had gone to the Duke because summoned by him; and he had given them to understand that he would release them from the pledge made the year before, but when they got there and the notary had been summoned to draw up the contract, the Duke asked in return for such annulment of the pledge certain special assistance in his present affairs in Romagna. Since they would not give it, having no instructions for it, he on his side would not annul that pledge; so the affair remained unsettled. The Protonotary added that the Duke has made a false move, because he should have showed himself liberal in such an annulment and not have wished to take his stand on the agreement drawn up, because in any case they are not intending ever to give him a soldo. He told me also that, when he talked about such a thing with the Cardinal Euna, the Cardinal had said that he believed the Duke out of his mind: not knowing what he wanted to do, he was confused and irresolute. I asked him if they were going to aid him in anything. He replied that the entrance of the Venetians into Romagna was so important that, if to aid the Duke was the means for checking them, he believed his father[1] and that state would be for helping him . . . .

1. *Giovanni Bentivoglio, ruler of Bologna.*

13.42

18 November 1503, 4 p.m., from Rome.

. . . It seemed good to the Most Reverend Monsignor of Volterra that I should again be at the feet of the Pope and read him your letters, to see what further His Holiness might say, and also to tell him your opinion about the affairs of the Duke, and altogether to learn his intention about it . . . . I went into the business of the Duke and gave the reason why you had not granted him the safeconduct. He said that was well enough and that he agreed with you about it; and he raised up his head.[1] You can see from this—something you were in doubt of before—that it seems to him a thousand years until he can get him out of his presence, and still the Duke is leaving, satisfied to such an extent with the Pope that he cannot complain about the keeping of his word; and yet if it happens that the Pope can employ him in the affairs of Romagna to his advantage,

1. *His spirits seemed to improve.*

he has not entirely closed the road to using him. But what you or any third person does against the Duke, he doesn't care . . . and perhaps he believes that the Duke, when he sees himself abandoned by you, will have to yield to him the territory still in his hands, and he believes that if he succeeds in getting hold of some of those towns, he can get hold of the others easily . . . .

The Duke having had letters indicating that Your Lordships had not granted him the safe-conduct, summoned me; hence, as soon as I had spoken with the Pope, I proceeded to him. His Lordship complained that his safe-conduct had been denied, saying that he had already sent on his cavalry, supposing they would be received in Your Lordships' domain, and he himself wished to leave with the hope that the safe-conduct would reach him after all, and he was not expecting this, and he cannot understand you, having on one side fear that those cities will get into the hands of the Venetians and on the other fear of closing the road to helpers, and by chance he might still be able to make a decision through which Your Lordships would be ruined. And though he knows that making peace with the Venetians would be dangerous, yet constraint might bring him to it, and he would get from them ex-cellent offers, which he might wish to accept, thus getting into such a position that he will injure you to the heart.

I answered that his safe-conduct had not been refused, but that he had been given to understand that Your Lordships wished to know how they were going to live with His Lordship, and to come to an agreement with him and define the alliance, as is proper for two who wish to live with a good understanding and to have con-sideration for one another; and that Your Lordships were not in the habit of going rashly or hastily into any of your affairs, and would not begin now. And therefore it would be well for him to send an experienced person and one who understood his intention, and that he must believe that Your Lordships would not fail to do what would be of advantage to you and be good for your friends.

He replied that he was about to leave; he had sent on his soldiers and was planning to go by water, and he would be glad to be clear before leaving on what he could hope from you.

I replied that I would write this morning to Your Lordships by the speediest way, and would give notice to Your Lordships that His Lordship had sent his soldiers and was dispatching a man, and that he begged Your Lordships to be hospitable to the said soldiers. Meanwhile his man would appear and would talk with Your Lordships; and I did not at all doubt that something of value could be decided, which his agent could make known to him wherever he was.

He was in part satisfied, and answered that if Your Lordships should keep limping under him[2]—which would be clear in four or five days, as soon as this man of his could go and write—then he would come to an agreement with the Venetians and with the devil, and he would go to Pisa, and all the money and forces and friends he had left he would employ in doing you harm.

The man he has decided shall come is a Messer Vanni, one of his favorites, and he should have left this morning; but it is noon, and I have not heard of his leaving; I do not know whether he has changed deliberately. The Duke too, as was agreed yesterday with Rouen, was to leave this morning and go by way of La Spezia, according to the first arrangement, and he plans to take with him in the ship and in his boats five hundred men in all, gentlemen[3] and infantry; but up to this hour I have not heard that he has left. I do not know whether he will decide to wait until he assures himself to some extent of you.

I have assured the Duke in the way you see, only to give him a bit of hope, that he may not have to delay, and that the Pope will not therefore have to urge you to give him the safe-conduct. Your Lordships, when the Duke's man comes, can treat him negligently, and conduct yourselves as you think best, considering the results both of cutting off the negotiation and of completing it. The cavalry have gone in your direction under Carlo Baglioni; there are a hundred men-at-arms and two hundred and fifty light horsemen; Your Lordships will find out their nature; and if it seems good to Your Lordships to act in such a way that they will turn back, you can do so. When I know Your Lordships' mind, I shall proceed with the Duke according to your intention. Your Lordships will not fail to write if anything else is required . . . .

2. *Figurative or semi-proverbial for* vacillating.
3. *Cf.* PRINCE 7 *for the Roman gentlemen who abandoned the Orsini for the Duke.*

13.44

19 November 1503, from Rome.

. . . Duke Valentino, to the pleasure of all this city, . . . has left for Ostia, and two or three days ago he sent his people by land in your direction; he says there are about seven hundred cavalry. When the weather is right, he will embark with four or five hundred per- sons, to go by way of La Spezia, as he has agreed here, and then to go by that road I mentioned in mine of the fourteenth. Yet there is reason to fear that he has been vexed by the actions of Your Lord- ships and that he intends to disembark at Pisa, as he hinted to me the last time I talked with him, in the way I explained to Your Lord- ships in yesterday's letter. What makes me suspect it is that he has not said a word to me about the man we agreed he should send there, as we engaged he should, because he needed to have letters and documents for his security; hence I suspect that he does not intend to have any more dealings with you . . . .

13.46

20 November 1503, from Rome [*second letter*].

. . . All the favors that the Pope, Rouen, and those here have done Valentino have been in order that he may go away, the sooner, the better. And therefore Your Lordships have the field clear for deciding without any hesitation what is for your advantage. And again I say that if because of some recent happening Your Lordships think you should aid him, you can change, though the Pope will like it better if he can give him a shove, as soon as his situation is such as I have mentioned . . . . The Duke himself is at Ostia, and is waiting for weather to go to La Spezia. He will occupy five vessels, and will have with him five hundred persons; nobody knows whether he has left yet. Perhaps he will leave tonight, if the weather is favorable. He has sent his men-at-arms by land in your direction, though from the Sienese and Gianpaolo Baglioni he has had no other pledge than from Your Lordships. Hence, everybody here laughs about his affairs. We shall see where the wind will carry him and how his soldiers will come out, and in the same way what Your Lordships decide . . . .

13.49

21 November 1503, from Rome.

. . . The Pope. . . sent again for the Monsignor of Volterra and told him that last night he had not been able to sleep on account of these affairs of Faenza and Romagna, and that he had considered whether it would be a good thing to test Duke Valentino again, to see whether he would put in His Holiness' hands the castle of Forlì and the other strongholds and places that he still holds in Romagna, with the promise that they would be restored—thinking it would be better to have the Duke rather than the Venetians in them; then he asked the said Monsignor of Volterra whether he would undertake the business of going to Ostia to see the Duke, to make this agree-ment. The Most Reverend Monsignor consented to do everything that His Holiness wished; but the Pope hesitated about saying he had decided on this, and charged him meanwhile to talk with Rouen, and see in what direction he had turned, and how he was inclined in these affairs. This plan—that Valentino should put these towns in the Pope's hands, with the promise that he should have them again—was considered many days ago, and the Duke acqui-esced; but the Pope would not consent to it, saying he was not going to break his word to anybody; not being satisfied that Valentino should be lord there, he would not consider the plan. Now he has gone over to it, if he does not change his purpose, forced by those necessities you know of, for he believes this defense the strongest there is and the most easily excused to the Venetians, since he does not think it to his advantage to reveal himself as their enemy.

Still again the Most Reverend Monsignor of Volterra was sum-moned by His Holiness at the dinner hour, was kept to dine, remained with His Blessedness until nearly midnight. And the aforesaid Monsignor told me that the Pope had sent a messenger to Ostia to see whether Duke Valentino had left, and if he had not left to have him wait, and tomorrow early the Monsignor will go to see him; on his return we shall know the agreement he has made. But if he has left, we shall have to stop thinking about this expedient . . . .

13.56

23 November 1503, from Rome.

. . . It is six p.m., and since the Most Reverend Monsignor has not yet returned, I believe he will delay until tomorrow. But I do not want to miss telling Your Lordships what is said publicly; and I write it because I have heard it from a responsible man, one who easily can know the truth. This is that early this morning a messenger came to the Pope, sent by those cardinals who went to the Duke, who announced to him that the Duke would not put the castle[1] in the Pope's hands. His Holiness, angered at their report, sent to arrest the said Duke, to have him held as his prisoner, and wrote at once to Perugia and to Siena, giving instructions in both places that those soldiers of the Duke who had gone in your direction should be plundered. I do not know whether this is true; we shall find out on the coming of the Most Reverend Monsignor, and Your Lordships will be fully informed.

1. *Apparently that of Forlì.*

13.57

24 November 1503, from Rome.

. . . Since the Duke did not wish to agree to give up those cities, the Pope has had him arrested; . . . it appears that the Pope is determined to have those towns and to make sure of the Duke's person. This Duke now is in the Pope's power, because he is on the King's galleys commanded by Mottino. Nobody thinks that any harm will be done him at present, and it is not known for certain that the Pope has sent to plunder his soldiers who have gone by land, but it is believed that nature will act for itself, since they have gone into that region without safe-conducts . . . .

13.61

26 November 1503, from Rome.

. . . It is not yet known whether the Duke is still on the ships at Ostia or whether he has been made to come here. It was talked of today in various ways. True it is that one man has told me that when last night at eight o'clock he was in the Pope's chamber, two men came from Ostia; at once everybody was excused from the chamber, but when he was in the other room he overheard that they carried news that the Duke had been thrown into the Tiber as the Pope had commanded. I do not confirm it and I do not deny it. I do believe, if it has not happened, it will. So we see that this Pope is already paying his debts very honorably, and that he cancels them with the cotton of the inkstand.[1] Nonetheless, everybody invokes blessings on his hands, and will so much the more, the further he goes onward. Now that Valentino is arrested, whether he is alive or dead, one can act without thinking further about his affair.

1. *Apparently proverbial; the meaning is to be inferred from the context.*

13.62

27 November 1503, from Rome.
 . . . Of the Duke . . . I know only that he is at Ostia in the Pope's power. I am told that last night Messer Gabriello returned from Fano and Messer Michele Romolino from Ostia. And they had settled things with the said Duke, that is, that he should give the fortress into the Pope's hands by treaty, and that the Pope should give him some recompense . . . .

13.64

28 November 1503, from Rome [*first letter*].
 . . . Last night the Pope's entire guard went to Ostia to bring Duke Valentino here, as some say; according to others they went not merely to bring him but to make surer of him, because the night before word came to the Pope that he had retired to some galleons with his people, and if forces were not sent there, he would leave. That was the reason why he had the guard ride off; . . . it is 6 p.m., and they have not yet returned. It was said in Rome today that he escaped; yet this evening it is said that they have him in their hands. However it may be, we shall know better tomorrow; and at any rate we see that this Pope is dealing with him *a ferri puliti* . . . .[1] We see that his sins have little by little brought him to penitence. May God grant that it come out the better! . . .
 Yesterday one of those men returned whom in the beginning the Pope sent into Romagna; he reports that the Church has a very small party in Imola and in Forlì, because they fear to be put back

1. *Apparently proverbial. With polished tools, deftly and vigorously.*

under Madonna;² in Imola the people want the Duke, and the castellan of Forlì is going to fortify himself, and will keep his fidelity to the Duke as long as he lives. This account angered the Pope . . . .

2. *The Lady of Forlì, Caterina Sforza. See the Index.*

13.67

29 November 1503, from Rome.

. . . The guard returned from Ostia today at 4 p.m.; Duke Valentino was brought at that hour on a galleon to San Paolo two miles from here, and it is believed that tonight he will be brought back to Rome. What then will be done will be learned day by day. At least, Your Lordships will no longer need to imagine where he is going to disembark; the infantry he led away have returned to Rome a few at a time; the gentlemen he took with him will have to go back to their homes; and Don Michele and the other people who went in your direction cannot accomplish much . . . .

13.68

30 November 1503, from Rome.

. . . It seems that the Pope does not yet treat Duke Valentino as a prisoner for life, and he has had him go to Magliano, where he is under guard; it is a place seven miles from here. So the Pope continues to soften him, and attempts to get the countersigns from him through agreement, so that it will not be learned that he has been forced to give them up, lest the castellans, in the belief that the Duke had been forced, make some trouble about turning over the castles to anybody except the Pope;¹ and therefore he wishes to have the countersigns by agreement, as I have said. And such an agreement will be under the condition that the Pope will have those fortresses, and the Duke then can go free. Certainly this condition will be laid down, and perhaps there will be discussion of some compensation, or a promise of restitution after a time. What will happen I do not know, and I cannot form a good judgment, because these affairs of the Duke, since I have been here, have gone through a thousand changes. True it is that they have always gone down . . . .

1. *The texts give* Pope. *The sense seems to require* Duke.

13.70

1 December 1503, from Rome [*a postscript*].

I forgot to tell Your Lordships that Duke Valentino is in the Palace, where he was brought this morning, and he has been put in the chamber of the Treasurer . . . .

13.72

2 December 1503, 9 p.m., from Rome [*second letter*].

. . . I found that the Most Reverend Monsignor of Volterra and the Pope . . . had got the countersigns of the fortresses of Romagna from Duke Valentino, and ordered that this evening or early to‑morrow morning Messer Pietro d'Oviedo, as a man for the Duke, and another man for the Pope should go with the said countersigns to Romagna, by way of Florence . . . .

Duke Valentino has been taken from the chamber of the Treas‑urer and is in the chamber of Rouen, and wants to go through Florence with the said Rouen . . . . Rouen has taken him into his chamber unwillingly, and more unwillingly will take him with him; as to receiving him, he has consented in order to satisfy the Pope. But as to taking him with him, perhaps they will not agree. And then if the Pope wishes, before the Duke leaves, to have those fortresses in his hands, and Rouen is ready to leave, they cannot be turned over in time. And so one doesn't know how to predict what end it will have . . . .

13.74

3 December 1503, from Rome.

I wrote yesterday . . . that Pietro d'Oviedo, with the agent of the Pope, was going to leave this morning to pass through Florence with the countersigns of the fortresses. Your Lordships should know that he has not yet gone. The reason is that, because the Pope has treated with the Duke about this surrender of the fortresses in a friendly way, the said Duke stands firm and wants to have securities and to look at it minutely; and the Pope does not want to compel him as yet. The securities he asks are that Rouen promise him, and subscribe with his hand, all that the Pope says he is going to do, in short, act as the Pope's bondsman for his promise. This Rouen up to now refuses, and nobody believes that he will promise in any way, or on any account; and so this thing has been debated all today, and in short it is thought that tomorrow, without other promise by Rouen, Messer Pietro will be on the way with the countersigns. So it seems that this Duke little by little is slipping into his grave . . . .

13.84

9 December 1503, from Rome.

. . . Duke Valentino remains in part of those rooms that were occupied in the Palace by the said Rouen, and last night he was guarded by the Pope's men. It is believed that to avoid this annoyance the Pope will put him in the Castle, although many rumors are spread, as that the Pope has promised Rouen to let the Duke go as soon as he gets possession of those fortresses . . . .

13.88

14 December 1503, from Rome [*postscript*].

. . . Duke Valentino is where I have earlier said he is. Let me remind Your Excellencies that if you wish to proceed against him, you should send an order to whomever you wish, with authority to substitute lawyers, etc.

ON THE METHOD OF DEALING WITH THE REBELLIOUS PEO﹍PLES OF THE VALDICHIANA

[A selection]

[*This fragment is usually assigned to the year 1503 because of its subject. But what Florentine body could Niccolò have addressed in such terms? Because of its affinities with the fictitious speeches of the* HISTORY OF FLORENCE, *this address may be considered as written for the book planned to deal with the events in Valdichiana in 1503; in connection with these, Machiavelli wrote official letters (Canestrini,* SCRITTI INEDITI DI MACHIAVELLI, 1857, *pp. 29﹍39). Some twenty years later, looking back on the mistakes of Florentine government, Machiavelli as historian put in the mouth of some prominent citizen a fictitious speech urging a wiser policy. The fragment is, then, dated in the 1520's.*

Much of the material had already been more briefly used in the DIS﹍COURSES 2. 23. *The section on Cesare, which has some air of composition after the fact, is, then, among Machiavelli's last formal references to that adventurer.*]

. . . Anybody who has observed the Duke [*Cesare Borgia, Duke Valentino*] sees that, in maintaining the states he holds, never has he planned to lay his foundation on Italian friendships, always having put a low value on the Venetians, and on you a lower one. If this is true, it follows that he thinks of building himself so large a state in Italy that it will make him safe by himself and that it will make his friendship desirable to any other ruler. And if this is his purpose, we may suppose that he looks forward to the rule of Tuscany as closest by the other states he possesses and fit to form a kingdom along with them; that he has made this plan we conclude necessarily both from the things already said, and from his ambition, and from his having played along with you about the agreement and never having been willing to settle anything with you. We have left only to see if the time is suited for giving effect to these plans of his. I remember having heard the Cardinal de'Soderini say that among the reasons for praise permitting anyone to call the Pope and the Duke *great* was this: they are men who recognize the right time and know how to use it very well. This opinion is confirmed by our experience of the things they have carried through when they had an opportunity. And if you are to debate whether this is a time opportune and safe for them to put pressure on you, I should say not. But considering that the Duke cannot wait for a sure thing, little time being left him by the short span of life remaining to the Pope, he must use the first opportunity that offers itself, and entrust a good part of his cause to Fortune. At present in two ways opportunity can come to the Duke for hoping to conquer you, etc.[1]

1. *For this sentence, with which the manuscript breaks off, see Tommasini,* VITA DI MACHIAVELLI, 1. 662.

A DESCRIPTION OF THE METHOD USED BY DUKE VALENTINO IN KILLING VITELLOZZO VITELLI, OLIVEROTTO DA FERMO, AND OTHERS

[The last event mentioned in this work, the execution of Pagolo Orsini and the Duke of Gravina Orsini, took place on 18 January 1503. Since Machiavelli was at the court of Duke Valentino from 7 October to 18 January, he may be called an eyewitness of the events he narrates. He wrote almost daily reports to the Florentine government; a selection from them is given above. The present description is generally supposed later than the reports. Its literary quality (noticed by Roberto Ridolfi in his VITA DI NICCOLÒ MACHIAVELLI, *Rome, 1954, second edition, p. 98) suggests that it was intended for the* HISTORY OF FLORENCE; *if so, its composition falls in the 1520's.]*

BY THIS TIME DUKE VALENTINO HAD RETURNED FROM Lombardy, where he had gone to clear himself with Louis the King of France from many charges laid against him by the Florentines as the result of the rebellion of Arezzo and the other towns of Valdichiana,[1] and had reached Imola. There he was intending to halt with his army and carry out his design against Messer Giovanni Bentivoglio, despot in Bologna, because he planned to bring that city into his power and to make her head of his dukedom of Romagna. When the Vitelli and the Orsini and their followers learned this, they felt that the Duke was getting too powerful and that they might well fear, when he had conquered Bologna, that he would try to destroy them in order to be the only armed man in Italy.

And on this subject they held a council at Magione, in the territory of Perugia, at which appeared the Cardinal, Pagolo, and the

---

1. *On 9 August 1502, Machiavelli wrote to Antonio Giacomini: "Valentino has come to court and is trying to justify himself with the King and put blame on Vitellozzo." On 11 September, he alludes to the return of Valentino (Canestrini,* SCRITTI INEDITI DI MACHIAVELLI, *1857, pp. 23, 36).*

Duke of Gravina Orsini, Vitellozzo Vitelli, Oliverotto da Fermo, Gianpagolo Baglioni the ruler of Perugia, and Messer Antonio da Venafro, sent by Pandolfo Petrucci lord of Siena; there they dis, cussed the greatness of the Duke and his purpose, and their need to bridle his ambition; otherwise there was danger that with others they would be destroyed. So they determined not to desert the Bentivogli and to try to win over the Florentines; hence to the two cities they sent their agents, promising aid to one and encouraging the other to unite with them against the common enemy.

This council was at once reported throughout Italy, so that the peoples who were unhappy under the Duke's rule, among them the citizens of Urbino, formed hopes of making a change in affairs. While their intentions were thus uncertain, some men from Urbino made a plan for seizing the fortress of San Leo, held by the Duke's forces. They took the following opportunity.[2] The castellan was strengthening the fortress and had brought there some carpenters. So the conspirators arranged that some beams that were being dragged into the castle should be left on the bridge, which, being thus encumbered, could not be raised by the garrison. On this opportunity, the conspirators, fully armed, rushed over the bridge into the castle. As a result of this capture, as soon as it was known, all that state rebelled and summoned back the old Duke, taking hope not so much from the seizure of the castle as from the council at Magione, which gave them hope of assistance.

Those who had taken part in the council, learning of the rebellion at Urbino, decided that they should not lose the opportunity. So gathering their soldiers, they moved forward to assail any city in that territory which had been left in the Duke's power. And again they sent to Florence to urge that republic to decide to join them in putting out this general fire, demonstrating the plan that had been carried out, and that they had an opportunity such that they could not expect another. But the Florentines, because of their hatred against the Vitelli and the Orsini for various reasons, not merely did not join them but sent Niccolò Machiavelli, their secretary, to offer the Duke asylum and aid against these new enemies of his.

The Duke was then in Imola, in great fear, because suddenly and against all his expectations, since his soldiers had become hostile to him, war was upon him and he was unarmed. But regaining

2. *Machiavelli learned of this from Cesare himself* (LEGATION 11, 8 Oct. 1502).

courage on the offer of the Florentines, he decided to protract the war with the few soldiers he had and with negotiations for truce, and meanwhile to obtain help. That he obtained in two ways, partly by sending to the King of France for soldiers, and partly by hiring some men-at-arms and anybody else who in any way could serve on horse-back; and to all he gave money.

In spite of this, his enemies advanced and came toward Fossom-brone, where some of the Duke's soldiers had gathered; these were defeated by the Vitelli and the Orsini. This news caused the Duke to turn entirely to seeing if he could settle this rebellion with negotia-tions for an agreement. And being a very skilful dissembler, he did not fail in any effort to make them think that they had moved their troops against a man who intended what he took to become theirs, and that it was enough for him to have the title of prince, but that he intended the princedom to be theirs. And he so far convinced them that they sent Lord Pagolo to him to negotiate an agreement, and halted their army. But the Duke did not at all halt his own prepara-tions, and with the utmost haste kept increasing the number of his cavalry and infantry; and in order that his preparations might not be evident, he scattered his soldiers through all the towns of Romagna. Meanwhile five hundred French lances came to him.[3] Although he was now so strong that he could in open war revenge himself on his enemies, nevertheless he decided that to deceive them would be a more secure and profitable method and that he therefore would not stop the negotiations for an agreement. And he so labored at the matter that he did make a peace treaty with them, in which he con-firmed their old military contracts; he gave them four thousand ducats at that time; he promised not to injure the Bentivogli and formed a marriage alliance with Messer Giovanni; and in addition he relin-quished all right to require them to come into his presence more than they wished to. On their side, they promised to restore to him the dukedom of Urbino and all the other regions they had occupied, to aid him in all his expeditions, and not to engage in any war or take any military employment without his permission.

After this agreement was made, Guidobaldo Duke of Urbino again fled and returned to Venice, first securing the destruction of all the fortresses in his state because, trusting in the people, he did not

3. *A lance consisted of a heavy-armed horseman and several other men, some of them light-armed cavalry. The French sent perhaps twenty-five hundred men.*

wish the enemy to possess fortresses which he knew he could not defend, and through them to hold his friends in check. But Duke Valentino, after making this treaty and scattering his soldiers throughout the Romagna with the French menatarms, at the beginning of November left Imola and went to Cesena. There he remained many days to negotiate with men sent by the Vitelli and Orsini, who were with their soldiers in the dukedom of Urbino, where a campaign was again to be carried on. When the negotiations produced nothing, Liverotto da Fermo was sent to make him an offer: if he wished to carry on a campaign in Tuscany, they were ready for it; if not, they would besiege Sinigaglia. The Duke replied that he would not begin war in Tuscany because the Florentines were his friends, but that he would be much pleased if they went to Sinigaglia.

As a result, not many days later he received a dispatch that Sinigaglia had surrendered to them but that the castle had not consented to surrender, because the castellan was determined to give it to the Duke in person and to no one else; hence they urged him to come to the city. To the Duke the opportunity seemed good and not such as to rouse suspicion, since he was invited by them and was not going of himself. To reassure them further, he dismissed all his French soldiers, who returned to Lombardy, except a hundred lances under Monsignor di Ciandales his brotherinlaw. So leaving Cesena about the middle of December, he went to Fano, where with all the crafty and prudent words he could use, he persuaded the Vitelli and the Orsini to wait for him in Sinigaglia, showing them that such timidity could not make their agreement either reliable or lasting, and that he was a man who wished to avail himself of the weapons and the counsels of his friends. And though Vitellozzo was very reluctant, and the death of his brother had taught him that one ought not to injure a prince and then trust him,[4] nonetheless, persuaded by Paulo Orsini, whom the Duke had bribed with gifts and promises, he agreed to wait for him.

So the Duke, on the evening (which was the thirtieth day of December, 1502) before he was going to leave Fano, revealed his intention to eight of his most trusted followers, among whom were

4. *Evidently the word* prince *here refers to the city of Florence. In the* FIRST DECENNALE *229, Machiavelli speaks of Pagolo Vitelli's deceit, and in an official letter to the Commissioners in charge of the war against Pisa, of his perfidy (27 Oct. 1499, in Canestrini,* SCRITTI INEDITI DI MACHIAVELLI *119). Pagolo was executed by the Florentines.*

Don Michele and Monsignor d'Euna, who was later Cardinal, and charged them that as soon as Vitellozzo, Pagolo Orsini, the Duke of Gravina, and Oliverotto met him, that each two of them should put between them one of the others (giving in charge a certain man to certain men), and should take care of them until they were inside Sinigaglia, and should not let them go until they had come to his quarters and were arrested. He ordered also that all his soldiers, both mounted and on foot, who were more than two thousand cavalry and ten thousand infantry, should be at daybreak the next morning at the Metaurus, a river five miles from Fano, where they were to wait for him in person. Being then on the last day of December on the Metaurus with these soldiers, he sent riding ahead about five hundred cavalry; next he set in motion all the infantry, and after them he went in person with all the rest of the menatarms.

Fano and Sinigaglia are two cities of the Marches situated on the shore of the Adriatic Sea, fifteen miles apart, so that he who goes toward Sinigaglia has on his right hand the mountains, the bases of which sometimes are so close to the sea that between them and the water there is very little space, and where they give most room, the distance does not reach two miles. The city of Sinigaglia stands little farther than a bowshot from the bases of these mountains, and from the sea is distant less than a mile.[5] Close to this city runs a little river, which washes that part of its walls that looks toward Fano. The road, until it gets close to Sinigaglia, runs for a large part of the journey alongside the mountains, and when it gets to the river that flows by Sinigaglia, it turns to the left along the bank until, having covered a bowshot, it comes to a bridge that crosses the river and almost connects with the gate that leads into Sinigaglia, not by a straight line but diagonally. In front of the gate, outside the wall, is a group of houses with a public square which on one side is bounded by the embankment of the river.

The Vitelli and Orsini, having thus determined to await the Duke and in person to do him honor, in order to make room for his soldiers, withdrew theirs into certain towns six miles distant from Sinigaglia, and left in Sinigaglia only Liverotto with his force, amounting to a thousand infantry and a hundred and fifty cavalry, who were lodged in those houses outside the wall of which I spoke

5. *Sinigaglia at present (as apparently in Machiavelli's time) is much less than a mile from the sea; in fact, it is on the sea.*

above. The state of things being thus, Duke Valentino came toward
Sinigaglia, and when the cavalry reached the bridge, they did not
pass, but, halting, turned the croups of the horses, half of them
toward the river, the other half toward the country, and left a passage
in the middle by which the infantry marched, who without halting
entered the town. Vitellozzo, Pagolo, and the Duke of Gravina,
riding mules, went to meet the Duke, accompanied by a few cavalry.
And Vitellozzo, unarmed, in a cloak lined with green, very dis-
consolate, as though he were aware of his coming death, caused (to
those who knew the valor of the man and his past fortune) some
astonishment. Moreover, it is said that when he left his soldiers to
come to Sinigaglia to meet the Duke, he took as it were his final
leave from them; and from his officers he asked aid for his house and
its fortune, and exhorted his nephews that not the fortune of their
house but the capacity of their fathers and their uncles should be
present in their minds.

When these three, then, came into the presence of the Duke and
saluted him courteously, he welcomed them with a pleasant face, and
being immediately greeted by those to whom they were committed,
they were placed between them. But when the Duke saw that
Liverotto was missing (he had remained with his soldiers at Sinigaglia and was waiting by the front of the public square at his
quarters near the river to keep them to the arrangement and to
instruct them in it), he winked at Don Michele, to whom the charge
of Liverotto was entrusted, as a sign that he should take such measures that Liverotto would not escape. So Don Michele rode on
ahead, and when he reached Liverotto, told him that it was not the
right time to keep his soldiers in their ranks outside of their quarters
because the space would be taken from them by the Duke's men;
and therefore he advised him to send them to their quarters and to
come with him to meet the Duke. And as soon as Liverotto had
carried out this order, the Duke came up and on seeing him spoke to
him. Liverotto, having paid his respects, joined the others. And
having entered Sinigaglia, all of them dismounted at the quarters of
the Duke and went with him into a private room, where the Duke
made them prisoners.

He at once mounted his horse and ordered the soldiers of Liverotto and of the Orsini to be plundered. Those of Liverotto were all
pillaged, because they were near. Those of the Orsini and Vitelli,

being at a distance and having foreseen the ruin of their leaders, had time to assemble; and remembering the courage and discipline of the house of Vitelli, in firm order, against the will of the country and of their enemies, they saved themselves. But the soldiers of the Duke, not being satisfied with the plunder of the followers of Liverotto, began to sack Sinigaglia; and if the Duke had not with the death of many restrained their excesses, they would have sacked it entirely.

And when night came on and the disturbances had been stopped, the Duke decided to have Vitellozzo and Liverotto killed; and taking them into a place together, he had them strangled. At that time neither of them used words worthy of their past lives: Vitellozzo begged that the Pope be petitioned to give him plenary indulgence for his sins; Liverotto, weeping, put on Vitellozzo all the blame for the injuries done to the Duke. Pagolo and the Duke of Gravina Orsini were left alive until the Duke learned that at Rome the Pope had arrested the Cardinal Orsini, the Archbishop of Florence, and Messer Jacopo da Santa Croce; after that news, on the eight-eenth of January at Castel della Pieve they too were in the same fashion strangled.

AN EXHORTATION TO PENI- TENCE

[*There is an autograph manuscript of undetermined date.*

Orations of this sort, before religious companies, were common in Flor- ence.[1] In 1495 Machiavelli became a member of the Company of Piety.[2] To the Company of Charity, Pope Clement VII in 1523 directed a Brief;[3] for that fraternity Machiavelli's oration, in its praise of charity, would have been especially suitable.

Part of the oration is conventional in lauding the outward signs of penitence, even in taking as models the saints who inflicted on themselves bodily pain. Machiavelli may have accepted these things as normal without much consideration, or he may have been ironical in a way apparent to few hearers or later readers. At least, he characteristically declares weeping not enough; action is necessary. Similarly he said in THE PRINCE *that the sins of the Italians were not those charged by the preachers, but such ones as reliance on mercenary soldiers. Even the instruments of self-chastisement used by the saints immediately become allegories for good deeds directed against conduct injurious to one's fellows. Machiavelli's friend Vettori stated thus his view of religion:*

> *The theologians are the chief ones of our religion who have made and continue making so many books, so many debates, so many syllogisms, so many clever doctrines that they fill not merely the libraries but the shops of the booksellers. Nevertheless, our Savior Jesus Christ says in the Gospel: "You shall love God your Lord with all your heart, with all your mind, with all your spirit, and your neighbor as yourself; in these two precepts are summed up all the laws and the prophets." What need is there then for debates about the Incarnation, the Trinity, the Resur- rection, the Eucharist?*

This or an even simpler religion is that of Machiavelli. In his letters espe- cially there are frequent and apparently spontaneous references to God. But always he considers what religion will do for one's neighbors, as when in THE

1. Tommasini, VITA DI MACHIAVELLI, 2. 734.
2. Ibid., 386.
3. Ibid., 734.

ART OF WAR *he attributes much of the wickedness of mercenary troops to lack of religion, and makes the soldier who serves society a religious man. In the* HISTORY OF FLORENCE, *in his account of a violent storm as a divine warning, occurs the harmonious reverse of his suggestion in this little work that the goodness of God is shown in providing the world for the happiness of man.*]

"From the depths I have called upon you, O Lord; O Lord, hear my voice" (Psalm 130).

SINCE THIS EVENING, HONORED FATHERS AND SUPERIOR Brothers, I am to speak to Your Charities, in order to obey my superiors, and am to say something on penitence, it has seemed to me good to begin my exhortation with words of that teacher of the Holy Spirit, David the Prophet, so that those who have sinned with him may, according to his words, hope they can receive mercy from God all-powerful and all-merciful. And that they can obtain it, since David obtained it, they should not fear, because neither greater transgression nor greater penitence for a man than in his instance can be conceived, nor in God can greater generosity to pardon be found. And therefore with the words of the Prophet we shall say: "O Lord, I, imprisoned in the depths of sin, with a voice humble and full of tears have called upon you, O Lord, for mercy; and I pray you that in your infinite goodness you may be willing to grant it to me." There should be no one, then, who should despair of obtaining it, if only with eyes full of tears, with distressed heart, with sad voice he asks for it. O immense pity of God! O boundless goodness! It was known to the most high God how easy it was for man to rush into sin; he saw that, if he had to endure the harshness of vengeance, it was impossible that any man should be saved; he could not with a more merciful remedy provide against human frailty than by admonishing the human race that not sin but persistence in sin could make him unforgiving; and therefore he opened to men the way of penitence so that, having lost the other way, they could by it rise to heaven.

Penitence therefore is the only means for annulling all the ills, all the sins of men, which, though they are many and in many and various ways are committed, nonetheless for the most part can be divided into two groups: one is to be ungrateful to God, the second is to be unfriendly to one's neighbor.

But in order to realize our ingratitude, it is necessary to consider how many and of what sort are the benefits we have received from God. Consider, then, how all things made and created are made and created for the benefit of man. You see first of all the huge extent of the land, which, in order that it could be inhabited by men, he did not allow to be wholly covered over with water but left in part exposed for their use. Then he made to grow on it so many animals, so many plants, so many grasses, and whatever upon it is produced, for their benefit; and not merely did he wish that the earth should provide for their living, but commanded the waters also to support countless animals for their food.

But let us leave these earthly things; let us raise our eyes to the sky; let us consider the beauty of the things we see. Of these, part he has made for our use, part in order that, as we observe the glory and the marvelous workmanship of these things, upon us may come a thirst and a longing to possess those other things that are hidden from us. Do you not see how much toil the sun undertakes, to cause us to share in his light, to cause to live, through his energy, both ourselves and those things that have been created by God for us? So every object is created for the glory and good of man, and man is alone in being created for the good and glory of God, who gave him speech that he might praise him, gave him sight, turned not to the ground as for the other animals but turned to the sky, in order that he might always see it, gave him hands in order that he might build temples, offer sacrifices in His honor, gave him reason and intellect in order that he might consider and understand the greatness of God. See, then, with how much ingratitude man rises against such a great benefactor! And how much punishment he deserves when he per-verts the use of these things and turns them toward evil! That tongue made to glorify God blasphemes him; that mouth, through which he must be fed, he makes into a sewer and a way for satisfying the appetite and the belly with luxurious and excessive food; those thoughts about God he changes into thoughts about the world; that desire to preserve the human species turns into lust and many other dissipations. Thus with these brutish deeds man changes himself from a rational animal into a brute animal. Man changes, therefore, by practicing this ingratitude to God, from angel to devil, from master to servant, from man to beast.

These who are ungrateful to God—it is impossible that they are not unfriendly to their neighbors. Those are unfriendly to their neighbors who are without charity. This, my Fathers and Brothers, is the only thing that takes our souls to Heaven; this is the only thing that has more worth than all the other virtues of men; this is that of which the Church says at such length that he who does not have charity does not have anything. Of this Saint Paul says: "If I speak with all the tongues of men and of angels, and do not have charity, I am just like a worthless musical instrument."[4] On this is based the Christian faith. He cannot be full of charity who is not full of religion, because charity is patient, is kindly, is not envious, is not perverse, does not show pride, is not ambitious,[5] does not seek her own profit, does not get angry, meditates on the wicked man, does not delight in him, does not take pleasure in vanity, suffers everything, believes everything, hopes everything. Oh divine virtue! Oh, happy are those that possess you! This is that heavenly garment in which we must be clad if we are to be admitted to the celestial marriage feast of our Emperor Jesus Christ in the heavenly kingdom! This is that in which we must be dressed if we are not to be driven from the banquet and put in the everlasting fire! Whoever, then, lacks it must necessarily be unfriendly to his neighbor: he does not aid him, he does not endure his faults, he does not console him in tribulation, he does not teach the ignorant, he does not advise him who errs, he does not help the good, he does not punish the evil. These offenses against one's neighbor are grave; ingratitude against God is very grave.

Because into these two vices we often fall, God the gracious creator has showed us the way for raising ourselves up, which is penitence. The might of this he has shown with his works and his words: with words when he commanded Saint Peter to forgive seventy times seven in one day the man who asked forgiveness from him; with his works when he forgave David for his adultery and murder, and Saint Peter for the offense of having denied him not once but three times. What sin will God not forgive you, my

4. *A translation of Machiavelli's Italian rendering of the Latin Bible, I Corinthians 13:1.*
5. *I Corinthians 13:4-7. The word* ambitious *does not occur in the English version. For its importance to Machiavelli, see his* TERCETS ON AMBITION.

brothers, if you sincerely resort to penitence, since he forgave these to them? And not merely did he forgive them, but he honored them among the highest of those chosen in heaven; merely because David, prostrate on the earth, full of affliction and of tears, cried out: "Pity me, God"; merely because Saint Peter without ceasing wept bitterly for his sin. David wept for his. They deserved, both of them, forgiveness.

But, because it is not enough to repent and to weep (for it is necessary to prepare oneself by means of the actions opposed to the sin), in order not to sin further, to take away opportunity for evil, one must imitate Saint Francis and Saint Jerome; they, in order to re-strain the flesh and take from it means for forcing them into sinful deeds, would, one of them, roll himself in thorns, the other with a stone would tear his breast. But with what stones or what thorns shall we keep down our appetite for usury, for slander, for deceptions practiced against our neighbor, if not with alms and with honoring him and doing good to him? But we are deceived by lust, involved in transgressions, and enmeshed by the snares of sin; and we fall into the power of the Devil. Hence, to get out of it, we must resort to penitence and cry out with David: "Have mercy upon me, oh God!" and with Saint Peter weep bitterly, and for all the misdeeds we have committed feel shame

And repent and understand clearly
that as much as pleases the world is a short dream.[6]

6. *Petrarch,* SONNET 1.

DISCOURSES ON THE FIRST DECADE
OF TITUS LIVIUS

Book 2

Book 3

[*Probably written in 1513–1517.*

In THE PRINCE, *chap. 2, Machiavelli says he has elsewhere written on republics. The* DISCOURSES *do not deal exclusively with republics, and they cannot have been finished in 1513, the only date we have for* THE PRINCE, *because they refer to events as late as 1517. Yet the years mentioned are those when, so far as we know, Machiavelli would have had most leisure for writing, and the close relation of* THE PRINCE *and the* DISCOURSES *makes contemporary composition plausible.*

The general method of the DISCOURSES *is comment on passages of the first ten books of Livy in order, each of Machiavelli's three books making a fresh beginning with Livy's first. But there are many exceptions to this rule, including irregular inversions in order, omission of various books, discourses without dependence on Livy, and grouping of discourses according to subject. Other matters than Livian order influenced Machiavelli, though he returned to that order when he had no other determinant. Subjects are assigned for the three books of the* DISCOURSES: *for Book 1, the decisions of the Romans on internal affairs; for Book 2, their decisions pertaining to the expansion of their empire; for Book 3, the effect on the Roman republic of the actions of individuals. Yet these topics are not strictly adhered to. It is reasonable, indeed, to suppose with the first Florentine publisher that Machiavelli did not consider the work ready for the press. Readers should beware of treating it as a finished product, in the smallest matters as well as in the largest.*

Its irregular and unconstricted method, or almost lack of method, permitting Machiavelli to write on such political and military matters as he chose, and at such length as he chose, was admirably suited to his unpedantic temperament. The DISCOURSES *may be considered a group of familiar essays, in which we listen to the informal conversation of the Florentine secretary.*

He who is to read but a little of Machiavelli should turn to THE PRINCE *and* MANDRAGOLA, *but he who hopes to understand Machiavelli's thought and attitude should begin with the* DISCOURSES. *They are in the atmosphere of* THE PRINCE, *but being written with more feeling of leisure and at greater length, they can give reasons for what the shorter work leaves unexplained. For example, a reader of the* DISCOURSES *could never wonder why Machiavelli, believing in the superiority of republics, could write a book for princes; at times only the kingly hand can master the difficulties of government. The ethical problem is more fully stated; some of the methods necessary to a ruler who is to maintain himself are unchristian and inhuman; a man ought to fly from them and choose to live a private life rather than become or remain a king by means of such cruelty; but choosing to be a king, to abandon the good way, he has no alternative to severity or cruelty itself (1. 26). Machiavelli does not deny what is good, but, as in* THE PRINCE, *he reveals what the world's rulers do. Some have been shocked by* THE PRINCE, *as Bacon knew, because it uncovers the evils normal to governments; they can learn from the* DISCOURSES *that the evils themselves are inhuman.*

Between the topics of THE PRINCE *and of the* DISCOURSES *there is no division. In the first, Machiavelli cannot refrain from treating republics, and in the second are sections addressed directly to the ruler, according to the habit of the shorter work. Whatever in politics Machiavelli wished to discuss has its place in the* DISCOURSES.]

DISCOURSES ON THE FIRST DEC-ADE OF TITUS LIVIUS

NICCOLÒ MACHIAVELLI TO ZANOBI BUONDELMONTI AND COSIMO RUCELLAI, GREETINGS

[Dedication]

I AM SENDING YOU A GIFT WHICH, IF IT DOES NOT BEFIT my obligations to you, is such that beyond doubt it is the largest Niccolò Machiavelli is able to send you; in it I have set out all I know and all I have learned in the course of my long experience and steady reading in the affairs of the world. And since it is not possible for you or anyone to ask more from me, you cannot grieve if I have not given you more. You can indeed mourn over the poverty of my talents, if these discussions of mine are poor, and over the fallacy of my judgment, if, as I go along, in many places I deceive myself. That being true, I do not know which of us needs to be less under obligation to the other—whether I should be to you, who have forced me to write what I of myself never would have written; or you should be to me if, though I have written, I have not satisfied you. Take this, then, in the way in which everything is taken from friends, where one always considers rather the intention of him who sends than the quality of the thing that is sent. And be assured that in this affair I have just one reason for satisfaction: namely, when I reflect that though I may have deceived myself in many of its particulars, in one thing I know that I have made no error, that is, in choosing you as those to whom, before all others, I should dedicate these *Discourses* of mine, both because in doing so I think I have shown some gratitude for the benefits I have received, and because I believe I have got away from the common custom of those who write, who always address their works to some prince and, blinded by ambition and avarice, praise him for all the worthy traits, when they ought to blame him for every quality that can be censured. So in order not to run into this error, I have chosen not those who are princes, but those who because of their countless good qualities deserve to be; not those able to load me with offices, honors, and riches, but those who, though unable, would like to do so. If men wish to judge justly, they must esteem those who are liberal, not those who merely have the power to be so, and likewise those who know how to rule a kingdom, not those who, without knowing how, have the power to do it. Thus historians praise Hiero of Syracuse more when he was in private life than Perseus of Macedon when he was king, because Hiero lacked nothing of being a prince except a princedom; the other had no attribute of a king except his kingdom. Enjoy, then, that good or that ill that you yourselves have asked; and if you continue in the error of being pleased by these opinions of mine, I shall not fail to go through the rest of the *History*, as in the beginning I promised you. Farewell.

BOOK ONE

[PREFACE: THE VALUE OF HISTORY]

[A new path]

On account of the envious nature of men, it has always been no less dangerous to find ways and methods that are new than it has been to hunt for seas and lands unknown, since men are more prone to blame than to praise the doings of others. Nevertheless, driven by the natural eagerness I have always felt for doing without any hesitation the things that I believe will bring benefit common to everybody, I have determined to enter upon a path not yet trodden by anyone; though it may bring me trouble and difficulty, it can also bring me reward, by means of those who kindly consider the purpose of these my labors. And if my poor talents, my slight experience of present affairs, and my feeble knowledge of ancient ones make this my attempt defective and not of much use, they will at least show the way to someone who, with more vigor, more prudence and judgment, can carry out this intention of mine, which, though it may not gain me praise, ought not to bring me blame.

[The value of ancient example]

When I consider, then, how much respect is given to antiquity and how many times (to pass over countless other examples) a fragment of an antique statue has been bought at a high price in order that the buyer may have it near him,[1] to bring reputation to his house with it, and to have it imitated by those who take pleasure in that art, and when I know that the latter then with their utmost skill attempt in all their works to imitate it, and when I see, on the other hand, that the most worthy activities which histories show us, which have been carried on in ancient kingdoms and republics by kings, generals, citizens, lawgivers, and others who have labored for their native land, are sooner admired than imitated (rather they are so much avoided by everyone in every least thing that no sign of that ancient worth remains among us), I can do no other than at the

---

1. *By a construction according to the sense unusual even with him, Machiavelli here begins to talk of the buyer without having mentioned him.*

same time marvel and grieve over it. And I marvel so much the more when I see that in the differences that come up between citizens in civil affairs, or in the illnesses that men suffer from, they ever have recourse to the judgments or to the remedies that have been pronounced or prescribed by the ancients; for the civil laws are nothing else than opinions given by the ancient jurists, which, brought into order, teach our present jurists to judge. And medicine too is nothing other than the experiments made by the ancient physicians, on which present physicians base their judgments. Nonetheless, in setting up states, in maintaining governments, in ruling kingdoms, in organizing armies and managing war, in executing laws among subjects, in expanding an empire, not a single prince or republic now resorts to the examples of the ancients.

[*The* HISTORY *of* Titus Livius *to be explained*]

This I believe comes not from the weakness into which the present religion[2] has brought the world, or from the harm done to many Christian provinces and cities by a conceited laziness, as much as from not having a true understanding of books on history, so that as we read we do not draw from them that sense or taste that flavor which they really have. From this it comes that great numbers who read take pleasure in hearing of the various events they contain, without thinking at all of imitating them, judging that imitation is not merely difficult but impossible, as if the sky, the sun, the elements, men, were changed in motion, arrangement, and power from what they were in antiquity. Wishing, then, to get men away from this error, I have decided that on all the books by Titus Livius which the malice of the ages has not taken away from us,[3] it is necessary that I write what, according to my knowledge of ancient and modern affairs, I judge necessary for the better understanding of them, in order that those who read these explanations of mine may more easily get from them that profit for which they should seek acquaintance with books. And though this undertaking may be difficult, all the same, aided by those who have encouraged me to take up this

2. *The Rome edition of 1531 reads* educazione.

3. *Machiavelli's intention to deal with all of Livy that was extant appears also in the publisher's dedication in the first Florentine edition, 1531. The same purpose is asserted at the end of Machiavelli's Dedication, and is implied at the end of bk. 3, chap. 1, in a reference to the first decade, or ten books, of Livy. Apparently he wrote nothing on the remaining three and a half decades.*

burden, I hope to carry it in such a way that only a short journey will
be left for some other who will bring it to its destined place.

CHAPTER 1. OF WHAT SORT THE BEGINNINGS OF ALL CITIES EVERYWHERE HAVE BEEN, AND OF WHAT SORT THAT OF ROME WAS

[Why cities are founded]

Those who read in what way the city of Rome began, and by
what lawgivers and how she was organized, will not marvel that so
much vigor was kept up in that city for so many centuries, and that
finally it made possible the dominant position to which that republic
rose. And intending first to consider her origin, I say that all cities
are built either by men native to the place where they are built or by
foreigners. The first situation comes about when the inhabitants,
dispersed in many little places, perceive that they cannot live in safety,
since, each one by itself, because of both site and small numbers,
cannot resist the attack of those who may assail it, and as to uniting
for their defense, when the enemy comes, they are too late. Or if they
are not, they have to leave many of their dwelling places deserted, and
so these become the ready prey of their enemies. Hence, to escape
these perils, either on their own initiative or on that of some one
among them who is of greater authority, they unite to dwell together
in a place chosen by them, more convenient for living in and easier
to defend.

[Athens and Venice]

Of this sort, among many others, have been Athens and Venice.
The first, under the authority of Theseus, was for such reasons built
by a scattered population. As to the other, many people gathered in
certain little islands at the end of the Adriatic Sea, to escape those
wars that every day, because of the coming of new barbarians after
the decline of the Roman Empire, sprang up in Italy; without any
special ruler to direct them, they began for themselves to live under
such laws as they thought most fit to preserve them. This came out
happily for them because of the long repose the site gave them, since
that sea had no harbor, and the people who were afflicting Italy had
no ships with which to molest them. So the least little beginning
was enough to allow them to come to such greatness as is now theirs.

[*Alexandria and Florence*]

The second case, when a city is built by foreigners, originates either with free men or with those who depend on others, such as the colonies sent by a republic or a prince to disburden their lands of inhabitants or for the defense of territory newly acquired, which they wish to hold securely and without expense. The Roman people built many cities of this sort all through their empire. Or they may be built by a prince, not in order that he may live there, but for the sake of his fame, as the city of Alexandria by Alexander. And because these cities are by origin not free, it rarely happens that they make great progress and can be numbered among the chief cities of kingdoms. Such was the building of Florence, because (built either by the soldiers of Sulla, or perhaps by the inhabitants of the moun-tains of Fiesole, who, trusting in the long peace that began in the world under Octavian, came to live in the plain by the Arno) she was built under the Roman Empire, and could not at first make other advances than the kindness of the sovereign allowed her.

[*Free cities*]

Free men are the builders of cities when any peoples, either under a prince or of themselves, are forced, either by pestilence or by famine or by war, to abandon their native land and to find a new seat. Such as these either inhabit the cities they find in the countries they con-quer, as did Moses, or they build them anew, as did Aeneas. This is the case where we can observe the wisdom of the builder and the fortune of what he builds, for the latter is more or less astonishing according as he is more or less able who has been its cause. His ability is made known in two ways: the first is the choice of its site, the second the establishment of its laws.

[*A barren or a fertile site*]

And because men act either through necessity or through choice, and because ability appears the more where choice has less power, it must be considered whether for the building of cities it would be better to choose barren places, in order that men, forced to keep at work and less possessed by laziness, may live more united, having because of the poverty of the site slighter cause for dissensions, as happened in Ragusa and in many other cities built in like places.

Such a choice would without doubt be most wise and most useful if men were content to live on their own resources and were not inclined to try to govern others. All the same, since men cannot make themselves safe except with power, it is necessary for them to avoid such barrenness of country and to establish themselves in very fertile places, where, since the richness of the site permits the city to expand, she can both defend herself from those who assail her and crush whoever opposes himself to her greatness. As to that laziness which the site brings on her, she should arrange that the laws will force upon her those necessities which the site does not force upon her; she should imitate wise cities placed in countries very pleasant and fertile and likely to produce men lazy and unfit for all vigorous activity. They, to forestall the losses which the pleasantness of the country would have caused through laziness, have laid such necessity for exercise on those who are to be soldiers that through such an arrangement better soldiers have been produced there than in those countries that naturally are rough and barren. Among these was the kingdom of the Egyptians, in which, notwithstanding that the country was most pleasant, so strong was that necessity laid down by the laws that it produced very excellent men; and if their names had not been destroyed by their antiquity, we should see that they merit more praise than Alexander the Great and many others whose memory is still fresh. And anyone considering the kingdom of the Soldan and the organization of the Mamelukes and of that army of theirs before Selim, the Grand Turk, destroyed it, would see many exercises for the soldiers and would, indeed, learn how much they feared that laziness which the fertility of the land might bring upon them, if with the stongest laws they did not forestall it.

[*A fertile site calls for wise government*]

I say, then, that it is the more prudent choice to build in a fertile spot, when by laws that fertility is kept within proper limits.[1] When Alexander the Great intended to build a city for his glory, Dinocrates, the architect, came to him and showed him that he could build it on Mount Athos, a place which, besides being strong, could be treated in such a way that a human form could be given to a city built there, which would be a thing marvelous and rare and worthy

1. *That is, the influence of that fertility.*

of his greatness. But on Alexander's asking him what those inhabitants would live on, he answered that he had not thought of that. At which the King laughed and, giving up that mountain, built Alexandria, where the inhabitants were glad to live because of the richness of the country and the convenience of the sea and of the Nile.

[*Rome*]

Anyone who examines, then, the building of Rome, if Aeneas is taken as her first founder, will put her among the cities built by foreigners; if Romulus, among those built by the natives of the place; and in any case, he will see that she had a free beginning, without depending on anyone. He will also see, as will be told below, how many necessities the laws made by Romulus, Numa, and the others forced upon her—so that the fertility of the site, the convenience of the sea, her frequent victories, and the greatness of her empire could not for many centuries corrupt her—and they kept her full of vigor as great as that by which any city or republic was ever distinguished.

[*The subject of the First Book*]

Because the things she performed, which Titus Livius celebrates, came about either through the wisdom of the public or of an individual, and either inside or outside the city, I shall begin by discoursing on those things happening inside and through public wisdom that I judge most worthy of note, adding to them everything that depended on them; to such *Discourses* this first book, or this first part, will be limited.

CHAPTER 2. HOW MANY KINDS OF REPUBLICS THERE ARE, AND THE KIND OF THE ROMAN REPUBLIC

[*Free cities; Sparta and Florence*]

I intend to omit discussion of those cities that at their beginning have been subject to somebody, and I shall speak of those that at their beginning were far from all external servitude, but at once governed themselves by their own judgment, either as republics or as princedoms. Just as they have had diverse beginnings, they have had diverse laws and institutions. Because to some, either at their be

ginning or not long afterward, laws have been given by a single man
and at once, like those that were given by Lycurgus to the Spartans.
Some have had them by chance and at several times and as the result
of unforeseen events, as did Rome. Hence, happy is that republic
whose lot it is to get a man prudent enough to give her laws so
planned that without any need for revision she can live safely under
them. And it appears that Sparta observed them more than eight
hundred years without debasing them and without any dangerous
rebellion. And on the contrary, that city is in a somewhat unhappy
position which, not having chanced upon a prudent founder, is
obliged to reorganize herself. And of these again, that one is most
unhappy that has departed farthest from good order; and that one is
farthest from it which in its customs is wholly out of the straight
road that might lead it to a perfect and true end, because for those in
this class it is almost impossible that through any happening they
can set themselves right again. Those others that, if they do not have
a perfect constitution, have made a beginning that is good and
adapted for getting better, can through the meeting of unexpected
circumstances become perfect. But it will certainly be true that they
will never put themselves in order without peril, because enough
men will never agree to a new law that looks toward a new order in
the city, if some necessity does not show them that they need to do it.
And since this necessity cannot arise without danger, it is an easy
thing for such a state to crash before its organization is made perfect.
This is fully confirmed by the republic of Florence, which because of
what happened at Arezzo in 1502 was reorganized, and because of
what happened at Prato in 1512 was disorganized.

[Kingdoms, aristocracies, republics]

Since I am, then, to consider the nature of the institutions of the
city of Rome, and what events brought them to their perfection, I
say that some who have written of states say that they have one of
three kinds of government, called princedom, aristocracy, and popular government, and that those who organize a state ought to make
use of one of these, according as it seems to them more to the purpose.
Some other and, as many think, wiser men hold that there are six
kinds of government, of which three are very bad; the three others
are good in themselves, but so easily corrupted that even they come

to be pernicious. Those that are good are the three indicated above; those that are bad are three others, which evolve from these three, and each of these is in such a way like the one to which it is nearest that they all easily jump from one form to the other, for the princedom easily becomes tyrannical; the aristocracy with ease becomes a government by a few; the popular form without difficulty changes itself into one that abuses liberty. Hence if the founder of a state organizes one of these three governments in a city, he organizes it there for a short time only, because no precaution can be used to make certain that it will not slip into its contrary, on account of the likness, in this case, of the virtue and the vice.

[*The origin of government*]

These varieties of government sprang up by chance among men because in the beginning of the world, since the inhabitants were few, they lived for a while scattered in the fashion of the beasts. Then as their numbers increased, they gathered together, and so that they could better defend themselves, deferred to him among them who was strongest and bravest, and made him chief and obeyed him. From this came understanding of things honorable and good, as different from what is pernicious and evil, because if one injured his benefactor, there resulted hate and compassion among men, since they blamed the ungrateful and honored those who were grateful. Moreover, since they thought also that these same injuries could be done to themselves, they undertook, in order to escape such evils, to make laws and to establish punishments for those who broke them. Thence came the understanding of justice. As a result, when afterward they had to choose a prince, they did not prefer the strongest, but him who was most prudent and most just.

[*The governmental cycle*]

But when later they set up princes by inheritance and not by choice, the heirs quickly degenerated from their ancestors and, leaving off actions requiring ability, thought that princes needed to do nothing else than to surpass the others in lavishness and in lust and in every other sort of licentiousness. Hence, as the prince became hated, and on account of such hate became afraid, and quickly went from fear to violence, the speedy result was tyranny. From this came, next, causes for destruction and for conspiracies and plots against princes, not made by those who were either timid or weak, but by those who in nobility, greatness of spirit, riches, and rank were superior to the others, such as could not endure the shameful life of their prince. The multitude, then, following the authority of these powerful men, took arms against the prince, and when he was destroyed, obeyed them as its liberators. The latter, hating the name of a single ruler, formed a government of themselves, and at first, taking thought of the past tyranny, conducted themselves according to the laws they had laid down, subordinating all of their own advantage to the common good, and with the greatest diligence cared for and pre- served things private and public. Then when later the control of affairs came to their sons, they, not knowing the variations of fortune, never having experienced evil, and refusing to content themselves with equality among citizens, but turning to avarice, to ambition, to violence against women, caused a government by the best men to become a government by the few, without having regard to any civil rights, so that in a short time it happened to them as to the tyrant, because, wearied out by their conduct, the multitude became the instrument of whoever intended in any way to injure those rulers; and so quickly one rose who, with the aid of the multitude, de- stroyed them.

[*The governmental cycle continued*]

And while the memory of the prince and of the injuries received from him was still fresh, those who had overthrown the government of the few, and did not wish to set up again that of the prince, turned to popular control and organized the state in such a manner that neither the few powerful men nor one prince could have any authori- ty. And because all governments get some respect at the beginning, this popular government was kept up for a while, but not long, especially after the death of the generation that had established it, because it rapidly went on to abuse of liberty, in which there was no fear either of private or of public men, so that since each one lived as he pleased, every day a thousand wrongs were done. Hence, forced by necessity, or according to the suggestion of some good man, or to escape such abuses, they returned once more to the princedom; and from that, step by step, things went on again toward abuse of free- dom, in the ways and for the reasons given.

And this is the circle in which all states revolve as they are governed and govern themselves, but only a few times do they return to the same forms of government, for almost no state can have so much life that it can pass many times through these shifts and continue on its feet. But it probably happens that, as it struggles, a state that always lacks prudence and strength becomes subject to a neighboring power that is better organized. But, granted that this does not happen, a state might circle about for an infinite time in these forms of government.

[*The superiority of the mixed form of government*]

I say, then, that all the said types are pestiferous, by reason of the short life of the three good and the viciousness of the three bad. Hence, since those who have been prudent in establishing laws have recognized this defect, they have avoided each one of these kinds by itself alone and chosen one that partakes of them all, judging it more solid and more stable, because one keeps watch over the other, if in the same city there are princedom, aristocracy, and popular government.

[*Lycurgus and Solon*]

Among those who have deserved most praise for such a constitution is Lycurgus, who so prepared his laws in Sparta that, giving their shares to the king, to the aristocrats, and to the people, he made a state that lasted more than eight hundred years, with the highest reputation for himself and peace for the city. The opposite happened to Solon, who prepared the laws in Athens, because, organizing there a state governed only by the people, he made it of such short life that before he died he saw arise the tyranny of Pisistratus. And though, after forty years, his heirs were driven out and Athens returned to liberty, yet because she took up again popular government according to Solon's design, she did not keep it more than a hundred years, although in order to preserve it she enacted many laws that Solon had not thought of, through which she restrained the rich men's arrogance and the people's license. Nonetheless, because she did not mix them with the power of the princedom and with that of the aristocrats, Athens, as compared with Sparta, lived a very short time.

[The mixed government of Rome]

But let us come to Rome. In her case, in spite of her not having a
Lycurgus to organize her at the beginning in such a way that she
could continue free for a long time, nonetheless so many unexpected
events happened, on account of the disunion between the plebeians
and the Senate, that what an organizer had not done was done by
Chance. Because if Rome did not gain the first fortune, she gained
the second; because her first laws, though they were defective, nevertheless did not turn from the straight road leading them to perfection.
Romulus and all the other kings made many good laws, adapted
also to a free society. But because their purpose was to found a
kingdom and not a republic, when that city became free, she lacked
many things that had to be enacted for the sake of freedom, which
those kings had not enacted. And even though those kings lost their
dominion through the causes and means discussed, nonetheless those
who drove them out, since they at once decreed two Consuls to take
the place of the king, succeeded in driving from Rome the name
but not the power of kings. So, since in that state there were the
Consuls and the Senate, it had become a mixture of two only of the
three elements mentioned above, that is, of princedom and aristocracy. It remained only to make place for the popular part of the
government. As a result, when the Roman nobility became insolent
for the reasons that will be given below, the people rose up against it;
hence, in order not to lose the whole, the nobility was obliged to
grant the people their share, and on the other side the Senate and the
Consuls continued to hold so much power that in such a republic
they were able to keep their rank. And thus came about the establishment of the Tribunes of the People; after that, the condition of that
republic became firmer, since then all of the three types of government
had their shares. And so favorable to her was Fortune that even
though she passed from the government of the king and the aristocrats
to that of the people, through the same steps and for the same reasons
that are discussed above, yet never, in order to give authority to the
aristocrats, did she take all authority away from the kingly element,
nor did she entirely remove the authority of the aristocrats to give it
to the people, but continuing her mixed government, she was a
perfect state. To this perfection she came through the discord be-

tween the people and the Senate, as will be shown at length in the next two chapters.

CHAPTER 3. WHAT EVENTS CAUSED TRIB⁄UNES OF THE PEOPLE TO BE ESTABLISHED IN ROME—A THING THAT MADE THE STATE MORE PERFECT

[*A lawgiver must assume that all men are evil*]

As is demonstrated by all those who discuss life in a well⁄ordered state—and history is full of examples—it is necessary for him who lays out a state and arranges laws for it to presuppose that all men are evil and that they are always going to act according to the wickedness of their spirits whenever they have free scope; and when any wickedness remains hidden for a time, the reason is some hidden cause which, in the lack of any experience of the contrary, is not recognized, but then its discovery is brought about by Time, which they say is the father of every Truth.

[*Tyranny kept the nobility humble*]

It seems that in Rome after the Tarquins were driven out the people and the Senate were very closely united, and that the nobles had put away that pride of theirs and become democratic in spirit and could be tolerated by anyone however humble. This falsity was concealed and its cause was not seen as long as the Tarquins lived, for the nobility, fearing them and being afraid that the people, if treated badly, would not take their side, bore themselves kindly toward the people, but as soon as the Tarquins were dead and the fear the nobles felt had departed, they began to spit out against the people the poison they had kept in their breasts, and injured them in any way they could.

[*Necessity makes men good*]

This thing bears testimony to what I have said above, that men never do anything good except by necessity, but where there is plenty of choice and excessive freedom is possible, everything is at once filled with confusion and disorder. Hence it is said that hunger and poverty make men industrious, and the laws make them good. And where without law a thing of itself works well, law is not necessary, but when such a good custom is lacking, at once law is necessary. Hence when the Tarquins were gone, who with fear of themselves had kept the nobility in check, Rome needed to think of a new arrangement that would have the same effect as the Tarquins had when they were alive. And therefore, after much confusion, uproar, and danger of civil war from the dissensions between the people and the nobility, they came, for the security of the people,[1] to the setting-up of the Tribunes; and they established them with such position and such dignity that always thereafter they were middle-men between the people and the Senate, able to head off the arrogance of the nobles.

1. *Livy* 2. *33.*

CHAPTER 4. THE DISCORD BETWEEN THE PEOPLE AND THE ROMAN SENATE MADE THAT REPUBLIC FREE AND POWERFUL

[*Good soldiers indicate good government*]

I do not intend to omit the dissensions in Rome between the deaths of the Tarquins and the establishment of the Tribunes;[1] then I shall bring up some things against the opinion of the many who say that Rome was a disorderly republic and so full of confusion that, if good Fortune and military vigor had not supplied her defects she would have been inferior to all other republics. I cannot deny that Fortune and the military system were sources of the Roman power; but it surely seems that these objectors do not realize that wherever there are good soldiers there must be good government,[2] and it seldom happens that such a city does not also have good Fortune.

[*Roman dissensions not injurious*]

But let us come to other details about this city. I say that those who condemn the dissensions between the nobility and the people seem to me to be finding fault with what as a first cause kept Rome free, and to be considering the quarrels and the noise that resulted from those dissensions rather than the good effects they brought

1. *Livy* 2. 7-32.
2. *Good government precedes good military organization. See* THE PRINCE *12, and n. 1.*

about; they are not considering that in every republic there are two opposed factions, that of the people and that of the rich, and that all the laws made in favor of liberty result from their discord. We easily see that this was true in Rome, because from the Tarquins to the Gracchi, more than three hundred years, the dissensions in Rome rarely caused exile and very rarely bloodshed. It is impossible, therefore, to pronounce these dissensions injurious, or a republic divided, which in so long a time sent into exile by reason of its disagreements not more than eight or ten citizens, put to death very few, and levied fines on not many more. Nor can a republic in any way reasonably be called unregulated where there are so many instances of honorable conduct; for these good instances have their origin in good education; good education in good laws; good laws in those dissensions that many thoughtlessly condemn. For anyone who will properly examine their outcome will not find that they produced any exile or violence damaging to the common good, but rather laws and institutions conducive to public liberty.

[*The desires of free people not harmful*]

And someone may say: such methods were unlawful and almost inhuman, for the people were shrieking against the Senate, the Senate against the people, there was disorderly running through the streets, locking of the shops, the people all leaving Rome—all which things strike with horror him who merely reads of them. But I reply that every city ought to have methods with which the people can express their ambition, and especially those cities that intend to make use of the people in important affairs. Among such methods, the city of Rome had this one: when the people wished to secure a law, either they did some one of the things I have mentioned or they did not consent to give their names for going to war, so that to soothe them it was necessary in some way to satisfy them. The aspirations of free peoples are seldom harmful to liberty, because they result either from oppression or from fear that there is going to be oppression. And whenever their beliefs are mistaken, there is the remedy of assemblies, in which some man of influence gets up and makes a speech showing them how they are deceiving themselves. And as Cicero says, the people, though they are ignorant, can grasp the truth, and yield easily when by a man worthy of trust they are told what is true.

[Roman dissension protected liberty]

Men ought, then, to be more sparing in their blame for the Roman procedure, and to consider that all the many good effects the republic produced resulted from only the best causes. If these dissensions brought about the installation of the Tribunes, they deserve the greatest praise, for the reason that, besides giving its share to popular control, these officials were designed for the protection of Roman liberty, as will be shown in the following chapter.

CHAPTER 5. WHERE IS THE GUARDIAN-SHIP OF LIBERTY MOST SECURELY PLACED, IN THE PEOPLE OR IN THE GREAT? AND WHICH HAS MORE CAUSE TO RAISE A RIOT, HE WHO WISHES TO GAIN OR HE WHO WISHES TO KEEP?

[Sparta, Rome, Venice]

As to those who have prudently set up a republic, one of the most necessary things they have arranged has been to set up a guardian for liberty, and according as they have placed him well, that free government is more or less lasting. And because in every republic there are rich men and men of the people, there has been doubt in the hands of which of these the said guardianship is better placed. And among the Lacedaemonians and, in our day, among the Venetians, it has been put in the hands of the nobles. But among the Romans, it was put in the hands of the people. Therefore it is necessary to consider which of these republics made the better choice. And if one should follow out the reasons, there is something to be said on either side; but if one should examine their outcome, one would take the side of the nobles, because the liberty of Sparta and of Venice had a longer life than that of Rome. And coming to the reasons, I say, taking first the side of the Romans, that those should be put on guard over a thing who are least greedy to take possession of it. And without doubt, if one will look at the purpose of the nobles and of those who are not noble, there will be seen in the former great longing to rule, and in the latter merely longing not to be ruled, and as a consequence greater eagerness to live in freedom, since they can have less hope of taking possession of it than the great can. Hence, if the common people are set up to guard liberty, it is reasonable that they will care for it better, and since they cannot seize it themselves, they will not allow others to seize it.

[*The nobles in Sparta and Venice*]

On the other hand, he who defends the Spartan and Venetian arrangement says that those who put the guardianship in the hands of the powerful do two good things: one is that they satisfy their ambition better, for, having a better share in the republic—since they have this club in their hands'—they have reason to be satisfied better; the other is that they take away from the restless spirits among the people a sort of authority that is the cause of numberless quarrels and troubles in a republic and likely to bring the nobility to a state of desperation that in time will bring forth evil effects. And they give as an example of this Rome herself, in which, because the Tribunes of the People had this authority in their hands, it was not enough for them to have one Consul who was plebeian, but they wanted both of them. After that, they wanted the censorship, the praetorship, and all the other offices in the city government. Nor was this enough for them, because, moved by the same madness, they were in time ready to idolize men whom they saw qualified to beat down the nobility. From this sprang the power of Marius and the ruin of Rome. And truly he who considers well one thing and the other may be in doubt which he would chose for the guardian-ship of such liberty, not knowing which human tendency is more injurious to a republic, whether that which hopes to keep the position it has already gained or that which hopes to gain what it does not have. And in the end he who will keenly examine the whole will come to this conclusion about it: either you are talking of a republic that wishes to set up an empire, like Rome, or of one to which it is enough to maintain itself. In the first case it is necessary to do everything as Rome did; in the second, Venice and Sparta can be imitated, for the reasons and in the way the following chapter will tell.

[*Hope of gain and fear of loss*]

But to turn to discussing what sort of men do more harm in a republic, those who hope to gain or those who fear to lose what they

1. *Their club is governmental power.*

have gained, I say that when Marcus Menenius had been made Dictator and Marcus Fulvius Master of the Horse, both of them plebeians,[2] in order that they might look into certain conspiracies that were made in Capua against Rome, the people gave them authority also to seek out anybody in Rome who through ambition and by irregular methods was exerting himself to obtain the con, sulate and the other city offices. And since the nobility believed that such authority was given to the Dictator against them, they spread through Rome the idea that the nobles were not the ones who were seeking offices through ambition and by unlawful methods, but that men of low rank, not trusting in their blood and in their ability, were those who were seeking by unlawful methods to come to these positions; and especially they accused the Dictator. And so powerful was this accusation that Menenius, calling an assembly and complaining of the calumnies put on him by the nobles, laid down the dictatorship and submitted himself to any decision the people might make about him; and then, after his case had been considered, he was cleared. It was much disputed there who is more ambitious, he who wishes to keep or he who wishes to gain, because easily either passion can be the cause of very great disturbances.

[The rich fear loss]

At any rate most of the time they are caused by those who already possess, because the fear of loss produces in them the same desires as exist in those who wish to gain, because it is generally held that a man is not in secure possession of what he has if he does not gain something new in addition. And, besides, there is this, that since they have great possessions, they can use greater power and greater force in causing revolutions. And there is still this besides, that their unrestrained and ambitious conduct kindles, in the breasts of those who do not possess, the wish to possess, either in order to get revenge on the rich by plundering them or in order to be able themselves to enter upon those riches and those offices that they see badly used by others.

2. *Livy* 9. 26.

CHAPTER 6. WHETHER IT WAS POSSIBLE TO SET UP IN ROME A GOVERNMENT THAT COULD TAKE AWAY THE ENMITY BETWEEN THE PEOPLE AND THE SENATE

We have discussed above the results of the controversies between the people and the Senate. Now since these continued until the time of the Gracchi, when they caused the ruin of free government, one may wish that Rome could have produced the great results she did without there being such enmities within her. Therefore I have thought it useful to consider whether a government could have been organized in Rome able to dispose of those controversies. And if we are going to look into this, it is necessary to turn to those republics that without so many enmities and disturbances have been for a long time free, and to see of what sort their government was and whether it could have been introduced into Rome.

[The Venetian government]

As an example among the ancients there is Sparta, among the moderns Venice—states I have named above. Sparta set up a king, with a small senate, to govern her. Venice has not divided control according to names,[1] but under one appellation all those able to hold office are called gentlemen. This method was given to them by chance rather than by the prudence of those who gave them laws. For the reasons mentioned above, many inhabitants were brought together on those islands where the city now is; hence, when they had increased to such a number that, if they wished to live together, they needed to make themselves laws, they established a form of government. And as they often met in councils to deliberate about the city, when they saw that their numbers were sufficient for political organization, they closed the road to any share in their government against all those who might later come there to live. And in time, when the place had enough inhabitants outside the government to give reputation to those who governed, they called the latter gentle/men and the others the people. It was possible for this form to originate and to keep going without rebellions because, when it originated, whoever then lived in Venice was included in the

1. *There are no distinctions within the ruling class.*

government, so that nobody could complain. Those who afterward came there to live, finding the administration solid and limited, had neither reason nor opportunity for rebelling. Reason there was not, because from them nothing had been taken. Opportunity there was not, because those who ruled held them in check and did not employ them in things through which they could seize authority. Besides this, those who later came to live in Venice were not many, nor were they so numerous that there was a disproportion between those who ruled and those who were ruled, for the number of the gentlemen is equal to theirs or is superior. Hence, for these reasons, Venice could organize that government and keep it united.

[The government of Sparta]

Sparta, as I have said, was ruled by a king and a limited Senate. She maintained herself so long because—since there were few inhabitants in Sparta and the road had been blocked against those who might have come there to live and the laws of Lycurgus (through which they removed all reasons for disturbances) were received with respect—they were able to live united a long time. For Lycurgus with his laws made in Sparta more equality of property and less equality of rank, so that there was equal poverty there, and the common people were less ambitious because the offices of the city were open to but few citizens and were kept entirely away from the common people; nor did the nobles by treating the people badly ever make them wish to hold the offices. This was the effect of the Spartan kings, who, being set up in that princedom and placed in the midst of that nobility, had no better means to hold their office firm than to keep the people secure from every injury. As a result, the people had no fear and did not desire authority. And not having authority and not being afraid, the strife they might have had with the nobility and the reason for rebellions were taken away; and they could live united for a long time. But there were two chief causes for this union: one was that the inhabitants of Sparta were few, and for this reason they could be governed by a few; the other was that, since they did not receive foreigners into their state, they did not have occasion either to be corrupted or to increase so much that the government was too heavy a weight for the few who ruled her.

[*Expansion demands popular participation; a choice of evils*]

So considering all these things, we see that Rome's lawgivers needed to do one of two things if Rome was to remain quiet like the republics mentioned above: either not to make use of the populace in war, like the Venetians, or not to open the way to foreigners, like the Spartans. Yet they did both of these. This gave the people power and increase in numbers and countless reasons for rioting. But if the Roman state had become quieter, this difficulty would have followed, namely, that it would also have been weaker, be⁄ cause the way to come to the greatness it reached would have been cut off from it. Hence, if Rome had planned to take away the causes of riot, it would also have taken away the causes of growth. And in all human affairs he who examines them well will see this: that one difficulty cannot be removed without another's coming up. So then, if you try to make a people so numerous and so well⁄armed that it can produce a great empire, you make it such that you cannot manage it as you wish. If you keep it either small or unarmed, so that you can manage it, when you gain territory you cannot hold it, or your state becomes so weak that you are the prey of whoever assails you. Hence in all our thinking we must consider where the fewest inconveniences are and take that for the best decision, because what is entirely clear, entirely without uncertainty, is never found. Rome, then, like Sparta, might have established a prince for life, might have established a small senate. But she could not, like Sparta, prohibit any increase in the number of her citizens, if she were going to build a great empire. In her situation the king for life and the small numbers of the senate would in the matter of union have helped her little.

[*The small state*]

If anyone sets out, therefore, to organize a state from the be⁄ ginning, he needs to examine whether he wishes it to expand like Rome, in dominion and power, or whether it is to remain within narrow limits. In the first case, it is necessary to organize it like Rome and to give scope to disturbances and discords among the inhabitants, as well as one can, because without a large number of men, and well armed, a republic never can grow larger, or, if it does grow larger, never can maintain itself. In the second case, you can organize it like Sparta and like Venice. But because expansion is the poison of such republics, he who organizes them ought in all possible ways to prohibit their making conquests, because such conquests, based on a weak state, are its total ruin. So it happened to Sparta and to Venice. The first of these, having subjugated almost all Greece, revealed upon a very slight occasion her weak foundation, because, when other cities rebelled after the rebellion of Thebes led by Pelopidas, that state completely collapsed. Likewise, Venice, having taken possession of a large part of Italy, for the most part not with war but with money and with craft, when she had to make a test of her forces lost everything in one battle.[2] I am sure that the method for making a city that will last a long time is to organize her internally like Sparta or Venice, and to put her in a place naturally strong and so fortified that no one will believe he can quickly conquer her. Yet on the other hand she should not be so large as to give reason for fear to her neighbors. Thus she might enjoy her independence for a long time; for war is made on a city for two reasons: one, to become her master; the second, for fear she may conquer you. The method just mentioned almost entirely removes these two causes. Because this city is hard to attack, as I assume she is, being well prepared for defense, seldom or never will conditions be such that somebody will plan to conquer her. If she remains within her boundaries, and experience shows her without ambition, never will anyone through fear for himself make war on her. And such fear will be the less likely if her constitution or law forbids her to grow greater. Without doubt, I believe, if affairs could be kept balanced in this way, they would produce the true good government and the true calm of a city.

[Government adapted to change]

But since all human affairs are in motion and cannot remain fixed, they must needs rise up or sink down; to many things to which reason does not bring you, you are brought by necessity. Hence, if a republic is so organized that she is adapted to main‑ taining herself provided she does not grow, and necessity then forces her to grow, the process will remove her foundations and make her fall more speedily. Thus, on the other side, if Heaven is so kind to her that she does not have to make war, the effect might be that ease

2. *Cf.* PRINCE *12;* HISTORY OF FLORENCE *1. 29.*

would make her effeminate or divided; these two things together, or either one alone, would cause her ruin. Therefore, since I believe it impossible to balance these affairs or to keep exactly this middle way, it is essential in organizing cities to think of the most honorable courses, and to organize them in such a way that if necessity causes them to grow, they can keep what they have taken.

[*The Roman method the best*]

To return to the beginning of our discussion, then, I believe the Roman method must be followed, and not that of the other states, because to find a course half way between one and the other I believe not possible. Those enmities rising between the people and Senate must be borne, being taken as an evil necessary to the attainment of Roman greatness. Besides the other reasons I brought forward when I showed the authority of the Senate necessary as a guard for liberty, I easily observe the benefit a republic gains from the right to make charges. This among other rights was entrusted to the Tribunes, as I shall show in the following chapter.

CHAPTER 7. IN A REPUBLIC THE RIGHT TO BRING CHARGES IS ESSENTIAL TO KEEPING HER FREE

Those who are set up in a city to guard her liberty can receive no more useful or necessary authority than the power to bring before the people, or before some magistrate or council, charges against citizens who in any way sin against free government. This arrangement has two effects very valuable to a republic. The first is that the citizens, for fear of being accused, do not attempt things against the state; and if they do attempt them, they are put down instantly and without favor. The other effect is that it provides an outlet for the discharge of those partisan hatreds that develop in cities in various ways against various citizens. When these hatreds do not have an outlet for discharging themselves lawfully, they take unlawful ways that make the whole republic fall. Therefore nothing makes a republic so firm and solid as to give her such an organization that the laws provide a way for the discharge of the partisan hatreds that agitate her.

[*The people hated Coriolanus*]

This appears in many examples and especially in that of Coriolanus, brought up by Titus Livius,[1] who says that the Roman nobles
were irritated against the plebeians because they thought the people
had too much authority as a result of the creation of the Tribunes
who were to defend them and that there happened to be a great
scarcity of food in Rome, and the Senate had sent to Sicily for grain.
Coriolanus, an enemy to the popular party, advised that the time
had come when the Senate, keeping the people hungry by with-
holding the grain, could punish the people and take from them the
authority they had grasped to the injury of the nobility. When this
opinion reached the ears of the people, they became so resentful
against Coriolanus that, when he left the Senate, the mob would
have killed him if the Tribunes had not cited him to appear to
defend his case.

[*Private revenge ruins states*]

This happening illustrates what I said above, namely that it is
useful and necessary for republics with their laws to provide an outlet
by which the masses can discharge the anger they have formed
against a single citizen. Because when there are no lawful methods,
unlawful ones are resorted to; and without doubt the latter produce
much worse effects than do the former. Because if a citizen is oppressed by lawful means, even though injury is done to him, little or
no disorder in the republic comes of it, because the action is carried
on without private forces and without foreign forces, which are the
ones that ruin free government. But if they are done with public
forces and means, which have their definite limits, they do not go on
to something that may destroy the republic. And as to corroborating
this opinion with examples, I think this of Coriolanus is enough
from the ancients. Each one may observe from it how much ill for
the Roman republic would have resulted if he had been killed by a
mob, because thereby injury would have been done by individuals
to individuals. Such injury produces fear; fear seeks for defense; for
defense partisans are obtained; from partisans rise parties in states;
from parties their ruin. But since the affair was managed by one

1. Livy 2. 34-35.

who had authority over it, all those ills were avoided that might have arisen if it had been managed with private power.

[*Florentine instances: Francesco Valori*]

We have seen in our times how much rebellion there has been in the republic of Florence because the multitude could not give vent to its rage against one of the citizens in a lawful way. There was such an event in the time when Francesco Valori was as it were prince of the city. By many he was thought ambitious and a man who with his rashness and his courage would try to rise above lawful govern- ment, and there was not in the republic any way by which he could be resisted, except by a party opposed to his. The result, since he had fear only of measures that were unlawful, was that he gathered partisans who would defend him. On the other side, since those who opposed him had no lawful way in which to repress him, they turned their attention to ways that were unlawful; thus they resorted to arms. And if he could have been opposed lawfully, his authority would have been destroyed with damage to him alone, but when he had to be destroyed unlawfully, the result was damage not merely to him but to many other noble citizens.

[*Piero Soderini*]

In support of the conclusion stated above, I further allege what happened also in Florence in the case of Piero Soderini—all of which went on because in that republic there was no method for bringing charges against the ambition of powerful citizens. In any republic to bring a charge against a powerful man before eight judges is not enough. It is essential that the judges be many, because a few always act in the normal method of a few. At any rate, if such methods had existed in Florence, either the citizens would have brought charges against him, if he was acting wickedly, and by such means would have vented their rage without bringing in the Spanish army, or if he was not acting wickedly, they would not have dared to work against him for fear of being accused themselves. So in either case the impulse[2] that caused the dissension would have disappeared.

2. *The impulse to express wrath against an ambitious citizen.*

[*The danger of foreign arms in domestic quarrels*]

At least this conclusion can be drawn: Whenever outside forces are summoned by one party of men that live in a city, her bad constitution is evidently the cause, since inside her wall she has no method by which, without unlawful measures, the malignant humors that spring up in men can find vent. This is fully provided against by arranging there for the bringing of charges before a large number of judges, and by giving those judges high standing. These methods were so well arranged in Rome that, in the many quarrels between the people and the Senate, neither the Senate nor the people nor any individual citizen planned to avail himself of foreign arms because, having a remedy at home, they were not obliged to go outside for one.

[*A Roman instance*]

And though the examples given above are enough to prove it, nonetheless, I wish to add another, related by Titus Livius in his *History*.[3] He tells how in Chiusi, a city in those times very important in Tuscany, a sister of Aruns was violated by a certain Lucumo, and when Aruns could not avenge himself because of the power of the violator, he went to the French, who then were ruling in the region that today is called Lombardy, and he encouraged them to come in arms to Chiusi, showing them that with benefit to themselves they could avenge for him the injury he had received. But if Aruns had seen that he could avenge himself according to the institutions of the city, he would not have sought the forces of the barbarians. But as such bringing of charges is valuable in a republic, so slanders are without value and harmful, as we shall show in the discussion in the following chapter.

3. *Livy 5. 33.*

CHAPTER 8. SLANDERS ARE AS DAMAG-
ING TO A REPUBLIC AS THE BRING-
ING OF CHARGES IS VALUABLE

[*Manlius slanders Camillus*]

Notwithstanding that the valor of Furius Camillus, when he had freed Rome from the oppression of the French, made all the Roman citizens defer to him without thinking that reputation or rank was taken from them—in spite of this, Manlius Capitolinus could not endure having so much honor and so much glory attributed to him, since it was his own belief that, as to the safety of Rome, he himself had by saving the Capitol deserved as much as Camillus, and that in other soldierly merits he was not inferior to him. Hence, overcome with envy, unable to remain quiet because of the other's fame and without possibility of sowing discord among the Fathers, he turned to the people and sowed various dangerous ideas among them. And among other things he said that the treasure gathered to give to the French, and then not given to them, had been taken for themselves by individual citizens, and if it could be recovered, it could be turned to the public benefit, relieving the people of taxes or of private debts. These words were very powerful with the people, causing them to hold gatherings and freely to make many disturbances in the city. Since this matter displeased the Senate and seemed to them serious and dangerous, they appointed a Dictator to look into the business and check Manlius' fury. As a result the Dictator had him at once cited, and the two appeared in public confronting one another—the Dictator in the midst of the nobles and Manlius in the midst of the plebeians. Manlius was asked whom he could mention who had this treasure that he talked of, because the Senate was as eager to know of it as were the people. To this Manlius did not answer specifically, but kept evading them and saying that it was not necessary to tell them what they knew. As a result the Dictator had him put in prison.[1]

[Slanders must be dealt with by law]

It can be learned from this passage how detestable slanders are in free cities and in every other kind of community, and how, to repress them, no plan that fits the conditions should be neglected. Nor can there be a better plan for getting rid of them than to give enough openings for bringing charges, because however much lawful charges help republics, so much do slanders hurt them. And from the one side to the other, there is this difference, that slanders have no need of a witness or of any other particular information to prove them, so that anybody can be slandered by anyone; but not everybody can be subjected to legal charges, since such charges need true information

1. Livy 6. 11, 15-16.

and circumstances that show the truth of the accusation. Men are charged with offenses before the magistrates, the people, the councils; they are slandered in the public squares and the arcades. This method of slander is used most where that of lawful charges is used least and where cities are least organized to deal with them. Hence the organizer of a republic ought to arrange that charges can be brought against any citizen in it, without any fear or without any hesitation. And when a charge has been made and well investigated, slanderers should be severely punished. They cannot complain when they are punished, since places are open for hearing complaints against those whom they slander in the public arcades. And where this matter is not well arranged, there always follow great disorders, because slanders irritate but do not punish the citizens. And those who are irritated think of avenging themselves, rather hating than fearing the things that are said against them.

[How slanders injured Florence]

This matter, as has been said, was well arranged in Rome, and has always been badly arranged in our city of Florence. And as in Rome this provision did much good, in Florence this lack of provision did much harm. And he who reads the history of this city will see how many slanders have at all times been uttered against citizens who have been employed in its important affairs. Of one it has been said that he stole public money; of another that he did not succeed in an undertaking because he was bribed; and that this other because of his ambition committed this or that improper action. From whence it came that on every side hate sprang up; hate went on to divisions; from divisions to parties; from parties to ruin. But if there had been in Florence an arrangement for bringing charges against citizens and punishing slanderers, countless troubles would not have followed that did follow. For those citizens, whether they had been condemned or acquitted, could not have harmed the city and would have been legally accused much less often than they have been slandered, since, as I have said, it is not so easy to accuse formally as to slander someone.

And chief among the things that a citizen is likely to employ in becoming great, are these slanders. When directed against powerful citizens who oppose themselves to his thirst for power, they are much to his advantage, because, by taking the side of the popular party and confirming its low opinion of its opponents, he makes it friendly to himself.

[*Giovanni Guicciardini slandered in Florence*]

And though I might bring forward many examples, I intend to be content with only one. The Florentine army was besieging Lucca, commanded by Messer Giovanni Guicciardini, its commissioner. As a result either of his bad arrangements or of his bad fortune, the city was not captured. At any rate, however the thing was, Messer Giovanni was blamed, since it was said that he had been bribed by the Lucchese. This slander, being encouraged by his enemies, brought Messer Giovanni almost to complete despair. And though to clear himself he wished to be put in the hands of the Captain, nevertheless he was never able to clear himself because there were no methods in that republic by which he could do it. The affair caused great indignation among Messer Giovanni's friends, who formed the majority of the rich and were among the number hoping to cause revolution in Florence. For this and similar reasons, the trouble grew so great that it caused the ruin of that republic.

Manlius Capitolinus, then, was a slanderer and not a lawful accuser. In this very case the Romans showed how slanderers should be punished. They must be obliged to make charges according to law. If a charge turns out true, they must be rewarded, or at least not punished; when it turns out untrue, they must be punished as Manlius was punished.

CHAPTER 9. A MAN MUST BE ALONE IF HE IS TO ORGANIZE A REPUBLIC AFRESH OR REMODEL HER WITH COMPLETE ANNULMENT OF HER OLD LAWS

[*The murder committed by Romulus*]

Perhaps some will think I have run too far along in Roman history without making any mention of the founders of that republic or of the ordinances that concern religion or military affairs. Therefore, since I do not wish to hold in suspense the minds of those who want to know something about these matters, I say that many will perhaps think it a bad example that the founder of a state, such as

Romulus, should first have killed his brother, and then have been a
party to the death of Titus Tatius the Sabine,¹ who was his partner
in authority. From this they infer that the citizens, in ambition and
wish to rule, might follow their prince's example in attacking those
who opposed their authority. This opinion would be true if the
purpose causing him to commit such a murder were not regarded.

[A state can be founded by one man only]

This we must take as a general rule: seldom or never is any
republic or kingdom organized well from the beginning, or totally
made over, without respect for its old laws, except when organized
by one man. Still more, it is necessary that one man alone give the
method and that from his mind proceed all such organization.
Therefore a prudent organizer of a republic and one whose intention
is to advance not his own interests but the general good, not his own
posterity but the common fatherland, ought to strive to have authority
all to himself. Nor will a prudent intellect ever censure anyone for
any unlawful action used in organizing a kingdom or setting up a
republic. It is at any rate fitting that though the deed accuses him,
the result should excuse him; and when it is good, like that of
Romulus, it will always excuse him, because he who is violent to
destroy, not he who is violent to restore, ought to be censured.

[The wise founder prepares for the future]

He ought, moreover, to be so prudent and high-minded that he
will not leave to another as a heritage the authority he has seized,
because, since men are more prone to evil than to good, his successor
might use ambitiously what he had used nobly. Besides this, though
one alone is suited for organizing, the government organized is not
going to last long if resting on the shoulders of only one; but it is
indeed lasting when it is left to the care of many, and when its
maintenance rests upon many. The reason is that just as a large
number are not suited to organize a government, because they do not
understand what is good for it on account of their diverse opinions,
so after they become familiar with it they do not agree to abandon it.
And that Romulus was among those, that he deserved excuse for
the death of his brother and his companion, and that what he did
was done for the common good and not for his own ambition, is

1. Livy 1. 7, 14.

shown by his immediate organization of a Senate, with which he could consult and according to the opinion of which he would decide. And he who will consider well the authority that Romulus reserved for himself will see that nothing was reserved except the command of the armies, when war was decided on, and the power to assemble the Senate. This appeared later, when Rome became free through the expulsion of the Tarquins, when the Romans changed no arrangement from the past except that, in place of a king for life, there were two annual consuls. This testifies that all the first arrangements for that city were more in conformity with a con- stitution free and according to law than with one that was absolute and tyrannical.

[*Wise founders: Moses, Solon, Lycurgus, Cleomenes*]

In support of what I have written above, I could give countless examples, such as Moses, Lycurgus, Solon, and other founders of kingdoms and republics, who, because they appropriated to them- selves sole power, could form laws adapted to the common good. But I wish to pass them by, as things that are known. I shall bring forward only one, not so celebrated, but worth considering by those who wish to be framers of good laws. This is that when Agis king of Sparta wished to bring the Spartans back within the boundaries that the laws of Lycurgus had marked off (since it appeared to him that because they had deviated from them, his city had lost much of her former energy, and consequently of her power and her authority), almost at his beginning he was killed by the Spartan Ephors, as a man who wished to seize the tyranny. But when Cleomenes came after him in the kingdom, and there grew up in him the same wish (as a result of the memorials and writings of Agis that he found, where it appeared of what sort his mind and intention were), he knew that he could not do this good to his fatherland if he did not become the only one in authority, since he saw that on account of the ambition of men he could not do good to the many against the will of the few. And he took a convenient chance and killed all the Ephors and everyone else who could oppose him; then he wholly restored the laws of Lycurgus. This decision might have been enough to make Sparta rise up again and to give Cleomenes such a reputation as Lycurgus had, if it had not been for the power of the Macedonians and the weakness of the other Greek states. But when after such organizing he was attacked by the Macedonians, being inferior in strength when alone and not having anybody from whom he could get help, he was conquered. So his plan, though suitable and praiseworthy, was not carried out.

Considering all these things, then, I conclude that to found a state it is necessary to be alone; and Romulus deserves excuse and not blame for the death of Remus and of Titus Tatius.

CHAPTER 10. THE FOUNDERS OF A TYRANNY ARE AS DESERVING OF CENSURE AS THOSE OF A REPUBLIC OR A KINGDOM ARE DESERVING OF FAME

[The tyrant is deceived by false glory]

Among all famous men those are most famous who have been heads and organizers of religions. Next after them are those who have founded either republics or kingdoms. After these, they are famous who, when set over armies, have enlarged their own dominion or that of their native land. Next to these are put men of letters. And because these are of many kinds, they are famed, each one of them, according to his rank. To various other men, the number of whom is countless, is given some measure of praise brought by their profession or their occupation. On the contrary, those men are infamous and detestable who have been destroyers of religions, squanderers of kingdoms and republics, enemies of virtue, of letters, and of every other art that brings gain and honor to the human race, such as the impious, the violent, the ignorant, the noaccount, the lazy, the cowardly. And no one will ever be so foolish or so wise, so bad or so good, that, if there is put before him the choice between the two kinds of men, he will not praise what is to be praised and blame what is to be blamed. Yet in the end, almost all, deceived by a false good and a false glory, allow themselves to go, either willingly or ignorantly, into the positions of those who deserve more blame than praise. And though able, to their perpetual honor, to set up a republic or a kingdom, they turn to a tyranny. Nor do they realize how much fame, how much glory, how much honor, security, quiet, along with satisfaction of mind, they abandon by this decision, and into what great infamy, censure, blame, peril, and disquiet they run.

[*History condemns the tyrant*]

And it is impossible that those who live in private stations in a republic or who through fortune or through ability become princes of it, if they read histories and get profit from the records of ancient things, should not wish as private citizens to live in their fatherland as Scipios rather than as Caesars, and those who are princes as Agesilauses, Timoleons, Dions, rather than as Nabises, Phalarises, and Dionysiuses, because they will see that the latter are censured to the utmost and the former exceedingly praised. They will see also that Timoleon and the others did not have in their native cities less authority than did Dionysius and Phalaris, and will see that by far they had more security.

[*Historians did not speak sincerely of Caesar*]

Nor should anyone be deceived by the glory of Caesar, on seeing him especially celebrated by the historians, for those who praise him are bribed by his fortune and awed by the long duration of the Empire, which, being ruled under his name, did not allow writers to speak freely of him. But a reader wishing to know what free historians would say of Caesar may see what they say of Catiline, for Caesar is so much the more blameworthy in proportion as one is more to blame who has done evil than one who has intended to do it. Let a reader observe too with what great praises they laud Brutus, as though, unable to blame Caesar because of his power, they laud his enemy.[1]

[*The good ruler is defended by the love of the people*]

Let any man who has become prince in a republic consider also how much more praise those emperors deserved, after Rome had become an empire, who lived according to the laws and as good princes than did those who lived in the opposite way. And he will see how Titus, Nerva, Trajan, Adrian, Antoninus, and Marcus did not need the praetorian soldiers nor the multitude of the legions to defend them, because their qualities, the good will of the people, the

---

1. Cf. *Machiavelli's own method in writing about the Medici* (HISTORY OF FLORENCE, *introductory note*).

love of the Senate defended them. The prince will see also that for
Caligula, Nero, Vitellius, and many other wicked emperors, the
eastern and the western armies were not enough to protect them from
those enemies which their evil habits, their vile lives had produced
for them. And if the history of these emperors is well pondered, it is
a sufficient body of instruction for any prince, to show him the way to
glory or to censure and to security or to fear. Because, of twenty-six
emperors between Caesar and Maximinus, sixteen were killed, ten
died normal deaths. And if any one of those who were killed was
good, as were Galba and Pertinax, he was killed by the corruption
his predecessor had left among the soldiers. And if among those
who died normally there was a wicked ruler, like Severus, it can be
explained by his very great good fortune and ability—two things
that few men have as companions. A prince will see also, through
the reading of this history, how he can organize a good kingdom.
For all the emperors who succeeded to the empire through heredity,
except Titus, were bad; those through adoption were all good, as
were those five from Nerva to Marcus; and when the empire was left
to heirs, it went back to confusion.

[*The world under good and under bad government*]

Let a prince put before himself, then, the times from Nerva to
Marcus and compare them with those that went before and those
that came later, and then choose in which he would like to be born
or over which he would like to be put in charge. In those governed
by good emperors, he will see a prince secure in the midst of his
secure citizens, the world full of peace and justice; he will see the
Senate with its authority, the magistrates with their honors, the rich
citizens enjoying their riches, nobility and virtue exalted; he will see
the utmost tranquillity and the utmost good, and on the other side all
hatred, all license, corruption, and ambition wiped out; he will see
golden days, in which every man can hold and defend what opinion
he wishes. He will see, in short, the world rejoicing, the prince
satisfied with respect and glory, the people with love and security.
If then he considers with care the times of the other emperors, he will
see them savage through wars, at variance through seditions, cruel
in peace and in war, many princes slain with steel, many civil wars,
many foreign ones, Italy afflicted and full of hitherto unknown misfortunes, the cities of that land destroyed and sacked. He will see

Rome burned, the Capitol laid waste by her own citizens, the ancient temples desolate, their ceremonies corrupted, the city full of adulteries; he will see the waters covered with exiles, the islands full of blood. He will see enacted in Rome countless cruelties, while nobility, riches, past honors, and above all virtue, are counted capital sins. He will see false accusers rewarded, servants bribed against their masters, freedmen against their former owners, and those who have no enemies oppressed by their friends. Then he will understand very well what great obligations Rome, Italy, and the world owe to Caesar.

[*The ruler's true glory*]

Without doubt, if a prince is of human birth, he will be frightened away from any imitation of wicked times and will be fired with an immense eagerness to follow the ways of good ones. Truly if a prince is seeking glory in the world, he should wish to possess a corrupt city, not to ruin it wholly like Caesar but to reform it like Romulus. Truly the heavens cannot give a greater opportunity for glory, nor can men desire a greater. If indeed for the sake of organizing a city well, the princedom had to be laid down, a man who refused to organize her, to avoid falling from that position, would deserve some excuse; but if he could keep his princedom and organize her, he would deserve no excuse. In short, then, those to whom the Heavens give such an occasion should observe that two roads are put before them: one makes their lives secure and after death renders them famous; the other makes them live in continual anxieties and after death leave an ill repute that never ends.

CHAPTER 11. ROMAN RELIGION

[*Respect for religion*]

Though Rome had Romulus as her first lawgiver, and as a daughter must acknowledge that she owed him her birth and her education, nevertheless, since the Heavens judged that the laws of Romulus would not be sufficient for so great an empire, they inspired the Roman Senate to choose Numa Pompilius as Romulus' successor, so that Numa might establish the things he had omitted. The latter, finding a very savage people and wishing to bring it to obey

the laws by means of the arts of peace, turned to religion as something
altogether necessary if he wished to maintain a well-ordered state.
And he established it in such a way that for many ages there was
never so much fear of God as in that republic; this facilitated whatever undertaking the Senate or those great men of Rome planned to
carry on. And he who will go over countless actions both of the
people of Rome altogether and of many of the Romans for themselves, will see that these citizens feared much more to break an oath
than to break the laws, since they respected the power of God more
than that of men.

[Instances of Roman respect for religion]

This is made clear by the examples of Scipio and of Manlius
Torquatus.[1] After Hannibal defeated the Romans at Cannae, many
citizens met together who, despairing of their native land, agreed to
abandon Italy and go to Sicily. Scipio, hearing of this, went to them
and, with his naked sword in his hand, forced them to swear not to
abandon their native land. Lucius Manlius, father of Titus Manlius, who was later called Torquatus, was accused of crime by
Marcus Pomponius, Tribune of the People; but before the day of the
trial came, Titus went to Marcus and, threatening to kill him if he
did not swear to withdraw the accusation against his father, forced
him to the oath; so he, having sworn through fear, withdrew the
accusation. Thus those citizens whom love of their country and its
laws did not keep in Italy were kept by an oath that they were forced
to take. And that Tribune laid aside his hate for the father, the
injury that the son had done him, and his own honor, to obey the
oath he had taken. This came from nothing else than the religion
Numa had brought into that city.

[Numa's use of religion in government]

Thus he who examines Roman history well sees how helpful
religion was in controlling the armies, in inspiring the people, in
keeping men good, in making the wicked ashamed. Hence if there
should be a debate on the prince to whom Rome was most under
obligation, whether Romulus or Numa, I believe that Numa would
sooner get the first place. Because where there is religion, it is easy to
bring in arms; but where there are arms and not religion, only with

1. Livy 22. 53; 7. 4-5.

difficulty can the latter be brought in. We see that Romulus, in establishing the Senate and making other civil and military pro-visions, had no need for the authority of God. Yet it was necessary to Numa, who pretended he was intimate with a nymph who advised him about what he was going to advise the people.[2] He did so because he planned to introduce new and unwonted laws into the city, but feared that his own authority would not be enough.

[*The reformer has recourse to God*]

And truly no one who did not have recourse to God ever gave to a people unusual laws, because without that they would not be accepted. Because many good things are known to a prudent man that are not in themselves so plainly rational that others can be persuaded of them. Therefore wise men, who wish to remove this difficulty, have recourse to God. So Lycurgus did, so Solon, so many others who have had the same purpose as they did. Aston-ished, then, at Numa's goodness and prudence, the Roman people yielded to his every decision. To be sure, it is true that since those times were very religious and those men with whom he had to labor were untaught, he found it very easy to carry out his designs, since he was able easily to stamp on them any new form whatever. And without doubt anyone who at present wishes to build a state will find it easier among mountaineers, where there is no culture, than among those who are used to living in cities, where culture is corrupt. And a sculptor will more easily get a beautiful statue out of a rough piece of marble than from one badly blocked out by someone else.

[*Either a strong prince or religion; a wise prince provides against weak successors*]

Having considered everything, then, I conclude that the religion introduced by Numa was among the chief reasons for the prosperity of that city. Because religion caused good laws; good laws make good fortune; and from good fortune came the happy results of the city's endeavors. And as the observance of religious teaching brings about the greatness of states, so contempt for it brings about their ruin. Because, where fear of God is lacking, it is necessary either that a kingdom fall or that it be sustained by fear of a prince which atones for what is missing in religion. And because princes are

2. *Livy* 1. 19.

short-lived, it is probable that a kingdom will quickly fail just as the strength and wisdom of the prince fails. Hence it comes about that kingdoms depending on the vigor of one man alone are not very lasting because that vigor departs with the life of the man, and seldom is it restored in the course of heredity, as Dante prudently says:

> Seldom does human probity move out along the branches;
> and this is the will of Him who gives it, that it may get its
> name from Him.[3]

It is not, then, the salvation of a republic or a kingdom to have a prince who will rule prudently while he lives, but to have one who will so organize it that even after he dies it can be maintained. And though rude men are more easily won over to a new order or opinion, it is still not for that reason impossible to win over to it also cultured men and those who assume they are not rude. The people of Florence do not suppose themselves either ignorant or rude; neverthe-less they were persuaded by Brother Girolamo Savonarola that he spoke with God. I do not intend to decide whether it was true or not, because so great a man ought to be spoken of with reverence, but I do say that countless numbers believed him without having seen anything extraordinary to make them believe him, because his life, his teaching, the affairs he dealt with were enough to make them lend him faith. No one therefore should fear that he cannot carry out what has been carried out by others, because, as I said in the preface, men are born, live and die, always, with one and the same nature.

3. PURGATORIO 7. 121–3: not exact.

CHAPTER 12. HOW IMPORTANT IT IS TO TAKE ACCOUNT OF RELIGION, AND HOW ITALY, HAVING BEEN WITHOUT IT BECAUSE OF THE ROMAN CHURCH, IS RUINED

[The pagan oracles]

Those princes or those republics that wish to keep themselves uncorrupted must above everything else keep the ceremonies of their religion uncorrupted and hold them always in respect, because one can have no better indication of the ruin of a country than to see divine worship little valued. This is easy to understand if it is known on what the religion of a man's birthplace is founded, because the life of every religion has its foundation in some chief usage of its own. The life of the heathen religion was founded on the responses of the oracles and on the cult of diviners and augurs. All their other ceremonies, sacrifices and rites depended on these, because they easily believed that any god who was able to foretell your future good and your future ill was also able to grant it to you. From these came the temples, from these the sacrifices, from these the supplications and every other ceremony in showing them respect; through these came the oracle of Delphi, the temple of Jupiter Ammon, and other famous oracles, which filled the world with admiration and devo- tion. Then when these turned to speaking so as to please the powerful, and their falsehood was discovered by the people, men became unbelieving and ready to upset any good custom whatever. It is the duty, then, of the rulers of a republic or of a kingdom to preserve the foundations of the religion they hold. If they do this, it will be an easy thing for them to keep their state religious, and consequently good and united. Also whatever comes up in favor of religion, even though they think it false, they are to accept and magnify. And so much the more they are going to do it as they are more prudent and as they have better understanding of natural things.

[*Pagan miracles*]

And because this method has been followed by wise men, there has risen from it the belief in miracles, which are celebrated even in false religions. Because whatever the beginning in which they originate, they are magnified by the prudent, whose authority then gains them credit with everybody. Of these miracles there were at Rome a great many. Among them was this: As the Roman soldiers were sacking the city of the Veientians, some of them went into the temple of Juno, and when they approached her statue and said, "Do you wish to come to Rome?" (Livy 5. 22), one thought he saw her nod and another that she said "Yes." Because, since these men were full of religion (which Livy makes plain because, on entering the temple, they entered it without disorder, all devout and full of reverence), they believed they heard the reply to their question which perhaps they expected. Camillus and the other chief men of the city in every way favored and magnified this opinion and belief.

[*Christianity has degenerated*]

If religion of this sort had been kept up among the princes of Christendom, in the form in which its giver founded it, Christian states and republics would be more united, much more happy than they are. Nor can a better estimate of its decline be made than by seeing that those peoples who are nearest to the Roman Church, the head of our religion, have least religion. And he who considers its foundations and sees how different its present habit is from them, will conclude that near at hand, beyond doubt, is its fall or its punishment.

[*The Church has harmed Italy*]

And because many are of the opinion that the well-being of the cities of Italy comes from the Roman Church, I am going, in opposition to this, to discuss some reasons that occur to me. And I shall bring forward two very strong ones that, as I think, are not to be refuted. The first is that through the bad examples of that court this land has lost all piety and all religion. This brings about countless evils and countless disorders, because, just as we assume everything good where we find religion, so when it is lacking we assume the contrary.

[*The Church keeps Italy divided*]

We Italians, then, have as our first debt to the Church and to the priests that we have become without religion and wicked. But we have one still greater, which is the second reason for our ruin: this is that the Church has kept and still keeps this region divided. And truly no region is ever united or happy if all of it is not under the sway of one republic or one prince, as happened to France and to Spain. The reason why Italy is not in that same condition and why she too does not have one republic or one prince to govern her is the Church alone; because, though she has dwelt there and possessed temporal power, she has not been so strong or of such ability that she could grasp sole authority in Italy and make herself ruler of the country. Yet on the other hand she has not been so weak that, when she feared to lose dominion over her temporal possessions, she could not summon a powerful man to defend her against anyone who in Italy had become too powerful. In ancient times there were many instances of this, as when by means of Charlemagne she drove out the Lombards, who were then almost masters of all Italy, and when in our times she took away the power of the Venetians with the help of France; then she drove out the French with the aid of the Swiss.

[*The Church brought the barbarians into Italy*]

Since, then, the Church has not been powerful enough to take possession of Italy and has not permitted any other to possess it, she is the cause why the land has been unable to unite under one head. But Italy has been under many princes and lords, who have brought about the great disunion and the great weakness that have made her the prey not merely of powerful barbarians but of whoever assails her. For this we Italians are indebted to the Church and not to any other. And he who would like by sure test to see the truth more plainly would need to be of such power that he could send the Roman court, with all the influence it has in Italy, to live in the cities of the Swiss, who are today the only people who, in respect to both religion and military usages, live as did the ancients. And he would see that in a short time the evil habits of that court would do more to break down law and order in that region than any other event which at any time could occur there.

CHAPTER 13. HOW THE ROMANS MADE USE OF RELIGION IN REORGANIZING THEIR CITY AND CARRYING ON THEIR ENTERPRISES AND STOPPING RIOTS

[*Religion used in managing the plebeians*]

I think it not beside the point to bring forward some instances in which the Romans made use of religion in reorganizing their city and carrying on their enterprises. And though there are many of them in Titus Livius, still I intend to be satisfied with the following.[1] After the Roman people had chosen Tribunes of consular power who, with one exception, were all plebeians, that same year there was pestilence and famine, and certain marvelous signs appeared. In the next choice of Tribunes, the nobility used the opportunity afforded by these portents, saying that the gods were angered because Rome had used badly the majesty of her power, and that

1. *Livy* 5. 13–16; 3. 10, 15.

there was no other device for placating the gods than to put the selection of Tribunes back where it had been before. The result was that the people, terrified by this resort to religion, chose only nobles as Tribunes.

[A complacent oracle]

It can also be seen in the conquest of the city of the Veientians how the generals of the armies employed religion to keep the people intent on an undertaking. For when that year Lake Albanus rose greatly, and the Roman soldiers were tired by the long siege and wished to return to Rome, the Romans found that Apollo and certain other responses[2] said that the city of the Veientians would be taken in the year when Lake Albanus overflowed its banks. This thing made the soldiers bear the hardships of the siege, caught by this hope of taking the city, and they were willing to continue with the enterprise until Camillus, being made Dictator, captured that city after it had been besieged for ten years. And so religion, well used, aided both in the taking of that city and in the restoration of the tribunate to the nobility, though without the said means, it would have been difficult to carry out either of them.

[The Senate uses religion against the Tribunes]

I do not wish to neglect another example on this subject. Many disturbances had arisen in Rome because of Terentillus the Tribune, who wished to propose certain laws, for reasons that will be given below in their place. And one of the first defenses used against him by the nobility was religion, which served them in two ways. As the first, they had the Sibylline Books looked at and the response given that because of civil sedition, the city was that year in danger of losing her liberty. Though exposed by the Tribunes, this prediction still put so much fear into the breasts of the plebeians that their ardor for following the Tribunes was cooled. The other way was this: Appius Erdonius, with a multitude of outlaws and slaves to the number of four thousand men, had occupied the Capitol by night; hence it was easy to fear that the Aequi and the Volsci, perpetual enemies to the Roman state, would come to Rome and capture her. Yet the Tribunes did not for that reason give up their persistence in proposing the Terentillian law, saying that the menace of invasion

2. *The oracle of Apollo and other oracles in their responses.*

was pretended and not real. Whereupon Publius Ruberius, a grave citizen and a man of authority, came out of the Senate and with words partly friendly, partly threatening, showed the city's dangers and their unseasonable demand; thus he brought the people to swear not to depart from the wish of the Consul. So the people, obedient, by force recovered the Capitol. But since in that assault Publius Valerius, the Consul, was killed, at once they again chose as Consul Titus Quintius. He, in order not to let the people rest or to give them a chance to think about the Terentillian law, ordered them to go out from Rome against the Volsci, saying that because of the oath they had taken not to abandon the Consul, they were obliged to follow him. The Tribunes opposed this, saying that their oath had been given to the dead Consul and not to him. Nonetheless Titus Livius shows how the people, in their fear of religion, determined rather to obey the Consul than to believe the Tribunes, saying in favor of the ancient religion these words: "Not yet this neglect of the gods, that now possesses the age, had come to pass; nor that each man should make for himself laws suited to interpreting his oath" (3. 20). Because of this, the Tribunes, then fearing they would lose all their importance, agreed with the Consul to obey him, and that for a year there should be no discussion of the Terentillian law and the Consuls should not for a year take the people outside the city for war. And so religion enabled the Senate to overcome those difficul- ties that without it could never have been overcome.

CHAPTER 14. THE ROMANS INTERPRET- ED THE AUSPICES ACCORDING TO NECESSITY, AND PRUDENTLY MADE A SHOW OF OBSERVING RELIGION EVEN WHEN THEY WERE FORCED NOT TO OBSERVE IT; AND IF ANYONE RASHLY BELITTLED IT, THEY PUNISHED HIM

[Divination by Poultry]

Not merely were the auguries, as has been said above, in good part the foundation of the ancient religion of the pagans, but they also caused the well-being of the Roman republic. Hence the Ro- mans had more concern about them than about any other law in the republic, and they employed them at the elections of Consuls, in beginning enterprises, in leading out their armies, in undertaking battles, and in all their important actions, either civil or military; nor would they ever go on an expedition without convincing the soldiers that the gods promised them victory. And among the other auspices, they had in their armies certain orders of diviners whom they called *pullarii*; and whenever they decided to fight a battle with the enemy, they required the *pullarii* to take the auspices; then if the fowls ate, they fought with good augury; when they did not eat, they kept out of battle. Nonetheless, when reason showed them a thing that ought to be done, notwithstanding that the auspices were adverse, they did it just the same, but with expedients and schemes they turned it around so cleverly that they did not seem to do it with any disre-spect to religion.

[Deception about the oracular poultry]

Such an expedient was used by the Consul Papirius in a very important battle he fought against the Samnites, after which they were in every way very weak and miserable. Because when Papirius was encamped near the Samnites and believed that he was sure of victory in the combat and therefore wished to join battle, he com-manded the *pullarii* to take the auspices. But though the fowls did not eat, the chief of the *pullarii*, observing the strong disposition of the army for combat and the belief held by the general and all the soldiers that they would win, told the Consul that the auspices went well, in order not to take from that army an opportunity for a good action. But when Papirius was drawing up his forces, some of the *pullarii* told certain soldiers that the fowls had not eaten, and they told it to Spurius Papirius, the nephew of the Consul. Yet when he passed it on to the Consul, the latter at once told him that he should try to do his own duty well, because for himself and the army, the auspices were good, and if the *pullarius* had told lies, they would turn out to his disadvantage. And that the result might correspond to the prophecy, he ordered the legates to put the *pullarii* in the very front of the combat. Thence it came about that, as they went toward the enemy, a dart that was thrown by a Roman soldier by chance killed the chief of the *pullarii*. When he heard this, the Consul said every-thing was going well and with the favor of the gods, because by the death of that liar the army was purged of every fault and of all the wrath that they had conceived against it. And thus, by knowing well how to fit his plans to the auspices, he made his decision to engage in combat without the army's perceiving that in any respect he had neglected the rules of their religion.

[*Prudent contravention of the auspices*]

Appius Pulcer did the opposite in Sicily in the first Punic war, for, wishing to fight with the Carthaginian army, he had the *pullarii* take the auspices; and when they announced to him that the fowls did not eat, he said: "We will see if they want to drink," and had them thrown into the sea. Thereupon, joining battle, he lost the day; for this he was sentenced to punishment at Rome, but Papirius was honored, not so much because one had won and the other lost, as because one had acted against the auspices prudently and the other rashly. Nor was this custom of taking auspices directed to any other end than to make the soldiers go confidently to battle; from which confidence almost always issues victory. This was practiced not merely by the Romans but by foreigners; of this I think it well to give an instance in the following chapter.

CHAPTER 15. THE SAMNITES, AS A LAST REMEDY FOR THEIR DISTRESSES, TURNED TO RELIGION

After the Samnites had often been defeated by the Romans and had at last been ruined in Tuscany and their soldiers and their generals killed, and their allies—the Tuscans, the French, and the Umbrians—had been conquered, they could no longer stand "either by their own or by foreign strength; nevertheless they did not refrain from war, since they were not weary even of an unsuccessful defense of liberty, and preferred to be conquered rather than not to strive for victory" (Livy 10. 31). Hence they determined to make a last effort. So because they knew that if they expected to conquer they must put determination into the minds of their soldiers, and that there was no better means for putting it there than religion, they decided to repeat an ancient sacrifice of theirs, with the aid of Ovius Paccius their priest. They arranged it as follows.[1] When the proper sacrifice had been offered and, between the dead victims and the altar fires, all the

1. *Livy* 10. 38.

leaders of the army had sworn that they would never abandon the combat, they summoned the soldiers one by one; and among those altars, in the midst of many centurions with naked swords in their hands, they first had them swear not to repeat anything that they saw or heard. Then, with the words of a curse and verses full of terror, they had them vow to the gods to go quickly wherever the generals sent them, and never to flee from the combat, and to kill anybody they saw fleeing. If this were not observed, it was to come back on the heads of their families and of their tribes. And when some of them were terrified and unwilling to swear, at once their centurions killed them; hence those who came next, horrified by the savage spectacle, all took the oath. And to make their muster of forty thousand men more magnificent, they clad half of them in white garments, with crests and feathers above their helmets; so equipped they placed themselves near Aquilonia.

[*The appeal to religion fails*]

Against them came Papirius, who, to encourage his soldiers, said: "Crests do not cause wounds, and painted and gilded shields can be pierced by the Roman pilum" (Livy 10. 39). Moreover, to weaken the opinion his soldiers had of the enemy because of the oath they had taken, he said that it moved them to fear and not to forti-tude, because they were obliged to be at the same time in terror of citizens, gods and enemies. And having entered the conflict, the Samnites were defeated, because Roman valor and the fear derived from past defeats overcame whatever determination they had been able to form by virtue of their religion and through the oath they had taken. Nonetheless they evidently believed that they had no other resource and could try no other means for gaining some hope for the recovery of their lost valor. This testifies in full how much confidence can be acquired by means of religion well used.

[*The structure of the* DISCOURSES]

Though this section rather demands, perhaps, to be put in my discussion of foreign affairs,[2] yet since it relates to one of the most important institutions of the republic of Rome, I have decided to bring it all together in this place, in order not to divide the material and have to return to it several times.

2. *See* DISCOURSES *1. 16; 2. pref., end.*

CHAPTER 16. A PEOPLE ACCUSTOMED TO LIVING UNDER A PRINCE, IF BY SOME ACCIDENT IT BECOMES FREE, WITH DIFFICULTY KEEPS ITS FREEDOM

What great difficulty a people accustomed to living under a prince has later in preserving its liberty, if by any accident it gains it, as the Romans gained it after the expulsion of the Tarquins, is shown by countless examples in the records of ancient history. And such difficulty is reasonable, because that people is none other than a brute beast, which, though of a fierce and savage nature, has always been cared for in prison and in slavery. Then, if by chance it is left free in a field, since it is not used to feeding itself and does not know the places where it can take refuge, it becomes the prey of the first one who tries to rechain it.

This same thing happens to a people that, being accustomed to living under the orders of others, not knowing how to think about defense or offense by the state, not understanding monarchs and not being understood by them, returns quickly beneath a yoke that usually is heavier than the one that a little earlier it threw off its neck. And it finds itself in these difficulties even though its matter is not corrupted. Because a people into which corruption has fully entered cannot live free even for a short time, in fact not at all, as will be explained below. Hence we are dealing with those peoples where corruption has not spread much and where there is more of the good than of the spoiled.

[*A state newly freed has zealous enemies but not zealous friends*]

There is added to the aforesaid another difficulty, which is that the state that becomes free makes itself partisan enemies and not partisan friends. All those become its partisan enemies who profited from the tyrannical government by feeding on the riches of the prince; and when the possibility of profit is taken away, they cannot live contented but are forced, all of them, to try to get the tyranny back in order to get back into their offices. As I have said, it does not gain partisan friends, because the free community confers honors and rewards for certain honorable and established causes, and except for these does not reward or honor anybody. And when a man has those honors and those good things that he believes he deserves, he does not admit that he is obliged to those who recompense him. Besides this, the common benefit gained from a free community is recognized by nobody while he possesses it: namely, the power of enjoying freely his possessions without any anxiety, of feeling no fear for the honor of his women and his children, of not being afraid for himself, because no one will ever admit that he has any obligation to a government which does not harm him. Therefore, as I said above, the state that is free and that is newly established comes to have partisan enemies and not partisan friends.

[Killing the sons of Brutus]

If a state wishes to provide against these troubles and disorders that the aforesaid difficulties bring with them, there is no more powerful remedy, none more effective nor more certain nor more necessary, than to kill the sons of Brutus. As history shows,[1] they, along with other Roman youths, were led to conspire against their native city by no other reason than that they could not profit unlaw-fully under the consuls as they had under the kings. Hence it seemed that the people's liberty had become their slavery. And he who undertakes to govern a multitude, whether by the method of freedom or by that of a princedom, and does not secure himself against those who are enemies to the new government, establishes a short-lived state. It is true that I consider those princes unlucky who have to take unlawful methods for securing their positions for them-selves, when the multitude are his enemies. Because he who has the few as his enemies easily and without many occasions for violence makes himself safe, but he who has the people as his enemies generally never makes himself safe. And the more cruelty he uses, the weaker his princedom becomes. So the strongest resource he has is to try to make the people friendly.

[Advice to a prince on making his throne secure]

And though this *Discourse* is out of harmony with its title, since here I am speaking of a prince and there I spoke of a republic, yet, in order not to have to return to this matter afterward, I wish to speak of it briefly. If a prince, then, intends to win over a people that is hostile to him (I am speaking of those princes who have become

1. Livy 2. 1–5.

tyrants of their native lands) I say that he ought first to investigate what the people want, and he will always find that they wish two things: one, to avenge themselves on those who are the cause of their being slaves; the second, to get their liberty again. The first wish the prince can satisfy wholly, the second in part.

As to the first, here is an example to the point. When Clearchus, tyrant of Heraclea, was in exile, a quarrel arose between the people and the aristocrats of Heraclea; the aristocrats, knowing that they were weaker, turned to support Clearchus and, by conspiring with him, brought him into Heraclea against the popular wish and took away the people's liberty. Then Clearchus, finding himself between the arrogance of the aristocrats, whom he could in no way satisfy or control, and the rage of the citizens, who could not endure the loss of their liberty, determined at one blow to free himself from the annoyance of the rich and to win over the people. And taking a suitable occasion for this, he cut to pieces all the aristocrats—to the utter satisfaction of the people. And so in this way he satisfied one of the wishes of the people, that is, to avenge themselves.

[*The prince must govern according to law*]

But as to the second popular wish, that of having their freedom again, since the prince cannot satisfy it, he should investigate what the reasons are that make them wish to be free; and he will find that a small part of them wishes to be free in order to rule; but all the others, who are countless, wish freedom in order to live in security. For in all republics, in whatever way organized, positions of authority cannot be reached by even forty or fifty citizens. And because this is a small number, it is an easy thing to secure oneself against them, either by getting rid of them or by bestowing on them so many honors that according to their stations they are for the most part contented. Those others, for whom it is enough to live secure, are easily satisfied by the making of ordinances and laws which provide for the general security and at the same time for the prince's own power. When a prince does this and when the people see that under no circumstances will he break those laws, in a short time they feel secure and contented. An example is the kingdom of France, which lives safely for no other reason than that those kings are restrained by countless laws in which is included the security of all her people. And he who organized that state planned that about arms and money the kings should do as they wished, but that they could deal with nothing else except as the laws prescribe.

[*Liberty secured better late than never*]

That prince, then, or that republic that does not make itself secure at the beginning of its rule must make itself secure at the first opportunity, as the Romans did. He who lets that pass repents too late of not having done what he should. Hence, because the Roman people was still not corrupt when it regained its liberty, it could keep it, after killing the sons of Brutus and getting rid of the Tarquins, with all those ways and means that have before been discussed. But if that people had been corrupt, neither in Rome nor elsewhere would there have been expedients strong enough to maintain it, as will be shown in the following chapter.

CHAPTER 17. A CORRUPT PEOPLE, IF IT ATTAINS FREEDOM, HAS THE GREATEST DIFFICULTY IN KEEPING ITSELF FREE

[*A corrupt princedom can hardly become free*]

I judge it was necessary either for the Roman kings to be abol/ ished or for Rome in a very short time to become weak and without energy. Because, in view of the great corruption to which those kings came, if two or three in succession had continued in the same way, and the corruption that was in them had extended through the members, when the members became corrupt, it would have been impossible ever to reform her. But since they lost the head when the body was sound, they easily adapted themselves to a free and well/ ordered life. And it should be granted as a thing very true that a corrupt city living under a prince, even though that prince with all his race is destroyed, never can bring itself back to freedom. On the contrary, one prince must destroy another; for without setting up a new lord she is never quiet, unless indeed the goodness of one man, together with his ability, keeps her free. But that freedom lasts only as long as the life of that man lasts. Thus it was in Syracuse with respect to Dion and Timoleon, whose ability at different times, as long as they lived, kept that city free. When they were dead, it went back to its old tyranny.

[*The uncorrupted Rome of Brutus; the corrupt Rome of Caesar*]

But there is no stronger example than that of Rome. When the Tarquins were driven out, she was at once able to take and keep her freedom. But after Caesar was dead, Caius Caligula dead, Nero dead, all the race of Caesar destroyed, not merely could she never maintain her freedom but she could not even begin it. So great a difference in result in the same city came from nothing other than that in the time of the Tarquins the Roman people were not yet corrupt, but in these later times they were very corrupt. In early times the keeping of the people firm and determined to avoid kings required merely that they be made to swear that they would never agree that anyone should be king in Rome.[1] Yet in later times the authority and severity of Brutus, with all the Eastern legions, were not enough to keep them determined to maintain that freedom which he, in the likeness of the first Brutus, had restored to them. This resulted from the corruption spread among the people by the Marian parties; hence Caesar, as the head of these parties, could so blind the multitude that it did not recognize the yoke it was putting on its own neck.

[*Freedom impossible for Milan and Naples*]

And though this instance of Rome is to be preferred to any other, I shall illustrate the subject also from peoples known in our times. Therefore I say that no chance event, though violent and severe, could restore Milan or Naples to freedom, because their members are wholly corrupt. This was evident after Filippo Visconti's death, because when Milan tried to restore her freedom, she could not, and did not know how to maintain it. Great, therefore, was the good fortune of Rome in that her kings became corrupt early, so that they were driven out before their corruption had passed into the vitals of that city. Because she was not corrupted, the countless uprisings that took place in her—so long as the purpose of the men was good—did not injure but rather benefited the republic.

[*Reform depends on a single able man*]

So it can be concluded that where the matter is not corrupt, uprisings and other disturbances do no harm. Where it is corrupt,

1. *Livy* 2. 1.

well-planned laws are of no use, unless indeed they are prepared by one who with the utmost power can force their observation, so that the matter will become good. I do not know that this has ever happened or if it can happen, because, as I said a little above, evidently when a city has declined by corruption of her matter, if ever she rises, she does so through the virtue of one man who is then living, not through the virtue of the masses in supporting good laws. And as soon as such a man is dead, she goes back to her early habits, as did Thebes, which, through the virtue of Epaminondas, could while he lived keep the form of republic and sovereign state; but when he died, she returned to her earlier misgovernment. The reason is that one man cannot live so long that he has time enough to give good customs to a city that for a long period has had bad ones. Hence if one man of exceedingly long life or two vigorous reigns in succession do not make her reformation thorough, the lack of them, as I have said above, ruins her, unless the reformer before his death has with many perils and much blood caused her to be born again. Such corruption and slight aptitude for free life spring from inequality in a city; and anyone who tries to bring her back to equality must use entirely extralegal means, such as few can or will use, as elsewhere I shall show in more detail.[2]

2. DISCOURSES *1. 18 end, 26.*

CHAPTER 18. HOW FREE GOVERNMENT
CAN BE MAINTAINED IN CORRUPT
CITIES, IF IT IS ALREADY THERE; AND
IF IT IS NOT THERE, HOW IT CAN BE
SET UP

[*"It is well to reason about everything"*]

I believe that it is not out of order or inharmonious with the *Discourse* above to consider if in a corrupt city free government can be preserved, when it already exists there; or when it does not exist, if it can be established: on this I say that to do either one or the other is very difficult. And although to give rules for it is almost impossible, because I should need to proceed according to the degree of corruption, nevertheless, since it is well to reason about everything, I do not wish to omit this. And I shall assume a city very corrupt, by which I shall the more increase such a difficulty, because there are no laws or rules sufficient to restrain a universal corruption. Because just as good morals, if they are to be maintained, have need of the laws, so the laws, if they are to be observed, have need of good morals. Besides this, the customs and the laws formed in a republic at its origin, when men were good, are no longer applicable when they have become wicked. Moreover if according to events in a city its laws vary, its customs never, or seldom, vary. This keeps the new laws from being adequate, because the customs, which remain fixed, corrupt them.

[*The constitution and the specific laws*]

And to make this discussion better understood, I say that in Rome there existed the basic organization of the government or of the state; and after that the laws which, along with the magistrates, restrained the citizens. The basis of the government was the authority of the people, of the Senate, of the Tribunes, of the Consuls, the manner of choosing and setting up magistrates, and the manner of making the laws. This basis changed little or not at all with circum⁄stances. There were changes in the laws that restrained the citizens, such as the law about adultery, the sumptuary law, that on canvassing for office, and many others, according as the citizens gradually grew corrupt. But since the basis of the government, which in corruption was no longer good, stood fixed, those laws, as they were revised, were not enough to keep men good. But they would have been quite enough if with the revision of the laws the basis had been changed.

[*The corruption of basic methods*]

And that it is true that the basis in the corrupt city was not good, is plain in two chief matters, with respect to choosing the magistrates and the laws. The Roman people did not give the consulate and the other chief offices of the city to any except those who asked for them. This habit was in the beginning good, because only those citizens asked for them who judged themselves worthy, and to be refused was ignominious, so that in order to be judged worthy every⁄body conducted himself well. Later, in the corrupt city, this method became very harmful, because not those who had most ability but those who had most power asked for the magistracies; and those without power, however worthy, abstained from asking for them through fear. This bad condition came about not all at once but gradually, as happens for all other objectionable things. Because, after the Romans had conquered Africa and Asia and brought almost all Greece under their rule, they felt sure of their freedom, and believed they had no more enemies who could cause them fear. This security and this weakness of their enemies caused the Roman people, in awarding the consulate, no longer to consider ability, but favor, putting in that office those who knew best how to please men, not those who knew best how to conquer enemies. Then from those who had most favor, they descended to giving it to those who had most power, so that the good, because of the weakness of such a procedure, were wholly excluded from office. A Tribune, and any other citizen whatever, had the right to propose a law to the people; on this every citizen was permitted to speak, either for or against, before it was decided. This custom was good when the citizens were good, because it has always been desirable that each one who thinks of something of benefit to the public should have the right to propose it. And it is good that each one should be permitted to state his opinion on it, in order that the people, having heard each, may choose the better. But when the citizens became wicked, such a basic custom became very bad, because only the powerful proposed laws, not for the common liberty but for their own power, and for fear of such men no one dared to speak against those laws. Thus the people were either deceived or forced into decreeing their own ruin.

[A difficult reform demands a prince]

It was necessary, therefore, if Rome when corrupt was to keep herself free, that, just as in the course of her life she formed new laws, she should also form new basic methods, because the methods and ways of living suitable for adoption by a bad subject are not like those for a good one, nor can matter of entirely different sorts have the same form. But since these basic methods must be replaced either all at once, when they evidently are no longer good, or little by little, before they generally are recognized as bad, I say that both of these two things are almost impossible. The cause of any attempt to replace them little by little must be a prudent man who can see these evils at a great distance as they originate. Yet it can easily be that no man of that sort will ever appear in a city. And if indeed such a man does appear, never will he succeed in persuading others of what he himself understands, because when men are used to living in one way, they do not like to change, and so much the more when they do not look the evil in its face but need to have it indicated to them through reasoning. As to reforming these basic methods at one stroke, when everybody knows they are not good, I say that their injurious quality, then easily recognized, is hard to correct because to accomplish it the use of lawful devices is not enough, since lawful methods are futile, but it is necessary to resort to unlawful ones, such as violence and arms, and before anything else to become prince of that city and have power to manage it in one's own way. To reorganize a city for living under good government assumes a good man, and to become prince of a state by violence assumes an evil man; therefore a good man will seldom attempt to become prince by evil methods, even though his purpose be good; on the other hand a wicked man, when he has become prince, will seldom try to do what is right, for it never will come into his mind to use rightly the authority he has gained wickedly.

[*Kingly power makes reform possible*]

From all the things explained above comes the difficulty or impossibility of maintaining a government in a corrupt city or of setting up a new government there. Indeed when in such a city one is to be set up or maintained, necessity demands that it be inclined more toward kingly rule than toward popular rule, in order that those men who, on account of their arrogance, cannot be controlled by law may in some fashion be restrained by a power almost kingly. To try to make them become good in other ways would be either a most cruel undertaking or altogether impossible, as I said above on what Cleomenes did. If he, in order to stand alone, killed the Ephors, and if Romulus, for the same reasons, killed his brother and Titus Tatius, the Sabine, and then they used well the power they gained, it is still to be remembered that neither of them had a subject spotted with that corruption of which we are speaking in this chapter, and therefore they had reason to hope and, hoping,[1] to justify their design.

1. *Having a good subject to work on, they could expect to succeed.*

CHAPTER 19. AFTER AN EXCELLENT PRINCE A WEAK PRINCE CAN MAINTAIN HIM-SELF, BUT AFTER A WEAK ONE NO KING-DOM CAN BE MAINTAINED BY ANOTHER WEAK ONE

[*One strong king after another can do great things*]

Having considered the ability and the methods of Romulus, Numa, and Tullus, the first three Roman kings, one can see how Rome chanced upon most excellent fortune, for her first king was very violent and warlike, her second quiet and religious, her third of the same violence as Romulus and more a lover of war than of peace.[1] Because in Rome it was necessary that there should appear among her first princes an organizer of a law-abiding community, but it was quite as necessary afterward that other kings should possess the same ability as Romulus; otherwise that city would have become effeminate and the prey of her neighbors. From this it can be learned that a successor not of so great ability as the first can maintain a government as a result of his predecessor's ability, and can enjoy the fruit of his labors. But if it comes about either that he is of long life or that after him there does not rise up another who repeats the ability of the first, that kingdom must fall. So, on the other side, if two, one after the other, are of great ability, they often do very great things and their fame rises to the sky.

[*David, Solomon, Bajazet*]

David, without doubt, was a man of the highest excellence in arms, in learning, in judgment. So great was his ability that, having conquered and crushed all his neighbors, he left to Solomon his son a peaceful kingdom, which could be retained with the arts of peace and without war. And so he could happily enjoy the result of his father's ability. But he could not at all leave it to Rehoboam his son, who, since he was not like his grandfather in ability nor like his father in fortune, had difficulty in inheriting a sixth part of the kingdom. Bajazet, Sultan of the Turks, who loved peace more than war, without difficulty enjoyed the labors of his father Mahomet, who, like David, having crushed his neighbors, left him a settled

1. Livy 1. 21, 22.

kingdom and one that could easily be preserved with the arts of peace. Yet if his son, Sali, the present ruler, had been like his father and not his grandfather, that kingdom would have fallen; but he seems likely to surpass the glory of his grandfather. By means of these instances then, I assert that after an excellent prince a weak prince can maintain himself. But if one weak one comes after another, no kingdom can be maintained, unless it is like that of France, which would be maintained by its old institutions. So those princes are weak who do not give constant attention to war.

[*Soldierly ability maintains a kingdom*]

I conclude therefore from this discussion that the ability ot Romulus was great enough to give Numa Pompilius opportunity to rule Rome many years with the arts of peace. After him came Tullus, who by his courage gained a reputation like that of Romulus, and after him came Ancus, so gifted by nature that he could both enjoy peace and carry on war. First he gave his attention to walking in the way of peace, but quickly he found that his neighbors, judging him effeminate, esteemed him little. As a result he decided that to maintain Rome he must turn to war and be like Romulus, and not like Numa.

[*Ruin comes from a succession of weak kings*]

In all this, princes who possess states should find their example. For he who is like Numa will hold his state or will not hold it according as the times and fortune turn under him. But he who is like Romulus, and like him armed with prudence and weapons, will hold it under all conditions if it is not taken from him by persistent and excessive force. Certainly we may suppose that if Rome had chanced to have as her third king a man unable to give her reputation with arms, she later could not at all or with very great difficulty have stood on her feet or produced the results she did. Hence as long as she lived under kings, she was subject to the danger of falling in ruin under a king who was either weak or bad.

CHAPTER 20. TWO ABLE PRINCES IN SUCCESSION PRODUCE GREAT EFFECTS; WELL-ORGANIZED REPUBLICS OF NECESSITY HAVE A SERIES OF ABLE RULERS, AND THEREFORE THEIR GAINS AND INCREASES ARE GREAT

When Rome had driven out the kings, she was without those dangers which I said above she was subject to, if there came to her throne a king who was weak or bad. Because the weight of authority fell on the consuls, who not through heredity or through deceits or through violent ambition, but through free votes, came to that authority, and were always very excellent men. Since Rome enjoyed their abilities and fortune, as time went on, she reached her final greatness in a course of years equaling in number those she had spent under kings. Because it can be seen that two successive reigns by able princes are enough to gain the world. Such were Philip of Macedon and Alexander the Great. For a republic this should be still more possible, since the method of choosing allows not merely two able rulers in succession but countless numbers to follow one another. Such a succession of able rulers will always be present in every well-ordered republic.

CHAPTER 21. WHAT GREAT BLAME IS DESERVED BY PRINCES AND REPUBLICS THAT LACK THEIR OWN ARMIES

[Where there are men there are soldiers]

Living princes and modern republics, when for defense and offense they lack soldiers of their own, ought to be ashamed and, from Tullus' example, to decide that this defect comes not from a lack of men fit for warfare but from their own error, because they have failed to make their men soldierly. For Tullus, after Rome had been at peace for forty years, when he came to the throne did not find one man who had ever been in war. Nonetheless, when he planned to make war, he did not consider resorting to the Samnites or the Tuscans or others who were in the habit of bearing arms. But he determined, as a very prudent man, to avail himself of his own people. And so great was his ability that under his direction he immediately made them into very excellent soldiers.[1] So it is truer than any other truth that if where there are men there are not soldiers, the cause is a deficiency in the prince and not a deficiency in the position or nature of the country.

[*Military training in England*]

Of this there is a very late instance. For everybody knows that in very recent times the King of England attacked the realm of France and did not take any soldiers except his own people, and because that kingdom had been more than thirty years without making war, he had no soldiers and no general who had ever seen service. Nevertheless, with them he did not hesitate to attack a kingdom full of generals and of good armies, who had been continually in active service in the Italian wars. It all came from that king's being a prudent man and that kingdom well organized; for in time of peace she does not suspend arrangements for war.

[*The Thebans became soldiers*]

Pelopidas and Epaminondas the Thebans, after they had freed Thebes and brought her out of the slavery of Spartan rule, though they were in a city accustomed to obey and in the midst of effeminate people, did not hesitate (so great was their competence) to put those people under arms and with them to engage the Spartan armies in the field and conquer them. And he who writes of it says that these two in a short time showed that warriors were born not merely in Lacedaemon but in every other region where men are born, if only there is someone who can direct them toward soldiership, as Tullus could direct the Romans. And Virgil could not better have expressed this opinion or shown that he agreed with it in other words than where he writes:

Tullus will stir indolent men to arms.[2]

1. *Livy* 1. 31.
2. Aeneid 6. *813–814.*

CHAPTER 22. WHAT IS NOTEWORTHY IN THE AFFAIR OF THE THREE ROMAN HORATII AND THE THREE ALBAN CU-RIATII[1]

Tullus King of Rome, and Metius King of Alba agreed that the kingdom whose above-mentioned three men should conquer would be master of the other. All of the Alban Curiatii were killed; one of the Roman Horatii was left alive. Because of this, Metius the Alban king and his people became subject to the Romans. And as that Horatius who was victor returned to Rome, he met a sister of his who was betrothed to one of the three dead Curiatii, and when she wept for the death of her betrothed, he killed her. As a result, that Horatius was brought into court for this crime and after much debate was freed, more through his father's prayers than through his own deserts. Three things are to be noted here: first, that on part of his forces a ruler should never risk all his fortune; second, that never in a well-ordered city are transgressions atoned for with good deeds; third, that never are treaties wise if their maker should or can be uncertain about their observance. Being a slave is so important to a city that we must never believe that either of those kings or those peoples would continue satisfied after three of their citizens had put them into subjection. This is evident in what Metius tried to do, for though right after the victory he confessed himself beaten by the Romans and promised submission to Tullus, nevertheless in the first expedition in which he had to join him against the Veientians, he sought to deceive Tullus, having too late become aware of the rashness of the treaty he had made. And because of this third note-worthy matter enough has been said, in the following two chapters we shall speak only of the other two.

1. *Livy 1. 24-27.*

CHAPTER 23. A GENERAL OUGHT NOT TO PUT IN JEOPARDY ALL HIS FORTUNE AND NOT ALL HIS FORCES; FOR THIS REASON THE GUARDING OF PASSES IS OFTEN HARMFUL

[The labor of years lost in a moment]

It never has been considered a wise decision to put in jeopardy all your fortune and not all your forces. This can be done in many ways. One is by acting like Tullus and Metius,[1] for they entrusted all the fortune of their fatherlands and the valor of all the men that both of them had in their armies to the valor and fortune of three of their citizens, who amounted to a very small part of the forces of each of them. They did not realize that as a result of this plan, all the labor their ancestors had undergone in organizing the state, in order to make it live free a long time and to make the citizens defenders of their freedom, was as though in vain, since it was in the power of so few to lose it. In this affair those kings could not have been more imprudent.

[The folly of relying on defense of mountain passes]

Into this difficulty they too almost always fall who, when the enemy comes, plan to hold the difficult places and to guard the passes. This decision is almost always harmful, unless you can conveniently keep all your forces in that difficult place. If you can, such a plan is to be adopted. But if the place is rugged, so that you cannot keep all your forces there, the plan is harmful. I am led to this judgment by the example of those who have been attacked by a powerful enemy in a country surrounded by mountains and precipitous places, for they never have tried to fight the enemy in the passes or on the mountains but have gone to meet them on the other side; or if they have not done so, they have awaited them on the inner side of those mountains, in places that were favorable and not precipitous. Their reason has been what I have said above, namely, that many men cannot be employed in the defense of precipitous places, both because they cannot live there long and because in confined places, capable of holding only a few men, you cannot resist an enemy who

1. *See the preceding* DISCOURSE.

comes with large numbers to assail you; but the enemy can easily come in large numbers, because their intention is to cross over and not to halt. Yet to wait with large numbers is impossible for him who is waiting, since he must encamp there for some time, not knowing when the enemy may attempt to pass through places that are, as I have said, confined and barren. If, then, you lose a pass which you have set out to hold and which your people and your army trust, almost every time such great terror seizes your people and the remainder of your soldiers that, without a chance to test their valor, you become a loser. Thus you lose all of your fortune with part of your forces.

[*The Romans fought Hannibal on the plains*]

Everybody knows with what difficulty Hannibal crossed the mountains that separate Lombardy from France and with what difficulty he crossed those that separate Lombardy from Tuscany.[2] Nevertheless the Romans waited for him first on the Ticino and then in the plain of Arezzo. And they preferred to have their army destroyed by the enemy in places where there was a chance for it to conquer, rather than to lead it among the mountains to be destroyed by an injurious site.

[*The French in 1515 found an Alpine pass unguarded*]

He who reads with perception all the histories will find very few able generals who have tried to hold such passes, both for the reasons given and because the passes cannot all be closed, for the mountains like the plains have not merely the roads that are normal and much used but many others which, though unknown to strangers, are known to the country people. With their aid you will always be led to any place whatever, against the expectation of your adversary. Of this I can bring up a very recent instance, in 1515. When Francis the King of France decided to go into Italy to recover the state of Lombardy, the chief reliance of those opposed to his undertaking was that the Swiss would hold the mountain passes. But, as their experience shows, that reliance of theirs was vain because, neglecting two or three places they were guarding, that king came over by another unknown way and was in Italy and upon them before they expected him. So they retired in confusion to Milan, and all the

2. *Livy* 21. *32–38, 58.*

people of Lombardy took the side of the French soldiers, having been disappointed in their belief that the French would be brought to a stop in the mountains.

CHAPTER 24. WELL-ORGANIZED REPUB-LICS ESTABLISH REWARDS AND PENAL-TIES FOR THEIR CITIZENS AND DO NOT CANCEL ONE WITH THE OTHER

The deserts of Horatius were very great, for with his valor he overcame the Curiatii;[1] his crime was horrible, for he killed his sister. So greatly did his homicide offend the Romans that they brought him to trial for his life, notwithstanding that his deserts were so great and so recent. To one looking at it superficially, their act seems an instance of popular ingratitude. Nonetheless, he who examines it more closely and with better attention considers what the methods of republics should be, blames that people rather for acquitting him than for considering his punishment.

The reason is that no well-ordered republic ever cancels the de-merits of its citizens with their merits, but after establishing rewards for good deeds and penalties for evil ones, if it rewards a man for doing well and then that same man does badly, it punishes him without regard to his good deeds. And when these customs are well observed, a city lives in freedom for a long time; otherwise it always soon falls. Because if, besides the reputation some excellent deed he does for the good of the city brings him, a citizen acquires such boldness and confidence that without fear of penalty he does some deeds that are not good, he will soon become so arrogant that all free government will disappear.

[*Small rewards may mean much*]

It is in fact necessary, if the penalty for wicked deeds is to be retained, always to give rewards for good ones, as Rome did. And though a republic be poor and able to give little, it should not hold back from that little, because the smallest gift given to anybody in recompense for a good deed, even though great, will always be esteemed by him who receives it as honorable and very great. Well

1. DISCOURSE *22, above.*

known is the story of Horatius Cocles and that of Mutius Scaevola:[2] the first held back the enemy on a bridge until it was cut; the other burned his own hand which had made a mistake when he tried to kill Porsenna King of the Tuscans. For these two deeds so excellent, the people rewarded these two men with two *stadera* of land apiece. The story of Manlius Capitolinus is also known.[3] When he saved the Capitol from the French who were investing it, those who were besieged there with him gave him a little dish full of flour. That reward, according to the fortune then current in Rome, was great, yet was of such a sort that when Manlius was later moved by envy or by his evil nature to try to arouse sedition in Rome and to gain the people to his side, he was, without any regard to his worthy actions, hurled headlong from that Capitol which earlier, with so much glory to himself, he had saved.

2. Livy 2. 10–13.
3. Livy 5. 47.

CHAPTER 25. HE WHO WISHES TO REMODEL A GOVERNMENT THAT HAS GROWN OLD IN A FREE CITY SHOULD KEEP AT LEAST THE SHADOW OF THE OLD METH-ODS

[The shadow of a king]

He who wishes or intends to remodel the government of a city, so that it will be accepted and can maintain itself to everybody's satisfaction, is under the necessity of retaining the shadow at least of the old methods, in order that to the people the government may seem not to have changed its form, even though in reality the new forms are altogether unlike those of the past. For the generality of men feed themselves as much on what seems to be as on what is; still more, many times they are moved more by the things that seem than by the things that are. For this reason the Romans, recognizing this necessity at the beginning of their free government, when in ex-change for one king they set up two consuls, decided they should have not more than twelve lictors, in order not to exceed the number of those who waited on the king.[1] Besides this, since an annual

1. Livy 2. 1.

sacrifice was offered in Rome, which could be offered only by the king in person, and since the Romans intended that the people should not because of the absence of the kings have reason to long for anything from the past, they made a director of the said sacrifice, whom they called the Sacrificing King, and subordinated him to the chief priest.[2] Thus the people in this way were satisfied about that sacrifice and never had occasion, through want of it, to desire the return of the kings.

[*New things upset the people's minds*]

And this ought to be observed by all those who wish to wipe out an old form of government in a city and bring in a new and free form of government. Because, since new things upset the minds of men, you ought to strive to have these upsetting changes retain as much of the old as is possible, and if the magistrates are different in number and authority and term from the old ones, they should at least keep their names. And this, as I have said, he should observe who intends to organize a constitutional government, whether of the type of a republic or of a kingdom. But he who intends to set up an absolute power, such as historians call a tyranny, ought to renew everything, as will be explained in the following chapter.

2. *Livy* 2. 2.

CHAPTER 26. A NEW PRINCE OUGHT TO MAKE EVERYTHING NEW IN A CITY OR PROVINCE HE CONQUERS

[*The tyrant makes all men depend on himself*]

If anyone who becomes prince of a city or of a state, especially when his foundations are weak, cannot move toward constitutional government by way of a kingdom or a republic, the best means he has for keeping that princedom (if he is a new prince) is to make everything in that state anew. That is, to set up in the cities new administrations with new names, new powers, new men, to make the rich poor, the poor rich, as David did when he became king: "the poor he filled with good things and the rich he sent away empty." Besides this, he should build new cities, overthrow those already built, change the inhabitants from one place to another; and in short he should leave nothing in that province untouched, and make sure that no rank or position or office or wealth is held by anyone who does not acknowledge it as from you.[1] He should aim at what was done by Philip of Macedon, father of Alexander, who, in the beginning a petty king, grew in these ways until he became lord of Greece. And he who writes of him says that he transferred men from province to province, as herdsmen transfer their herds.

[A good man rejects such cruel methods]

These methods are very cruel, and enemies to all government not merely Christian but human, and any man ought to avoid them and prefer to live a private life rather than to be a king who brings such ruin on men. Notwithstanding, a ruler who does not wish to take that first good way of lawful government, if he wishes to maintain himself, must enter upon this evil one. But men take certain middle ways that are very injurious; indeed, they are unable to be altogether good or altogether bad, as in the following chapter I shall show by example.

1. An instance of Machiavelli's frequent change to direct address to a prince.

CHAPTER 27. VERY RARELY DO MEN UNDER-STAND HOW TO BE ALTOGETHER BAD OR ALTOGETHER GOOD

[Giovampagolo of Perugia]

Pope Julius the Second, when going to Bologna in 1505 to drive out from that state the house of Bentivogli, which had held the princedom of that city for a hundred years (for the Pope had taken an oath against all the tyrants who occupied the cities of the Church), planned also to remove Giovampagolo Baglioni from Perugia, of which he was tyrant.[1] And having come near Perugia with this purpose and determination, known to everybody, he did not wait until he could enter that city with his army, which could guard him, but entered it unarmed, notwithstanding that Giovampagolo was inside with many soldiers that he had brought together there to defend him. So that, carried along by that impetuosity with which

1. Machiavelli was in Perugia at the time, as Florentine agent to the Pope. Giving some details about the soldiers, he writes: "Nevertheless, the Pope and the College [of cardinals] are in the power of Gio. Paolo" (LEGATION 20. 22, letter of 13 Sept. 1506 from Perugia).

he conducted everything, with only his bodyguard he put himself in the hands of his enemy, whom then he took off with him, leaving in that city a governor who would execute justice for the Church.

[*His failure to be splendidly wicked*]

All the sagacious men with the Pope observed the rashness of the Pope and the cowardice of Giovampagolo, and they could not reckon whence it came that the latter did not, to his everlasting fame, at one stroke put down his enemy and enrich himself with booty, since with the Pope were all the cardinals with all their precious things. Nor can it be believed that he abstained either through goodness or through conscience that held him back, because into the breast of a vicious man, who had taken his sister for himself, who had killed his cousins and nephews in order to rule, no pious scruples could come, but we must conclude that it happened be-cause men cannot be splendidly wicked or perfectly good, and when an evil deed has greatness in itself or is in some part noble, they cannot comprehend it.

[*Giovampagolo might have shown the prelates how low they should be estimated*]

So Giovampagolo, who did not mind being incestuous and an open parricide, could not or, to put it better, did not dare, when he had a perfect opportunity for it, do a deed for which everybody would have admired his courage and for which he would have left an everlasting remembrance of himself, as being the first who had shown to prelates what a low estimate was to be put on men who live and reign as they do. And he would have done a thing the greatness of which would have transcended every infamy, every peril that could have resulted from it.

CHAPTER 28. WHY THE ROMANS WERE LESS UNGRATEFUL TO THEIR CITIZENS THAN THE ATHENIANS

Whoever reads on the affairs of republics will find in all of them some sort of ingratitude against their citizens, but will find in Rome less of it than in Athens and perhaps than in any other republic. And seeking the reason for this, with relation to Rome and Athens,

I believe it came about because the Romans had less reason than the Athenians for being suspicious of their fellow citizens. Because if one considers Rome from the expulsion of the kings to Sulla and Marius, her liberty was never taken away by any of her citizens. Hence she had no strong reason for suspecting them and, consequently, for injuring them inconsiderately. To Athens, however, the opposite happened: since her liberty was taken away by Pisistratus in her most flourishing time and under a false appearance of goodness, as soon as she again became free, remembering the injuries she had received and her past servitude, she became very prompt to punish not merely the errors but the shadows of errors committed by her citizens. From this resulted the exile and the death of so many excellent men, from this the custom of ostracism and all the other violent deeds against her aristocrats done by that city at various times.

So with truth our writers on political theory say: people bite more savagely after regaining their liberty than after preserving it. He who considers, then, all that has been said, will not blame Athens in this matter nor praise Rome, but will blame only the necessity resulting from the difference in the events that came about in these cities. Because anybody considering the matter carefully will see that if the liberty of Rome had been taken away as was that of Athens, Rome would not have been kinder to her citizens than was Athens. One can base a perfectly true inference about this on what happened, after the expulsion of the kings, to Collatinus and Publius Valerius.[1] The first of these, though he was in favor of freeing Rome, was exiled for no other reason than that he bore the name of the Tarquins. The other, merely having caused suspicion of himself by building a house on the Caelian Hill, was also on the point of being exiled. If Rome against these two was so suspicious and severe, we infer that she would have shown ingratitude as did Athens, if her citizens, in early times and before her expansion, had injured her in the same way. And in order not to have to turn again to this matter of ingratitude, in the following chapter I shall say about it what is necessary.

1. *Livy* 2. 2, 7.

CHAPTER 29. WHICH IS MORE UNGRATEFUL: A PEOPLE OR A PRINCE?

[*The successful general*]

In connection with the matter discussed above, I think it proper to debate which shows this ingratitude in more striking instances: a people or a prince. And to argue this case better, I say that this vice of ingratitude comes from either avarice or suspicious fear. Because when a people or a prince sends a general out on an important expedition from which, by success, he gains much glory, that prince or that people is obligated on its part to reward him. But if a city or a prince is so moved by avarice as to dishonor or injure him, since cupidity forbids giving the general his due, that city or that prince commits a folly that has no excuse, but rather brings everlasting infamy. Yet there are many princes who sin in this way. And Cornelius Tacitus puts the reason in this sentence:

> We are more inclined to make a return for an injury than
> for a benefit, for gratitude is looked on as a burden, revenge
> as a gain (*History* 4. 3).

[*Fear excusable*]

But when the government does not reward a general, or, to put it better, injures him, moved not by avarice but by fear, then both people and prince deserve some excuse; we read about many such acts of ingratitude resulting from fear. Such fear arises because a general who has ably gained a dominion for his lord, by conquering the enemy and loading himself with glory and his soldiers with riches, necessarily gains with his soldiers and with the enemy and with that prince's own subjects such a great reputation that his victory cannot be relished by that lord who has sent him. And because the nature of men is ambitious and suspicious and does not know how to set a limit to its own fortune, such suspicious fear as suddenly rises in the prince after his general's victory cannot but be increased by the general himself with some act or word displaying arrogance. Hence the prince can think of nothing else than of securing himself against him, and to do this, he thinks either of putting the general to death or of taking away the reputation he has gained in his army and among his people, and he makes every effort to show that that victory has come about not through the general's ability but through fortune or through the enemy's cowardice or through the prudence of the other leaders who have been with him in the action.

[Vespasian's ingratitude to Antonius]

After Vespasian, then in Judea, was proclaimed emperor by his army, Antonius Primus, who was in Illyria with another army, took his part and came into Italy against Vitellius, who was ruling at Rome, and most ably defeated two Vitellian armies and occupied Rome. Hence Muzianus, sent by Vespasian, found that through Antonius' ability everything had been gained and every difficulty overcome. The reward Antonius got for it was that Muzianus at once took from him the command of the army, and little by little brought him down to utter impotence in Rome. So Antonius went to Vespasian, still in Asia, who so received him, allowing him no rank whatever, that soon he died as though in despair. Of such instances histories are full.

[Ferdinand's ingratitude to Gonsalvo]

In our time everybody knows with what labor and ability Gon-salvo Ferrante, campaigning in the Kingdom of Naples against the French for Ferdinand of Aragon, conquered and subdued that kingdom. Yet as the reward of his victories what he obtained was that Ferdinand, leaving Aragon and coming to Naples, first stripped away his command of the soldiers, then deprived him of the fortresses, and at last took him back to Spain, where after a short time he died unhonored. So natural to princes, then, is suspicious fear that they cannot defend themselves from it and cannot show gratitude to men who by victory have under the princely banners made great gains.

[The ingratitude of republics results from love of freedom]

So if a prince cannot defend himself against ingratitude, we need not think it a miracle or worthy of special notice if a people cannot defend itself. A city living in freedom has two ends: the first, to make gains; the second, to keep herself free. In both of these she probably will err through too much love. Her errors in making gains will be spoken of in their place.[1] Her errors in keeping herself free are, among others, these: injury to citizens whom she should reward; fear of citizens whom she should trust. And though such conduct brings about great evils in a republic that has come to corruption and many times makes her come all the quicker to tyranny—as happened to Rome with Caesar, who by force took for himself what ingratitude denied him—nonetheless it brings great benefits to an uncorrupted republic and makes her live in freedom longer, since by fear of punishment men are kept better and less ambitious.

[*Rome seldom ungrateful*]

It is true that among all the peoples that ever had authority, Rome, for the reasons discussed above, was the least ungrateful, because actually there is no other example of her ingratitude than Scipio, for Coriolanus and Camillus were made exiles because of injuries that both of them had done to the plebeians.[2] But the first was not pardoned because his spirit was always persistently hostile to the people; the second was not merely recalled but through the whole course of his life was adored as prince. But the ingratitude shown to Scipio sprang from fear that the citizens began to have of him, which they had not had of the others. This resulted from the greatness of the enemy Scipio had overcome, from the reputation given him by victory in so long and perilous a war, from its rapidity, from the favor that his youth, his prudence, and his other notable virtues were gaining him. These things were so great that the magistrates of Rome (not to mention others) feared his authority. This displeased wise men, as something strange in Rome. And his conduct seemed so astonishing that Cato Priscus, considered holy, was the first to act against him and to say that a city could not be called free in which there was one citizen whom the magistrates feared. Hence if the Roman people in this case followed Cato's opinion, they deserve such excuse as I have said above those people deserve, and those princes, who are ungrateful through fear.

[*Republics less ungrateful than princes*]

In concluding this *Discourse*, then, I say that this vice of ingratitude is practiced either through avarice or through fear. Obviously

1. DISCOURSES 2. *19.*
2. Livy 2. *34; 5. 23–32.*

the people never exercise it through avarice; through fear they practice it much less than do princes, since they have less reason to be afraid, as I explain below.

CHAPTER 30. BY WHAT METHODS A PRINCE OR A REPUBLIC CAN AVOID THE VICE OF INGRATITUDE, AND BY WHAT METH-ODS AN ABLE GENERAL OR CITIZEN CAN ESCAPE BEING CRUSHED BY IT

[*The prince should be his own general*]

A prince, in order to escape the necessity of living in fear or of being ungrateful, should go personally on his campaigns, as at first the Roman emperors did, as in our times the Turk does, and as prudent rulers always have done and now do. Because, if they conquer, the glory and the gain are all theirs, but when they are not present, since the glory goes to another man, they think they cannot enjoy the gain if they do not destroy for the winner such glory as they have not been wise enough to gain for themselves. Thus they become ungrateful and unjust, and without doubt lose more than they gain. So when through lack of care or through slight prudence they remain lazily at home and send a general, I have no precepts to give them other than those they already know.

[*The general must avoid weak middle courses*]

But I do say to a prince's general, since I judge he cannot avoid Ingratitude's teeth, that he should do one of two things. Either, immediately after his victory, he should leave his army and put himself in the prince's hands, avoiding every arrogant and ambitious act, so that the prince, relieved of all suspicious fear, will have reason either to reward him or not to injure him; or if the general is un-willing to do so, he should boldly take the opposite method. That is, he should use all the measures through which he believes his conquest can be his own and not his prince's: he should make soldiers and citizens well disposed to himself; he should form new alliances with neighbors, occupy the fortresses with his men, bribe the leaders of his army and make himself secure against those he cannot bribe. Through such means he should seek to punish his lord for the ingratitude he will show. There are no other ways. But as I said above,[1] men cannot be wholly good or wholly bad. So always a general is unwilling to abandon his army right after a victory; he cannot bear himself modestly; he does not understand the use of violent measures that have honor in them. Hence, remaining uncertain, he is crushed between his delay and his uncertainty.

[*A republic must send a citizen as general*]

To a republic that wishes to avoid this vice of ingratitude, I cannot advise the same resource as to a prince, that is, to go in person on her campaigns and not send a general, because she must send one of her citizens. Therefore I allow her as a resource the methods of the Roman republic for being less ungrateful than the others. This arose from her method of administration. Because since the whole city, both the noble and the ignoble, were employed in war, there rose up in Rome in every age so many valiant men, famous for various victories, that the people had no reason for fearing any of them, since they were many, and one watched another. And meanwhile they were kept so virtuous and so careful not to cast the shadow of any ambition or to give the people any reason for attacking them as ambitious, that he who came to the dictatorship got greater glory from it the sooner he laid it down. And thus, since such ways could not generate suspicion, they did not generate ingratitude. Hence a republic that does not wish to have cause for being ungrateful will conduct her affairs as Rome did, and a citizen who wishes to avoid Ingratitude's teeth will observe the rules observed by the Roman citizens.

1. DISCOURSES *1. 27.*

CHAPTER 31. THE ROMAN GENERALS WERE NEVER EXCESSIVELY PUNISHED FOR ANY MISDEEDS; NOR WERE THEY EVER PUNISHED WHEN THEIR INCAPACITY OR BAD PLANNING RESULTED IN INJURY TO THE REPUBLIC

As we have said above, the Romans were not merely less ungrateful than other republics, but were also more merciful and more considerate in the punishment of the leaders of their armies than any other state. If a general did wrong through malice, they punished him humanely; if through incapacity, they were so far from punishing him that they rewarded and honored him. This policy was wisely adopted, because they judged it very important for a man in com-mand of an army to have his mind free and unburdened, ready to make decisions without any outside considerations; they therefore did not wish to add new difficulties and dangers to a thing in itself difficult and dangerous, realizing that if they added them, never would any general act vigorously. For example, they might be sending an army into Greece against Philip of Macedon or into Italy against Hannibal or against those people that they conquered earlier. The general put in charge of such an expedition would be worried by all the cares that accompany such affairs, which are weighty and important. Now if to such cares were added many instances in which the Romans crucified or otherwise killed those who had lost battles, it would be impossible for that general among so many anxieties to decide with vigor. For this reason, judging the ignominy of having lost sufficient for such men, they did not wish to frighten them with some greater penalty.

Here is an example of a folly committed not through ignorance.[1] Sergius and Virginius were besieging Veii, each one in charge of a part of the army. Of the two, Sergius was facing in the direction from which the Tuscans might come, and Virginius on the other side. When in the course of events Sergius was attacked by the Faliscians and other peoples, he endured being defeated and put to flight rather than send for aid to Virginius. And on the other side, Virginius, waiting for him to humble himself, preferred rather to see the dishonor of his fatherland and the ruin of that army than to aid him. This was an affair truly wicked and worthy of consideration, and from which one could draw no good inferences about the Roman republic, if both of them had not been chastised. It is true that while another republic would have punished them with a capital penalty, that one punished them by fines. This came about not because their faults did not deserve greater punishment but because in this case the Romans preferred, for the reasons already stated, to keep their old customs.

Of blunders through incapacity, there is no finer instance than Varro's, when through his rashness the Romans were defeated by

1. Livy 5. 8-11.

Hannibal at Cannae, where that republic was in danger of losing its liberty.² Nevertheless, because he showed incapacity but not wickedness, they not merely did not punish him but honored him, and when he returned to Rome all the senatorial order went to meet him. And since they could not thank him for the battle, they thanked him because he had returned to Rome and had not despaired of Roman affairs. When Papirius Cursor wished to have Fabius put to death for having fought with the Samnites against his orders, among the other reasons that were brought forward by Fabius' father against the determination of the Dictator, was that the Roman people had not on any defeat of their generals done what Papirius wished to do in victory.³

2. *Livy 22. 61.*
3. *Livy 8. 30.*

CHAPTER 32. A REPUBLIC OR A PRINCE SHOULD NOT PUT OFF BENEFITING MEN UNTIL TIMES OF NECESSITY

[Governmental forethought]

The Romans indeed were successful with their liberality to the people just as danger was coming upon them, at the time when Porsenna attacked Rome in order to restore the Tarquins. At that time the Senate, fearing that the people would prefer to accept the King rather than to endure the war, tried to make sure of them by relieving them from the tax on salt and from every imposition, saying that the poor did enough for the public benefit if they brought up their children.¹ Because of this benefit, the people exposed themselves to endure siege, hunger, and war. Yet no one, relying on this example, should defer gaining over the people until times of peril. He will never succeed as the Romans succeeded, because the masses will reckon that they do not have that benefit from you but from your adversaries; and since they properly will fear that when the necessity has passed you will take back what you have been forced to give them, they will not feel any obligation to you. The reason why the Roman decision came out well was that the government was new and not yet settled, and the populace had earlier seen laws made for

1. *Livy 2. 9.*

their advantage, such as that for the appeal to the people. Hence they could be persuaded that the favor done them resulted not so much from the enemy's coming as from the Senate's inclination to benefit them.[2] Besides this, their memory of the kings, by whom they had been in many ways injured and insulted, was fresh. Nevertheless, because such needs seldom are found, it also seldom happens that such remedies are of value. Whoever is in power, therefore, whether a civil government or a prince, should consider beforehand what sorts of adverse times are likely to come upon him and what men he may need in times of trouble, and then treat them in just the way he thinks he would need to treat them in an emergency of any kind. He who conducts himself otherwise, whether prince or civil government—but especially a prince—and then believes that when the peril is on him he can in a moment regain men with benefits, deceives himself, because he not merely does not make sure of them but even hastens his own ruin.

2. *Livy 2. 8.*

CHAPTER 33. WHEN A DANGER WITHIN A STATE OR FROM WITHOUT HAS GROWN GREAT, THE SAFER POLICY IS TO PUT OFF DEALING WITH IT RATHER THAN TO ATTACK IT

[The dangerous growth of Rome]

As the Roman republic increased in reputation, force and power, her neighbors—who at first had not recognized how much that new republic could harm them—recognized their error, though too late. In order to remedy what they had not remedied earlier, as many as forty peoples conspired against Rome. Hence the Romans determined to use their chief remedy against urgent perils: they set up a Dictator;[1] that is, they gave power to one man to make decisions without any consultation, and without any appeal to carry out what he decided. This device, as it was useful then and was a cause of their overcoming the perils which hung over them, so it was always very useful in all the emergencies that as their dominion increased at various times endangered the Republic.

1. *Livy 2. 18.*

[*A dangerous citizen*]

Mention of such peril at once brings on discussion of the rise within a republic or in opposition to a republic of a danger resulting from some cause either internal or external. When such a danger is so serious that it frightens everybody, the safest plan is to put off dealing with it rather than to try to obliterate it, because almost always those who attempt to destroy it make its powers greater and hasten the ill that was feared from it. Such emergencies come up in a republic more often through an internal than through an external cause. Many times, indeed, a citizen is allowed to get more power than is safe, or corruption begins in a law that is the nerve and life of free institutions; then this mistake is allowed to run on so far that to attempt remedy is more harmful than to let it go on. Moreover the recognition of these evils when they spring up is more difficult inasmuch as it appears more natural for men always to approve the beginnings of things; and such approval for the actions of young men, if they seem of some value, is stronger than for the actions of others. So if in a state a young noble appears who possesses extraordinary ability, all the citizens turn their eyes toward him and agree, without reservation, in honoring him. Hence, if he has a bit of ambition, through the union of the aid Nature gives him with this situation, he soon gets to such a place that, if the citizens realize their mistake, they have few methods for putting a stop to the process, and if they try to make use of all those they have, they do nothing else than hasten his rise to power.

[*Cosimo de'Medici*]

Of this I might bring up many instances, but I shall give only one, from our city. Cosimo de'Medici, with whom the Medici family first grew great in our city, arrived at so high a reputation by means of the credit derived from his own prudence and other citizens' ignorance, that he so greatly frightened the government as to make other citizens judge it dangerous to attack him and exceedingly dangerous to let him continue. But in those days Niccolò da Uzzano was living, who in public affairs was considered highly expert. Though he made the first mistake of failing to recognize the dangers that might rise from Cosimo's reputation, yet as long as he lived he did not permit the second mistake, that is, an effort to put Cosimo out of the way, for Niccolò judged that such an attempt would completely destroy control by his own party. We see that after his death it really did, because those citizens who were left, not following Niccolò's advice, gathered their strength against Cosimo and drove him from Florence. The result was that Cosimo's party, resentful over this injury, a little later called him back and made him prince of the republic—a rank to which without that open opposition he never could have risen.

[Caesar]

The same thing happened in Rome for Caesar; his ability was supported by Pompey and others, but a little later that support changed into fear. Of this Cicero bears witness, saying that too late Pompey began to fear Caesar. This fear made them think about remedies, and the remedies they used hastened the ruin of their republic.

[Opposition made Rome more dangerous]

I say, then, that since it is difficult to recognize these ills when they rise up (this difficulty being caused by the way in which these affairs deceive you in the beginning), it is a wiser decision to give them time when they are recognized rather than to oppose them, because, if you give them time, they disappear, or at least the ill is deferred for a longer space. And under all conditions rulers ought to keep their eyes open, if they intend to destroy them or to oppose their power and momentum, so that they do not increase instead of check these ills, and when they believe they are pushing a thing on do not pull it back, or do not drown a plant by watering it. But they ought to examine well the power of the evil, and when you see you are prepared to cure it, set yourself at it without reservation; otherwise, let it go, and do not in any way attempt it. Because the same thing will happen, as I explain above, that happened to the neighbors of Rome. For since Rome had grown to such great strength, it would have been more to their safety to attempt with the ways of peace to placate her and hold her back than with the ways of war to make her consider new methods and new defenses. Because that league of theirs did nothing other than make the Romans more united, stronger, and intent on new ways, by means of which in a short time they increased their power. Among these was the setting up of the Dictator—a new device through which they not merely overcame the dangers hanging over them, but also avoided countless ills which except for that remedy the public would have incurred.

CHAPTER 34. THE AUTHORITY OF THE DICTATOR DID GOOD AND NOT HARM TO THE ROMAN REPUBLIC; AND THE POWERS CITIZENS TAKE FOR THEMSELVES, NOT THOSE GIVEN THEM BY FREE VOTES, DESTROY CIVIL GOVERNMENT

[*Forces easily acquire names; names do not acquire forces*]

Some writers have condemned those Romans who devised for that city the scheme of setting up a Dictator, believing that it was in time the cause of tyranny in Rome; for they allege that the first tyrant in that city ruled her under the title of Dictator, and that without that office Caesar could not with any lawful title have given good standing to his tyranny. Nevertheless anyone who holds this belief has not examined the matter well, but accepts it contrary to all reason. Because not the name or the rank of Dictator made Rome a slave, but the power citizens gained through prolonged military command; if Rome had not had the name of Dictator, they would have taken some other, for forces easily acquire names, but names do not acquire forces. The Dictator, in fact, as long as he was set up according to the general laws and not by his own authority, always did good to the city. To republics, indeed, harm is done by magistrates that set themselves up and by power obtained in unlawful ways, not by power that comes in lawful ways; it is apparent that never in Rome during so long a course of time did any Dictator do the republic anything but good.

[*Rome when uncorrupted was not harmed by a Dictator*]

For this there are very obvious reasons. First, if a citizen is to be capable of doing harm and seizing unlawful authority for himself, he must have many qualifications which in an uncorrupted city he can never have. For he needs to be very rich and to have many adherents and partisans, which he cannot have where the laws are observed. And if even then he does have them, such men are so dangerous that free votes do not unite on them. Besides this, the Dictator was set up for a limited term but not for life, and merely to dispose of that affair that caused him to be set up. His authority included the power to decide for himself about the remedies for that urgent peril and to do everything without consultation and to punish anybody without appeal; but he was not empowered to do things that might weaken the state, such as taking authority away from the Senate and the people, or doing away with the old institutions of the city and making new ones. Three things, then, worked together: the dictatorship lasted but a short time; the Dictator's power was limited; the Roman people was not corrupt. These conditions made it impossible for the Dictator to go beyond bounds and injure the city; experience shows that he always benefited her.

[Republics in emergencies move too slowly]

Certainly among all Roman laws this is one deserving to be considered and counted among those causing the greatness of so powerful an empire, for without such a law the citizens have difficulty in escaping from strange and unexpected afflictions. The normal legal procedures of republics are very slow, since no council or official can do anything independently, but each one must for many things have the approval of another; in reconciling their various opinions time is lost. Because of this delay, their provisions are very dangerous when they must provide against something that does not permit loss of time. Republics should therefore have among their laws one like this of the Romans. The Venetian republic, indeed, which ranks high among modern republics, has authorized a small group of citizens who, in great need, without consulting anyone, are empowered to make a unanimous decision. This is a wise custom, because when such a possibility does not exist in a republic, either she must through keeping her laws ruin herself, or in order not to be ruined, must break her laws. Yet it is not good that in a republic anything should ever happen that has to be dealt with extralegally. The extralegal action may turn out well at the moment, yet the example has a bad effect, because it establishes a custom of breaking laws for good purposes; later, with this example, they are broken for bad purposes. Therefore a republic will never be perfect if with her laws she has not provided for everything, and furnished a means for dealing with every unexpected event, and laid down a method for using it. In conclusion, therefore, I say that those repub-lics that cannot against impending danger take refuge under a dictator or some such authority will in serious emergencies always be ruined.

[*Envy avoided in choosing the Dictator*]

About this new law we should observe how wisely the Romans provided for electing their Dictator. His choice was an embarrass-ment for the Consuls who, having been the rulers of the city, had to submit to authority like other men. Foreseeing that this would lead the citizens to feel some contempt for them, the Romans decided that the power to choose the Dictator should rest with the Consuls, believing that when a time came that Rome had need of such kingly power, they would decide upon it. Since they did it themselves, they would feel less pain, because wounds and other injuries that a man voluntarily inflicts on himself, by choice, are much less painful than those inflicted by others. In later times, in fact, instead of choosing a Dictator, the Roman formed the habit of giving dicta-torial power to the Consul, with these words: "Let the Consul take care that the republic is not harmed."

[*Again the conclusion of Chapter 33*]

To return to our subject, I draw the conclusion that Rome's neighbors, by trying to crush her, forced her to organize in such a way that she could not merely defend herself but could with greater force, better planning, and more show of justice attack them.

CHAPTER 35. WHY THE CREATION OF THE DECEMVIRATE IN ROME WAS INJURIOUS TO THE LIBERTY OF THAT REPUBLIC, NOTWITHSTANDING THAT IT WAS SET UP BY FREE AND GENERAL VOTE[1]

Seemingly contradictory to what has been set forth above (name-ly, that authority taken by violence, not that given by votes, injures a republic) is the election of the Ten Citizens chosen by the Roman

1. Livy 3. 32–54.

people to make laws in Rome; they in time became tyrants and without any scruple usurped her liberty. As to this, one should consider the methods of giving authority and the time for which it is given. When free authority is given for a long time—that is, for a year or more—it will always be dangerous and will produce good or bad effects according as those to whom it is given are bad or good. And if the authority of the Ten is considered and that of the Dicta/tors, that of the Ten appears beyond comparison greater. When the Dictator was set up, there remained the Tribunes, the Consuls, the Senate with their authority, which the Dictator was not empowered to take from them. And even though he could exclude one man from the consulate, and another from the Senate, he could not blot out the senatorial order and make new laws. Hence the Senate, the Consuls, the Tribunes, remaining in their authority, were like a guard over him, to block any turn from the right way. But in the setting up of the Ten, everything ran contrary. The Consuls and the Tribunes were abolished; the Ten received authority to make laws and to do everything else, as though they were the Roman people. Hence standing alone, without Consuls, without Tribunes, without appeal to the people, and therefore without anybody to watch them, in their second year, influenced by Appius' desire for power, they easily became arrogant.

This shows that when I say that authority given by free vote never injures any republic, I presuppose a people never bringing itself to give it, except with proper limitations and at the proper times. But when, either deceived or blinded by something, they are brought to give it imprudently—as the Roman people gave it to the Ten—they will always have such an experience as the Romans did. This is easily proved by noting what causes kept the Dictators good and what made the Ten wicked, and by noting also how states that have been thought well ordered have acted in giving authority for a long time, as the Spartans gave it to their kings and the Venetians to their dukes, because it is clear that guards were placed over both of these, which allowed them no possibility for using their authority badly. That the matter is not corrupted gives no help in this in/stance, because an absolute authority in a very short time corrupts the matter, and makes itself friends and partisans. It is not harmed by being poor or not having relatives,[2] because riches and every

2. *Apparently in the sense of supporters or partisans.*

other advantage quickly follow it, as we shall explain in more detail
on the setting up of the said Ten.[1]

1. DISCOURSES 1. 40.

CHAPTER 36. CITIZENS WHO HAVE HELD HIGH OFFICES OUGHT NOT TO DESPISE THE LOWER ONES

[Venetian practice inferior to Roman]

The Romans had made Marcus Fabius and G. Manlius Consuls and had won a glorious battle against the Veientians and the
Etruscans; among those killed was Quintus Fabius, the Consul's
brother, who the year before had himself been Consul.[1] Here we
may observe how well the institutions of that city were adapted to
making it great, and how much other republics, which are far
different in their ways, deceive themselves. Because, though the
Romans were great lovers of glory, yet they did not think it a dishonorable thing to obey at one time a man whom at another time
they had commanded, and to serve in an army of which they had
been leaders. This custom is opposed to the opinions, institutions,
and ways of citizens in our times; in Venice there is still the bad
practice that a citizen, after holding a high rank, is ashamed to
accept a lower one, and the city allows him to reject it. This custom,
though it may be honorable for the individual, for the public is
wholly disadvantageous. A republic has a right to hope and confide
more in a citizen who descends from a high position to serve in a
lower one, than in him who ascends from a lower one to serve in a
higher place, because in this second person, the republic cannot
reasonably have confidence unless there are around him men of such
high quality and ability that his newness can be moderated by their
advice and standing. And if in Rome there had been the custom
there is in Venice and in other modern republics and kingdoms—
that he who once had been consul would never be willing to go
into the armies except as consul—it would have brought about
countless things opposed to free government, both through the mistakes the new men would make and through the ambition that they
could exercise more easily, not having men around them in whose

1. *Livy* 2. 46.

sight they would be afraid to do wrong; and so they would become more careless—all of which would have been to the public detriment.

CHAPTER 37. WHAT DISCORDS THE AGRAR-IAN LAW CAUSED IN ROME; AND FOR A REPUBLIC TO MAKE A LAW THAT LOOKS FAR BACKWARD AND IS OPPOSED TO AN ANCIENT CUSTOM OF THE CITY IS PRODUCTIVE OF DISCORD

[Ambition causes strife]

Ancient writers say that men usually worry in bad conditions and get bored in good ones, and that either of these afflictions produces the same results. Whenever men cease fighting through necessity, they go to fighting through ambition, which is so powerful in human breasts that, whatever high rank men climb to, never does ambition abandon them. The cause is that Nature has made men able to crave everything but unable to attain everything. Hence, since men's craving is always greater than their power to attain, they are discontented with their acquirements and get slight satisfaction from them. Men's fortunes therefore vary because, since some strive to get more and others fear to lose what they have gained, they indulge in enmity and war. These cause the ruin of one province and the prosperity of another.

[The state should be rich and the citizens poor]

I have written this discussion because it was not enough for the Roman populace to make sure of the nobles by setting up the trib-unes—a desire to which it was forced by necessity—but at once, having attained that, it began fighting through ambition and through its hope to share honors and wealth with the nobles, as things much esteemed by men. From this rose the disorder that brought forth the contention over the Agrarian Law,[1] which at last resulted in the destruction of the republic. So, because well-ordered republics ought to keep their treasuries rich and their citizens poor, it follows that in the city of Rome there was a defect in this law. Either it was not made at the beginning in such a way as not to need remaking every

1. *Livy* 2. 41.

day, or there was such delay in making it that application to the past would have been dangerous, or if it was well designed at first, it was later corrupted in application. However it was, this law was never spoken of in Rome without turning that city upside down.

[*The rich evade the Agrarian Law*]

This law had two main provisions. One of them laid down that no citizen was permitted to own more than so many acres of land; the other that the fields taken from enemies should be divided among the Roman people. Thus it did two sorts of injury to the nobles, because those who possessed more property than the law permitted (namely, the greater part of the nobles) were to be deprived of it; and if the property of the enemy was divided among the multitude, the nobles lost a means for getting rich. So since these attacks were made on powerful men, who believed they served the public by opposing the law, whenever it was alluded to, as I have said, all that city turned upside down. And the nobles with patience and ingenui⁄ty caused delays about it: either an army was led out, or to the Tribune who invoked the law another Tribune was opposed, or sometimes part was yielded, or a colony was sent to the place that was to be parceled out, as happened to the district of Anzio, for when this quarrel over the law came up about it, they sent to that place a colony taken from Rome, to which the district was turned over. In this case Titus Livius uses a noteworthy phrase, saying that there was difficulty in finding in Rome anybody who would give his name for going to the said colony, so much more prone was that multitude to hope for things in Rome rather than to possess them in Anzio.² The dissension over this law kept on giving trouble for a while, until the age when the Romans took their armies into the remote parts of Italy and outside Italy; after that time it apparently stopped. This happened because the land owned by enemies to Rome, being distant from the eyes of the multitude and in a place where they could not easily cultivate it, became less desirable; and also the Romans did not so much penalize their enemies in that way; and if they did despoil any city of its land, they placed a colony there.

2. Livy 3. 1.

[Danger in private remedies for public evils]

Hence, for such reasons, this law lay as though asleep until the Gracchi appeared; when they waked it up, it wholly ruined Roman liberty, because by that time the power of its adversaries was re′ doubled; as a result, it stirred up so much hatred between the multitude and the Senate that it led to arms and bloodshed, contrary to every lawful habit and custom. Since the public magistrates could not remedy it, the factions, placing no more hope in them, had recourse to private remedies, and each of the parties decided to get a leader to defend it. The multitude acted early in this turmoil and disorder by turning its support to Marius, so that four times it made him consul, and he continued his consulate so long with slight intervals that he was able to make himself consul three times more. Having no remedy against this plague, the nobility backed Sulla, and making him head of their party, entered the civil wars; after much bloodshed and variety of fortune, the nobility were victors. These feuds came to life again in the time of Caesar and Pompey, when Caesar made himself head of Marius' party, and Pompey of Sulla's. In the war that followed, the victor was Caesar, the first tyrant in Rome; as a result, that city was never again free.

[Danger in the ambition of the rich]

Such were the beginning and the end, then, of the Agrarian Law. And though we showed above how the enmities at Rome between the Senate and the multitude kept Rome free by producing laws in support of liberty, and therefore the result of this Agrarian law seems out of harmony with my belief, I say that I do not for that reason abandon my opinion. To a great extent the ambition of the rich, if by various means and in various ways a city does not crush it, is what quickly brings her to ruin. So if the quarrels over the Agrarian Law took three hundred years to make Rome a slave, she would perhaps have been brought much sooner to slavery if the people, with this law and with its other cravings, had not continually checked the ambition of the nobles. This also shows how much more men esteem property than they do positions of honor. For about such positions the Roman nobility always without great dis′ turbance yielded to the populace, but when they came to property, so great was their obstinacy in defense that the people, to satisfy its appetite, had recourse to the illegalities discussed above.

[*Wise procrastination*]

These troubles were started by the Gracchi, whose intention should be praised above their prudence. Because, to attempt to take away an irregularity that has grown serious in a republic, and for the sake of this to make a law that looks far into the past, is a badly considered decision; as was set forth at length above, it does nothing else than hasten the evil toward which that irregularity is taking you. But if you delay, either the evil comes later, or before it comes to its completion, with time it disappears of itself.

CHAPTER 38. WEAK REPUBLICS ARE IRRESO/LUTE AND CANNOT MAKE DECISIONS; IF EVER THEY ADOPT ANY PLAN, IT COMES MORE FROM NECESSITY THAN FROM CHOICE

Since there was a very severe pestilence in Rome, and for that reason the Volscians and the Equi believed that the time had come when they could crush Rome, these two peoples, forming a very large army, attacked the Latins and the Ernici and began to plunder their country.[1] Hence the Latins and the Ernici were obliged to make it known at Rome and to beg to be defended by the Romans. Since the Romans were afflicted by the pestilence, they replied that the Latins must take measures to defend themselves with their own arms, because the Romans could not defend them.

[*The Roman Senate faced facts*]

Here we observe the Senate's nobility and prudence and how always in every fortune it intended to be master of the decisions that its subjects would have to make. And it never felt shame in deciding on a thing contrary to its policy and to its other decisions, when necessity gave command. I say this because at other times the same Senate had forbidden those peoples to take arms and defend them/selves. A Senate less prudent than this would have thought its dignity lowered by granting them this defense. But that Senate

1. *Livy* 3. 6.

always judged things as they ought to be judged and always took the less bad decision as the better. It disliked inability to defend its subjects; it disliked their taking up arms without permission, for the reasons mentioned and for many others that can be understood. Nevertheless, knowing that they would necessarily be armed in any case, since the enemy were upon them, the Senate made the honorable decision and determined that what they had to do they should do with its consent, in order that they should not, by disobeying through necessity, get accustomed to disobeying through choice. And though this evidently is the decision any republic ought to make, nonetheless weak and badly advised republics do not know enough to make it and do not know how to gain themselves honor from such necessities.

[Florence treated Cesare Borgia foolishly]

In our day, Duke Valentino had taken Faenza and had made Bologna yield to his terms. Then, planning to return to Rome through Tuscany, he sent one of his men to Florence to ask passage for himself and his army. When there was debate in Florence on how they ought to conduct themselves in this matter, nobody ever advised that they should grant it. In this they did not follow the Roman method. Yet since the Duke was heavily armed and the Florentines so nearly unarmed that they could not thwart his passage, it would have been much more to their honor that he should seem to pass with their permission than by force, because, while in any case his passage was wholly disgraceful to them, it would have been so in a lower degree if they had conducted themselves otherwise. But the worst quality weak republics have is to be irresolute, so that all the decisions they make, they make as the result of force, and if ever they do anything good, they do it as something forced and not as a result of their prudence.

[Florentine folly about Pisa and Arezzo]

I wish to give two further instances of this which happened in our time in the government of our city. In 1500, when King Louis XII of France, after taking Milan, was eager to turn over Pisa to Florence in order to get fifty thousand ducats that had been promised him by the Florentines after such restitution, he sent his armies toward Pisa, led by Monsieur de Beaumont—a Frenchman indeed, nonetheless a man in whom the Florentines had much confidence.

This army and this general moved between Cascina and Pisa, in order to assail the walls. While he was pausing there some days to get ready for the assault, Pisan ambassadors came to Beaumont and offered to give over the city to the French army with the condition that, on the King's faith, he should promise not to put her in the power of the Florentines earlier than at the end of four months. This plan the Florentines wholly refused, so that in consequence they went ahead with the siege and left in disgrace. They refused the plan for no other reason than that they distrusted the King's faith, even though through their feeble planning they had of necessity put them-selves into his power. On the other hand, they did not trust him, and they did not see how much better it was for the King to turn Pisa over to them after he was inside the city, or if he did not turn her over, to reveal his purpose to them, than when he did not have it, for him to promise her to them and for them to be forced to buy his promises. Hence they would have acted much more profitably if they had consented that with any sort of promise Beaumont should take Pisa, as experience showed later in 1502 when, after Arezzo rebelled, Monsieur Imbault was sent by the French king to rescue the Florentines with French soldiers. Arriving in the neighborhood of Arezzo, he promptly negotiated an agreement with the Aretines, who were willing, under a certain pledge, to surrender the city like the Pisans. Florence refused such a plan. Whereupon Monsieur Imbault, seeing this and judging that the Florentines had little understanding of the affair, undertook the negotiations for the agree-ment by himself, without participation by the Commissioners. So finally he concluded it as he wished and according to it entered Arezzo with his soldiers, giving the Florentines to understand that they were mad and did not understand the affairs of the world, because if they wanted Arezzo, they might make it known to the King, who was much better able to give it to them when he had his soldiers inside the city than outside. In Florence they did not stop tearing to pieces and blaming the said Imbault; nor did they ever stop until at last they saw that if Beaumont had been like Imbault they would have had Pisa as they had Arezzo.

And so, to return to our subject, irresolute republics never make good decisions except through force, because when there is any doubt, their weakness never lets them come to a decision; and if that doubt is not canceled by some violence that drives them on, they always remain undecided.

CHAPTER 39. AMONG DIFFERENT PEOPLES THE SAME EVENTS OFTEN OCCUR

[Human nature always the same]

He who considers present affairs and ancient ones readily under-stands that all cities and all peoples have the same desires and the same traits and that they always have had them. He who diligently examines past events easily foresees future ones in every country and can apply to them the remedies used by the ancients or, not finding any that have been used, can devise new ones because of the similarity of the events. But because these considerations are neglected or are not understood by those who read or, if they are understood, are not known to rulers, the same dissensions appear in every age.

[Florentine instability]

The city of Florence after 1494, having lost part of her empire, such as Pisa and other towns, was obliged to make war on those who held them. Because those holders were strong, it followed that Florence spent much on the war, without any return. From much spending came high taxes; from the taxes came countless complaints by the people. And since this war was administered by a magistracy of ten citizens called the Ten of War, the populace were brought to hate the Ten, as the cause both of the war and the expense of it; so they persuaded themselves that if that magistracy were abolished, the war would be abolished. Hence when it was to be chosen again, new members were not selected, but it was allowed to come to an end and its duties were turned over to the Signory. This decision was so damaging that not merely did it not get rid of the war, as the populace was convinced it would, but through the lack of those men who had prudently administered it, so much confusion resulted that Arezzo and many other places, besides Pisa, were lost. Hence the people, seeing their mistake, and that the cause of the sickness was the fever and not the doctor, re-established the magistracy of the Ten.

[*A Roman instance*]

This same inclination appeared in Rome against the name of the Consuls. When the people saw one war springing from another, and that they could never rest, although they should have believed that the wars were caused by the ambition of their neighbors who wished to crush them, they did believe that those wars were caused by the ambition of the nobles, who, unable to punish the plebeians in Rome where they were defended by the power of the Tribunes, wished to get them out of Rome under the Consuls, in order to oppress them where they could get no aid. Because of this, the people decided that they must get rid of the Consuls or regulate their power in such a way that they would have no authority over the plebeians either abroad or at home. The first who attempted this law was one Terentillius, a Tribune, who proposed that five men should be set up to consider the power of the Consuls and limit it. This greatly disturbed the nobility, since they thought the majesty of their authority had wholly declined, so that the nobility no longer had any standing in that republic. Nevertheless such was the per sistence of the Tribunes that the consular name was blotted out; and finally they consented, after some other arrangements, rather to set up Tribunes with consular power than Consuls; so much more they hated their name than their authority. And so it continued a long time, until finally, recognizing their mistake, just as the Florentines returned to the Ten, so they established their Consuls again.[1]

1. *Livy 4. 6; 6. 35, 38–42.*

CHAPTER 40. THE ESTABLISHMENT OF THE DECEMVIRATE IN ROME AND WHAT IS TO BE LEARNED FROM IT;[1] WHEREIN I CONSIDER, AMONG OTHER THINGS, HOW THROUGH SUCH AN EVENT A REPUBLIC CAN BE SAVED OR SUBJECTED TO TYRANNY

Since I am going to discuss in detail what happened in Rome through establishing the Decemvirate, I think it not superfluous to tell, first, all that followed that establishment, and then to debate the

1. *Livy 3. 31–58.*

things that are noteworthy in these events. They are many and of great import, both for those who hope to keep a republic free and for those who plan to get one into their power. Such discussion will reveal many mistakes made by the Senate and by the populace to the detriment of liberty; and many errors made by Appius, head of the Decemvirate, to the detriment of the tyranny he planned to set up in Rome.

[Appius' hypocrisy]

After there had been many disputes and struggles between the populace and the nobility over establishing new laws in Rome, through which the city's liberty might be made firmer, the parties agreed to send Spurius Posthumus with two other citizens to Athens for copies of the laws Solon gave that city, so as to base the Roman laws on them. When these messengers had gone and returned, the next thing was the appointment of men to examine and establish the said laws. So they appointed ten citizens for a year, among whom was Appius Claudius, a man keen and restless. And in order that they might without restraint draw up such laws, they removed all the other Roman magistrates, especially the Tribunes and the Consuls, and took away the right of appeal to the people, so that the new magistracy was absolute ruler of Rome. Into Appius' hands came all the authority of his companions, by reason of the support he had from the people, for he had to all appearances so sided with the populace that it seemed a marvel how quickly he had taken on a new nature and a new disposition, since before this time he had been thought a cruel persecutor of the people.

[Appius shows his true character]

These Ten conducted themselves quite as in a free state, not keeping more than twelve lictors, who marched before the chief of the Ten. And though they had absolute authority, nonetheless, when they had to punish a Roman citizen for homicide, they cited him into the presence of the populace and had it judge him. They wrote their laws on ten tables which, before the laws were confirmed, they put in a public place to allow everyone to read and debate them, that any defects might be known which before confirmation could be amended. Thereupon Appius produced in Rome a general opinion that if two more tables were added to these ten, they would be perfect, so this belief gave the people opportunity to re-elect the Ten for another year. To this the people willingly agreed, both in order that the Consuls should not be brought back and because they assumed that they could get on without Tribunes, since they themselves were judges in law cases, as has been said above. After the decision to re-elect the Ten, all the nobility bestirred themselves to seek those positions, and among the first was Appius, who used such great courtesy to the populace in asking it that he roused the suspicions of his companions, "for they thought it unnatural that in such great arrogance there should be geniality" (Livy 3. 35). Fearing to act openly against him, they decided to do it artfully, and though he was younger than all the rest, they gave him authority to propose the future Ten to the people, believing that he would keep within the limits set by others in not proposing himself, since it was a thing contrary to custom and disgraceful in Rome. "He, however, turned the obstacle into an opportunity" (*ibid.*) and named himself among the first, to the astonishment and vexation of all the nobles; he then named nine others, such as he preferred. This new choice, made for another year, soon showed the people and the nobility their error. For suddenly Appius "put an end to playing an unnatural part" (*ibid.* 36), and displayed his inborn pride, and in a few days imparted to his companions his own habits. And to terrify the people and the Senate, in place of twelve lictors, he set up a hundred and twenty.

[Appius loses popular support]

Both parties were equally afraid for some days, but ere long the Ten were rousing the hopes of the Senate and oppressing the populace; and if anybody oppressed by one of the Decemvirs appealed to another, he was treated worse in the appeal than in the first sentence. Hence the populace, recognizing its error and full of woe, looked to the nobles for aid "and found hope of liberty in the place from which they had so greatly feared servitude that they had brought the city to its present condition" (*ibid.* 37). This woe of theirs was pleasing to the nobility "since the people themselves, in disgust at their present circumstances, wished for Consuls" (*ibid.*). The end of the year came. The two tables of the laws were finished but not made public. In this the Ten found opportunity for continuing in the magistracy, and they carried on the government with violence and made for themselves satellites among the young nobles, to whom they gave the goods of persons condemned. "Bribed with these gifts, the young men preferred license for themselves rather than liberty for all" (*ibid.*). At this time the Sabines and the Volscians began a war against the Romans. Through fear of that, the Ten were brought to see the weakness of their position, because without the Senate they could not carry on the war, and they believed that if the Senate met they would lose their position. Yet of necessity they resolved on this last plan. When the Senators had assembled, many spoke against the pride of the Ten, and in particular Valerius and Horatius. The authority of the Ten would have been wholly extinguished if the Senate, in hatred of the populace, had not been unwilling to show its authority, thinking that if the Ten laid down the magistracy voluntarily, the Tribunes of the People might not be restored. They determined, then, on war, and went out with two armies, led in part by the said Ten. Appius remained to govern the city. At that time he fell in love with Virginia, and since he wished to take her by force, her father Virginius killed her to free her. Then followed the rebellions in Rome and in the armies, which, uniting with the rest of the Roman populace, went off to Mons Sacer, where they remained until the Ten laid down the magistracy, Tribunes and Consuls were put in office, and Rome was brought back to the form of her ancient freedom.

[*Selfish desires by both the people and the rich*]

We first observe, then, in this account that in Rome the evil of establishing this tyranny came from the same causes as most tyrannies in cities, namely, the too great desire of the people to be free and the too great desire of the nobles to command. And when they do not agree to make a law in freedom's behalf, but one of the parties rushes to support a single person, then tyranny quickly appears. The people and the nobles of Rome agreed to set up the Ten and to set them up with such authority because of the desires of each of the parties, for one hoped to abolish the consular office, the other the tribunate. When they were in office, the plebeians, thinking that Appius had become one of the popular party and was attacking the nobles, turned to favor him. When a people thus brings itself to make this mistake of giving one man authority in order that he may attack those it hates, and that one is shrewd, he always becomes tyrant of that city, because with the aid of the people he undertakes to get rid of the nobility, and he never turns to the oppression of the people until he has got rid of the nobles. By that time, when the people realizes it is in slavery, it has no one with whom to take refuge. This has been the method used by all those who have founded tyrannies in republics. If Appius had used this method, that tyranny of his would have taken on more life and would not have failed so quickly. But he did everything contrary and could not have conducted himself more imprudently, because in order to hold the tyranny, he made himself an enemy to those who had given it to him and could keep it for him, and made himself a friend² to those who had not agreed to give it to him and could not keep it for him; and he lost those who were friendly to him and sought to have as friends those who could not be his friends. Because, though the nobles wish to tyrannize, that part of the nobility that is outside the tyranny is always hostile to the tyrant. He never can entirely win its support because of its great ambition and great avarice, for the tyrant cannot have so much wealth and so many high offices that he can satisfy all of them. So Appius, abandoning the people and taking the side of the nobles, made a very apparent mistake, both for the reasons given above, and because if a thing is to be held with violence, he who forces needs to be more powerful than he who is forced.

[*A wise tyrant secures the people's support*]

From this it results that those tyrants to whom the people are friendly and to whom the rich are hostile are more secure, because the forces supporting their violence are stronger than those supporting that of tyrants to whom the people are hostile and the nobility friendly. With the support of the people, internal forces are enough for preservation, as they were enough for Nabis, tyrant of Sparta; for when all Greece and the Roman people attacked him, he first made himself sure of a few nobles; then with the aid of the friendly populace he defended himself; yet he could not have done so if the people had been his enemies. In that other condition, when a prince has few friends in his city, internal forces are not enough, but he must try to get help from outside. And it needs to be of three sorts: one, hiring foreign satellites, who will guard your person; two, arming the

2. *The textual evidence is for* enemy, *but the sense requires* friend, *which occurs in many editions.*

country people, who will perform the duties that the citizens should perform; three, allying yourself with powerful neighbors who will defend you. He who uses these methods and practices them well, even though he has the populace as his enemy, can in various ways preserve himself. But Appius could not use the method of gaining the country people, since the country and Rome were one and the same; and what he might have done, he did not know how to do; hence he fell when he had hardly begun.

[*Party spirit*]

The Senate and the people made the most serious mistakes in establishing the Decemvirate, because—even though (as I said above in my discussion of the Dictator) those magistrates that set themselves up, not those the people set up, are harmful to liberty—when estab- lishing magistrates the people still need so to act that the magistrates will have to use some caution about becoming wicked. But whereas the people ought to put a guard over magistrates to keep them good, the Romans took it away, making the Decemvirate the only magis- tracy in Rome and annulling all the others, through the Senate's excessive desire (as we said above) to get rid of the Tribunes and the people's desire to get rid of the Consuls. This blinded them so completely that they agreed in such an evil. Indeed, as King Ferdi- nand said, men often act like some small birds of prey, who so strongly desire to catch their victims, as Nature urges them to do, that they do not see above them another larger bird that will kill them.

From this discussion, then, you can learn, as I stated at the beginning, the Roman people's mistake, if it wished to save its liberty, and Appius' mistakes, if he wished to hold the tyranny.

CHAPTER 41. TO LEAP FROM HUMILITY TO PRIDE, FROM MERCY TO CRUELTY, WITHOUT PROPER PAUSES MIDWAY, IS IMPRUDENT AND UNPROFITABLE

[*More on the Decemvirate*]

Among Appius' foolish proceedings, if he wished to maintain his tyranny, of no little importance was his leaping too quickly from one attitude of mind to another. Because his cleverness in deceiving the people, by pretending to be a man with popular sympathies, was well handled; also well handled were his proceedings for getting the Ten chosen a second time; also well handled was his boldness in setting himself up contrary to the expectation of the nobility; well handled was his choice of associates adapted to his purpose. But not at all well handled, when he had done these things, was his sudden change of nature, as I say above, by which he showed himself an enemy rather than a friend to the people; instead of courteous, proud; instead of easy to deal with, difficult; and he changed so quickly that, since he offered no excuse, no man could avoid seeing the falsity of his purpose. Because he who has for a while appeared good but intends, for his own purposes, to become bad, ought to do so with proper pauses midway; and in such a way to govern himself according to the circumstances that before your changed nature deprives you of your old support, it has given you so much that is new that you do not bring about any lessening of your authority. Otherwise, since you are revealed and without friends, you fall.

CHAPTER 42. HOW EASILY MEN CAN BE BRIBED

[*Illustrated by the Decemvirate*]

We note also in this affair of the Decemvirate how easily men are bribed and brought to assume a wholly different nature, however good and well brought up they may have been, when we observe how the group of young men that Appius chose to have around him grew friendly to tyranny because of a little profit they gained, and how Quintus Fabius,[1] one of the number of the second Ten, though a very good man, was blinded by a little ambition and influenced by Appius' wickedness, so that his good morals changed to utterly bad ones and he became like the tyrant. This when well examined will make the legislators of republics and kingdoms the more eager to bridle human appetites and to take from them every hope of erring without punishment.

1. *Livy 3. 41–42, 58.*

CHAPTER 43. THOSE WHO FIGHT FOR
THEIR OWN GLORY ARE GOOD AND FAITH﹐
FUL SOLDIERS

[*Against mercenary soldiers*]

One can also observe, in the discussion above, how much differ﹐
ence there is between an army that is satisfied and fights for its own
glory and an army that is ill disposed and fights for some leader's
ambition. Whereas the Roman armies were accustomed to be vic﹐
torious under the Consuls, under the Decemvirs they always lost.[1]
From this instance one can learn, in part, why mercenary soldiers are
useless, having no other reason that holds them firm than the little
pay you give them. This reason is not and cannot be enough to
make them faithful or so much your friends that they are willing to
die for you. Because in these armies where there is no affection for
him in whose behalf they fight, so that they do not become his
partisans, there never can be enough military vigor to resist an enemy
who has a little of that vigor. And because this love and this eager﹐
ness to excel cannot spring up in others than your own subjects, it is
necessary, if you expect to keep your position, if you expect to
maintain a republic or a kingdom, to provide yourself an army of
your own subjects, as we see they all have done who have gained
great advantages with their armies. The Roman armies under the
Ten had the same ability, yet because they did not have the same
inclination, they did not get their usual results. But as soon as the
magistracy of the Ten was wiped out and the Romans again fought
as free men, the same courage returned to them; in consequence their
undertakings had a successful outcome, according to their old habit.[2]

1. Livy 3. 41–42.
2. Livy 3. 61–63, 66–70.

CHAPTER 44. A MULTITUDE WITHOUT A HEAD IS HELPLESS; ONE SHOULD NOT FIRST MAKE THREATS AND THEN ASK AUTHORITY

[Conclusions from the Decemvirate]

The Roman populace, because of the incident of Virginia, had gone armed to Mons Sacer. The Senate sent its ambassadors to ask under what authority they had abandoned their officers and gone to the Mount. And so much was the authority of the Senate respected, that, since the people did not have leaders among them, nobody had the courage to answer. And Titus Livius says that they did not lack matter for answering but lacked somebody to give the answer. This situation shows exactly the helplessness of a multitude without a head.

This trouble was understood by Virginius, and according to his plan they set up twenty Military Tribunes to be their heads for answering and for dealing with the Senate. And when they asked that Valerius and Horatius should be sent, so that they could tell them what they wanted, these two did not wish to go if the Ten did not first lay down their magistracy. And when they arrived at the Mount where the populace was, they were asked to consent that Tribunes of the People should be set up, that there should be appeal to the people from every magistrate, and that all the Ten should be given to them, because they intended to burn them alive. Valerius and Horatius commended their first requirements. They blamed the last one as pitiless, saying: "You condemn cruelty; into cruelty you rush" (Livy 3. 53); and they advised them to omit making mention of the Ten and to wait until they got back their authority and their power; then they would not lack means for satisfying themselves.[1]

Here it is plain how much folly and how little prudence there is in asking a thing and saying first: I wish to do such an evil with it. One should not show one's mind but try to get one's wish just the same, because it is enough to ask a man for his weapons without saying: I wish to kill you with them. For when you have the weapons in your hands you can satisfy your desire.

1. *Livy 3. 44-53.*

CHAPTER 45. NOT TO KEEP A LAW THAT HAS BEEN MADE SETS A BAD EXAMPLE, ESPECIALLY FOR ITS AUTHOR. TO DO EVERY DAY NEW AND FRESH INJURIES IN A CITY IS VERY INJURIOUS TO A RULER

[*Appeal denied to Appius Claudius*]

When the agreement had been made and Rome was brought back to her old form, Virginius cited Appius before the people to defend his case.[1] He appeared accompanied by many nobles; Virginius ordered that he be put in prison. Appius cried out in appeal to the people. Virginius said he was not worthy to have that right of appeal which he had destroyed and to have as defender the people he had attacked. Appius replied that they ought not to violate that right which they had been so eager to enact. Nevertheless he was put in prison, and before the day of trial he killed himself. And though the wicked life of Appius deserved the utmost punishment, nonetheless to violate law was not in accord with good government, and so much the more when the law violated had just been made. For I do not think there is a thing that sets a worse example in a republic than to make a law and not keep it, and so much the more when it is not kept by him who has made it.

[*Savonarola failed to keep his own law*]

After 1494 Florence reorganized her government with the aid of Frate Girolamo Savonarola, whose writings show his learning, his prudence, and his mental power.[2] Among other enactments to give the citizens security, he got a law passed permitting appeal to the people from the sentences of the Eight and the Signory in political cases. This law he urged a long time and gained with very great

---

1. Livy 3. 54–58.
2. *This passage shows Machiavelli's respect for Savonarola's intellectual powers. Not only does he here approve the law giving the right of appeal, but in his* DISCOURSE ON REMODELING THE GOVERNMENT OF FLORENCE *he suggests the revival of Savonarola's great council of citizens. Probably the Frate's political writings were acceptable to him (Gilbert,* MACHIAVELLI, THE PRINCE AND OTHER WORKS, *Chicago, 1941, Index; J. H. Whitfield, "Savonarola and the Purpose of The Prince,"* Modern Language Review, XLIV, 1949, 44–59).

difficulty; but when, a short time after its confirmation, five citizens condemned to death by the Signory on behalf of the government attempted to appeal, they were not permitted to do so; thus the law was not observed. This took away more of the Frate's influence than any other event, because the right of appeal, if valuable, should have been observed; if it was not valuable, he should not have had it enacted. This happening was the more noticed inasmuch as the Frate, in all the sermons he delivered after this law was broken, never either condemned those who broke it or excused them; for he was unwilling to condemn their action, which was to his advantage, and excuse it he could not. This conduct, by revealing his ambitious and partisan spirit, took influence away from him and brought him much censure.

[*Subjects not to be made desperate*]

The harm done by a government is also very great when every day in the minds of your[3] citizens it renews and refreshes animosities by means of new injuries done to this one and that one, as happened in Rome after the Decemvirate. Because all the Ten and other citizens at different times were accused and condemned, to such an extent that there was the greatest terror in all the nobility, who judged that such condemnations would not end until all the nobility were destroyed. And it would have produced great trouble in that city it Marcus Duellius the Tribune had not provided against it, for he made an edict that for a year no one would be permitted to cite or accuse any Roman citizen; this reassured all the nobility. Here we see how damaging it is to a republic or to a prince to keep the minds of subjects uncertain and fearful with continual penalties and attacks. And without doubt there is no method more destructive, because men who suspect that they are going to suffer something bad take any means to make themselves safe in their peril and become more audacious and less cautious about attempting revolution. Therefore it is necessary either not to injure anybody or to inflict the injuries at once, and then to reassure men and give them opportunity to calm and settle their spirits.

3. *Here, as often in* THE PRINCE, *Machiavelli shifts to the second person, as though ad-dressing directly the rulers, whether of princedom or republic, mentioned below.*

CHAPTER 46. MEN CLIMB FROM ONE AMBI-TION TO ANOTHER; FIRST THEY TRY NOT TO GET HURT, THEN THEY HURT OTHERS

[*When men try to escape fear, they make others fear*]

After the Roman people had recovered their liberty and returned to their earlier level of strength, and indeed had gained a higher level, inasmuch as many new laws were made in confirmation of their power, it is reasonable that Rome would have a little rest. Neverthe-less, experience shows the opposite, for every day new quarrels and new discords arose there. Because Titus Livius very prudently sets forth the reason why this happened,[1] I think it not other than fitting to report exactly the words in which he says that always either the people or the nobility acted proudly when the other humbled itself; when the populace was quiet within its bounds, the young nobles wronged it, and the Tribunes could offer few remedies because they too were outraged. The nobility, on the other side, though they thought their young men too violent, nevertheless preferred that if bounds were to be overstepped, the overstepping should be by their men and not by the populace. Thus desire for defending its liberty made each party try to become strong enough to tyrannize over the other. For the law of these matters is that when men try to escape fear, they make others fear, and the injury they push away from them-selves they lay on others, as if it were necessary either to harm or to be harmed.

[*Citizens should not be allowed to gain influence dangerous to the free-dom of their city*]

From this you can see one way among others in which republics go to pieces, and in what way men climb from one ambition to another, and how a saying Sallust puts in the mouth of Caesar is quite true: "All instances of evil-doing arise from good beginnings." The first endeavor, as has been said above, of those citizens in a republic who act through ambition is to make it impossible for them-selves to be harmed not merely by private persons but also not even by the magistrates. They endeavor, in order to accomplish this, to make friendships; and these they gain in ways apparently honorable,

1. Livy 3. 65.

either by aiding men with money or by protecting them from the powerful; because this conduct seems honorable, it easily deceives everybody; hence no one uses any remedy against it. So, working on without hindrance, an ambitious man becomes so powerful that private citizens are afraid of him, and the magistrates regard him with deference.² When he has climbed to this level, if there has not already been some opposition to his greatness, he is in a position such that to attempt to oppose him is very dangerous, for the reasons I gave above on the danger of opposing a peril that has already greatly increased in a city.³ Thus the business comes to such a position that you must either try to annul it at the risk of sudden ruin or, by letting it go on, enter into evident slavery, if death or some accident does not liberate you. Because if it comes to the aforesaid pass, when the citizens and the magistrates are afraid of offending the ambitious man and his friends, he then does not have to take much trouble to make them pronounce judgment and do injury at his will. Hence a republic ought to have among its laws this: that the citizens are to be watched so that they cannot under cover of good do evil and so that they gain only such popularity as advances and does not harm liberty—something we shall discuss in its place.⁴

2. From this sentence on, Machiavelli speaks of the ambitious man in the singular.
3. DISCOURSES 1. 33, 37 end.
4. DISCOURSES 3. 28.

CHAPTER 47. HOWEVER MUCH MEN ARE DECEIVED IN GENERALITIES, THEY ARE NOT DECEIVED IN PARTICULARS

[*The Roman people would not elect incompetent officials*]

When the Roman people, as was said above,¹ became disgusted with the name of Consul and wished that men of the people should be made Consuls or that consular authority should be lessened, the nobility, in order not to blemish that authority with the one thing or with the other, took a middle course, and consented that there should be set up four Tribunes with consular power, who might be plebeians as well as nobles.² The populace was satisfied with this, since it thought it was getting rid of the consulate and having its

1. Chap. 39.
2. Livy 3. 9; 4. 1–6.

own part in this very high office. A noteworthy event resulted from this, for when in the choice of these Tribunes the Roman people were permitted to choose plebeians entirely, they chose only nobles. On this Titus Livius writes thus: "These elections by their outcome teach that there is one sort of spirit in contentions over liberty and honor, and another after strife has been laid aside, so that the judgment is unspoiled" (4. 6). And examining the reason for this, I believe it to be that in general things men deceive themselves a great deal, in specific things not so much. In general the Roman populace be- lieved that they deserved the consulate, since their part in the city was more important, for they were exposed to more danger in wars and they with their sinews kept Rome free and made her powerful. So feeling sure, as I have said, that this desire of theirs was reasonable, they determined to get this power no matter how. But when they had to judge men of their own class individually, they recognized their weakness and decided that no one of them deserved what they believed all of them together deserved. Hence, as ashamed of them, they turned to those who did deserve high office. Being rightly astonished at this decision, Titus Livius writes: "Such modesty, equity and nobility of spirit, where now will you find it in one man? which then the whole people possessed" (4. 6).

[Competence demanded in Capua]

In confirmation of this, I cite another notable instance, which occurred in Capua after Hannibal defeated the Romans at Cannae.[3] Though all Italy was upset by this defeat, Capua still went on with her quarrels, caused by the hate between the Senate and the people. Pacuvius Calanus was then in the supreme magistracy; realizing the city's peril on account of her quarrels, he planned to use his position to reconcile the populace with the nobility. Having formed his plan, he called the Senate together and told them of the popular hatred against them and of their danger that the populace would kill them and give the city to Hannibal, since the Roman state was in distress. Then he added that if they would put him in charge of the affair, he would manage to unite the two parties. He planned to lock the Senators into the Palace and, by giving the people power to punish them, to save them. To his opinion they yielded. So he

3. Livy 23. 2-4.

assembled the populace, after shutting up the Senate in the Palace. He told the assembly that the time had come when they could put down the pride of the nobility and revenge the injuries they had received from them, since they were all shut up under his charge. But because he believed the people would not wish their city to be left without government, they needed, if they were going to kill the old Senators, to choose new ones. Meanwhile he would put the names of all the Senators in a bag and draw them out before the assembly. Those drawn out should be put to death in order, as soon as their successors were chosen. When he drew out the first, a great uproar was raised at the man's name; he was called proud, cruel, and arrogant. Yet on Pacuvius asking that his successor be chosen, all the assembly was quiet. Then after some delay one of the populace was named; at his name one man whistled, one laughed, one spoke ill of him in one way and another in another. And so on and on, all those named were judged unworthy of senatorial rank. Then Pacuvius, using the opportunity, said: "Since you judge that this city is badly off without a Senate, and you do not agree in providing successors for the old Senators, I think you might well reconcile yourselves with them, because the fear which the Senators have felt has humbled them so much that you will find in them the kindness you are searching for elsewhere." And since they agreed to this, union with the senatorial order followed; thus the illusion they were under was revealed when they were forced to come to particulars. Besides this, the people deceive themselves in judging things in general and the events connected with them, but when later these things are individually known, they are not so deceived.

[*Agitators when put in office become conservative*]

After 1494, the chief men of Florence had been driven from the city, and there was no government there, but rather a sort of ambitious license, and public matters were going from bad to worse. Whereupon many of the popular party, seeing the ruin of the city and not finding any other cause for it, charged it to the ambition of some powerful persons who were feeding the troubles in order to set up a government according to their will and to take away the people's liberty. And such men stood around in the arcades and the squares speaking ill of many citizens and threatening that if ever they became Signors, they would reveal the rulers' trickery and punish them. It happens often that such a person rises to the supreme magistracy; and when he has climbed to that place and sees things nearer at hand, he realizes where the troubles come from and the dangers that impend and the difficulty of remedying them. And having seen how the times and not men cause the trouble, he becomes instantly of another mind and of another sort, because the knowledge of particular things destroys his belief in such trickery as he had taken for granted when considering things generally. Hence those who heard him speak earlier when he was a private citizen, and then see him sit quiet in the supreme magistracy, believe that the change has come not from a truer knowledge of affairs, but because he has been misled and bribed by the great. And since this has happened to many men and at many times, the people formed the proverb: "These fellows have one mind in the Public Square and another in the Palace."

Considering, then, all that has been presented, we see that though the people may be deceived by a generality, they quickly and easily open their eyes when anyone finds a method that will make them descend to particulars, as Pacuvius did in Capua and the Senate in Rome.[4]

[A prudent man will respect popular judgment of particulars]

I believe also that we may grant that a prudent man need not avoid the popular judgment in particular things about the distribution of offices and dignities, because in this alone the people do not deceive themselves, and if sometimes they are deceived, this happens so seldom that more often a few men who have to make such distributions will be deceived. Nor does it seem superfluous to show, in the following chapter, the method the Senate used for tricking the people in its distributions.

4. As appears in the next DISCOURSE.

CHAPTER 48. HE WHO WISHES THAT A MAGISTRACY SHOULD NOT BE GIVEN TO A MAN OF LOW RANK OR TO A WICKED MAN, SHOULD HAVE IT ASKED FOR EITHER BY ONE OF TOO LOW RANK AND TOO WICKED OR BY ONE OF TOO HIGH RANK AND TOO GOOD

When the Senate feared that Tribunes with consular power would be chosen from the plebeians, they used one of two ways: either they had the office asked for by the men of highest repute in Rome; or actually, by suitable means, they bribed some worthless plebeians of very low rank to ask for it along with the plebeians of better quality who ordinarily asked for it. This last method made the populace ashamed to give it; the first made them ashamed to accept it.[1] All this relates to the preceding discussion, in which it is shown that the people, if it is deceived about generalities, is not deceived about particulars.

1. *Livy* 4. 56, 57.

CHAPTER 49. IF CITIES OF FREE ORIGIN, SUCH AS ROME, WITH DIFFICULTY FIND LAWS THAT WILL PRESERVE THEM, CITIES OF ORIGIN IMMEDIATELY SERVILE HAVE SLIGHT POSSIBILITY FOR DOING SO

How difficult it is, in founding a republic, to provide all the laws that will keep her free, the course of the Roman republic very well shows. Notwithstanding the many laws laid down first by Romulus, then by Numa, by Tullus Hostilius and Servius, and last by the Ten Citizens chosen for such work, nevertheless in the operation of that city new necessities were always appearing; it was therefore necessary to devise new laws, as happened when they devised the Censors. Their office is one of the precautions that helped Rome to keep free, as long as she lived in freedom, because, becoming arbiters of the morals of Rome, the Censors were a power-ful reason why she was slower in growing corrupt. When instituting that office the Romans did, indeed, make a mistake, first giving it a five-year term; yet before long Mamercus the Dictator prudently remedied this by a new law reducing that magistracy to eighteen months.[1] The Censors who were then functioning took this change so badly that they excluded Mamercus from the Senate—an act much blamed both by the populace and by the Fathers. And because Livy's *History* does not show that Mamercus could protect himself against it, either the Historian must be inadequate or the Roman laws on this subject were not good; because it is not right for a republic to be so organized that a citizen can without any recourse be injured for promulgating a law in harmony with free government.

But going back to the beginning of this discussion, I say that from the introduction of this new office one must judge that if it is difficult for cities of free origin, which like Rome have ruled themselves, to find laws which will keep them free, we cannot wonder that it is not merely difficult but impossible for cities of origin immediately servile to organize themselves in such a way that they can live in peace and according to law.

[*Florence never a true republic*]

This is evidently true of the city of Florence. Since at her origin she was subject to Roman authority and had always lived under the control of others, she remained for a time humble, without planning for herself. Then, when there came a chance for taking breath, she undertook to make her own laws; these, being mingled with old ones that were bad, could not be good. And so she has gone on governing herself for the two hundred years for which there are trustworthy records, without ever having had a government because of which she could truly be called a republic. Difficulties like hers have always existed for all those cities whose beginnings were like hers. And though many times, through free and public votes, full power to reform her has been given to a few citizens, nevertheless they have never organized her for the common benefit, but always for the advantage of their own party; this has caused not order but greater disorder in that city.

1. *Livy 4. 8, 24.*

[*In Florence no court would punish the powerful*]

And to come to some particular instances, I say that one of the chief things that must be done by the founder of a republic is to look closely at the sort of men into whose hands he puts the power of death over the citizens. This was well arranged in Rome, because it was easy to appeal to the people in normal conditions, and if some/ thing important did happen which made deferred action as a result of appeal dangerous, they had as a resort the Dictator, who acted at once; to this remedy they never resorted except in necessity. But in Florence and other cities that originated in the way she did, as slaves, this authority was lodged in a foreigner, who, being sent by the prince, performed this duty. Then when they became free, they kept up this power in a foreigner, whom they called the Captain. Since he could easily be bribed by powerful citizens, this was a very harmful method. But later, when it was changed because of the change in governments, they set up eight citizens to carry out the duty of the Captain. This method went from bad to worse, for the reasons that have been given at other times; the few were always the servants of the few and of the more powerful.

[*In Venice powerful malefactors do not escape*]

From this the city of Venice has protected herself, for she has ten citizens who, without appeal, are empowered to punish any citizen. Yet because they might not be enough to punish the powerful, though they had authority for it, they have set up there the Council of Forty, and beyond that have decided that the Council of the *Pregai*, which is their greatest council, should have power to punish them. Hence, if an accuser is not lacking, there is no lack of a judge to keep powerful men in check.

Thus in Rome, organized by herself and by so many prudent men, there came up every day new reasons making necessary new laws in behalf of free government; it is no wonder, then, if in cities with more confused beginnings so many difficulties appear that they never can be put right again.

CHAPTER 50. ONE COUNCIL OR ONE MAGIS- TRACY OUGHT NOT TO BE ABLE TO BRING CITY BUSINESS TO A STANDSTILL

The Consuls in Rome were Titus Quintius Cincinnatus and Gneus Julius Mentus, who, being at variance, brought to a standstill all the business of that republic.[1] The Senate, seeing this, urged them to set up a Dictator, in order to do what they, because of their discords, could not do. But the Consuls, disagreeing in everything else, were in agreement on one matter, namely, in refusing to set up a Dictator. Hence the Senate, not having any other remedy, sought the aid of the Tribunes, who, through the authority of the Senate, compelled the Consuls to obey.

Here we note, first, the value of the tribunate, which was useful in checking not merely the ambition that the powerful exercised against the populace, but also that which they exercised among themselves; second, that it never should be lawful in a city for a few to impede decisions about things that according to law are needed for maintaining the republic. For the sake of example, if you give power to a Consul to make a distribution of offices and of property or to a magistracy to attend to a piece of business, you must either lay necessity on him to do it in any case, or arrange that, if he refuses, some other has the power and duty to do it. Otherwise, this method is defective and dangerous, as it evidently would have been in Rome, if they could not have opposed to the stubbornness of those Consuls the authority of the Tribunes.

[*Venetian wisdom*]

In the Venetian republic the Great Council distributes the offices and places of profit. It happened sometimes that that body, because of anger or some false conviction, did not choose successors to the magistrates of the city and to those who administered their empire abroad. Such failure was very dangerous, because at once both the subject towns and the city itself lacked their lawful judges; nor was it possible to obtain anything if the membership of that Council was not either appeased or undeceived. And this difficulty would have brought that city to a bad condition if it had not been

1. *Livy* 4. 26.

provided for by prudent citizens, who, taking a good opportunity, made a law that all the magistracies that are or may be, inside or outside the city, never can be vacant except when their substitutes and successors are chosen. And so there was taken from that Council the possibility that, with danger to the republic, it could put a stop to public business.

CHAPTER 51. A PRINCE OR A REPUBLIC OUGHT TO APPEAR TO DO THROUGH LIBERALITY ANY ACTION COMPELLED BY NECESSITY

Prudent men always and in all their actions win credit from circumstances, even though necessity forces them to such acts in any case. Such prudence was well used by the Roman Senate when it decided to give government pay to soldiers in the army, who had always before served at their own expense.[1] The Senate saw that they could not carry on a long war under such a system, which prevented their besieging towns and sending their armies to a distance. Yet since they judged that they needed the possibility of doing both, they determined that stipends should be given; but they so did it that an action to which necessity drove them won them gratitude. This gift was so acceptable that Rome was turned upside down with pleasure; the populace looked on it as a great benefit, such as they never hoped to have and which of themselves they never would have asked. And though the Tribunes made an effort to cancel this gratitude, showing that the measure burdened rather than relieved the populace—since this money had to be paid from taxes—yet they could not keep the populace from accepting it. The Senate also increased the benefit through their method of assigning the taxes, for the more annoying and heavier ones were laid on the nobility, and these were the first that were paid.

1. *Livy* 4. 59, 60.

CHAPTER 52. TO REPRESS THE ARROGANCE OF ONE WHO IS TRYING TO RISE TO SUPREME POWER IN A REPUBLIC, THERE IS NO MORE SECURE AND LESS DANGEROUS METHOD THAN TO GET AHEAD OF HIM ON THOSE ROADS BY WHICH HE IS MOVING TOWARD THAT POWER

The preceding discussion shows how much credit the nobility gained with the populace under the appearance of benefiting them through the pay they decreed and the manner of levying the tax. If the nobility had held to that method, all dissension would have been removed from that city, and the Tribunes would have been deprived of the credit they had with the populace, and consequently of their power.

[*How Cosimo de' Medici gained power*]

And truly in a republic, and especially in one that is corrupt, the ambition of any citizen cannot be opposed with a better method— less dangerous and easier—than by taking ahead of him those roads by which he evidently is moving toward the position he wants. This method, if it had been used against Cosimo de' Medici, would have been a much better choice for his adversaries than to drive him from Florence, because if those citizens who were his rivals had taken up his scheme of befriending the people, they would have succeeded without uproar and without violence in taking out of his hands the weapons he most relied on.

[*Methods open to Piero Soderini for keeping his power*]

Piero Soderini gained himself a reputation in the city of Florence simply by appearing to befriend the common people; this gave him among the common people a reputation as a lover of the city's liberty. Those citizens who envied his greatness, would unquestionably have found it easier, much more honorable, less dangerous and less harmful to the republic to adopt ahead of him those methods by which he made himself prominent than to try to oppose him, so that with his fall all that was left of the republic would fall. Because it they had seized from his hands those weapons with which he made himself strong (as they could easily have done), they could have opposed him in all the councils and all public deliberations without exciting suspicion and without any scruples. Someone may rejoin that if the citizens who hated Piero were mistaken in not adopting ahead of him those methods through which he was gaining himself reputation with the people, Piero also was mistaken not to adopt in advance those methods through which his opponents endangered him. But to that I should reply that Piero deserves excuse because it was difficult for him to do so, and because their ways were not honorable for him; they damaged him by supporting the Medici; yet if he had given such support, they would have attacked him for it and in the end ruined him.[1] By no possibility, then, could Piero honorably adopt that plan because he could not keep a good reputa tion if he destroyed that liberty over which he had been stationed as guard. Besides, since such support could not be given secretly and at one stroke, it would have been very dangerous for Piero, because if ever he had been exposed as friendly to the Medici, the people would have suspected and hated him. Thence there would have arisen for his enemies much better opportunity for crushing him than they had before.

[*The ingenious plan of Cicero ruined him*]

As to every plan, therefore, men should consider its defects and dangers and not accept it when there is in it more danger than value, even though they have been advised that it is in harmony with their intention. Because, if they do otherwise, in this situation the same thing may happen to them as happened to Cicero, who, by trying to get advantages away from Marc Antony, increased them for him. After Marc Antony had been judged an enemy by the Senate and had gathered a great army in large part from the soldiers who had been following the party of Caesar, Cicero, in order to get those soldiers away from him, encouraged the Senate to give authority to Octavian and to send him with Irtius and Pansa, the Consuls, against Marc Antony; Cicero asserted that as soon as the soldiers who followed Marc Antony heard the name of Octavian, Caesar's nephew, who was calling himself by the name of Caesar, they would leave the former and adhere to the latter; Marc Antony, thus stripped

1. *His enemies would have used any concessions to the Medici to show that Piero was a traitor to the cause of freedom.*

of support, would easily be crushed. But the affair came out altogether differently, for Marc Antony won Octavian over, and he,
leaving Cicero and the Senate, sided with Antony. That was the
complete destruction of the nobles' party. It should have been easy
to conjecture this, and they should not have believed what Cicero
thought certain, but they should have taken into account that name
which with such glory had annihilated its enemies and gained for
itself the position of prince in Rome, nor should they have believed
that from his heirs or supporters they could ever have anything in
harmony with the name of freedom.

CHAPTER 53. THE POPULACE, DECEIVED BY A FALSE APPEARANCE OF GOOD THINGS, MANY TIMES DECREES ITS OWN RUIN, AND GREAT HOPES AND MIGHTY PROMISES EASILY MOVE IT

When the city of the Veientians was taken,[1] the Roman people
formed the opinion that it would profit the city of Rome for half of
the Romans to go to live at Veii, the argument being that since it was
a city rich in land, full of buildings, and near Rome, half of the
Roman citizens could be enriched; yet because of the nearness of its
site, no public activity would be hindered. This proposal appeared
to the Senate and to the wiser Romans so unprofitable and so injurious that they freely said they were ready to suffer death rather than
agree to such a decision. Hence when this matter came to debate,
the populace grew so angry with the Senate that the affair would
have come to weapons and bloodshed if the Senate had not made
itself a shield of some old and respected citizens, esteem for whom
restrained the populace from going further with its arrogance.

Here two things are to be noted. The first is that the people,
deceived by a false image of good, many times desire their own ruin.
And if somebody in whom they have faith does not convince them
that what they want is bad and explain what is good, countless
dangers and losses come upon the republic. And when chance
causes the people to have faith in no one, as sometimes happens, since
they have been deceived in the past both by things and by men, of

1. *Livy* 5. 24, 25, 51.

necessity the republic is ruined. Dante says about this, in his discussion *On Monarchy*, that the populace many times shouts: "Long live its own death," and "Down with its own life."[2] The result of this lack of belief is that sometimes good decisions are not made in republics. Thus we said above of the Venetians that, when assailed by so many enemies, they could not adopt the plan of winning anybody's support by restoring what they had taken from other states (for the sake of which the war was begun and the league of princes made against them) before ruin came.

[*The populace likes courageous decisions*]

Therefore, considering when it is easy and when it is hard to get a people to accept something, one can make this distinction: either what you are trying to persuade them of shows on its surface gain or loss; or the decision to be made seems courageous or cowardly. When in a plan put before the people gain is apparent, even though loss be hidden beneath, and when it seems courageous, even though the ruin of the republic be hidden beneath, always the multitude is easily persuaded to approve. Likewise the multitude is always with difficulty persuaded to accept proposals in which either cowardice or loss appears, even if beneath them be hidden safety and gain.

[*Roman instances*]

What I have said is confirmed by countless instances, Roman and foreign, ancient and modern. From this came the bad opinion that grew up in Rome about Fabius Maximus,[3] who could not persuade the Roman people that it would be of benefit to the republic to proceed slowly in their war against Hannibal and to endure his invasion without engaging in battle, because the people thought his view cowardly and did not see its actual value; nor did Fabius have reasons sufficient to convince them. But by courageous opinions the people are badly blinded. The Roman people made their mistake of giving Fabius's Master of the Horse authority to engage in battle even though Fabius did not approve; through that authority the Roman army was at the point of defeat, when Fabius' prudence applied a remedy. Yet this experience was not enough for them; they made Varro Consul, not because of any merits of his but because in all

2. *Actually from* CONVIVIO *1. 11. 54.*
3. *Livy 22. 25–49.*

the squares and public places in Rome he promised to defeat Hanni⁄
bal whenever he received authority. From this came the battle and
defeat of Cannae and almost the ruin of Rome.

I shall bring up here still another instance from Rome.[4] Hanni⁄
bal, during eight or ten years in Italy, had slaughtered Romans
throughout the land. Then into the Senate came Marcus Centenius
Penula, a man of very low degree (though nevertheless he had held
some rank in the army) who promised that if they would give him
authority to raise an army of volunteers wherever he chose in Italy,
he would in a short time give them Hannibal, captive or dead. The
Senate thought his request rash. Nevertheless, they decided that if
they refused him and his offer were then known among the people,
some disturbance might result, and some hatred and ill feeling against
the senatorial order; hence they granted it to him, choosing rather to
put in danger all those who followed him than to excite new anger
in the people, who, as they knew, would be likely to accept such a
suggestion and could be dissuaded from it with difficulty. That
man, then, with an undisciplined and disorderly multitude attacked
Hannibal, and no sooner did he come to the encounter than with all
his followers he was routed and killed.

[A Greek instance]

In Greece, in the city of Athens, never could Nicias, a very
influential and prudent man, persuade the people that it was unwise
to attack Sicily; yet when that decision was made against the opinion
of the wise, the total ruin of Athens resulted. Scipio, becoming
Consul and applying for the province of Africa,[5] promised the total
ruin of Carthage. When, on the advice of Fabius Maximus, the
Senate did not agree, Scipio threatened to present it in the popular
assembly, since he very well knew how greatly plans of that kind
appeal to the multitude.

[A Florentine instance]

I can give pertinent instances from our city. Messer Ercole
Bentivogli, commander of the Florentine soldiers, along with An⁄
tonio Giacomini, after they had defeated Bartolommeo d'Alviano at
San Vincenti, besieged Pisa. This undertaking was resolved on by

4. Livy 25. 19.
5. Livy 28. 40–45.

the people after mighty promises by Messer Ercole, though many wise citizens opposed it. Still they had no way to prevent it, driven by the general determination founded on the mighty promises of the commander.

[*Mighty enterprises ruin republics and individuals; Giacomini*]

I say, then, that there is no easier way to cause the fall of a republic where the people have authority than to get it into mighty enterprises, because where the people are of any influence, such enterprises will always be approved; and against them those of another opinion will have no recourse. But if the ruin of the city results, there also results—and more often—the ruin of the citizen put at the head of such an undertaking, because after the people have counted on victory, and loss comes, they accuse neither Fortune nor the weakness of him who managed it, but his wickedness and ignorance; almost every time they inflict on him death or prison or exile, as happened to countless Carthaginian generals and many Athenians. Nor are any victories the man has gained in the past of any avail, because by the present loss they all are canceled. Thus it happened to our Antonio Giaco-mini, who, not having taken Pisa (which the people counted on and he promised) came into such popular disfavor that, in spite of his countless good works in the past, he lived rather through the humani-ty of those who held authority over him than through any argument that would protect him from the people.

CHAPTER 54. THE GREAT POWER OF AN INFLUENTIAL MAN TO CHECK AN IN-CENSED MULTITUDE

The second thing of note in the passage discussed in the preceding chapter is that nothing is so suited to check an incensed multitude as their respect for some man of influence and standing who opposes them. Not without reason does Virgil say: "Then if they see some man weighty in his piety and his high qualities, they stand silent and with open ears" (*Aeneid* 1. 151–152). Therefore he who commands an army or he who is in a city where there is a riot should appear in public at such a time with the utmost elegance and dignity, putting on the ensigns of his rank, to make himself more respected.

[*The Bishop of Volterra and a Florentine mob*]

A few years ago Florence was divided into two factions, the Fratesca and the Arrabbiata, as they were called. And when there was a fight, the Fratesca were defeated. Among them was Pago-lantonio Soderini, a citizen of high repute in those times. During the riots, the people went armed to his house to plunder it. But Messer Francesco his brother, then Bishop of Volterra and today Cardinal, chanced to be in the house; as soon as he heard the noise and saw the crowd, he put on his most dignified garments, with the Bishop's rochet over them, met those armed men, and with his aspect and his words stopped them. All through the city this act was for many days talked of and praised. I conclude, then, that there is no more reliable or more necessary means for checking an incensed multitude than the presence of a man whose aspect makes him appear worthy of veneration and who is worthy of it.

[*The conclusion from this and the preceding* DISCOURSE]

We see, then, turning to the passage mentioned above,[1] how stubbornly the Roman populace took up that idea of going to Veii, judging it profitable, and not recognizing the harm underneath. Their attempt caused much disorder and would have caused re-bellion if the Senate by means of influential men, full of dignity, had not checked their fury.

1. *Livy* 5. 24, 25, 51.

CHAPTER 55. PUBLIC AFFAIRS ARE EASILY MANAGED IN A CITY WHERE THE POPU-LACE IS NOT CORRUPT. WHERE THERE IS EQUALITY A PRINCEDOM CANNOT BE ESTABLISHED; WHERE THERE IS NONE, A REPUBLIC CANNOT BE ESTABLISHED

[*Roman honesty*]

Though I have already discussed at length what is to be hoped and feared from corrupt cities, nevertheless it is not apart from my subject to consider the Senate's decision about Camillus' vow to give Apollo a tenth part of the Veientian spoils.[1] Since these spoils

1. *Livy* 5. 23, 25.

had gone into the hands of the Roman people, and there was no way to reckon the accounts, the Senate decreed that each man should turn over to the government the tenth part of what he had seized. Though the Senate did not put that decree into effect but took another method and in a different way satisfied Apollo by atoning for the populace, nonetheless such a decision shows how much the Senate trusted in the people's goodness, judging that nobody would fail to present exactly what the edict required. And on the other side, we see that the populace did not think of defrauding the edict in any amount by giving less than was due, but did think of liberating itself from the tax by showing open indignation. This instance, with many others presented above, shows how much goodness and how much religion that people possessed and how much good was to be expected from it.

[Social honesty in Germany]

Truly, where this goodness does not exist, nothing good can be expected, as nothing good can be expected in regions that in our times are evidently corrupt, as is Italy above all, though in such corruption France and Spain have their share. If in those countries fewer disorders appear than we see daily in Italy, the cause is not so much the goodness of the people—which for the most part no longer exists—as that they have a king who keeps them united, not merely through his ability but also through the still unruined organization of those kingdoms. In Germany this goodness and this religion are still important among the people. These qualities enable many republics to exist there in freedom and to observe their laws so well that nobody outside or inside the cities dares to try to master them. How true it is that a large part of this ancient goodness still reigns there, I wish to show by an example like that mentioned above of the Senate and the Roman people. These German republics, when they need to spend a quantity of money on the public account, have the magistrates or councils in charge assess all the inhabitants of the city one or two per cent of each man's property. And after they have made such a decision, according to the law of the place, each man presents himself before the collectors of that tax; and having first taken an oath to pay the proper amount, he throws into a chest prepared for this what, according to his conscience, he thinks he ought to pay; of this payment there is no witness except him who pays. From this one can infer how much goodness and how much religion there still are in those men. And it must be supposed that each one pays the proper sum, because if it were not paid, that tax would not bring the amount they plan on, according to the old taxes they have been accustomed to collect, and if it did not bring it, the fraud would become known, and when it was known, they would take some other way than this. Such goodness is the more to be admired in these times, inasmuch as it is more infrequent. Indeed it seems to have survived only in that region.

[Simplicity and hatred of inequality in Germany]

This comes from two things: one, that they have not had many dealings with their neighbors; the latter have not come to their cities nor have they visited neighboring places; they have been content to enjoy the goods, to live on the food, and to be clothed with the wool provided by their country. Thus the reason for all intercourse has been removed, and the beginning of all corruption, because they have had no chance to take up the customs of either France or Spain or Italy—nations which altogether are the corruption of the world. The other reason is that those republics where government has been kept orderly and uncorrupted do not allow any citizen of theirs to be a gentleman or to live in the fashion of one, but they preserve among themselves a complete equality. To the lords and gentlemen who live in that region they are entirely hostile; if by chance any come into their hands, they put them to death as the beginners of corruption and the causes of all evil.

[The idle gentry are dangerous]

To explain what this name of gentleman means, I say that they are called gentlemen who without working live in luxury on the returns from their landed possessions, without paying any attention either to agriculture or to any other occupation necessary for making a living. Such men as these are dangerous in every republic and in every country, but still more dangerous are they who, besides the aforesaid fortunes, command castles and have subjects who obey them. These two kinds of men crowd the Kingdom of Naples, the City of Rome, the Romagna, and Lombardy. From this it comes that in those lands there never has arisen any republic or well-ordered government, because men of these types are altogether hostile to all free government.

[*Remodeling demands kingly power*]

To introduce a republic into those regions would be impossible; if a man who were their master attempted to reorganize them, he could find no other way than to set up a kingdom there. The reason is this: where the matter is so corrupt that the laws are not restraint enough, along with them some greater force must of necessity be established, namely, a kingly hand that with absolute and surpassing power puts a check on the over-great ambition and corruption of the powerful.

[*Tuscany has had no savior*]

This explanation can be verified with the example of Tuscany, where in a small extent of territory there long have been three republics, Florence, Siena, and Lucca; the other cities of that region have been servants of such a sort that from their courage and their organization we see that they maintain or would like to maintain their liberty. The reason is that in that region there are no lords of castles and no gentlemen or very few, but there is equality so great that a prudent man, understanding the ancient forms of society, could easily have introduced there well-regulated government. Yet to her great misfortune, up to these times she has found no man who has had power or wisdom to do it.

[*The strong man subject to local conditions*]

So from this discussion I draw these conclusions. He who attempts to set up a republic in a place where there are many gentlemen cannot do so unless he first wipes them all out. Where there is great equality, he who wishes to set up a kingdom or a principality cannot do so unless he draws away from that equality many of ambitious and restless spirit and makes them gentlemen in fact and not in name only, granting them castles and possessions and giving them aid with property and men, so that, standing in their midst, by their means he supports his power. They, by his means, support their ambition. The others are obliged to endure the yoke that force and nothing else can make them endure. And since in this way he who forces and he who is forced are in proportion to each other, men stand fixed, each one in his rank. So then, to make a province fitted to be a kingdom into a republic or to make one fitted to be a republic into a kingdom is a matter for a man who is rare in brain and in authority; many have tried to do it and few have succeeded, because the greatness of the affair partly frightens men, partly hinders them so much that they fail at the very beginning.

[*The Venetian government*]

I am aware that my opinion that where there are gentlemen a republic cannot be organized appears contrary to the practice of the Venetian republic, in which no position can be held except by those who are gentlemen. To this I answer that this instance does not oppose my belief, because the gentlemen in that republic are so rather in name than in fact; they do not have great incomes from landed possessions, but their great riches are based on trade and movable property; moreover none of them holds castles or has any jurisdiction over men. Thus that name of gentleman among them is a name of dignity and reputation, without being founded on any of those things in other cities signified by the word *gentleman*. And as the other republics have all their classes under various names, so Venice is divided into gentlemen and people; and the rule is that the first shall hold or be eligible to hold all the offices; the others are wholly excluded from them. This does not make trouble in that city, for the reasons mentioned elsewhere.[2]

[*The wise founder; a conclusion reaffirmed*]

The would-be founder,[3] then, will establish a republic where there is, or has been brought about, great equality; on the other hand, he will organize a princedom where there is great inequality. Otherwise he will produce a state out of proportion and not durable.

2. DISCOURSES 1. 6.

3. *Here Machiavelli goes back two paragraphs, to the beginning of "The strong man subject to local conditions," repeating from there the pronoun* colui *(He who . . . attempts to set up" etc.). The paragraph on the Venetians is parenthetical.*

CHAPTER 56. BEFORE GREAT EVENTS OC-CUR IN A CITY OR A REGION, THERE ARE SIGNS THAT PRESAGE THEM OR MEN WHO PREDICT THEM

[Signs predicting the death of Lorenzo de' Medici]

What causes it I do not know, but both ancient and modern instances indicate that nothing important ever happens in a city or in a region that has not been foretold either by diviners or by revela-tions or by prodigies or by other celestial signs. And in order not to go far from home in proving this, everybody knows how much was predicted by Frate Girolamo Savonarola before the coming of King Charles VIII of France into Italy; moreover throughout Tuscany people said that in the air above Arezzo were seen and heard men-at-arms who fought together. Everybody knows, besides this, that before the death of Lorenzo de'Medici the elder the cathedral was struck on its highest point by a lightning flash, with very great damage to that building. Everybody knows also that a little before the day when Piero Soderini—who had been made Gonfalonier for life by the Florentine people—was driven out and deprived of his rank, the Palace itself was struck by a thunderbolt. I could bring forward more instances than this, which, to avoid boredom, I shall omit. I shall tell only what Titus Livius says,[1] before the coming of the French to Rome; that is, that one Marcus Cedicius a plebeian reported to the Senate that he had heard at midnight, as he was passing through the Via Nuova, a voice louder than human that bade him report to the magistrats that the French were coming to Rome.

[Airy intelligences]

The cause of this I believe should be considered and interpreted by a man who has knowledge of things natural and supernatural, which we do not have. Yet it could be that since, as some philoso-phers hold, the air about us is full of intelligences—and these through their natural abilities foreseeing future things and having compassion on men—these spirits warn men with such signs, so they can prepare

1. *Livy* 5. 32.

for resistance. At any rate, however it is, so the truth seems to be; and always after such events strange and new things happen to countries.

CHAPTER 57. THE POPULACE UNITED IS STRONG; EACH MAN BY HIMSELF IS WEAK

[A Roman instance]

When the ruin of their native city followed the French invasion, many Romans went to Veii to live, against the decree and order of the Senate, which, to remedy this evil, commanded by its public edicts that everybody within a fixed time and under fixed penalties should come back to live in Rome. At first these edicts were ridi-culed by those against whom they were issued. Then, when the time for obeying drew near, all obeyed them. Titus Livius says: "Though bold when united, by the individual fear of each they were made obedient" (6. 4). Truly the nature of a multitude in this matter cannot be shown better than in this passage. The multitude is bold in speech, many times, against its ruler's decisions; then when they look the penalty in the face, not trusting one another they run to obey. Hence it seems certain that to what a people says about its favorable or its unfavorable inclination, you should pay no great attention when you are in a position to keep it steady if it is favorably inclined, or if it is unfavorably inclined, when you can provide that it will not harm you.[1]

[A multitude without a head is both formidable and weak]

This is to be understood of those bad inclinations of the people derived from some other source than the loss either of their liberty or of a beloved prince who is still living. The bad inclinations resulting from these sources are dangerous above everything else and have need of strong remedies to check them, but the people's other disinclina-tions are easily dealt with when they do not have leaders to whom to turn. On one side there is nothing more formidable than a multitude unrestrained and without a leader; on the other side nothing is weaker; even though it has arms in its hands, it is easily put down, if only you have a refuge where you can escape the first onset.[2] When

1. *Direct address here, in a passage for rulers, suggests* THE PRINCE.
2. *Also a passage intended for a prince. The refuge might be a fortress such as is mentioned*

their minds are a bit cooled and each man sees that he must return to his house, they distrust themselves and think of safety either by flight or by treaty. Therefore a multitude so stirred up, if it is to escape these perils, must at once choose from its number a leader who will direct it, keep it united, and think about its defense. So the Roman populace did when after Virginia's death it marched out of Rome and for security chose twenty Tribunes.[3] If a multitude does not do this, it experiences what Titus Livius, quoted above, says: when they are all together they are strong, but as soon as each man gets to thinking about his personal danger, he becomes worthless and weak.

near the end of the twentieth chapter of THE PRINCE. *This is one of the many passages in the* DISCOURSES *suggesting that* THE PRINCE *was excerpted from that work or that the DIS-COURSES contain matter left over from the briefer work.*

3. Livy 3. 50, 51.

CHAPTER 58. THE MULTITUDE IS WISER AND MORE CONSTANT THAN A PRINCE

[*The many-headed multitude*]

Nothing can be more unreliable and more inconstant than the multitude, as, like all other historians, our Titus Livius affirms. In the narratives of men's doings we often read that the multitude condemns a man to death and afterward weeps for that same man and greatly regrets him. So the Roman people did for Manlius Capito-linus, first condemning him to death, then greatly regretting him. The author's words are: "The people in a short time, when they were no longer in danger from him, regretted him" (Livy 6. 20). Elsewhere, when he narrates events in Syracuse after the death of Hieronymus, Hiero's grandson, he writes: "This is the nature of the multitude: either humbly it serves or arrogantly it domineers" (Livy 24. 25).

[*Not a sin to defend an opinion with reason*]

I do not know whether I am undertaking a task so hard and full of difficulties that I shall be forced to give up in disgrace or to continue with reproach when I try to defend something that, as I have said, has been condemned by all the writers. But however that may be, I do not judge and I shall never judge it a sin to defend any opinion with arguments, without trying to use either authority or

force. I say, then, about that fault of which writers accuse the multitude, that all men individually can be accused of it, and chiefly
princes; for he who is not regulated by the laws will commit the same
errors as the ungoverned multitude. And it is easy to make sure of
this, because there are and have been many princes, and the good and
wise ones have been few.

[Princes and peoples unrestrained by law]

I speak of princes who have broken that bridle intended to
restrain them, among which are not those kings who were born in
Egypt when, in remote antiquity, that land was governed with laws,
not those who were born in Sparta, nor those who in our times are
born in France, a kingdom more tempered by the laws than any
other kingdom of which we have notice in our times. And these
kings who are born under such constitutions are not to be put in that
number.[1] Hence it is necessary to consider each man's nature for
itself and to see if he is like the multitude, because the comparison
ought to be made with a multitude regulated by the laws in the same
way as those princes are, and it will be found to have the same goodness as we see in them, and it will appear neither arrogantly to
domineer nor humbly to serve.

[The people less rash than a prince]

Such was the Roman people, which, while the republic lasted
without corruption, never served humbly nor domineered arrogantly;
on the contrary with its laws and magistrates it kept its place honorably. And when it was obliged to take action against a powerful
man, it did so, as is seen in Manlius' case, in that of the Ten, and of
others who sought to oppress it. And when it needed to obey Dictators and Consuls, for the sake of the public safety, it did so. And if
the Roman people regretted Manlius Capitolinus when he was dead,
that is not strange, for they regretted his virtues, which were such
that their recollection caused sorrow to everybody; they would have
had power to produce that same effect in a prince, for it is the opinion
of all the writers that ability is praised and admired even by its
enemies. And if Manlius in the midst of such regret had been
brought back to life, the Roman people would have given the same

1. By using four times the word born, Machiavelli emphasizes that he is thinking of native
kings, who fit easily into a constitutional pattern of long standing.

judgment upon him as it did when, after taking him from prison, it soon condemned him to death. Yet we also see some princes, thought wise, who have put some person to death and then greatly regretted him, as Alexander did Clitus and others of his friends, and as Herod did Mariamne.

[*The people when regulated by law*]

But what our historian says of the nature of the multitude, he does not say of one that is regulated by the laws, as was the Roman, but of one that is unrestrained, like that at Syracuse, which committed such crimes as do men infuriated and unrestrained, just as Alexander the Great and Herod did in the cases mentioned. Hence the nature of the multitude is no more to be blamed than is that of princes, because all err equally when all are free to err without considering right and wrong. Of this, in addition to what I have given, there are many instances, both among the Roman emperors and among other tyrants and princes, who show as much inconstancy and variation of feeling as ever was found in any multitude.

[*The people not worse than princes*]

I conclude, then, against the common opinion, which says that the people, when they are rulers, are variable, changeable, and ungrateful, for I affirm that in those sins they do not differ from individual princes. And anybody who accuses both the people and the princes surely tells the truth, but in excepting the princes he deceives himself, because a people that commands and is well organized will be just as stable, prudent, and grateful as a prince, or will be more so than a prince, even though he is thought wise. And on the other hand, a prince set loose from the laws will be more ungrateful, variable and imprudent than a people. And the variation in their actions comes not from a different nature—because that is the same in all men, and if there is any superiority, it is with the people—but from having more or less respect for the laws under which both of them live. And he who will consider the Roman people will see that it was for four hundred years an enemy to the name of king, and a lover of the glory and the common good of its native city; he will see many examples displayed by it that testify to both of these things. And if anybody alleges to me its ingratitude to Scipio, I answer with what I said above at length on this subject, where I showed that the people are less ungrateful than princes. But as to prudence and stability, I say that a people is more prudent, more stable, and of better judgment than a prince. Nor is it without reason that the voice of a people is likened to that of God, because general opinion possesses marvelous power for prediction; indeed through some mysterious efficacy it appears to foresee its own happiness and misery.

[The people make better choices of officials]

As to judging things, very seldom does it happen, when a people hears two men orating who pull in opposite directions, that if the two are of equal ability, the people does not accept the better opinion and does not understand the truth it hears. And if in matters relating to courage or that seem profitable, as we said above, it errs, many times a prince too errs as a result of his own passions, which are many more than those of the people. It also appears that in choosing magistrates a people makes far better choices than a prince, nor will a people ever be persuaded that it is wise to put into high places a man of bad repute and of corrupt habits—something a prince can be persuaded to do easily and in a thousand ways. A people when once it abhors things can remain of that opinion for many ages—something not seen in a prince. And of both of these things I think that the Roman people is witness enough, which in so many hundreds of years, in so many elections of Consuls and of Tribunes, did not make four elections of which it needed to repent. And the Roman people, as I have said, so hated the name of king that no obligation to any Roman citizen who tried to get that name was enough to let him escape the penalties he deserved.

[Princes better to establish, people to preserve]

Besides this, we see that cities where the people are in control grow enormously in a very short time, and much more than those that have always been under a prince, as Rome did after she expelled the kings and Athens after she freed herself from Pisistratus. This comes from nothing else than that governments by the people are better than those by princes. Nor do I admit that this opinion of mine is refuted by all our historian says on it in the aforementioned passage and in any others, because if we consider all the people's faults, all the faults of princes, all the people's glories and all those of princes, the people will appear in goodness and in glory far superior. And if princes are superior to the people in establishing laws, forming communities according to law, setting up statutes and new institutions, the people are so much superior in keeping up things already organized that without doubt they attain the same glory as those who organize them.

[*A faulty people cured by words, a wicked prince by steel*]

In short, to conclude this subject, I say that governments by princes have lasted long, republican governments have lasted long, and both of them have needed to be regulated by the laws; because a prince who can do what he wants to is crazy; a people that can do what it wants to is not wise. If, then, we are discussing a prince obliged to keep the laws and a people chained by the laws, we shall see more worth in the people than in the prince. If we are to discuss either people or prince when unrestrained, fewer defects will be seen in the people than in the prince, and they will be smaller and easier to remedy. The reason is that an uncontrolled and rebellious people can be spoken to by a good man and easily led back into a good way. A wicked prince nobody can speak to, and the only remedy is steel. This lets us guess at the seriousness of the diseases both suffer from, since for the curing of the people's disease words are enough, but for the prince's disease steel is required. Hence no one can do other than conclude that the greater the faults the more the attention needed.

[*The people's cruelties are less selfish than the prince's*]

When a people is wholly unrestrained, the foolish things it does are not to be dreaded; no existing evil is to be feared, but rather what such evil can produce, for amid confusion it can produce a tyrant. For a bad prince the opposite is true: we fear the evil at hand and for the future we hope, since men persuade themselves that the wicked ruler's life can bring on an era of freedom. So you see the difference between the two, which is the difference between things that are and things that are to come. The cruelties of the multitude are against a man who they fear will seize the property of them all; the cruelties of a prince are against any man who the prince fears will seize his individual property.

[*The people can be censured; the prince cannot be*]

A bad opinion about the people arises because everybody says bad things of them without fear and freely, even while they are in power. Of princes everybody speaks with a thousand fears and a thousand cautions.

It seems to me not off the subject, because the preceding matter leads me on, to debate in the next chapter which alliances can be more trusted, those made with a republic or those made with a prince.

CHAPTER 59. WHICH ALLIANCE OR LEAGUE IS MORE TRUSTWORTHY, ONE MADE WITH A REPUBLIC OR ONE MADE WITH A PRINCE?

Because every day one prince with another, or one republic with another, makes a league and a friendly agreement, and similarly alliance and amity is contracted between a republic and a prince, I wish to consider which loyalty is more stable and of which more account should be taken, whether that of a republic or that of a prince. After considering everything, I for my part believe that in many cases they are the same, and in a few they differ somewhat. I believe, therefore, that neither a prince nor a republic will keep with you agreements made by force; I believe that when they fear for their positions, either of them, in order not to lose, will break faith with you and show you ingratitude. Demetrius, called the Stormer of Cities, had done the Athenians countless favors. But nevertheless after he was defeated by his enemies and went for refuge to Athens as a city friendly and under obligation to him, she did not receive him. This grieved him more than the loss of his people and his army. Pompey, after his defeat by Caesar in Thessaly, took refuge in Egypt with Ptolemy, whom in the past he had put back into his kingdom, and was killed by him. These things clearly had the same origins; nevertheless more humanity and less violence were used by the repub-lic than by the prince. Wherever, then, there is fear, in practice one will find the same loyalty.

[*Republics stable because slow-moving*]

And if you find either a republic or a prince who, to be loyal to you, will look forward to ruin, this also comes from like origins. For as to the prince, he well may be the friend of a stronger prince who, though not just then having means for defending him, will sometime, he hopes, restore him to his princedom; or indeed, having followed the strong prince as a partisan, he does not hope to find loyalty or amity with his ally's enemies. Of this sort have been those princes in the Kingdom of Naples who have followed the French party. As to republics, of this sort was Saguntum in Spain, which looked for ruin because she adhered to the Roman party;[1] likewise Florence, which in 1512 adhered to the French party. And I believe, everything considered, that in these cases, where there is urgent peril, some sort of stability will be found in republics sooner than in princes. Because, even though republics have the same courage and the same desire as a prince, their sluggish movement will always make their decisions more protracted than those of a prince; hence their faith-breaking will be more protracted than his.

[*Alliances are broken for profit*]

Alliances are broken for profit. At this point, republics are far more observant of their agreements than princes. There are instances in which a very small profit has made a prince break a pledge, and in which a great profit has not made a republic do so. An instance of the second appears in Themistocles' proposal to the Athenians: in their assembly he told them that he could make a suggestion very advantageous to their city, but he could not tell it because, if he revealed it, the opportunity for carrying it out would be lost. The people of Athens therefore chose Aristides to learn about the matter; then according to his judgment they would decide. So Themistocles explained to him that the fleet of all Greece, though protected by their pledge, was in a place where it could easily be taken or destroyed; this would make the Athenians complete masters of that region. Aristides reported to the people that Themistocles' plan was very profitable but very dishonorable. For that reason the people wholly rejected it—which would not have been done by Philip of Macedon and other princes who have sought for and gained more profit by breaking their pledges than by any other method. As to breaking treaties for some reason of nonobservance, I am not talking about that, for it is a proper thing. I am talking of those broken for improper reasons; in this I believe, according to what I have said, that a people commits smaller sins than a prince; therefore one can rely on a people more than on a prince.

1. Livy 21. 5-16.

CHAPTER 60. THE CONSULATE AND EVERY OTHER MAGISTRACY IN ROME WERE GIVEN WITHOUT REGARD TO AGE

It appears in the course of history that the Roman republic, as soon as the consulate was opened to the people, granted it to citizens without consideration of age or family, that indeed there never was any requirement as to age in Rome but that she always went looking for ability, whether in a young man or an old one. This is proved by the instance of Valerius Corvinus, who was made consul at twenty-three years of age; and this same Valerius, speaking to his soldiers, said that the consulate was the "reward of ability, not of family" (Livy 7. 32). Whether this policy was well considered or not might be much debated.

With respect to family, disregard was necessary; the same necessity as existed in Rome exists in every city intending to get the results Rome did, as I say elsewhere,[1] because men cannot be given trouble without reward, and without danger they cannot be deprived of the hope of gaining the reward. And therefore it was fitting that the populace should early have the hope of getting the consulate; on this hope they fed for a time, without getting it; then the hope was not enough, but they had to come to the reality. A city, on the other hand, that does not make use of her populace for anything glorious can treat them as she likes as I have said elsewhere,[2] but if she hopes to do what Rome did, she cannot make a distinction against the people.

If this be granted, that custom about age cannot be objected to; on the contrary, it is necessary, because a youth chosen to an office in which he needs the prudence of an older man must, since the multitude elects him, attain that office through some very striking action. And when a young man is of such ability as to make himself known by something remarkable, a city is damaged if she cannot at once make use of him but must wait until years affect the vigor of mind and the readiness which at an early age his country can use, as Rome used Valerius Corvinus, Scipio, and Pompey, and many others who triumphed when very young.

1. DISCOURSES 1. 6. *Cf.* 2. 3.
2. *See n. 1 above.*

BOOK TWO

[*PREFACE*]

[*Mistakes about ancient times*]

Men are always praising ancient times and finding fault with the present, but not always reasonably; and they are such partisans of things gone by that they praise not merely those ages they know through the accounts left by writers, but also those which they, now being old, remember to have seen in their youth. And though this opinion of theirs be false, as usually it is, I am persuaded that there are various reasons that bring about their mistake. The first of these is, I believe, that about ancient affairs we do not know the whole truth, and usually things are concealed that would bring those times bad repute, and other things that would bring them glory are made splendid and tremendous. Most writers are so subservient to the fortune of conquerors as not merely, in order to make their victories splendid, to increase what they have done ably, but also to give such renown to the actions of their enemies that anyone born afterward in either of the two lands, whether the victorious or the defeated, has reason to wonder at those men and those times, and is obliged to praise them and love them to the utmost.

[*The present may be superior to the past*]

Besides this, since men hate things either through fear or through envy, two very powerful reasons for hatred do not affect things past. But the opposite applies to things you deal with and see: in your complete knowledge of these, since they are in no respect hidden from you and you recognize in them along with what is good many other things that displease you, you are forced to judge them much inferior to the ancient. Yet in truth those of the present may be superior, if you are not considering the matter of the arts, which are so glorious that time can take from them or give them little more fame than in themselves they deserve. If you are speaking of the lives and habits of men, about which we do not see such clear evidence, the present may deserve much greater fame and renown than the past.

[*The condition of states varies*]

I repeat, therefore, that the habit of praising the old and finding fault with the new truly exists, but it is not true that those who do so are always wrong. Sometimes their judgment is necessarily true, for since human affairs are always in motion, either they rise or they fall. So a city or region can be organized for well-planned government by some excellent man, and for a time, through that organizer's efficiency, it can keep on always growing better. He who then is born in such a state and praises ancient times more than modern ones deceives himself, and the deception is caused by those things that have been mentioned above. But they who are born later in that city or region, when the time has come for it to descend toward a worse condition, do not then deceive themselves.

[*The world as a whole is always the same*]

When I meditate on how these things move, I judge that the world has always gone on in the same way and that there has been as much good as bad,[1] but that this bad and this good have varied from land to land, as anyone understands who knows about those ancient kingdoms which differed from one another because of the difference in their customs, but the world remained the same. There was only this difference, that whereas the world first placed excellence in Assyria, she later put it in Media, then in Persia, and finally it came to Italy and Rome. If the Roman Empire was not succeeded by any empire that lasted and kept together the world's excellence, that excellence nevertheless was scattered among many nations where men lived excellently, such as the kingdom of the French, the kingdom of the Turks, and that of the Soldan, and today the people of Germany, and earlier that Saracen tribe that did such great things and took so much of the world after it destroyed the Eastern Roman Empire.

[*The low state of Italy and Greece*]

In all these regions, then, since the Romans fell, and in all these peoples, has existed, and in some part of them still exists, this high ability that is longed for and praised with true praise. He who is

1. *Machiavelli is probably not insisting on an exact division of good and bad, perhaps means hardly more than both good and bad. For the mingling of good and evil, see* Discourses 3. 37; The [Golden] Ass 5. 104. *For the world as the same,* Discourses 3. 43.

born in them and praises past times more than the present may be
deceiving himself; but he who is born in Italy or in Greece, and in
Italy has not turned Northerner or in Greece turned Turk,[2] has
reason to find fault with his own time and to praise others. For in
the others there are many things that make them admirable; in these
there is nothing to redeem them from every sort of extreme misery,
bad repute and reproach; in these no care is given to religion, none
to the laws, none to military affairs, but they are foul with every sort
of filth. Moreover these vices are so much the more detestable the
more they are found in those who sit in judgment seats, give orders
to everybody and expect to be adored.

[*The faulty opinions of old men*]

But returning to our subject, I say that if men's judgment is
partial in judging whether the present age or the ancient one is better
in those things of which, through their antiquity, it is impossible to
have perfect knowledge such as men have of their own times, it
ought not to be partial when old men judge the times of their youth
and their old age, since they have equally seen and known both.
This conclusion would be true if in all times of their lives men were
of the same judgment and had the same appetites; but since these
change, the times, although they do not change, cannot appear the
same to men who have other appetites, other pleasures, other interests
in old age than in youth. For as men lessen in vigor as they grow
old, and improve in judgment and prudence, of necessity those
things that in their youth seemed to them tolerable and good become
intolerable and bad as they grow old. And though for this they
ought to blame their own judgments, they blame the times.

[*Men commonly find fault with the present*]

Moreover, human wants are insatiable, since man has from
Nature the power and wish to desire everything and from Fortune
the power to attain but little; the result is unending discontent in
human minds and weariness with what is attained. Hence the
present is blamed, the past is praised, and the future is desired, even
though men are not moved to act in this way by any reasonable cause.

2. *The French and other invaders of Italy and the Turkish conquerors of Greece.*

[It is a good man's duty to teach]

I do not know, then, whether I deserve to be numbered with those who deceive themselves if in these *Discourses* of mine I over-praise ancient Roman times and find fault with our own. And truly, if the excellence that then prevailed and the corruption that now prevails were not clearer than the sun, I would keep my speech more cautious, fearing to bring upon myself the very deception of which I accuse others. But since the thing is so clear that everybody sees it, I shall be bold in saying clearly what I learn about Roman times and the present, in order that the minds of the young men who read these writings of mine may reject the present and be prepared to imitate the past, whenever Fortune gives them opportunity. For it is the duty of a good man to teach others anything of value that through the malice of the times and of Fortune you have been unable to put into effect, in order that since many will know of it, some of them more loved by Heaven may be prepared to put it into effect.

[The subject of this book is Roman expansion]

Now since in the *Discourses* of the preceding book I spoke of the decisions made by the Romans with respect to affairs within the city, in this one I shall speak of what the Roman people did pertaining to the expansion of their empire.

CHAPTER 1. WHETHER THE ROMANS CON-QUERED THEIR EMPIRE MORE THROUGH ABILITY OR THROUGH FORTUNE

Many hold the opinion, among them Plutarch, a very weighty writer, that the Roman people in gaining their empire were more favored by Fortune than by ability. Among the reasons he brings forward, he proves by the Romans' admission that they attributed all their victories to Fortune, since they built more temples to Fortune than to any other god. Livy seems to embrace the same opinion, because he seldom has any Roman make a speech in which he refers to ability without adding Fortune. But I am not willing to grant this in any way nor do I believe it can be supported. Because if no republic ever produced such results as Rome, there has never been another republic so organized that she could gain as Rome did. The efficiency of her armies caused her to conquer her empire, and the order of her proceedings and her method, which was her very own and discovered by her first lawgiver, caused her to keep it when con‑ quered, as I shall fully explain below in later *Discourses.*

[*The Romans never were forced to carry on two wars at the same time*]

These writers say that if two very important wars never came upon Rome at the same time, the fortune and not the ability of the Roman people was the cause. The Romans had war with the Latins only when they not merely had entirely defeated the Samnites but were actually waging war in their defense. They did not fight the Tuscans until they had subjugated the Latins and with frequent defeats taken from the Samnites almost all their strength. If two of these powers in their full strength, when they were fresh, had united, we can easily infer that without doubt the result would have been the ruin of the Roman republic. But whatever the reason, they never had two very important wars at the same time; on the contrary, always either when one began the other was got rid of, or as they were getting rid of one, the other began.

This is evident in the succession of their wars, for, omitting those fought before Rome was taken by the French, never, while they were fighting with the Equi and Volsci, and those peoples were powerful, did any other nation rise against them. After they were defeated, the war against the Samnites began. And though before this war ended, the Latin people rebelled against the Romans, nevertheless while that rebellion was going on, the Samnites were in league with Rome and with their armies aided the Romans in mastering the Latin pride. When the Latins were defeated, the war with Samnium broke out again. When the Samnite forces were beaten down by many defeats inflicted on them, the war with the Tuscans began. When this was settled, the Samnites rose up anew on the crossing of Pyrrhus into Italy. When he was repulsed and sent back into Greece, they began the first war with the Carthaginians. No sooner was that war over than all the French on both sides of the Alps leagued together against the Romans; finally between Popolonia and Pisa, where today the Tower of Saint Vincent stands, with the greatest slaughter they were conquered. After this war was finished, for the space of twenty years they had wars of no great importance, for they did not fight with anybody except the Ligurians and that remnant of the French who

were in Lombardy. So they remained until the Second Carthaginian War, which for sixteen years kept Italy busy. When this was
finished with the greatest glory, the Macedonian War began. This
being finished, there came one with Antiochus and with Asia.
After that victory, there remained in the whole world neither prince
nor republic that by itself, or if all were united, could oppose the
Roman forces.

[Rome's prudent foreign policy]

But before this last victory, he who will consider well the order
of these wars and the way in which the Romans proceeded, will see
mixed with their fortune the utmost ability and prudence. Hence he
who looks for the cause of this fortune will find it easily, because it is
a very sure thing that, when a prince—or a people—attains such a
high reputation that every prince or people near at hand is afraid to
attack him alone and fears him, it will always happen that no one of
them ever will attack him unless compelled to, so that it will always
be as it were almost in the choice of that strong man to make war
with such of his neighbors as he likes, and with skilful negotiation
to keep the others quiet. They, partly in their respect for his power,
partly deceived by the methods he takes to put them to sleep, are
quieted easily. Such other powers as are far away and have no
dealings with him, look upon the affair as something at a distance
and not pertaining to them. In such a mistake they remain until
this fire comes near them. When it has come, they have no means for
putting it out except their own forces, which then are not adequate,
since the other has become very powerful.

I am going to omit how the Samnites stood watching while the
Roman people conquered the Volsci and the Equi. In order not to
be too lengthy, I shall begin with the Carthaginians, who were of
great power and in high esteem when the Romans fought with the
Samnites and with the Tuscans, because they already held all Africa,
Sardinia and Sicily, and were masters of part of Spain. Such power,
together with their borders being far away from the Roman people,
was the cause why they never thought of attacking Rome or of aiding
the Samnites and the Tuscans; on the contrary they acted, as men do
about affairs that are prospering, rather for the Romans' advantage,
making agreements with them and seeking their friendship. They
never realized their mistake until the Romans, having conquered all

the peoples between themselves and the Carthaginians, began to fight with them for the mastery of Sicily and Spain. The same thing happened to the French as to the Carthaginians, and so to Philip King of the Macedonians, and to Antiochus, for each of them believed, while the Roman people were occupied with the other, that the other would overcome them and that he himself would be in time, either with peace or with war, to defend himself from them. Hence I believe that the fortune the Romans had in this matter would have been enjoyed by all those princes if they had acted like the Romans and had been of the same ability as they.

[*How Rome gained footholds abroad*]

I should take this opportunity for showing the method used by the Roman people in entering into the lands of others, if in my tractate *On Princedoms*[1] I had not spoken of it at length, because in that work this matter is amply discussed. I shall say briefly just this: that they always tried to have in a new province some friends who would be a ladder or a gate for them to climb there or go in there, or a means by which to hold it. By means of the Capuans they went into Samnium, of the Camertini into Tuscany, of the Mamertines into Sicily, of the Saguntians into Spain, of Massinissa into Africa, of the Aetolians into Greece, of Eumenes and other princes into Asia, of the Massiliensians and the Aedui into France. And so they never lacked such supports with which they could make their under-takings easy, both in gaining their provinces and in holding them. Those peoples who are careful about this seem to have less need of Fortune than those who do not observe it well. In order that every-body may understand more easily that their ability was much more effective than their fortune in gaining that empire, in the following chapter we shall discuss the quality of those peoples with whom they had to fight and how stubborn they were in defending their freedom.

1. THE PRINCE 3.

CHAPTER 2. WITH WHAT KINDS OF PEOPLE THE ROMANS HAD TO FIGHT, AND HOW STUBBORNLY THOSE PEOPLE DEFENDED THEIR FREEDOM [*WITH DISCUSSION OF THE EFFECTS OF CHRISTIANITY*]

[*The free peoples of Italy*]

Nothing made it harder for the Romans to conquer the people around them and part of the lands at a distance than the love that in those times many peoples had for their freedom, which they defended so stubbornly that never except by the utmost vigor could they be subjugated. We learn from many instances in what perils they put themselves in order to maintain or regain that freedom, and what revenge they wreaked on those who took it from them. We also learn from the reading of histories what injuries peoples and cities receive from servitude. In our times there is but a single land that can be said to have in it free cities,[1] yet in ancient times there were in all lands many peoples completely free. In those times of which we are at present speaking in Italy, from the mountains that divide what is now Tuscany from Lombardy all the way to the point of Italy, the peoples were all free, such as the Tuscans, the Romans, the Samnites, and many others that lived in that section of Italy. Nor do we read that there was ever any king there except those who ruled in Rome, and Porsenna, King of Tuscany. How his family was wiped out, history does not tell, but it is very plain that in the times when the Romans went to besiege Veii, Tuscany was free, and it so much enjoyed its liberty and so much hated the name of prince that when the Veientians for their protection had established a king in Veii and were asking aid from the Tuscans against the Romans, the Tuscans, after holding many consultations, determined not to give aid to the Veientians so long as they lived under a king, thinking it not good to defend the country of those who had already submitted it to another.[2]

1. *Germany; see Index.*
2. *Livy* 5. 1.

[*Freedom has brought prosperity*]

It is easy to learn why this love for free government springs up in people, for experience shows that cities never have increased in dominion or in riches except while they have been at liberty. Truly it is a marvelous thing to consider to what greatness Athens came in the space of a hundred years after she freed herself from the tyranny of Pisistratus. But above all, it is very marvelous to observe what greatness Rome came to after she freed herself from her kings. The reason is easy to understand, because not individual good but com٬ mon good is what makes cities great. Yet without doubt this common good is thought important only in republics, because everything that advances it they act upon, and however much harm results to this or that private citizen, those benefited by the said common good are so many that they are able to press it on against the inclination of those few who are injured by its pursuit.

[*Under tyranny countries stagnate*]

The opposite happens when there is a prince; then what benefits him usually injures the city, and what benefits the city injures him. For that reason, as soon as a tyranny is established over a free com٬ munity, the smallest evil that results for those cities is that they no longer go forward and no longer increase in power or in riches; but in most instances, in fact always, they go backward. If chance brings about the rise of a vigorous tyrant, who through courage and through force of arms increases his dominion, no advantage comes from it to that state, but only to himself, because he cannot honor any of those citizens he tyrannizes over who are strong and good, unless he is willing to fear them. Nor can he, moreover, subordinate or make tributary to that city where he is tyrant the cities he conquers, because making his city powerful does not benefit him, but it does benefit him to keep his state disunited and to have each city and each province acknowledge him. Hence he alone profits from his con٬ quests—not his country. Let any man who wishes to support this opinion with countless other arguments read the tractate Xenophon composed *On Tyranny*.

[*The ancients loved freedom*]

We need not wonder, then, that the ancient peoples with such great hatred strove to overthrow tyrants and that they loved free government and highly esteemed the name of liberty. This was shown when Hieronymus, grandson of Hiero of Syracuse, was killed in Syracuse, for when the news of his death came to his army, which was not very far from Syracuse, at first they began to riot and to take arms against his murderers, but when they heard that in Syracuse there was a proclamation of freedom, being attracted by that name, they entirely quieted down, laid aside their anger against the tyran-nicides, and considered how in that city they could organize a free government.[3]

[*Revenge on the enemies of freedom*]

We also need not wonder that the people take awful revenge on those who deprive them of their liberty. Of this there have been many instances, of which I am going to mention but one. It hap-pened in Corcyra, a city in Greece, in the times of the Peloponnesian War. Greece was then divided into two parties, of which one followed the Athenians, the other the Spartans; consequently in many divided cities one party sought the friendship of Sparta, the other that of Athens. When it happened that in Corcyra the nobles won the mastery and took away the people's freedom, the popular party with Athenian aid regained its strength and, laying hands on all the nobility, shut them up in a prison that would hold them all. From this they took them out eight or ten at a time, under the pretext of sending them into exile in different places, and with many spec-tacular cruelties put them to death. Those who remained, being informed of this, determined to make every effort to escape that ignominious death; so, arming themselves as best they could, they fought against those who tried to enter, and defended the prison gates. Thereupon the people, running there as soon as they heard the noise, unroofed the upper part of that place and with the ruins smothered them. In that country there ensued many other similar events both horrible and striking; hence it clearly is true that freedom taken from you is avenged with greater fury than freedom which someone plans to take from you.

[*Modern religion does not favor freedom*]

Pondering, then, why it can be that in those ancient times people were greater lovers of freedom than in these, I conclude it came from

3. *Livy* 24. 21.

the same cause that makes men now less hardy. That I believe is the difference between our religion and the ancient. Ours, because it shows us the truth and the true way, makes us esteem less the honor of the world; whereas the pagans, greatly esteeming such honor and believing it their greatest good, were fiercer in their actions. This we infer from many of their institutions, beginning with the magnificence of their sacrifices, compared with the mildness of ours. There is in ours some pomp, more delicate than magnificent, but no action either fierce or vigorous. In theirs neither pomp nor magnificence was lacking in the ceremonies, and in addition there was the deed of sacrifice, full of blood and ferocity in the slaughter of a multitude of animals; this terrible sight made the men resemble it. Ancient religion, besides this, attributed blessedness only to men abounding in worldly glory, such as generals of armies and princes of states. Our religion has glorified humble and contemplative men rather than active ones. It has, then, set up as the greatest good humility, abjectness and contempt for human things; the other put it in grandeur of mind, in strength of body, and in all the other things apt to make men exceedingly vigorous. Though our religion asks that you have fortitude within you, it prefers that you be adapted to suffering rather than to doing something vigorous.

[Christianity has been interpreted according to sloth]

This way of living, then, has made the world weak and turned it over as prey to wicked men, who can in security control it, since the generality of men, in order to go to Heaven, think more about enduring their injuries than about avenging them. Though it may appear that the world has grown effeminate, and Heaven has laid aside her arms, this without doubt comes chiefly from the worthlessness of men, who have interpreted our religion according to sloth and not according to vigor. For if they would consider that it allows us the betterment and the defense of our country, they would see that it intends that we love and honor her and prepare ourselves to be such that we can defend her.

[Modern peoples show little love for freedom]

By reason of this education, then, and such false interpretations, there are in the world fewer republics than in ancient times, and, as a result, the people do not have such great love for freedom as then.

Still I believe that the cause of this is rather that the Roman Empire
with her arms and her greatness wiped out all the republics and all
the self-governing communities. And though later that Empire was
liquidated, the cities have not yet united themselves or reorganized
themselves for government according to law, except in a very few
places in that Empire.

[Roman efficiency]

However that may be, the Romans in every smallest part of the
world did find a league of republics well armed and very stubborn in
the defense of their freedom. This shows that the Roman people
without unusual and immense ability could never have overcome
them. To give an instance of some weight, I am sure that of the
Samnites is enough. It seems a wonderful thing—and Titus Livius
admits it—that they were so powerful and their armies so strong that
as late as the consulate of Papirius Cursor, son of the first Papirius,
they could resist the Romans (which was a space of forty-six years)
after the many defeats and destructions of cities and the many slaugh-
ters suffered in their country, especially when one sees that that
country, where there were so many cities and so many men, is now
almost uninhabited.[4] Yet then there was such good organization and
such force there that it would have been unconquerable, if it had not
been attacked with Roman efficiency.

[Why free countries prosper]

It is easy to determine whence that organization emerged and
whence this confusion is derived; it all comes from living in freedom
then and living in slavery now. All cities and provinces that live in
freedom anywhere in the world, as I said above, make very great
gains. They do so because their populations are larger, since marriages are freer and more attractive to men, and each man gladly
begets those children he thinks he can bring up, without fear that his
patrimony will be taken from him; he knows not merely that they are
born free and not slaves but that by means of their abilities they can
become prominent men. Riches multiply in a free country to a
greater extent, both those that come from agriculture and those that
come from industry, for each man gladly increases such things and
seeks to gain such goods as he believes, when gained, he can enjoy.

4. Livy 10. 31.

Thence it comes that men in emulation give thought to private and public advantages; and both kinds keep marvelously increasing.

[*The worst slavery is that under a republic*]

The opposite of all these things happens in those countries that live as slaves; and the more they fall away from their wonted good, the harder their slavery is. Of all hard slaveries, the hardest is that subjecting you to a republic: first, because it is more lasting and there is less hope of escape from it; second, because the purpose of a republic is to enfeeble and weaken, in order to increase its own body, all other bodies. This is not done by a prince who subjugates you, if that prince is not some barbarian prince, a destroyer of cities and a waster of all the civilization of men, as are the Oriental princes. But if he has in himself human and ordinary qualities, he usually loves equally the cities subject to him and leaves them all their industries and almost all their old institutions. Hence, if they do not prosper like free men, they also do not go to ruin like slaves. I refer to the slavery of cities subject to a foreigner, because of those subject to one of their own citizens I have spoken above.[5]

He who considers, then, all that has been said, will not be astonished at the power of the Samnites when they were free and at their weakness later when they were slaves. Titus Livius gives us assurance of it in several places and especially in the war with Hannibal,[6] where he shows that when the Samnites were oppressed by a legion of men that was in Nola, they sent ambassadors to Hannibal begging him to rescue them; and in their speech they said that they had for a hundred years fought the Romans with their own soldiers and their own generals, and many times had resisted two consular armies and two consuls, and that then they had come to such a low condition that they were scarcely able to defend themselves from one little Roman legion in Nola.

5. DISCOURSES *1. 40. Cf.* THE PRINCE *9.*
6. *Livy 23. 42.*

CHAPTER 3. ROME BECAME A GREAT CITY BY DESTROYING THE CITIES ROUND ABOUT AND BY EASILY ADMITTING FOREIGNERS TO HER OWN HIGH OFFICES

"Meanwhile Rome flourished on the ruins of Alba" (Livy 1. 30). Those who plan that a city should become a great power ought with all their ingenuity to strive to make it full of inhabitants, because without this abundance of men there will never be any success in making a city great. This is done in two ways: through love and through force. Through love, by keeping the ways open and safe for foreigners who wish to come to live in it, in order that everyone may live there gladly; through force, by destroying the cities nearby, and sending their inhabitants to dwell in your city. This was to such an extent practiced by Rome that in the time of the sixth king there lived in Rome eighty thousand men fit to bear arms.[1] For the Romans were accustomed to following the method of the good farmer, who, in order that a plant may grow and produce and ripen its fruit, cuts off the first branches it sends out, so that, since their vigor remains in the root of that plant, they will in time grow out greener and more fruitful. That this method, used that she might expand and become powerful, is necessary and good, is shown by the example of Sparta and of Athens, which, though they were two republics well armed and organized with the best of laws, nonetheless did not attain the greatness of the Roman Empire; yet Rome seemed more rebellious and not so well organized as those.

For this no reason can be brought forward other than the one already spoken of, because Rome, in those two ways having made the body of her state large, could at last put under arms two hundred and eighty thousand men; Sparta and Athens never exceeded twenty thousand each. This was not because the site of Rome was more favorable than that of the others but merely because of her different policy. For Lycurgus, founder of the Spartan state, believing that nothing would more quickly relax his laws than the mixture of new inhabitants, did everything to keep foreigners from having dealings there, and besides not accepting them in marriage, in citizenship, and in the other relations that make men come together, he decreed

1. *Livy* 1. 44.

that in his state leather money should pass current, in order to take away from everybody the desire for coming there to bring merchan/ dise or to bring any trade, so that the city never could increase in inhabitants.

Because all our actions imitate nature, it is not possible or natural for a slender stem to bear up a large limb. Therefore a little state cannot take possession of cities or kingdoms that are stronger and greater than itself; if it does get possession of them, it suffers what a tree suffers when it has a branch larger than its trunk, which, holding the branch up with difficulty, is broken down by the least wind. This we see happened to Sparta; after she had taken possession of all the cities of Greece, Thebes no sooner rebelled than all the other cities rebelled, and the stem remained without branches. This could not happen to Rome, whose trunk was so large that easily it could bear up any branch whatever. This way of acting, then, together with the others that will be told of below, made Rome great and very powerful, as Titus Livius makes clear in a few words when he says: "Meanwhile Rome flourished on the ruins of Alba" (1. 30).

CHAPTER 4. REPUBLICS HAVE USED THREE METHODS FOR INCREASING THEIR SIZE

[*The league of republics*]

On studying ancient history, we learn that republics have used three methods for increasing their size. That followed by the ancient Tuscans was a league of several republics in which none went beyond any other in authority or in rank. As they conquered, they made the new states their companions, as the Swiss do now and as the Achaians and Aetolians did in ancient times in Greece. Be/ cause the Romans made many wars against the Tuscans, I shall go to some length in giving an account of them, to show better the nature of this first method.

In Italy, before the Roman empire, the Tuscans had great power on sea and on land;[1] though there is no detailed history of their affairs, yet some little record and some signs of their greatness remain. We know that they sent to the shore of the upper sea a colony called Adria, which was so noble that it gave its name to the sea that the

1. *Livy* 5. 33.

Latins still call the Adriatic. We also know that from the Tiber as far as the foot of the Alps that circle the mass of Italy, men submitted to their arms. Notwithstanding this, two hundred years before the Roman forces grew great, the Tuscans lost their authority over the region today called Lombardy; that province was occupied by the French, who, moved by necessity or by the sweetness of her fruits and especially of her wine, came into Italy under Bellovesus their Duke. Having defeated and driven out the people of the region, they settled in that place, where they built many cities and, from the name that they then bore, called that region Gaul, which they held until they were conquered by the Romans.

The Tuscans, then, lived with that equality and proceeded in their expansion in the first manner mentioned above, and there were twelve cities, Chiusi, Veii, Arezzo, Fiesole, Volterra, and the like, which by the method of a league governed their empire. They were not able to go outside Italy in their conquests, and the greater part even of that remained untouched, for the reasons that will be given below.

[The central state with subordinate associates]

The second method is to get associates for yourself; not to such an extent, however, that you do not retain the position of command, the seat of authority, and the fame of the enterprises—the method observed by the Romans.

[The powerful state with subjects]

The third method is to get for yourself mere subjects and not associates, as the Spartans and the Athenians did.

[The last method sure to fail]

Of these three methods, this last is totally ineffective, as we see it was for the two republics mentioned above; they fell for no other reason than that they gained such dominion as they were unable to keep. Indeed to attend to the business of governing cities by violence, especially those accustomed to live in freedom, is difficult and laborious. If you are not armed and powerful in arms, you cannot command or rule; so if you hope to be in that situation, it is necessary to get yourself associates who will aid you and to increase your city's population. Because Athens and Sparta did neither one nor the other, their way of acting was ineffective.

[How the second method works]

Rome, an instance of the second method, by doing both rose to such tremendous power, and because she was the only one to conduct herself thus, she was also the only one to become so powerful. Throughout Italy she obtained many associates, who in most respects lived under the same laws as herself; and yet on the other hand, as is said above, she always reserved for herself the seat of authority and the reputation of command; hence these associates of hers found that without realizing it they had subjected themselves with their own labors and their own blood. For Rome sent armies outside Italy and turned kingdoms into provinces and made subjects of peoples who, accustomed to living under kings, did not mind being subjects; then these peoples, having Roman governors and having been conquered by armies called Roman, did not recognize any other superior than Rome. Hence these associates of Rome who were in Italy found themselves at once encircled by Roman subjects and kept down by such a very great city as Rome. When they realized the deception under which they had been living, they were not in time to remedy it—so great was the power Rome had gained by means of the external provinces and so great was the force in her breast, since her own city was very large and very well armed. Even though those associates of hers, to revenge themselves for their injuries, leagued together against her, they were in a short time losers in the war, making their condition worse, because they too became not associates but subjects. This method of proceeding, as has been said, has been observed only by the Romans; a republic that wishes to expand cannot use any other method, because experience has not shown us any other more certain or more true.

[How leagues operate]

The method of leagues earlier mentioned, according to which the Tuscans, the Achaians and the Aetolians lived, and according to which the Swiss live today, is, after that of the Romans, the best. Though through it you cannot grow very great, two good things result: first, you do not easily draw wars down on yourself; second, all you take, you keep easily. The reason why it is impossible to grow greater is that you have a republic disunited and placed in various seats; this makes it hard for the parts to consult and decide. It also causes them not to be eager to rule, because the many communities participating in that rule do not value such an acquisition so high as does a single republic that hopes to be able to enjoy the whole. Beside this, disunited republics are governed by a council, and it is necessary that they be slower in every decision than those who live within one and the same wall.

[The limited possibilities of the league]

Experience makes plain that this method of procedure has a fixed limit, for we have no example to show that it can be exceeded. A league may attain twelve or fourteen communities, and then not try to go any farther, because when it reaches such strength as to believe it can defend itself from anybody, it does not strive for more dominion, both because necessity does not force it to gain more power and because it sees no profit in conquests, for the reasons given above. So the members of the league must do one of two things: either they continue getting associates for themselves, and this multi/tude causes confusion; or they must make subjects, and because in that they see difficulty and not much profit, they do not value it. Hence, when they have arrived at such a number that they can live in security, they turn to two procedures. One is to receive those who entrust themselves to them and to undertake protectorates, and by this means to get from all quarters money they can easily distribute among themselves. The other is to carry on war for others and to take pay from any prince who hires them for his campaigns, as the Swiss do today, and as we read that those mentioned earlier did. Titus Livius bears witness to this, saying that when Philip, King of Macedonia, was conferring with Titus Quintius Flaminius and spoke of a treaty in the presence of a praetor of the Aetolians, and then this praetor spoke with Philip, the King charged him with avarice and lack of faith, saying that the Aetolians were not ashamed to take the field with one party and then to send their soldiers also into the service of the enemy, so that often in two opposing armies one saw Aetolian banners.[2]

Evidently, then, the method of using leagues has always been the same and has produced the same effects. It appears also that

2. Livy 32. 32.

this method of making subjects has always been feeble and has produced slight benefits, and when leagues have gone beyond their limit they have quickly fallen. If this method of getting subjects is of little value to armed republics, to unarmed ones, such as the Italian republics of our times, it is completely valueless. Clearly, then, the right method is that of the Romans, which is so much the more wonderful in that before Rome there was no instance of it, and after Rome no state has imitated her. As to leagues, there are only the Swiss, and the Suabian league that imitates them.

[*The methods of antiquity have not been imitated*]

As will be said at the conclusion of this matter,[3] many methods followed by Rome, pertinent to matters inside as well as to those outside, have in our present times not merely not been imitated, but no account has been taken of them, some judging them not true, some impossible, some without fitness and unprofitable. Altogether, since we are in this ignorance, we are the prey of whoever has wished to overrun this land. Yet if the imitation of the Romans seems difficult, that of the ancient Tuscans ought not to appear so, especially to the present Tuscans, because, if the former could not, for the reasons given, set up an empire like that of Rome, they were able to gain in Italy the power that their manner of proceeding yielded them. This was for a long time secure with the utmost glory of authority and of arms, and with the highest reputation in manners and religion. This power and glory were first decreased by the French, then destroyed by the Romans; it was indeed so completely destroyed that, although two thousand years ago the power of the Tuscans was great, at present there is scarcely any record of it.

This has made me wonder why things are thus forgotten, and I shall discuss it in the following chapter.

3. *For modern failure to imitate Rome, see* DISCOURSES 2. 18, 33.

CHAPTER 5. CHANGE IN RELIGIOUS SECTS AND LANGUAGES ALONG WITH THE COMING OF FLOODS AND PLAGUES WIPES OUT RECORDS

To those philosophers who have held that the world is eternal, I believe it can be replied that, if such antiquity is correct, it is reasonable that there should be record of more than five thousand years, except that such records of the past are blotted out by various causes, part of which come from men, part from Heaven.

[Religious sects]

Those that come from men are variations in religious sects and languages. On the rise of a new sect, that is, a new religion, its first effort, in order to give itself reputation, is to extinguish the old, and when the founders of the new sect are of a different language, they blot it out easily. This is evident if one considers the methods that the Christian sect has used against the Pagan, for it has brought to nothing all its laws, all its ceremonies, and blotted out every reminder of that old theology. It has not, we admit, succeeded in blotting out wholly the knowledge of the things done by excellent men who were of that sect; this has come about because the Christian sect kept the Latin language, which they did perforce, having to write these new laws in it; if they had been able to write in a new language, the other persecutions they carried on indicate that we should have no record of things past. On reading of the methods used by Saint Gregory and the other heads of the Christian religion we see with how much persistence they tried to get rid of all ancient records, burning the works of poets and historians, throwing down images, and destroying everything else that might give any suggestion of antiquity. Hence if to this persecution they had added a new language, in a very short time everything would have been forgotten. Moreover, what the Christian sect tried to do against the Pagan, the Pagan probably did against any sects preceding itself. But because these sects change two or three times in five or six thousand years, we have lost the record of things done before that time, and if there does remain any trace of them, it is looked upon as fabulous, and no faith is put in it. This applies to the history of Diodorus Siculus, which, though it gives an account of forty or fifty thousand years, yet is reputed—truly I be-lieve—full of lies.

[Natural cataclysms]

As to the causes that come from Heaven, they are those that wipe out the race of men and bring down to a few the inhabitants of part of the world, either through plagues or through famine or through a flood. The most important is this last, both because it is the most universal and because those who are saved are all mountaineers and ignorant men who, having no knowledge of anything ancient, can, not leave it to posterity. If among them anybody is saved who has any knowledge of antiquity, he conceals and modifies it as suits him, to get himself a reputation and a name, so that for his successors what he has chosen to write about it remains, but nothing more. That these floods, plagues and famines do come, I believe is not to be doubted, both because histories are full of them and because we see the result—that things are forgotten—and because in reason it should be so. Just as in the instance of simple bodies when a great deal of superfluous matter is brought together in them, Nature many times moves of herself and makes a purgation for the health of those bodies, the same process appears in this mixed body of the human race. When all the lands are full of inhabitants, so that men cannot live where they are and cannot go elsewhere, since all places are settled and filled full, and when human craft and malice have gone as far as they can go, of necessity the world is purged in one of the three ways mentioned, so that by becoming few and humble, men can live more comfortably and grow better.

Thus as I said above, Tuscany was once powerful, religious and vigorous, having her own customs and her native language. All this achievement, as I have mentioned, was wiped out by the Roman power, so that there remains only a record of the name.

CHAPTER 6. HOW THE ROMANS WENT ABOUT MAKING WAR

[*Wars are fought for profit*]

Having discussed how the Romans went about their expansion, we shall now discuss how they went about making war. In all their actions they appear to have deviated with great prudence from the methods universal among others, in order to make easy their way for attaining supreme greatness. Whoever makes war through choice or ambition has the intention of making gains and keeping them, and of acting in such a way as to enrich his city and his country and not to make them poor. He must, then, both in the gaining and in the keeping, take care not to spend, but rather to do everything to the profit of the public.

[*Short and vigorous wars*]

He who wishes to do these things must hold to the Roman custom and method. This first of all was to make their wars, as the French say, short and big. Coming into the field with large armies, they finished in a very short time their wars with the Latins, Samnites, and Tuscans. On observing all the wars they fought from the founding of Rome to the siege of Veii, we see that they finished them all, some in six, some in ten, some in twenty days. This resulted from their method. As soon as war was declared, they led their armies against the enemy and at once fought a battle. When this was won, the enemy, so that their country would not be completely laid waste, came to terms, and the Romans fined them in land; this land they changed into private property or assigned to a colony. This colony, placed on the frontiers of the vanquished, became a guard of the Roman boundaries, with profit to the colonists who received those fields and with profit to the Roman public, which without expense kept up this garrison. Nor could any method be safer or stronger or more profitable, because while their enemies were not in the field, that garrison was enough, and when they came out in force to crush that colony, the Romans also came out in force and joined battle; having fought and won the day, they laid heavier terms on the vanquished and returned home. So the Romans succeeded in gradually gaining a reputation higher than that of the others, and power for themselves. They kept on using this method until they changed their procedure in war. This happened after the siege of Veii, during which, to be able to carry on that war for a long time, they arranged to pay the soldiers,[1] whom before, since it was not necessary because the wars were short, they did not pay.

[*Short and profitable wars*]

Though the Romans paid their soldiers, and therefore could make their wars longer, and when they made them at a greater distance necessity kept their armies longer in the field, nevertheless they never varied from their first method of finishing wars quickly, according to the place and the time; nor did they ever vary from sending out colonies. To their first rule, that of making wars short, they were kept not only by natural habit but by the ambition of the

1. *Livy* 4. 60; 5. 4.

Consuls, who, holding office only one year and having to spend six months of that year at home, wished to finish a war in order to triumph. The Romans were held to their custom of sending out colonies by the great profit and advantage in which it resulted. They did somewhat change their custom about the spoil, with which they were not so liberal as they had been earlier, both because it was not so necessary when the soldiers had their pay and because, since the spoil was greater, they planned so to increase the public funds with it that they would not have to carry on expeditions by means of taxes from the city. This plan in a short time made their treasury very rich. These two methods then, that of distributing the booty, and that of sending colonies, caused Rome to grow rich by war, though other princes and unwise republics grow poor. And the matter went so far that a Consul thought he could not triumph if with his triumph he did not bring a great amount of gold and silver and booty of every other kind to the public treasury.' Thus the Romans, by the aforesaid methods and by finishing wars quickly—though they were strong enough to wear out their enemies by delaying—and by means of victories and inroads and treaties to their advantage, became always richer and more powerful.

2. Livy 10. 46.

CHAPTER 7. HOW MUCH LAND THE RO-MANS GAVE TO EACH COLONIST

The amount of land the Romans distributed to each colonist is, I believe, difficult to learn exactly, because they clearly gave more or less according to the places where the colonies went. I judge that under all conditions and everywhere the distribution was sparing: first, in order to send more men, since they were deputed to guard the country where they were sent; then, since the Romans lived frugally at home, they could not reasonably intend their men abroad to be very abundantly supplied. Titus Livius writes that when Veii was taken, they sent a colony there and distributed to each colonist three and seven-twelfths *jugera* of land, which amount in our measure to. . . .' Moreover, besides the things just mentioned, they held that a small amount of land, well cultivated, would suffice. The

1. *Blank in the original. The amount would be about two and one-third acres. Livy 5. 30.*

colony as a whole, however, requires public fields where each man feeds his cattle, and forests where he gets fuel; without these a colony cannot be maintained.

CHAPTER 8. WHY PEOPLES LEAVE THEIR NATIVE PLACES AND FLOOD THE COUN⁄TRIES OF OTHERS

[Conquests by ambitious republics and monarchs]

Since I have discussed above the Roman method of carrying on war, and how the Tuscans were attacked by the French, the subject permits me to discuss two types of war. One results from the ambi⁄tion of princes or republics trying to extend their empires, such as the wars of Alexander the Great and of the Romans, and the wars that every day one power makes with another. These wars are dangerous but do not altogether drive out the inhabitants of a country, because to the conqueror the mere obedience of the people is enough; usually he lets them live under their own laws and always in their own houses on their own property.

[Conquests by whole peoples]

In the other type of war a whole people, forced by hunger or war, departs from its home to hunt for a new dwelling and a new country, not merely to rule it, like those mentioned above, but to occupy all of it as individuals, and to drive away or kill its ancient inhabitants. This kind of war is very cruel and very frightful. With such wars Sallust deals at the end of his *Jugurtha,* saying that after Jugurtha was defeated, the Romans felt the movement of the French who were coming into Italy. There he says that the Roman people fought with all the other peoples merely over who was going to rule, but with the French they always fought for the survival of one or the other. A prince or a republic that assails a country does enough in wiping out only those who rule, but necessarily these peoples I have mentioned wipe out everybody, because they wish to live on what the others lived on.

[The French in Italy]

The Romans had three of these very dangerous wars. The first was when Rome was captured, for she was taken by those French who, as I said above, had seized Lombardy from the Tuscans and made it their seat, for which Titus Livius gives two causes. The first cause, as I said above, is that they were attracted by the sweetness of the fruits and the wine of Italy, which they lacked in France. The second cause is that since in that French kingdom men had so greatly increased that they could no longer be fed, the princes of that kingdom decided that necessity compelled part of them to seek new land. Having made such a decision, they chose as leaders for those who had to depart Bellovesus and Sigovesus, two kings of the French; Bellovesus came into Italy and Sigovesus crossed into Spain. From the invasion by Bellovesus resulted the occupation of Lom/bardy and thence the first war the French made against Rome. After this came the war the Romans fought after the first Carthaginian war, when between Piombino and Pisa they killed more than two hundred thousand French. The third dangerous war was when the Germans and Cimbri came into Italy; after defeating several Roman armies, they were defeated by Marius. The Romans, then, won these three very dangerous wars. Nor was slight ability required to win them, because later, when Roman ability failed and her armies lost their ancient courage, her empire was destroyed by such migrating peoples—the Goths, the Vandals and the like—who con/quered the entire Western Empire.

[Changes resulting from conquest]

Such peoples come out of their countries, as has been said above, driven by necessity; this necessity arises either from hunger or from war and oppression inflicted on them in their own countries, so that they are obliged to seek new lands. Such persons may be very numerous; then with violence they enter into the countries of others, kill the inhabitants, seize their property, set up a new kingdom, and change the name of the country, as did Moses, and those peoples who took possession of the Roman Empire. So these new names to be found in Italy and the other provinces came from nothing else than the giving of names by new possessors. Such is Lombardy, which was earlier called Gallia Cisalpina; France was called Gallia Trans/alpina, and now is named after the French, for so were named those peoples who took it. Slavonia was called Illyria; Hungary, Pan/nonia; England, Britannia; and many other countries likewise have changed their names, as it would be tedious to repeat. Moses also gave the name of Judea to that part of Syria he conquered.

[Necessity makes migrating peoples dangerous]

Because I have said above that sometimes such peoples are driven from their own abodes by war, by which they are obliged to seek new lands, I wish to bring up the instance of the Maurusii, a people anciently in Syria. Observing the Hebrew people come and judging they could not resist them, the Maurusii thought they would be wiser to save themselves by leaving their own country rather than, in attempting to save it, to lose themselves with it. Hence, departing with their families, they went into Africa to make their abode, driving away the inhabitants they found there. Thus men unable to defend their own country were able to conquer that of others. Pro-copius, who writes of the war Belisarius fought against the Vandals, conquerors of Africa, reports that he read letters written on certain columns in places where these Maurusii lived, which said: "We are the Maurusii, who fled before the face of Joshua, the robber, the son of Nun." In this appears the cause of their departure from Syria. Such peoples, therefore, are very formidable, being driven by the utmost necessity; if they do not meet good armies, they will never be repelled. But when those who are obliged to leave their native land are not many, they are not so dangerous as those peoples of whom I have spoken, because they cannot use so much force; necessity re-quires them to use craft in getting possession of some place and, after getting possession of it, to maintain themselves there by means of friends and allies, as we see was done by Aeneas, Dido, the Mas-silians and the like, all of whom sustained themselves through the allowance of the neighbors where they settled.

[The Scythians]

Such peoples in great numbers—indeed almost all of them—have come from the Scythian lands, regions cold and poor. Since their numbers are great and the country is such that it cannot feed them, they are forced to go out, for many things drive them and nothing keeps them. If for five hundred years now none of these peoples has flooded any country, the causes are many. The first is the great out-pouring from that country at the decline of the Empire; from it more than thirty peoples came out. The second cause is that Germany and

Hungary, from which also these peoples come, have now improved their land to such an extent that they can live there easily; hence they are not forced to change their abode. On the other hand, since their men are very warlike, they are like a fortress to keep the Scythians, who live on their borders, from supposing they can defeat them or pass through their country. Oftentimes there are great movements among the Tartars, which the Hungarians and the Poles repel. The latter indeed often boast that without their weapons Italy and the Church would many times have felt the weight of the Tartar armies. This I think enough on the aforesaid peoples.

CHAPTER 9. WHAT CAUSES COMMONLY GIVE RISE TO WARS BETWEEN POWERS

[*Wars resulting from circumstances*]

The cause of the wars between the Romans and the Samnites, who had long been allies, was such as is common among great powers. It appears either by chance or as devised by the power wishing to start the war. The conflict between the Romans and the Samnites began by chance,[1] because the Samnites, starting war against the Sidicini and then against the Campanians, had no intention of fighting the Romans. But the Campanians, being conquered, appealed to Rome against the expectation of both the Romans and the Samnites. Hence the Romans, since the Campanians had put themselves in their power, were forced to defend their clients by undertaking a war which they thought they could not with honor avoid. For the Romans thought they could reasonably refuse to defend the Campanians, their allies, against the Samnites, also their allies, but thought they could not without ignominy fail to defend the Campanians as subjects or as under their protection. Indeed they judged that if they did not undertake such defense, they would close the road against all those who might intend to come under their sway. Therefore, since Rome had as her end empire and glory, not tranquillity, she could not refuse this enterprise. The same sort of cause supplied a beginning to the first Roman war against the Carthaginians, because the Romans undertook the defense of the Messinians in Sicily—also by chance.

1. *Livy* 7. 19, 29–31.

[Deliberate wars with a good excuse]

But later the Second Punic War did not begin at all by chance, because Hannibal the Carthaginian general attacked the Saguntians, allies of the Romans in Spain, not to injure the former but to stir up the Roman armies and to have opportunity to fight them and cross into Italy.[2] This method of bringing on new wars has always been usual among those who are powerful and who have some regard both for their faith and for that of others. Because if I wish to make war with a prince when there are between us solid treaties for a long time observed, with more show of justice and with more excuse I can attack one of his allies rather than the prince himself, since I am certain that if I attack his friend, either he will resent it and I shall achieve my intention of making war on him, or, not resenting it, he will reveal his weakness and lack of fidelity by not protecting his dependent. Either of these two things tends to take away his reputation and makes easier my designs. We can observe, then, by means of the surrender of the Campanians what has been said above about beginning war, and can also observe an expedient for a city that cannot defend herself and nevertheless wishes to be defended against one who assails her: it is to give yourself without reserve to him whom you count on to defend you,[3] as the Capuans did to the Romans and the Florentines to King Robert of Naples; though not wishing to defend them as allies, the King did defend them as subjects against the forces of Castruccio of Lucca, who was conquering them.

2. Livy 21. 5.
3. *Machiavelli shifts to the second person, as though addressing a prince directly.*

CHAPTER 10. RICHES ARE NOT THE SINEWS OF WAR, THOUGH COMMON OPINION HOLDS THEM SO

[Soldiers must be considered before riches]

Because anybody is able to begin a war at his liking but not to end it, a prince, before he undertakes an enterprise, ought to measure his forces and govern himself according to them. But he needs to have so much prudence as not to deceive himself about his forces; and he will deceive himself every time when he measures them by money or by topography or by the good will of men, if on the other hand he lacks an army of his own. For the things aforesaid do increase your forces but do not at all give them to you, and by themselves they are nothing, and they avail nothing without faithful armies. For a large amount of money does not suffice you without them; the strength of the country does not avail you; the loyalty and good will of men do not last, because these cannot be faithful to you if you cannot defend them. Every mountain, every lake, every inaccessible place becomes a plain, when powerful defenders are lacking. Riches, too, not merely do not defend you but get you robbed sooner.

[*Imprudent princes rely on treasure only*]

Nothing can be more false than that common maxim that says riches are the sinews of war. This dictum is pronounced by Quintus Curtius on the war between Antipater of Macedon and the Spartan king, in the passage where he tells that because of want of money the Spartan king was obliged to engage in battle and was defeated; for if he had put the battle off a few days, the news of the death of Alexander would have come to Greece, and because of that he would have remained victor without fighting; but lacking money and fearing that his army because of the want of it would abandon him, he was forced to tempt the fortune of battle; hence Quintus Curtius for this reason affirms that riches are the sinews of war. This dictum is brought up every day and, by princes not prudent enough to make use of it, it is followed. Because, depending on it, they believe that it is enough for them, in order to defend themselves, to have plenty of treasure, and they do not realize that if treasure were sufficient for victory, Darius would have conquered Alexander; the Greeks would have conquered the Romans; in our times Duke Charles would have conquered the Swiss; and a few days ago the Pope and the Florentines together would not have had difficulty in conquering Francesco Maria, nephew of Pope Julius II, in the war of Urbino.[1] But all the above named were conquered by those who thought not riches but good soldiers to be the sinews of war.

[*Wars are made with steel*]

Among the things that Croesus King of the Lydians showed to Solon the Athenian was treasure beyond reckoning; and when he

---

1. *Urbino surrendered 17 Sept. 1517.*

asked what Solon thought of his power, Solon answered that he did
not for that consider him very powerful; war is made with steel and
not with gold, so a king who had more steel than he might come and
take his treasure away from him. Besides this, when after the death
of Alexander the Great a host of French crossed into Greece and then
into Asia, and the French sent ambassadors to the King of Macedonia to arrange a firm truce, that King, in order to show his power
and to awe them, showed them gold and silver to a great amount.
As a result those French, who up to then held the peace as settled,
broke it—so great a desire sprung up in them to get that gold; and so
that King was plundered as a result of the thing he had accumulated
for his defense. The Venetians, a few years ago, having their treasury
still full of money, lost all their state without being defended by it.

I say, therefore, that not gold, as common opinion proclaims, but
good soldiers are the sinews of war; for gold is not enough to find
good soldiers, but good soldiers are quite enough to find gold. For
the Romans, if they had planned to make war with gold rather than
with steel, it would not have been enough to have all the treasure in
the world, considering the great undertakings they completed and
their difficulties. But since they made their wars with steel, they
never suffered from scarcity of gold, because by those who feared
them it was brought to them even in their camps.

[Lack of money may compel battle]

And if that Spartan king through scarcity of money had to tempt
the fortune of battle, what happened to him on account of money has
many times happened for other reasons; for when an army lacks food
and is obliged either to die of hunger or to join battle, it always
decides to join battle, for that is more honorable and in it Fortune
can in some way favor you. It also has happened many times that
when a general has seen that aid was coming to an army opposed to
him, it has been necessary for him either to join battle and tempt the
fortune of combat, or, waiting until his enemy grows strong, to fight
in any case, under a thousand disadvantages. Also (as happened to
Hasdrubal when he was assailed in the Marches by Claudius Nero
together with the other Roman Consul) a general when he is obliged
either to flee or to fight, almost always chooses to fight, since perhaps
by this method, though it is very doubtful, he may be able to win; in

the other, he must lose in any case. There are, then, many necessities that make a general, contrary to his intentions, take the decision to fight. Among these sometimes there can be lack of money; but riches should not therefore be held the sinews of war, more than the other things that bring men to such a necessity. Again I repeat that riches are not, then, the sinews of war; but good soldiers are.

[*Good soldiers find money*]

Money is indeed necessary in the second place, but it is a necessity that good soldiers gain for themselves, because it is quite as impossible for good soldiers to lack money as it is for money of itself to find good soldiers. Every history shows in a thousand places that what we are saying is true—notwithstanding that Pericles advised the Athenians to make war with all the Peloponnesus, showing that they were able to win that war by ingenuity and with the power of money. And though in that war the Athenians were sometimes successful, at last they lost it; and the prudence and the good soldiers of Sparta were of more avail than the ingenuity and the money of the Athenians. But Titus Livius is a truer witness to this opinion than anybody else, in the place where, discussing whether if Alexander the Great had come into Italy he would have conquered the Romans, he shows that three things are necessary in war: many soldiers and good ones, prudent generals, good fortune.[2] Discussing there whether Rome or Alexander was superior in these things, he then comes to his conclusion without ever speaking of money.

The Capuans, when they were asked by the Sidicini to take arms for them against the Samnites, must have measured their power by money and not by soldiers, because, when they had decided to aid them, after two defeats they were obliged to become tributaries of the Romans, if they wished to save themselves.

2. Livy 9. 17. "*War must be measured with soldiers, money, generalship, and fortune. He who has most of these things can believe he will conquer*" (DISCOURSE ON THE AFFAIRS OF GERMANY).

3. *Livy 7. 30, 31.*

CHAPTER 11. IT IS NOT WISE TO FORM AN ALLIANCE WITH A PRINCE WHO HAS MORE REPUTATION THAN FORCES

[*A Florentine mistake*]

When Titus Livius is trying to show the error of the Sidicini in trusting to the aid of the Campanians, and the error of the Campanians in believing that they could defend them, he could not have put it in more lively words than when he says: "The Campanians brought a name to the assistance of the Sidicini, rather than strength for their defense" (7. 29). From this you can learn that leagues made with princes who cannot easily aid you because of the distance of the place, or who do not have forces to do it because of some trouble of their own or some other cause, bring more glory than help to those who trust in them. So it happened in our time to the Florentines when in 1479 the Pope and the King of Naples attacked them, because, being allied with the King of France, they had from that alliance "a name rather than defense." So it would happen also to any prince who, trusting in Maximilian the Emperor,¹ should undertake some enterprise, because this is one of those alliances that brings to him who makes it "a name rather than defense," as it is said in this passage that the alliance of the Capuans did to the Sidicini.² The Capuans, then, erred in this matter, since they believed they had more forces than they did.

[*A foolish attempt to defend others*]

Thus men are sometimes so imprudent that though they do not know how to defend themselves, and cannot do it, they undertake to defend others. The Tarentines also did this, for when the Roman armies were opposed to the Samnite army, they sent ambassadors to the Roman Consul, to let him know that they wished peace between those two peoples and that they were ready to make war against him who rejected peace. Hence the Consul, amused at this statement, in the presence of the said ambassadors had the trumpet sound for

---

1. *Since Maximilian died 12 Jan. 1519, this passage must have been written before that date*
2. *The Capuans are the Campanians of the first sentence. Capua, the chief city of Campania, is often mentioned by Livy in the narrative Machiavelli here follows.*

battle, and commanded his army to attack the enemy, showing the Tarentines with action and not with words what answer they deserved.

And having in the present chapter discussed the decisions that princes make, unwisely, for the defense of others, I intend, in the following to speak of those they make for their own defense.

CHAPTER 12. IF IT IS BETTER, WHEN FEARING ATTACK, TO BEGIN OR TO AWAIT WAR

[*A war of invasion*]

I have sometimes heard men much experienced in affairs of war debate this question: if there are two princes of almost equal forces, and the stronger one has proclaimed war against the other, which is the better plan for the other? Is he to wait for the enemy within his own boundaries or is he to seek him at home and attack him there? I have heard reasons brought up on both sides. Those who argue for attack bring up the advice that Croesus gave to Cyrus on his arrival at the frontiers of the Massageti to make war on them. Their Queen Tomyris sent him the message that he might choose either of the two plans he wished: he might enter her kingdom, where she would wait for him; or he might let her come to attack him. When the matter was debated, Croesus, against the opinion of the others, said that Cyrus should attack her, arguing that if he should conquer her at a distance from her kingdom, he would not take the kingdom away from her, because she would have time to reorganize; but if he should overcome her within her boundaries, he could pursue her in flight and, not giving her time to reorganize, take possession of her country. They cite also the advice that Hannibal gave to Antiochus when that king planned to make war on the Romans, in which he showed that the Romans could not be overcome except in Italy, because an invader could make use of their arms and their riches and their friends, but he who fought them outside Italy, and left Italy free to them, would leave them a never-failing source to supply them with forces at need. And he concluded that Rome could be taken sooner than the empire, and Italy sooner than the other provinces.[1] They cite also Agathocles, for when he could not support a war at home, he assailed the Carthaginians, who were fighting against him,

1. *Livy 34. 60.*

and brought them to asking peace. They cite Scipio, who, to get the war away from Italy, attacked Africa.

[A war of defense]

Those who speak on the other side say that one who wishes to make an enemy have a hard time gets him away from home. They cite the Athenians, who, while they made war conveniently near home, were successful; and when they moved to a distance and went with their armies into Sicily, they lost their liberty. They cite the fables of the poets, in which it appears that Antaeus, King of Libya, when attacked by Hercules the Egyptian, was unconquerable while he waited for him within the bounds of his own kingdom, but when he departed from it because of the cleverness of Hercules, he lost his state and his life. This has given support to the fable that Antaeus, being on the earth, got his strength back from his mother, who was the Earth, and that Hercules, realizing this, raised him aloft and got him away from the earth.

They cite also modern opinions. Everybody knows that Ferdinand King of Naples was in his day thought a very wise prince. On a rumor, two years before his death, that the King of France, Charles VIII, intended to attack him, he made great preparations; then he fell sick; and at the point of death, among his other pieces of advice to his son Alphonso, he said he should wait for the enemy within his kingdom, and for nothing in the world take forces outside his state but wait within his own bounds with his complete army. This was not observed by Alphonso, for by sending an army into Romagna, without fighting he lost that army and his state.

[The risking of all one's fortune but not all one's forces]

The reasons, in addition to those already given, brought up on either side of this debate are these: an attacker comes with more courage than he who awaits, which makes his army more confident; in addition to this, the attacker deprives his enemy of the power to make convenient use of many of his resources, since the defender cannot make use of subjects who have been plundered and a ruler having an enemy in his country is obliged to be more careful in taking money from his subjects and burdening them; thus the invader can dry up that source which, as Hannibal said, makes it possible for the defender to endure the war. Besides this, his soldiers, being in another ruler's country, necessarily fight, and such necessity gives them vigor, as we have said many times. On the other hand, it is said that, waiting for the enemy, you wait with great advantage, because without any trouble you can give him many troubles about supplies and about everything an army needs; you can more easily impede his plans through your knowledge of the country, which is better than his; you are able to meet him with greater forces, because you can easily bring all of yours together, but you cannot take them all to a distance from home; if you are defeated, you can easily reorganize, both because much of your army is saved through having places of escape close by and because the reinforcement does not have to come from a distance. Hence you succeed in risking all your forces but not all your Fortune; and if you go to a distance, you risk all your Fortune and not all your forces. And there have been some who, better to weaken their enemy, have let him enter some days' marches into their country and take many towns, so that, leaving garrisons in all of them, he may weaken his army and they then can fight him more easily.

[*Unarmed countries. Castruccio and the Florentines*]

But to say now what I myself think about it, I believe that this distinction is to be made: either my country is armed, like that of the Romans or like that of the Swiss at present, or it is unarmed, like that of the Carthaginians or like that of the King of France and the Italians. In the latter case, the enemy ought to be kept distant from your home, because, since your strength is in money and not in men, whenever the course of the former is impeded, you are finished; and there is nothing that hinders you in using it so much as war at home. The Carthaginians are instances of this, who, while their own home was free from enemies, could by means of their income make war with the Romans; but when it was attacked, they could not resist Agathocles. The Florentines had no remedy against Castruccio, Lord of Lucca, because he made war against them in their own country, so that to be defended they had to give themselves to King Robert of Naples. But when Castruccio was dead, these same Florentines had the courage to attack the Duke of Milan in his own country and to strive to take his dominion from him—so much vigor they showed in distant wars and so much weakness in those nearby.

[Armed countries more formidable at home]

But when kingdoms are armed, as Rome was armed and as the Swiss are, they are more difficult to conquer the nearer you get to them, because these bodies can unite more forces to resist an attack than they can to assail somebody else. Nor does Hannibal's authority move me in this case, because passion and his own profit made him say what he did to Antiochus. I believe that if the Romans had had in France in the same space of time those three defeats that Hannibal gave them in Italy, they would have been finished; they could not have made use of the remainders of their armies, as they made use of them in Italy; they would not have had the same opportunity for reorganizing, nor would they have been able to resist the enemy with such forces as they employed. We never find them sending out to attack a province an army exceeding fifty thousand men, but in order to defend their country they sent out in arms against the French, after the first Punic War, eighteen hundred thousand. And moreover they could not have defeated them in Lombardy as they defeated them in Tuscany, because against so large a number of enemies they could not have led such large forces to such a distance or have fought so conveniently. The Cimbri defeated a Roman army in Germany, and the Romans had no resource there. But when the Cimbri arrived in Italy and the Romans put all their forces together, they finished them. The Swiss can easily be overcome outside their own country, where they cannot send more than thirty or forty thousand men, but to overcome them at home, where they can bring together a hundred thousand, is very difficult.

[The decision according to circumstances]

I conclude, then, again, that a prince whose people are armed and disciplined for war should always wait at home for a mighty and dangerous war and not go to meet it; but he whose subjects are unarmed and whose country is unused to war should always get as far away from home as he can. And so both of them, according to their circumstances, will defend themselves best.

CHAPTER 13. MEN GO FROM LOW TO HIGH FORTUNE MORE OFTEN THROUGH FRAUD THAN THROUGH FORCE

[*Force without fraud is not enough*]

I believe it very true that rarely or never do men of humble fortune come to high rank without force and without fraud, except that a rank which another has attained may be given to such men or left them by inheritance. Nor do I believe that force alone will ever be enough, but fraud alone certainly will be enough, as anyone will see clearly who reads the life of Philip of Macedon, that of Agatho-cles, the Sicilian, and of many others like them, who from the lowest, or at least from low fortune, have attained either kingdoms or very large empires.

[*An ambitious prince must learn to deceive*]

Xenophon presents in his *Life of Cyrus* this necessity for deceiving, if we consider that Cyrus' first expedition against the King of Arme-nia is full of fraud, and that with deception and not with force he gained his kingdom.[1] No other conclusion is to be drawn from such an action than that a prince who wishes to do great things must learn to deceive. Xenophon says that Cyrus deceived also Cyaxares, King of the Medes, his maternal uncle, in many ways; without such fraud, Cyrus could not have attained the greatness he did. I do not believe that ever any man originally placed in humble fortune has come to great authority only by open force and honestly, but I firmly believe they have done it by fraud alone, as did Giovan Galeazzo Visconti when he took the state and the rule of Lombardy from Messer Bernabò his uncle.

[*Republics also use fraud*]

And what princes are obliged to do when they begin to grow great, republics are also obliged to do, until they have become power-

1. Xenophon, CYROPAEDIA 2. 4. 16, 23; 3. 1. 19. *None of these, however, illustrates other deception than military stratagem, such as covering an expedition by a pretended hunt. There seems to be in the* CYROPAEDIA *no instance in which Cyaxares is deceived by his nephew, though he is annoyed by the effect on himself of Cyrus' vigor (4. 1. 12–21; 4. 5. 8–13, 18–34; 5. 5. 5–41). In his desire to prove his point, Machiavelli seems to have supposed he remembered what in fact is not in Xenophon.*

ful, and force alone is enough. And because Rome used in every way, either through chance or through choice, all the methods needed for attaining to greatness, she did not fail to use this one too. She could not have adopted in the beginning a more important deception than her method, discussed by us above,[2] of making herself associates, because under this name she made them slaves, as were the Latins and other peoples round about. Because first she availed herself of their armies in subduing the neighboring peoples and getting reputa/ tion as a power. Then, after they were conquered, she attained such greatness that she could overcome anyone. And the Latins never realized that they were wholly slaves until they saw that the Samnites were twice defeated and were forced to make peace.[3] This victory, as it greatly increased the reputation of the Romans with princes at a distance, who by means of it learned the name of Rome but not her arms, so it gave rise to envy and suspicion in those who saw and felt her arms, among whom were the Latins. And this envy and this fear were so powerful that not merely the Latins but the colonies the Romans themselves had in Latium, together with the Campanians, who a little earlier had been defended, conspired against the Roman name. And the Latins began this war in the manner in which it is said above that the larger number of wars are made,[4] that is, not by assailing the Romans but by defending the Sidicini against the Sam/ nites, who were making war on the Sidicini with the permission of the Romans. And that the Latins began the war because they recognized this deception, Titus Livius shows by the tongue of Annius Setinus the Latin praetor, who in their council spoke these words: "For if even now under the cover of a bilateral treaty we can endure slavery," etc. (Livy 8. 4).

So it is plain that the Romans too in their early growth were also not lacking in fraud, which it has always been necessary for those to use who from little beginnings wish to climb to high places—some/ thing which is the less to be censured the more it is concealed, as was this of the Romans.

2. DISCOURSES *2. 4.*
3. *Livy* 7. *33, 36, 37.*
4. DISCOURSES *2. 9.*

CHAPTER 14. MEN MANY TIMES DECEIVE THEMSELVES, BELIEVING THEY WILL OVER﹣COME PRIDE WITH HUMILITY

It is often true that humility not merely does not profit but that it harms, especially when it is used toward arrogant men who, for envy or for some other reason, have conceived hate against you. Our historian bears witness to it in this matter of the war between the Romans and the Latins. Because, when the Samnites complained to the Romans that the Latins had assailed them, the Romans were not willing to forbid such a war to the Latins, wishing not to irritate them[1]—something that not merely did not irritate them but made them become bolder against the Romans, and they more quickly revealed themselves as enemies. Testimony to this is given by the words of the aforesaid Latin praetor, Annius, in the same council, where he said: "You have tested their patience by denying them troops; who can doubt that they were angry? Yet they endured that pain. They heard that we were getting ready an army against the Samnites, their con﹣federates, and yet they did not move from their city. Why are they so modest, unless they are aware of our forces and of their own" (Livy 8. 4)? So therefore we clearly see by means of this passage how much the patience of the Romans increased the arrogance of the Latins.

[*You had better lose by force than through fear*]

Never, therefore, should a prince consent to lower his dignity, and never should he give up anything by agreement, if he wishes to give it up honorably, except when he can hold it or believes he can. Almost always, when things have come to such a pass that you can﹣not give up a possession in the way just mentioned, you had better let it be taken from you by force rather than through the fear of force. If you let it be taken through fear, you do so to avoid war; yet usually you do not avoid it, because he to whom you have with evident cowardice resigned something does not stand still but hopes to take other things from you and is hotter against you, valuing you lower. And on the other side you find defenders colder in aiding you, since they think you weak and cowardly. But if, as soon as the purpose of your adversary is revealed, you prepare forces, even though they are

1. *Livy* 8. 2, 3.

inferior to his, he esteems you. You are also more esteemed by neighboring princes, and when you are under arms, some decide to aid you
who, if you abandon yourself, never will aid you.

[*Divide your enemies by prudent concessions to some of them*]

The foregoing applies when you have one enemy. But when you
have several, to give up some of your possessions to one of them in
order to gain him to your side, even though war is already declared,
and to cut him off from your other allied enemies, always is a
prudent measure.

CHAPTER 15. WEAK STATES WILL ALWAYS BE UNCERTAIN IN COMING TO A DECISION, AND SLOW DECISIONS ARE ALWAYS INJURIOUS

[*Firm purpose will find itself words*]

In this same material and in these same beginnings of war between the Latins and the Romans, we can observe how in every
council it is well to come to the specific in that which is to be decided
and not to remain always in doubt and uncertainty about the matter.
This is plainly seen in the council the Latins held when they were
thinking of detaching themselves from the Romans. Because the
Romans, having foreseen this bad disposition that had affected the
Latin people, in order to make themselves sure of the matter and to
see if without laying hands on their weapons they could gain back
those people, notified them to send eight citizens to Rome, because
they needed to consult with them. The Latins, learning this and
realizing that they had done many things against the will of the
Romans, held a council to arrange who should go to Rome and to
give them instructions on what they had to say. And being in the
council at this debate, their praetor, Annius, spoke these words to
them: "I judge it of the greatest importance for our affairs that you
should consider rather what we ought to do than what is to be said.
It will be easy, when the plans are settled, to fit words to things"
(Livy 8. 4). These words without doubt are very true and ought to
be chewed on by every prince and every republic, because when
they hesitate and are unsure what to do, they cannot find fit words,

but once having fixed their purpose and decided what they are going to do, they can easily find words.

[*Machiavelli's observation in Florence*]

I have stressed this matter the more gladly, inasmuch as in many instances I have seen such hesitation injure public acts, with damage and disgrace to our republic. And in doubtful questions, and where courage is needed for deciding them, this hesitation will always appear when weak men must discuss and decide.

[*Dilatory decision*]

Not less injurious than hesitating decisions are slow and late ones, especially those that have to be made in favor of some friend, because dilatory men aid nobody and damage themselves. Decisions of this sort come either from weakness in courage and in forces or from the wickedness of those who decide, for, moved by selfish passion to attempt to ruin the state or to carry out some other desire of theirs, they do not allow the decision to be made but impede it and oppose it. Because good citizens, even when they see popular impulse turning itself in an injurious direction, never impede their verdict, especially in things for which there is not plenty of time.

After the death of the tyrant Hieronymus in Syracuse, when there was a serious war between the Romans and the Carthaginians, the Syracusans got to disputing whether they ought to hold to the friendship of Rome or of Carthage. So great was the ardor of the parties that the thing was uncertain and they did not come to any resolve about it until finally Apollonides, one of the leaders in Syracuse, in an oration full of prudence showed that no one was to be blamed who held the opinion that they should adhere to the Romans, nor was anyone blameworthy who wished to take the Carthaginian side, but that it was good to abhor such uncertainty and delay in making their resolution, because in such uncertainty he saw the utter ruin of their republic. But if the resolve were made, whatever it might be, it was possible to hope for something good. Nor could Titus Livius show better than he does in this section the harm that hesitation brings on.[1] He shows it also in the following instance of the Latins: the Lavinians, when solicited by them for aid against the Romans,

1. *Livy* 24. 28.

put off deciding so long that when they had just got outside their gate with soldiers to give such aid, news came that the Latins were defeated. On this their praetor Milionius said: "This bit of marching will cost us plenty with the Roman people" (Livy 8. 11). Because, if they determined early either to aid or not to aid the Latins, by not aiding them they would not irritate the Romans; by aiding them, when their aid was in time, they might with the addition of their forces enable them to win. But by putting it off they were sure to lose in any case, as happened to them.

[Florentine procrastination]

And if the Florentines had heeded this passage, they would not have suffered from the French so many losses or so many troubles as they did at the time of the expedition of King Louis XII of France into Italy against Lodovico Duke of Milan. For when the King was considering such an expedition, he sought alliance with the Florentines; and the ambassadors who were with the King agreed with him that they would remain neutral and that the King, coming into Italy, should support them in their position and receive them under his protection; and he gave the city a month's time for ratifying. Such ratification was put off by those who with little prudence favored the affairs of Lodovico until finally, the King being on the very point of victory and the Florentines then wishing to ratify, their ratification was not accepted, for the King knew that perforce and not willingly the Florentines were allying themselves with him. This cost the city of Florence a great deal of money, and she was close to losing the power to govern herself, as at a later time and for a similar reason happened to her.[2] And so much the more to be condemned is that policy because it also did no service to Duke Lodovico, who, if he had won, would have showed many more signs of hostility against Florence than did the king.

[The structure of the Discourses]

And though the injury done to republics by this weakness has been discussed above in another chapter,[3] nonetheless, having a new chance for it because of a new circumstance, I have chosen to repeat

2. In 1512, when the Medici returned.
3. DISCOURSES 1. 38.

it, since it seems to me, strikingly, a matter that republics like ours ought to observe.

CHAPTER 16. HOW FAR THE SOLDIERS OF OUR TIMES HAVE TURNED AWAY FROM ANCIENT DISCIPLINE

[The stubborn courage of the Romans]

The most important battle ever fought by the Roman people in any war with any nation was that fought with the Latin people in the consulate of Torquatus and Decius. Every reason assures us that just as the Latins by losing it became slaves, so the Romans would have become slaves if they had not won it. And of this opinion is Titus Livius, since he makes the armies in every respect equal in discipline, in quality, in stubbornness and in number.[1] The only difference between them was that the Roman army had leaders more competent than the leaders of the Latin army. Further, as they directed this battle two events happened such as had not happened before and of which afterward there are few instances: namely, to keep the spirits of the soldiers firm and obedient to their orders and determined to fight, one Consul killed himself and the other killed his son. The equality between the armies that Titus Livius asserts came about because, having served together a long time, they were alike in speech, discipline and arms; in drawing up for battle they used just the same method, and the military bodies and the leaders of those bodies had the same names. It was necessary, then, since they were equal in forces and equal in efficiency, that something extraor-dinary should arise that would establish and make more stubborn the spirits of one army than of the other. On this stubbornness, as has been said at other times, depends victory, because while it lasts in the breasts of the fighters, armies never turn their backs. And that it might last longer in the breasts of the Romans than of the Latins, partly chance, partly the devotion of the Consuls brought Torquatus to kill his son, and Decius to kill himself.

1. *Livy* 8. 4-9.

[*Roman military organization*]

In connection with showing this equality of forces, Titus Livius shows the entire method that the Romans used in armies and in battles. Since he sets it forth at length, I shall not repeat it, but shall only run over what I think noteworthy and what, being neglected by all the generals of our times, has produced in armies and in battles many difficulties. I say, then, that from the passage in Titus Livius we gather that the Roman army had three principal bodies, which in Tuscan would be three *schiere*. They called the first *hastati*, the second *principes*, the third *triarii*, and each of these had its own cavalry. In drawing up for battle, they put the *hastati* in front; in the second place, straight behind them, they put the *principes*; in the third, right in the same file, they put the *triarii*. The cavalry of the three bodies they put to right and to left of the three. The squadrons of cavalrymen, from their form and from their position, were called *alae* because they seemed like two wings of that body. They drew up the first body, that of the *hastati*, which was in front, in such tightly locked order that it could push back and resist the enemy. The second body, that of the *principes*, was not the first to fight but had the duty of aiding the *hastati* when they were beaten or forced back; it did not, therefore, form in close order, but kept its ranks open in such a way that without being disordered it could receive the first into itself, whenever the *hastati* were pushed back by the enemy. The third body, that of the *triarii*, kept its ranks yet more open than did the second, in order to receive into itself, if there was need, the first two bodies, those of the *principes* and the *hastati*. These bodies then, drawn up in this form, entered the fight; if the *hastati* were forced back or overpowered, they retired into the spaces left in the ranks of the *principes*; thereupon, with the two bodies joined in one unit, they re-entered the fight. If these also were thrown back, they retired into the openings left in the ranks of the *triarii*, and all three bodies as a unit renewed the fight. If still they were beaten, since they could not again reform, they lost the day. And because whenever this last body, that of the *triarii*, was used, the army was in danger, the proverb arose: "The business has been brought to the *triarii*" (Livy 8. 8). This means in Tuscan form: "We have risked our last stake."

[*Modern armies fail to provide reserves*]

The generals of our day, as they have abandoned all the other methods of ancient discipline, and do not follow any part of it, have abandoned this part. Yet it is not of slight importance, because he who draws up his army for battle in such a way that he can reorder it three times, must have Fortune as his enemy three times if he is to lose, and must have against him an efficiency that three times is enough to conquer him. But he who relies only on the first push, as do all the Christian armies today, can easily lose, because any lack of order, any half-way efficiency can take the victory away from him. That which makes our armies lack the power to reorganize themselves three times is that they have lost the method of receiving one body into another. This comes about because at present battles are planned with one of these two defects. The first is that our generals put their groups shoulder to shoulder and make their array wide across and of slight depth, which makes it weak because it is thin from the front to the rear. And whenever, to make it stronger, they put bodies at the rear in the fashion of the Romans, if the first line is broken, since there is no method for it to be received by the second, they are all mixed together and break themselves: if the one in front is pushed back, it crowds upon the second; if the second tries to go forward, it is impeded by the first. Hence, the first crowding the second, and the second the third, so much confusion results that often a very slight unforeseen event ruins an army.

[*The battle of Ravenna*]

The Spanish and French armies at the battle of Ravenna, where Monsieur de Foix, leader of the French soldiers, died (which was, for our times, a very well-fought field), were drawn up according to one of the methods given above; that is, both armies came with all their men drawn up shoulder to shoulder, so that neither of them had more than one front, and they were much more extensive across than in depth. And so they always do where they have a large field, as they did at Ravenna, because, knowing the disorder they cause if they draw back, they escape it when they can by putting themselves in one line, by making their front wide, as has been said. But when the country limits them, they arrange themselves in the bad order mentioned above, without seeking for a remedy.

[The Florentines defeat themselves at Santo Regolo]

In this same bad order they ride through a hostile country, whether they are plundering or carrying on any other affair of war. At Santo Regolo in the territory of Pisa, and elsewhere, where the Florentines were defeated by the Pisans in the time of the war between the Florentines and that city (on account of its rebellion after Charles the King of France crossed into Italy), the damage from the friendly cavalry was greater than that from any other source; being in front and driven back by the enemy, it plunged into the Florentine infantry and broke it; thereupon all the remainder of the soldiers turned back. And Messer Ciriaco dal Borgo, the old leader of the Florentine infantry, has affirmed in my presence many times that he was never defeated except by the cavalry of his friends. The Swiss, who are the masters of modern war, when they serve with the French, above all things take care to put themselves to one side, where the friendly cavalry, if driven back, does not strike them.

[Modern armies subject to one fortune]

And though these things seem easy to understand and very easy to do, nevertheless none of our contemporary generals imitates the ancient methods and corrects the modern ones. And though they still have their army in three parts, calling one part the advance guard, another the battle,[2] and another the rear guard, they do not in any way use them except in giving orders in camps. But in handling them it is very seldom, as has been said above, that they do not make all these bodies subject to one and the same fortune.

[Artillery]

And because many, to excuse their ignorance, assert that the destructive force of artillery does not at the present permit many of the ancient methods to be used, I shall debate this matter in the following chapter, and I shall inquire whether the artillery is such an impediment that we cannot use the good methods of antiquity.

2. *Main body (Italian,* battaglia*). The word* battle *to signify one of the principal divisions of an army was frequently used as late as the seventeenth century.*

CHAPTER 17. HOW ARMIES AT THE PRESENT TIME SHOULD ESTEEM ARTILLERY AND IF THE OPINION UNIVERSALLY HELD OF IT IS TRUE

[Do cannon make courage useless?]

As I have considered, in addition to the things aforesaid, how many combats in the field (called in our times, with a French word, *giornate*, and by the Italians *fatti d'arme*) were fought by the Romans at different times, I have encountered an opinion common to many, that if artillery had been used in their times, the Romans could not—or not so easily—have taken provinces and made peoples tributary to them, as they did; nor would they in any way have made such mighty acquisitions. Many say also that as the result of these fire-weapons, men cannot use and show their courage as they could in antiquity.[1] And they add a third thing: that we come to battle with more difficulty than they came then, and that we cannot now keep the order of battle of those times; so that war will be turned over, in the course of time, to the artillery. And judging that it is not apart from the subject to discuss whether such opinions are true, and how much artillery has increased or diminished the forces of armies and if they take away or give opportunity to good generals for acting with ability, I shall begin to speak as to their first opinion, namely, that the ancient Roman armies would not have made the gains they did if artillery had existed. On that, I say in answer that war is made either by defending or by attacking. Hence I must first consider to which of these two aspects of war artillery brings more profit or more loss.

[Cannon favor the offensive]

And though there is something to say on either side, nonetheless I believe that without comparison it causes more loss to him who defends than to him who attacks. I say this for the reason that he who defends is either inside a city or he is in the fields inside a stockade.

1. *Cf. Ariosto's address to the musket: "Through you the soldier's glory is destroyed, through you the business of arms is without honor, through you valor and courage are brought low, for often the bad man seems better than the good; through you valor no more, daring no more can come to a test in the field"* (ORLANDO FURIOSO *11. 26*).

If he is inside a city, either this city is little, as most fortresses are, or it is large. In the first case he who defends himself is wholly lost, because the battering power of artillery is such that there is no wall, even though very great, that it does not break down in a few days; and if he who is inside does not have good places for retiring to, with both ditches and embankments, he is lost. He cannot repel the rush of the enemy who attempt then to enter through the break in the wall, nor will any artillery he has avail him against them, because it is an axiom that when men go in a crowd and with a rush, artillery does not repel them. Therefore, in the defense of towns the furious charges of the Northerners are not repelled. Italian assaults are indeed repelled, for not in a body but in small numbers they are led to battles—which they, by a name very suitable, call skirmishes. And these who go in this disorder and with this lukewarmness to a breach in a wall defended by artillery go to an obvious death, and against them artillery is effective. But those who, formed in a close body, and so that one pushes on the other, go against a breach, if they are not repelled by ditches or by embankments, enter in every place and artillery does not hold them back; if some of them die, they cannot be so many as to prevent victory.

[De Foix braved the cannon at Brescia]

That this is true is known from many assaults made by the Northerners in Italy, and especially from that on Brescia, because, when that town had rebelled against the French and the fortress still held out for the French King, the Venetians, in order to resist the onslaught that might come from it against the city, had provided with artillery the entire street that descended from the fortress into the city, and placed them in front and on the flanks and in every other suitable place. To these Monsieur de Foix paid no attention. On the contrary, he with his squadron, which had dismounted, passing through the midst of them occupied the city, nor do we hear that he received any remarkable damage. Hence, he who defends himself in a small town, as has been said, and sees the walls fallen to the ground and has no space for embankments and ditches to which he can retire, and has to trust in his artillery, loses quickly.

[*The defense of a large city against cannon*]

If you are defending a large city, and do have opportunity for retiring, artillery is nonetheless without comparison more useful to those outside than to those inside. The reason is, first, that if a piece of artillery is to injure those outside, you are obliged to raise yourself with it above the level of the city, because, if you remain on that level, if the enemy makes the slightest bank or ridge, he is safe, and you cannot injure him. Hence, since you must raise yourself and get on the passageway along the walls or in some fashion raise your-self above the ground, you run into two difficulties. The first is that you cannot hoist up there pieces of the greatness and the power with which he can shoot from outside, since in small spaces one cannot manage big things. The other is that if you actually can get them up there, you cannot make such trustworthy and secure embankments in order to protect the said artillery as the enemy outside can, being on the solid ground and having such opportunities and such space as they themselves wish. Hence it is impossible for one who is defending a city to keep his artillery in high places, when those outside have many pieces and powerful ones. And if he must put them in low places, they are then for the most part useless, as I have said. Thus the defense of the city becomes a matter of defending it with the hands, as was done in antiquity, and with light artillery.[2] If such light artillery is of some use for that purpose, a disadvantage results that counterbalances the advantage of the artillery; because of it, the walls of towns have come to be built low and almost buried in the ditches, so that if there is resort to hand-to-hand combat, either through the beating down of the walls or through the filling up of the ditches, he who is within has many more drawbacks than he had earlier. And therefore, as was said above, these weapons give much more help to him who besieges cities than to him who is besieged.

[*Cannon against a fortified camp; cannon at the battle of Ravenna*]

As to the third thing, that of going into a camp within a stock-ade, in order not to fight a battle except at your advantage or with superiority, I say that in this position you have no better means, ordinarily, to keep yourself from fighting than did the ancients, and

2. *Probably cannon of small caliber. There seems to be no instance in which Machiavelli clearly includes hand firearms under artillery.*

sometimes, on account of the artillery, you have a greater drawback. Because if the enemy comes upon you and has a little superiority in ground, as easily can happen, and is higher than you, or if on his arrival you have not yet made your embankments and covered your‚ self well with them, at once, and without your having any defense, he dislodges you, and you are forced to move out of your fortress and enter into combat. This happened to the Spaniards in the battle of Ravenna; where they encamped between the River Ronco and an embankment; since they had not built their bank high enough to be adequate, and the French had a little advantage in the lay of the land, the artillery forced the Spaniards to move out of their fortifica‚ tions and enter into combat. But granting that, as usually happens, the place you have occupied with your camp will be higher than the others opposed to it and that the embankments are good and secure, so that, because of the site and your other preparations, the enemy dare not assail you, in that case you come to the methods used in antiquity, when an army was in a place that could not be attacked. These are to overrun the country, to take or besiege the towns friendly to you, to hinder you in getting supplies, until some necessity forces you to remove and come to battle, where the artillery, as I shall say further on, does not accomplish much. Considering, then, the kinds of war the Romans waged and seeing that they made almost all their wars by attacking others and not by defending themselves, it is plain, if the things said above are true, that they would have had more advantage and would have made their gains more quickly if there had been guns in those times.

[Courage and fire‚arms]

As to the second thing, that on account of artillery men are un‚ able to show their courage as they could in antiquity, I say that it is true that where men have to show themselves in small groups they are exposed to greater dangers than at that time, whenever they have to scale a city wall or make like attacks, where men are not in close order but have to appear by themselves, one at a time. And it is also true that the generals and heads of the armies are more exposed to peril of death than then, since the artillery can reach them every‚ where, and it does not help them to be in the rear squadrons and to be defended by the strongest men. Nevertheless we see that the one and the other of these two dangers seldom do extraordinary harm, because cities well fortified are not scaled, and no army makes a feeble assault on them, but if they are to be taken, the matter is brought to a siege as was done in antiquity. And even in those that are taken by assault, the perils are not much greater than in ancient times, because then those who defended cities did not lack things to shoot with, which, if they were not so violent, had the same effects as to killing men.

[Generals killed by cannon fire]

As to the deaths of generals and leaders, the twenty-four years covered by the wars in Italy in times just past[3] give fewer examples than do ten years among the ancients. After Count Lodovico della Mirandola, who died at Ferrara when the Venetians some years ago assailed that state, and after the Duke of Nemours, who died at Cirignuola, not one has been killed by the artillery; for Monsieur de Foix at Ravenna died from steel and not from fire. Hence if men do not show their ability individually, it comes not from the artillery but from bad discipline and from the weakness of the armies, which, lacking ability as a whole, cannot show it in part.

[Cannon against infantry]

As to the third thing they say, that it is not possible to come to close quarters and that war will be carried on entirely by the artillery, I say that this opinion is entirely false; so it will always be held by those who try to handle their armies with the efficiency of the ancients, because he who wishes to turn out a good army must, with proce- dures either simulated or real, accustom his men to getting close to the enemy and to exchanging sword-blows with them and standing up to them. Moreover we should rely more on infantry than on cavalry, for reasons that will be given below. When we do rely on infantry, and on the methods aforesaid, artillery becomes wholly use- less, because in approaching the enemy, infantry can with greater ease escape the discharge of artillery than in antiquity they could escape the rush of elephants, of scythed chariots and of other strange opponents that the Roman infantry opposed; yet against these they always found a remedy. And so much the more easily they would have found one against artillery, to the extent that the time in which

3. *Presumably Machiavelli began to reckon with Charles VIII's invasion in 1494. If so, he was writing this sentence in 1517.*

it can injure you is shorter than that in which elephants and chariots could do injury. The latter throw you into confusion in the midst of close combat; the former hinder you only before combat. This hindrance infantry easily escape either by moving in the shelter given by the nature of the site or by lying down on the ground when the guns are fired. Yet even this is shown by experience to be unnecessary, especially in order to defend oneself from heavy pieces of artillery, which cannot be in such a way balanced, if they aim high, that they do not miss you, or if they aim low, that they do not fall short of you. But when armies then come to hand strokes, it is clearer than noonday that neither heavy nor light can harm you, because if the artillerymen are in front, they become your prisoners; if they are behind, they injure their friends before they do you. If the guns are on the flanks, they still cannot strike you in such a way that you cannot attack them, and the effect mentioned will follow. This cannot be much disputed. The Swiss give an example. At Novara, in 1513, without artillery and without cavalry, they attacked in its fortifications the French army, furnished with artillery, and defeated it without being halted by cannon fire. The reason, in addition to the things aforesaid, is that artillery must be protected, if it is going to function, either by walls or by ditches or by embankments, for when it lacks such protection, it is captured or becomes useless, just as when it is defended by men, as happens in battles and combats in the field. On the flank, cannon cannot be used except as the ancients used their instruments for shooting, which they placed outside their squadrons, so that they could fight outside the order of battle; and every time they were charged by cavalry or others, they took refuge behind the legions. He who otherwise relies on them does not well understand them and is trusting himself to a thing that easily can deceive him. If with artillery the Turk has won victories against the Sophy and the Soldan, he has done so not because of its effect, other than that the unaccustomed noise frightened their cavalry.

[*Cannon are useful to the brave*]

I conclude, then, coming to the end of this discussion, that artillery is useful in an army when the valor of the ancients is combined with it, but that without that, it is quite useless against a valorous army.

CHAPTER 18. ON THE AUTHORITY OF
THE ROMANS AND BY THE EXAMPLE
OF THE ANCIENT SOLDIERY, INFANTRY
OUGHT TO BE VALUED HIGHER THAN
CAVALRY

With many reasons and with many instances I can show clearly
how much higher in all military actions the Romans valued soldiers
on foot than on horseback; on it they based all the plans of their
forces. This appears in many instances: among them is their battle
with the Latins at Lake Regillus; there, when the Roman army was
falling back, they had their men on horseback dismount to fight on
foot, to give it aid; renewing the battle in that way, they gained the
victory.[1] Here it is evident that the Romans had more confidence in
their horsemen when they were on foot than when they were on
horseback. They used this same plan in many other battles, and
always found it the best remedy for their dangers.

[Hannibal on cavalry]

To this we should not oppose the opinion of Hannibal, who,
seeing in the battle of Cannae that the Consuls had made their
knights dismount, said in mockery of such a plan: "Quam mallem
vinctos mihi traderent equites" (Livy 22. 49)! That is: "I should
prefer that they would give them to me in chains." Though this
opinion came from the mouth of a very able man, nevertheless, if one
has to follow authority, one ought to believe a Roman republic and
her many very able generals rather than a single Hannibal.

[The foundation of an army is infantry]

Besides, without authorities, there are obvious reasons for it. A
man on foot can go into many places where a horse cannot go. He
can be taught to keep in formation and, if disordered, to re-form; it is
difficult to make horses keep their formation, and impossible, after
disorder, to get them back into it. Besides this, there are some horses
that, like some men, have little courage, and some that have plenty;
and many times it happens that a courageous horse is ridden by a
cowardly man, and a cowardly horse by a courageous man. In

1. *Livy* 2. 20.

whatever way this disparity goes, it causes loss and disorder. Infantry, in good order, are able easily to defeat cavalry, and are with
difficulty defeated by them. This opinion is corroborated, in addition to many instances ancient and modern, by the authority of those
who give rules for civil affairs, in places where they show that in
early times wars were first made with cavalry, because there was as
yet no discipline for the infantry, but when these were disciplined, at
once it was realized how much more valuable they were than cavalry.
It is not, however, for this reason true that cavalry are not necessary
in armies, to do scouting, to overrun and lay waste the country, to
follow the enemy when they are in flight, and also in part to oppose
the hostile cavalry. But the foundation and the strength of an army,
and that which ought to be most highly valued, are the infantry.

[Foolish neglect of infantry in Italy]

Among the sins of the Italian princes, who have made Italy the
slave of foreigners, none is greater than to have made little account of
this type, and to have turned all their attention to soldiers on horseback. This fault has arisen because of the malice of the leaders and
the ignorance of those who rule states. When Italian warfare was
turned over, twenty-five years ago and earlier, to men who had no
territory, but were like soldiers of fortune, they at once went to considering how they might maintain their reputations, since they were
armed and the princes were unarmed. Because they could not pay
regularly a great number of infantry, and they did not have subjects
of whom they could make use, and a small number did not give
them reputation, they turned to keeping cavalry, because two hundred or three hundred cavalry that were paid by a *condottiere* would
keep up a reputation for him, and the payment was not such that it
could not be met by men who had territory. That this might more
easily continue, and to keep their reputation higher, they took away
all the esteem and reputation of infantry and turned it over to their
cavalry. And they so prospered in this mistake that in the largest
army there was the least possible number of infantry. This practice,
together with many other mistakes mixed with it, made this Italian
soldiery of ours so weak that this country has easily been trampled on
by all the Northerners.

[A Roman instance]

More plainly this folly of esteeming cavalry higher than infantry is shown by another Roman instance.[2] The Romans were besieging Sora, and when a squadron of cavalry came out of the town to attack the camp, the Roman Master of Horse moved against them with his cavalry, and as they met face to face, chance brought about that at the beginning of the fight the leaders of both the armies were killed. The others remaining without leadership and the fight nevertheless going on, the Romans, to conquer the enemy more easily, dismounted and forced the hostile cavalry, if they wished to defend themselves, to do the same. And with all this the Romans carried off the victory. There could not be a better example than this for showing how much more strength there is in infantry than in cavalry, because if in other actions the Consuls had the Roman cavalry dismount, it was to aid infantry that was suffering and had need of help. But in this place they dismounted not to aid infantry nor to fight with footmen of the enemy, but when they were fighting on horseback with cavalry, they judged that since they could not overcome them on horseback, they could by dismounting more easily defeat them. I conclude, then, that well-ordered infantry cannot without the greatest difficulty be overcome except by other infantry.

[Roman infantry and Parthian cavalry]

Crassus and Marc Antony, Romans, moved freely through the domain of the Parthians many days with very few cavalry and many infantry, and had opposed to them the countless cavalry of the Parthians. Crassus was left there with part of his army, dead. Marc Antony ably saved himself. Nevertheless these hardships of the Romans make plain how much the infantry was superior to the cavalry, because, being in an open country where the mountains are few, the rivers very few, the seas far off, and distant from every convenience, nonetheless Marc Antony, in the judgment of the Parthians themselves, very ably saved himself; nor did all the Parthian cavalry ever have the courage to attempt the ranks of his army. If Crassus died there, anyone who reads of his actions will see that he was rather deceived than overpowered, and never in all his troubles did the Parthians dare to charge him. On the contrary,

2. *Livy 9. 22.*

always keeping on his flanks, impeding his supplies, and making him promises and not observing them, they brought him to a state of utter misery.

[The Swiss at Novara and Marignano]

I should believe I had to take more trouble in demonstrating how much the strength of infantry surpasses that of cavalry if there were not many modern instances that give testimony in great abundance. We have seen nine thousand Swiss at Novara, mentioned earlier, go to confront ten thousand cavalry and the same number of infantry and overcome them, because the cavalry could not damage them; the infantry, for the most part men from Gascony, badly disciplined, they did not respect. Later, near Milan, we see twenty-six thousand Swiss attack Francis, the King of France, who had with him twenty thousand cavalry, forty thousand infantry, and a hundred cannon.[3] And if they did not win the battle as at Novara, they fought valor- ously for two days; and then, when they were defeated, half of them escaped. With his infantry, Marcus Regulus Attilius was so bold as to resist not merely cavalry but elephants. And if his plan did not succeed, it was not because the efficiency of his infantry was so slight that he could not rely on them to overcome that difficulty.

[Good infantry yields only to better infantry]

I repeat, therefore, that to overcome disciplined infantry, one must oppose them with infantry better disciplined; otherwise one goes to obvious defeat. In the times of Filippo Visconti, Duke of Milan, about sixteen thousand Swiss descended into Lombardy. Hence that duke, then having Carmignuola as his general, sent him against them with about four thousand cavalry and a few infantry.[4] Not knowing their method of fighting, he attacked them with his cavalry, in the belief that he could defeat them quickly. On finding them immovable, he retired with loss of many of his men. But as a most vigorous man, able in new events to take up new plans, after getting more soldiers, he went to meet them. When he approached,

3. *Modern historians somewhat diminish the numbers on both sides, keeping about the same proportions.*

4. *My copy of the first Florentine edition of the* DISCORSI *(1531) reads* IIII. mila cavagli. *The usual reading is* mille, *but one thousand seems too few for sixteen thousand enemies. For this battle Machiavelli cannot have drawn on one of his important sources, the* DECADES *of Flavius Blondus (3. 1), who reckons the Swiss at four thousand.*

he dismounted all his men‑at‑arms and put them at the front of his infantry; then he attacked the Swiss. The latter had no remedy, because Carmignuola's men‑at‑arms, who were on foot and well armored, easily entered into the Swiss ranks without receiving any wounds, and when they had entered among them, they could easily destroy them; hence of all the Swiss there remained alive only that part which the humanity of Carmignuola preserved.[5]

[*Roman infantry discipline must be revived*]

I believe that many realize this difference in efficiency between the one and the other of these types, but so great is the misfortune of these times that neither ancient instances nor modern ones nor the confession of the error is enough to make modern princes take heed. Yet they should consider that if they are going to give reputation to the soldiers of a province or of a state, they must revive those methods, stick to them, give them reputation, give them life, in order that in return they may give him[6] life and reputation. As they deviate from these ways, so they deviate from the other ways spoken of above. From this it comes that acquisitions bring harm rather than greatness to a state, as I shall explain below.

5. *Modern historians decrease both the number of the Swiss and the completeness of the victory (Charles Oman,* The Art of War in the Middle Ages *[London, 1924], II, 263).*

6. *him. Singular in the original, though* them *is required to fit with* they *(i.e., modern princes). Such shifts are characteristic of Machiavelli's style.*

CHAPTER 19. CONQUESTS BY REPUB‑ LICS NOT WELL ORGANIZED AND NOT PROCEEDING IN ACCORD WITH RO‑ MAN ABILITY BRING THEM RUIN, NOT PROSPERITY

[*The power of infantry shown at Novara*]

These opinions contrary to the truth, founded on the evil exam‑ ples that have been introduced by these corrupt ages of ours, keep men from any attempt to deviate from the accustomed ways. Was it possible, up to thirty years ago, to persuade an Italian that ten thousand infantry could attack ten thousand cavalry and the same number of infantry on level ground, and not merely fight with them but beat them, as happened, in the instance we have many times brought forward, at Novara? And though the histories are full of these, nevertheless men would not put any faith in them. Or if they did, they would say that in these times arms are better, and that a squadron of men-at-arms is fit to charge a rock and not merely a body of infantry. And so with these false excuses they would corrupt their judgments, nor would they consider that Lucullus with a few infantry defeated a hundred and fifty thousand cavalry of Tigranes; and that among those horsemen there was a sort of cavalry in every way like our men-at-arms;[1] and also that this fallacy has been revealed by the example of the Northerners.[2]

[Conquests, except by Roman methods, are foolish]

And since this shows that about infantry everything the histories tell is true, they ought to believe that all the other ancient ways are true and useful. And if this were believed, republics and princes would make fewer mistakes; they would be better able to resist any attack made on them; they would not trust to running away; and those who had a commonwealth in their hands would know better how to direct it, whether in expanding it or in maintaining it. And they would believe that to increase the inhabitants of their city, to get for themselves associates and not subjects, to send colonies to guard countries conquered, to make capital of the spoil, to overcome the enemy with raids and battles and not with sieges, to keep the treasury rich, the individual poor, to support military training with the utmost zeal, is the true way to give greatness to a republic and to gain power. And if this method for growing great does not please them, they should remember that conquests through any other course are the ruin of a republic, and they will draw rein on every ambition, regulating their city well inside with laws and with customs, prohibiting its expansion, thinking only of self-defense and of keeping defenses well regulated. Thus the republics of Germany do, which by these methods are living free and have so lived for some time.

1. In THE ART OF WAR (2. oo, p. 601) Machiavelli is less sweeping, admitting that ancient cavalry did not have arched saddles and stirrups and that their armor was poorer. He might also have said that the Parthians fought with the bow as well as with the lance.

2. The Swiss. Apparently Machiavelli did not know of the English bowmen, so successful against the French chivalry in the Hundred Years War. They, however, could be effectively employed only in co-operation with other troops; the Swiss infantry acted alone.

[*It is difficult for a republic to stand still*]

Nevertheless, as I said before when I discussed the difference between organizing for expansion and organizing for maintenance, it is impossible for a republic to succeed in standing still and enjoying its liberties in its narrow confines, because if she does not molest some other, she will be molested, and from being molested rises the wish and the necessity for expansion; and when she does not have an enemy outside, she finds him at home, as it seems necessarily happens to all great states. And if the republics of Germany can live in that way and have lasted for some time, it results from certain conditions in that country, which do not exist elsewhere, without which such a mode of life could not be continued.

[*The free cities of Germany*]

That part of Germany of which I speak was, like France and Spain, subject to the Roman Empire. But when the authority of that Empire had declined and had grown slight in that province, the more powerful of those cities, according to the meekness or the necessity of the Emperors, began to free themselves, buying themselves off from the Empire by reserving to it a small annual tribute, so that, little by little, all those cities that were direct dependents of the Emperor, and were not subject to any prince, have in such a fashion bought themselves off. It happened in these same times when these cities were buying themselves off that certain communities subject to the Duke of Austria rebelled against him. Among these were Fribourg, and the Swiss, and the like, who, prospering in the beginning, little by little increased so much that not merely have they not returned under the yoke of Austria but are a cause of fear to all their neighbors. These are the people who are called the Swiss.

[*How the German cities live in peace*]

This region is, then, divided among Swiss, republics that are called free cities, princes, and Emperor. And the reason why, among so many different kinds of government, wars do not spring up there, or if they do spring up, do not last long, is that symbol of the Emperor, who, though he does not have forces, yet has such reputation among them that he is their conciliator and, with his authority interposing himself as mediator, quickly gets rid of all strife. And the greatest and the longest wars that have been fought there are those that have gone on between the Swiss and the Duke of Austria. And though for many years the Emperor and the Duke of Austria have been the same, he has not therefore been able to overcome the bold-ness of the Swiss, with whom there has never been a way of agreement except through force. Nor has the rest of Germany given him much aid, both because the communities do not like attacking anyone who wishes to live in freedom like themselves and because those princes partly cannot, because they are poor, partly do not wish to, because they envy his power. Those communities, then, live content with their small dominion because they do not have reason, on account of the imperial authority, to wish it greater. They live united within their walls, because they have an enemy who is near and would take his opportunity to seize them if ever they came to discord. But if conditions were different in that region, it would be necessary for them to seek to grow greater and to break that quiet of theirs.

[*Florence and Venice have grown weaker by their conquests*]

Because such conditions are not found elsewhere, this way of living cannot be adopted, so states must either grow greater by the method of leagues, or grow as did the Romans. He who conducts himself otherwise seeks not life but death and ruin, for in a thousand ways and for many causes gains are damaging, since he is very likely at one time to gain dominion and not strength. Yet he who gains dominion and not at the same time strength, must fall. He cannot gain strength who grows poor in wars even though he is victorious, because he lays out more than he gets from his conquests, as the Venetians and the Florentines have done, who have been much weaker since the one has had Lombardy and the other Tuscany than they were when one was content with the sea and the other with six miles of surrounding territory.³ The whole comes from having wished to make gains and not having known how to take the means. These cities deserve blame the more in so far as they have the less excuse, because they have seen the means the Romans used and could have followed their example, whereas the Romans, without any example, through their prudence, by themselves knew how to find means.

3. *Territory extending six miles from the walls in all directions.*

[*Conquest injured even Rome*]

Besides this, conquered territories sometimes do no small damage to the best-organized state, as when she conquers a city or province full of dissipations, from which she borrows some of their bad customs in the course of her dealings with them, as in the conquest of Capua happened first to Rome, later to Hannibal.[4] Indeed if Capua had been more distant, so that the soldiers' dissipation had not had a remedy near at hand, or if Rome had been to any extent corrupt, without doubt that conquest would have been the ruin of the Roman republic. Titus Livius confirms this with these words: "Even then not at all wholesome for military discipline, Capua, a storehouse of all the pleasures, turned away the captivated spirits of the soldiers from the remembrance of their country" (Livy 7. 38). Truly such cities or provinces revenge themselves upon the conqueror without combat and without bloodshed, because, filling him with their evil customs, they expose him to be conquered by whoever assails him. Juvenal in his *Satires* could not have dealt better with this matter, saying that because of their conquest of foreign lands, foreign customs had entered the breasts of the Romans, and instead of frugality and other very excellent virtues, "gluttony and luxury fastened upon her and revenged the conquered world." If, then, success in conquest was beginning to destroy the Romans in times when they were acting with such prudence and such vigor, what will happen then to those whose actions are far different from theirs, and who, besides the other mistakes they make, of which I have spoken at length above, depend on soldiers who are either mercenary or auxiliary? From this there often come upon them those afflictions of which mention will be made in the following chapter.

4. *Livy 7. 38–41; 23. 18.*

CHAPTER 20. THE SORT OF DANGER RISKED BY A PRINCE OR A REPUBLIC MAKING USE OF AUXILIARY OR MERCENARY SOLDIERS

If I had not treated at length, in another work of mine,[1] how valueless mercenary and auxiliary soldiers are, and how valuable

1. PRINCE *12 and 13. See also the Index. Possibly Machiavelli's reference is to his* ART OF WAR, *printed in 1521. With the ideas of that work he would have been familiar as early as*

one's own, I should linger further over this *Discourse*, but having elsewhere spoken of the subject at length, I shall be brief in this section. Yet I have not been willing to pass it by completely, since as to auxiliary soldiers I have found in Titus Livius so extensive an example. Auxiliary soldiers are those that a prince or a republic sends, officered and paid by him, for your aid.

And coming to the text of Livy,[2] I say that the Romans in two different places defeated two armies of the Samnites with their own armies, that they had sent to the aid of the Capuans, and by this freed the Capuans from the war that the Samnites were making on them; thereupon returning to Rome, they left two legions in the city of Capua to defend her, so that the Capuans, deprived of a garrison, would not again become the booty of the Samnites. These legions, rotting in idleness, were delighted with that city; hence, forgetting their native city and the respect due to the Senate, they determined to take arms and make themselves masters of that land which with their valor they should have defended, since they believed that the inhabit-ants were not worthy to have those goods they could not protect. Foreseeing this business, the Romans crushed it and set it right, as we shall show at length where we speak of conspiracies.[3]

[Auxiliaries the worst of soldiers]

I say therefore, again, that of all the types of soldier, the auxiliaries are most harmful, because that prince or that republic that uses them to aid him has no authority over them, but only the prince who sends them has such authority, because auxiliary soldiers are those who are sent to you by a prince, as I have said, under his own officers, under his own ensigns, and who are paid by him, as was the army the Romans sent to Capua. Such soldiers as these, when they have conquered, usually plunder the one who has hired them as much as the one against whom they have been hired, and they do it either through the wickedness of the prince who has sent them or through their own ambition. The intention of the Romans was not to break the agreement and the treaties they had made with the Capuans; nevertheless, those soldiers were persuaded by what they thought so

the time when he was organizing militia in rural Tuscany. Could he not have written much of it as early as that?

2. Livy 7. 32, 33.

3. DISCOURSES 3. 6.

easy a conquest to determine on taking from the Capuans their city and their state. It would be possible to give many instances of this, but I intend to stop with the preceding, and with that of the people of Regium, whose lives and whose city were taken away by a legion that the Romans had put there as a garrison.

[*Foolish ambition causes the employment of auxiliaries*]

A prince—or a republic—then, ought to adopt any other plan before he resorts to bringing auxiliary soldiers into his state for defense, if he must depend wholly on them; for any pact, any treaty, however hard, that he can make with the enemy will be easier on him than such a plan. When past things are carefully read and present ones reviewed, it appears that for one who has succeeded with this plan, great numbers have been deceived. Indeed a prince or an ambitious republic cannot have a better chance for seizing a city or a province than to be asked to send armies for its defense. Therefore anyone so ambitious as to call in such aid not merely to defend himself but to attack others is seeking to gain what he cannot hold and what can easily be taken from him by the ally who conquers it for him. But the ambition of men is so great that when they can satisfy a present desire, they do not imagine the ill that in a short time will result from it. Moreover, in this matter as in the others I have discussed, ancient examples do not move them, because if such examples did move them, they would see that the more liberality they show their neigh-bors and the less they incline to seizing them, the more those neighbors throw themselves into their laps, as I explain below with the example of the Capuans.

CHAPTER 21. THE FIRST PRAETOR THAT THE ROMANS SENT OUT THEY SENT TO CAPUA, AFTER THEY HAD BEEN MAKING WAR FOUR HUNDRED YEARS

[*The Romans allowed conquered cities to keep their old laws*]

How different in their way of going about expansion the Romans were from those who in the present times enlarge their dominion, has been sufficiently discussed above;[1] I have also said that they let

1. DISCOURSES 2. 3, 4, 19.

cities which were not destroyed live under their own laws, even those which surrendered themselves not as companions but as sub-jects. In such cities they did not leave any sign of control by the Roman People, but laid down certain conditions; if these were observed, the Romans kept the cities in their situation and dignity. We know that these methods were practiced until they went outside Italy and turned states and kingdoms into provinces. A very clear example is that the first praetor they sent anywhere went to Capua; they sent him not through their ambition but because the Capuans asked for him, for, being at variance with one another, they judged it necessary to have in their city a Roman citizen who would reor-ganize and reunite them. Moved by this example and forced by the same need, the people of Antium also asked for a prefect. Titus Livius says on this affair and on this new way of ruling, "because now not merely arms, but Roman laws were dominant" (Livy 9. 20). So we see how much this method facilitated the expansion of Rome.

[The advantages of local rule]

Those cities especially that are used to living in freedom or are used to being governed by their own countrymen are contented to live more quietly under a rule they do not see, even though there is some severity in it, than under one which they think reproaches them every day with their servitude, since they see it every day. In addition, it is a benefit to the prince that, since his ministers do not have under their power the judges and magistrates who judge civil and criminal cases in those cities, there never can be a sentence to the blame or reproach of the prince; hence there are few causes for slander and hatred against him.[2] Besides the ancient instances that might be brought up, there is a recent one in Italy. As everybody knows, Genoa has often been occupied by the French; at such times, except at present, the king has always sent there a French governor to govern in his name. Only now, not through the choice of the king, but because necessity has so ordered, he allows that city to be governed by herself and by a Genoese governor. And he who investigates which of these two ways brings more security to the king in his rule over the city, and more contentment to the people, without doubt will approve this last way.

2. *This and the following sentence suggest* THE PRINCE *rather than a work on republics.*

[*Ambitious protectors are suspected*]

Besides this, men so much the more quickly throw themselves into your lap as you appear the less inclined to take possession of them; and they fear you so much the less, with respect to their liberty, the more humane and friendly with them you are. This friendliness and liberality made the Capuans run to ask the praetor from the Romans; yet if the Romans had shown the least desire to send him, the Capuans would at once have been made suspicious and would have drawn back.

[*Florence dealt humanely with Pistoia*]

But why is it necessary to go for instances to Capua and to Rome, since we have them in Florence and in Tuscany? Everybody knows how long ago it was that the city of Pistoia came willingly under Florentine rule. Everybody also knows how much hatred there has been between the Florentines and the Pisans, the Lucchese, and the Sienese. And this diversity of feeling has not arisen because the Pistolese do not value their liberty as much as do the others and do not reckon themselves as high as the others, but because with them the Florentines have always conducted themselves like brothers, but with the others as enemies. For this reason the Pistolese have run willingly under their rule; the others have made and now make every effort not to come under it. And without doubt if the Floren-tines either by way of leagues or of aid had tamed their neighbors and not made them wild, at this hour they would be lords of Tuscany. It is not to be understood by this that I think one never has to use arms and force, but they ought to be reserved for the last place, where and when other methods do not suffice.

CHAPTER 22. HOW FAR WRONG IN JUDGING GREAT THINGS MEN'S OPINIONS OFTEN ARE

[*Corrupt republics employ excellent men only in necessity*]

How far wrong the opinions of men often are, those who witness their decisions have seen and still see, for often their decisions, if not made by excellent men, are contrary to all truth. Yet, especially in quiet times, excellent men in corrupt republics, as the result of envy and other ambitious reasons, are looked on as enemies; hence the people follow either someone who through general self-deception is thought good, or someone put forward by men interested in what they can get from the public, rather than in its good. In adverse times this deception is finally uncovered, and of necessity the people turn for help to those who in quiet times were almost forgotten. This matter will be fully considered in its place.[1]

[Inexperienced men easily deceived]

Various things also happen about which men of little experience in affairs are easily deceived, since there is in these happenings much that seems true, such as to make men believe about such a matter whatever they have been persuaded to think.

[Pope Leo's mistake]

I have spoken of these things because of what Numisius, the praetor, when the Latins were defeated by the Romans, convinced them of,[2] and because of what many believed a few years ago when Francis I, the King of France, came to take Milan,[3] which was defended by the Swiss. When Louis XII was dead, Francis of Angouleme, who succeeded to the Kingdom of France, desired to restore to his kingdom the dukedom of Milan, which a few years before had been captured by the Swiss with the aid of Pope Julius II; he wished therefore to have helpers in Italy who would make his undertaking easy. And besides the Venetians, whose friendship Louis had regained, he tried the Florentines and Pope Leo X, for he thought his undertaking would be easier when he had regained their friendship, since the King of Spain had forces in Lombardy, and the Emperor had forces in Verona. Pope Leo did not yield to the wishes of the King but was persuaded by those who advised him (it is said) to remain neutral; for they demonstrated that in this plan lay certain victory, because it did not tend to the good of the Church to have either the King or the Swiss powerful in Italy; if he wished to bring her back to her ancient liberty, he would have to free her from slavery to both of them. And because the Pope could not conquer either one, whether separate or united, the only possibility was that

---

1. DISCOURSES 3. 16.

2. Livy 8. 11. See also the end of this chapter.

3. In 1515. Can Machiavelli's "few years" be reckoned as fewer than three? If not, he wrote the passage in 1518 or later.

one should conquer the other, and that the Church with her friends should afterward attack the winner. And it was impossible to find a better occasion than the present, since both of them were in the field, and the Pope's forces were in such a condition that they could present themselves on the borders of Lombardy, and near both armies, with the excuse of wishing to guard his property, and there remain until they came to battle. It was probable, since both armies were valiant, that this would be bloody on both sides and would leave the victor so weak that the Pope could easily attack and defeat him. Thus with renown he would come to be lord of Lombardy and arbiter of all Italy. And how false this opinion was is shown by the outcome: when the Swiss were beaten after a long fight, the Pope's soldiers and the Spanish did not have courage to attack the victors; on the contrary, they prepared to flee. Even that would have been useless to them if it had not been for the kindness or the slug-gishness of the King, who did not seek a second victory, but thought it enough to make an agreement with the Church.

[*Victorious armies are formidable*]

There are certain reasons for this opinion that at a distance seem true but are altogether foreign to the truth. It rarely happens that the victor loses many of his soldiers; to the victors death comes in battle, not in flight,[4] yet in the heat of combat, when men are face to face, few of them fall, especially because it usually lasts but a short time. And if indeed it does last a long time and many of the victors are killed, so great is the reputation resulting from victory, and such is the terror it carries along with itself, that it far outweighs the damage the victor suffers through the death of soldiers. Hence an army that attacks him, believing him weakened, finds itself deceived, if indeed that army is not so strong that at any time, whether before the victory or after, it could engage the victor. In this case it might, according to its fortune and strength, win or lose, but the one that fought earlier and won would have the advantage rather than the other.

This is proved true by the experience of the Latins, by the fallacy that Numisius the praetor accepted, and by the damage suffered by those cities who believed him. When the Romans had beaten the Latins, he proclaimed through all the country of Latium that then was the time to attack the Romans, weakened by the battle they had

---

4. *A beaten army loses heavily when it flees, without organized resistance.*

fought, and that the Romans had nothing but the name of victory, but had borne all the other losses just as if they had been beaten, and that the smallest force that would assail them afresh would be enough to put an end to them. Therefore the cities who believed him formed a new army, and were at once defeated and suffered all the loss that those holding such an opinion always suffer.

CHAPTER 23. HOW FAR THE ROMANS IN PUNISHING SUBJECTS FOR SOME AFFAIR REQUIRING PUNISHMENT DEPART' ED FROM A MIDDLE COURSE

[A prince, or a republic, must measure his forces]

"Now in Latium such was the state of things that they could endure neither peace nor war" (Livy 8. 13). Of all unhappy condi' tions, the most unhappy is that of a prince—or a republic—brought to such extremities that he cannot accept peace or carry on war. In such a position are those too much injured by terms of peace, yet who, if they try to make war, are forced either to throw themselves away as the booty of those who aid them or to be the booty of the enemy. To these extremities men are brought by worthless theories and worthless plans, because of not measuring well their forces, as I said above.[1] For any republic or any prince that measures them well is with difficulty brought to such an extremity as were the Latins: when they should not have made an agreement with the Romans, they made one; when they should not have started war against them, they started one. Thus they succeeded in so acting that the hostility and the friendship of the Romans were equally harmful to them. The Latins, then, were beaten and altogether ruined, first by Manlius Torquatus and afterward by Camillus; the latter forced them to surrender and resubmit themselves to Roman power; then putting garrisons in all the cities of Latium, and taking hostages from all, he returned to Rome and reported to the Senate that all Latium was in the hands of the Roman people.

1. DISCOURSES 2. 10.

[*The Romans avoided half-way measures*]

And because this punishment is noteworthy and deserves to be heeded, so that princes can imitate it when they have similar opportunities, I wish to quote the words of Livy, put in the mouth of Camillus. They make certain the method of expansion used by the Romans, who in punishments of state always avoided half-way measures and turned to complete ones. For government is nothing other than holding your subjects in such a way that they cannot harm you or that they do not wish to. This is done either by making yourself entirely secure against them, taking from them every means for injuring you, or by benefiting them to such an extent that they cannot reasonably wish to change their fortunes. All this is covered, first, by Camillus' statement, and then by the Senate's decision on it. His words were these: "The immortal gods have made you so powerful in this matter that they have put in your power to decide whether Latium is to exist or not. Therefore, so far as Latium is concerned, you can provide peace for yourselves forever, either by destroying or by forgiving. Do you wish to make harsh decisions against those who have surrendered and are beaten? You can annihilate all Latium, make vast deserts of the places from which you have so often drawn an excellent allied army for many great wars. Do you wish, after the example of your fathers, to increase the Roman state by receiving the conquered as citizens? You have at hand material for rising to the greatest glory. Certainly the most solid rule by far is that under which subjects are happy. Therefore while the spirits of these Latins are benumbed with expectation, you must subdue them with either punishment or benefit" (Livy 8. 13). This statement was followed by the decision of the Senate, in accord with the words of the Consul. Bringing to judgment, city by city, all those of importance, they either showed them favor or destroyed them, granting exemptions and privileges to those who were favored, giving them citizenship, and in every way assuring their security. As for the others, they destroyed their cities, sent colonies there, brought their people to Rome, and scattered them in such a way that thereafter they could do no harm either with arms or with prudence. As I have said, the Romans never used indecisive measures.

[*The Valdichiana's rebellion against Florence*]

This decision princes should imitate. This the Florentines should have adopted when in 1502 Arezzo rebelled, with all the Valdi-chiana. If they had done so, they would have made the city of Florence very great, and provided her with those fields she lacked for food. But they used that half-way policy I have mentioned, which is very dangerous in punishing men; part of the Aretines they exiled, part they fined; from all they took away their offices and their ancient ranks in the city; they left the city unharmed. And if any citizen in the consultations advised that Arezzo be destroyed, those who thought themselves wiser said that it would be little credit to the republic to destroy her, because it would appear that Florence lacked forces to hold her. These reasons are of the sort that seem true and are not, because for this same reason it would not be possible to execute a parricide or a wicked and rebellious person, since it would be dis-graceful for a prince to show that he did not have force to restrain one man alone. And they do not see—such men as hold opinions of this kind—that men individually and a city as a whole sin sometimes against a state, so that, for an example to the others, for security to himself, a prince has no other remedy than to destroy them. And honor consists in being able and knowing how to punish such a city, not in being able with a thousand perils to hold her. For that prince who does not punish him who errs, in such a way that he cannot afterward err, is held ignorant or worthless.

[*Subjects to be either benefited or destroyed*]

As to this punishment that the Romans inflicted, its necessity is confirmed also by the judgment they gave on the people of Privern-um. In this we ought, according to the passage in Livy, to mark two things: one, what is said above, that subjects ought to be either benefited or wiped out; the other, how much nobility of spirit, how much speaking the truth helps, when it is spoken in the presence of wise men. The Roman senate was brought together to pronounce judgment on the inhabitants of Privernum, who, having rebelled, were then by force brought back under Roman sway. The people of that town sent many citizens to ask pardon from the Senate, and when they came into its presence, one of the senators asked one of them what punishment he thought the Privernati deserved. To this the man answered: "That which they deserve who think themselves worthy of liberty." To this the Consul replied: "And if we should remit the penalty to you, what sort of peace could we hope to have with you?" To which he replied: "If you grant a good one, loyal and lasting; if a bad one, not very long." Therefore the wiser part of the Senate, though many were disturbed by it, said "they had heard the voice of one who was free and a man, and they did not believe it possible for any people, or even an individual, to remain longer in a painful condition than they must. Peace would be sure where willing men had made it, and where they tried to get servitude, they could not hope to have loyalty" (Livy 8. 21). And on these words they determined that the men of Privernum should be Roman citizens, and honored them with the privileges of citizenship, saying that "only those who consider nothing except liberty are worthy to be Romans." So pleasing to noble minds was this true and noble reply, for every other reply would have been lying and cowardly. And those who believe otherwise about men, especially about any who are used either to being or to seeming to themselves to be free, are deceived; and under this deception they adopt plans not good for themselves and sure not to satisfy others. From which come frequent rebellions and the destruction of states.

[*Half-way measures imprudent*]

But to return to our theme, I conclude, both because of this and because of that judgment pronounced on the Latins, as follows: when one has to judge powerful cities and those used to living in liberty, it is necessary either to wipe them out or to treat them with kindness; otherwise, every decision is vain. And above all one should avoid any half-way measure, which is hurtful, as it was to the Samnites when they had shut up the Romans at the Caudine Forks; then they did not choose to follow the opinion of that old man who advised them that the Romans should be allowed to go away with honor or that they should all be killed.[2] But taking a half-way measure, after disarming them and sending them under the yoke, they allowed them to go away full of shame and anger. So a little later they learned to their damage that the opinion of that old man

2. *Livy 9. 3.*

had been valuable and their decision damaging, as in its place will be discussed more fully.[3]

3. DISCOURSES 3. *40–42.*

CHAPTER 24. FORTRESSES GENERALLY ARE MUCH MORE HARMFUL THAN USEFUL

[Free Rome did not build fortresses to overawe subjects]

It will seem perhaps to those who think themselves wise in our times a thing not well considered that the Romans, in their wish to make sure of the peoples of Latium and of the city of Privernum, did not consider building fortresses as a bridle to keep them faithful, especially since it is a saying in Florence, brought forward by our wise men, that Pisa and other like cities must be held with fortresses. And truly if the Romans had been of their sort, they would have decided to build them, but because they were of different ability, different judgment, different power, they did not build them. And while Rome was free and kept her laws and her wise and vigorous institutions, she never built any fortresses to hold either cities or provinces; she did, however, keep some of those already built. So, having seen the actions of the Romans in this matter and that of the princes of our times, I wish to consider whether it is good to build fortresses and if they bring loss or profit to him who builds them. We must observe, then, that fortresses are built either to defend one-self from enemies or to defend oneself from subjects. In the first case they are not necessary; in the second, harmful.

[A Prince cannot by means of fortresses retain subjects who hate him]

So giving the reasons why, in the second case, they are harmful, I say about a prince or a republic that is in fear of subjects and of their rebellion, first, that such fear must come from hate which the subjects feel for their ruler; that hate comes from his evil conduct; his evil conduct comes either from his believing he can hold them by force or from his imprudence as ruler. One of the things causing his belief that he can rule by force is that he has fortresses holding his subjects down; because the bad actions that are the cause of their hatred come in good part from that prince or that republic having such fortresses, which, when that is true, are far more harmful than profitable. Because, first, as I have said, they make you more rash and more violent with your subjects. Second, they do not give such security as you imagine, for all the forces, all the kinds of violence used to hold a people are worthless, except two: either you are always ready to put a good army in the field, as the Romans were; or you scatter, destroy, disarrange, and disunite the people, so that they cannot join together to attack you. If you make them poor, "weap-ons are left to the plundered"; if you disarm them, "rage supplies weapons";[1] if you kill their heads and go on to injure the others, the heads spring up again, like those of the Hydra. If you build for-tresses, they are serviceable in times of peace, because they give you more courage to mistreat your people, but in times of war they are most unserviceable, for they are attacked by your enemy and by your subjects, and it is not possible for them to resist both. And if ever they were unserviceable, they are in our times, because of artillery; through its destructive power small places, and those where embank-ments cannot be placed in the rear, are impossible of defense, as we said above.[2]

[*A good prince relies on his people's good will*]

I am going to debate this matter in more detail. Either you, prince, plan with these fortresses to hold in check the people of your city, or you, prince or republic, plan to curb a city taken in war. I am going to turn to the prince, and I say to him: to hold the citizens in check, nothing can be more useless than such a fortress, for the reasons given above, because it makes you quicker and less hesitant about oppressing your subjects, and that oppression makes them so disposed to your ruin and stirs them up in such a way that your fortress, which is the cause of it, cannot then defend you. So a wise and good prince, to keep himself good, in order not to give his sons reason or courage to become bad, will never build a fortress, so that his sons will rely not on fortresses but on the people's good will.

[*The Sforzas damaged by the Castle of Milan*]

Though Count Francesco Sforza, who became duke of Milan, was reputed wise, and yet he built a fortress in Milan, I say that

---

1. Juvenal, SATIRES 8. 124; Virgil, AENEID 1. 150.
2. In DISCOURSES 2. 17, Machiavelli tells of building additional fortifications to the rear of walls destroyed by bombardment. See also ART OF WAR, book 7.

therein he was not wise, for the outcome has shown that the fortress tended to the harm, not the safety, of his heirs. They, thinking it enabled them to live in security and they could do injury to their citizens and subjects, did not refrain from every sort of violence. Hence, becoming beyond measure hated, they lost that state as soon as an enemy attacked. That fortress did not defend them; in war it did them no good and in peace it did them harm in plenty. If they had not had it and through imprudence had dealt harshly with their citizens, they would have discovered their danger more quickly and would have drawn back. Then they could have resisted the French attack more courageously with friendly subjects, but having no fortress, than they could with hostile subjects, though having the fortress. Fortresses do not help you in any way, because you lose them either through the treachery of their garrisons or through vigorous attacks or through starvation. If you expect them to be of use in helping you recover a state you have lost, where only the fortress is left to you, you must have an army for attacking the enemy who has driven you out; if you have this army, you will get the state again in any case, just as though the fortress were not there—and more easily, in so far as men will be more friendly to you than they will after pride derived from the fortress has led you to mistreat them. Thus experi‑ ence has shown that this fortress of Milan, in times adverse either to the Sforza family or to the French, has done no good to either. On the contrary, it has brought much damage and injury to both, since, by reason of it, they have not tried to find more creditable ways for holding that state.

[*The Duke of Urbino destroyed fortresses*]

Guidobaldo Duke of Urbino, son of Frederick (who in his time was so greatly esteemed as a general), was driven out of his state by Cesare Borgia, Pope Alexander VI's son, and later, through an unexpected event, returned; thereupon he had all the fortresses in that province destroyed, thinking them injurious. Since he was loved by the people, he did not wish fortresses on their account; and as to the enemy, he saw that he could not defend his fortresses, since they need an army in the field to defend them. Hence he decided to destroy them.

[*Pope Julius and Niccolò da Castello*]

Pope Julius, after driving the Bentivogli from Bologna, built a fortress in that city and then allowed a governor of his to maltreat the people. So the city rebelled, and at once he lost the fortress. Thus the fortress was of no use to him and did him harm, though, if he had acted differently, it would have been of use to him. Niccolò da Castello, father of the Vitelli, having returned to his native city, from which he was an exile, at once demolished two fortresses that Pope Sixtus IV had built there, believing that not the fortress but the good will of the people must keep him in that state.

[*The fortress dominating Genoa*]

But of all examples the latest and the most worthy of note in every way, and fit to show the uselessness of building them and the value of demolishing them, is that of Genoa, in very recent times. Everybody knows that in 1507 Genoa rebelled against Louis XII King of France, who came in person and with all his forces to regain it. When he had got it back, he built a fortress, the strongest known up to the present, for in site and in every other way it was impregnable, placed on the summit of a hill, extending into the sea, which the Genoese call Codefà; with it he commanded all of the harbor and a great part of the city of Genoa. Then in 1512, when the French were driven from Italy, Genoa rebelled notwithstanding the fortress, and Ottaviano Fregoso took control of her. With the utmost effort, at the end of sixteen months he captured the fortress through famine. Everybody believed and many advised that he should preserve it as a refuge for himself in any unforeseen event, but as a very prudent man, knowing that not fortresses but the people's will keeps princes in power, he destroyed it. Thus founding his government not on the fortress but on his ability and his prudence, he has held and still holds it.[3] And whereas a thousand infantry are usually enough to change the government of Genoa, his adversaries have attacked him with ten thousand and have not been able to hurt him. We see, then, that the destruction of the fortress did not hurt Ottaviano and the building of it did not help the King. For if he had come into Italy with his army, he could have recovered Genoa, though he did

3. *Fregoso's rule as doge lasted until 1515. In that year he yielded to the French and became their governor of the city, so continuing until 1522.*

not have a fortress there; but when he could not come into Italy with his army, he could not hold Genoa, though he had the fortress there. It was, then, expensive for the King to build it and disgraceful for him to lose it. To Ottaviano, glorious was its recovery and profitable its destruction.

[Fortresses in conquered cities]

But let us come to republics that build fortresses not in their own country but in cities they acquire. And to show the fallacy of this, if the example I have given—that of France and Genoa—does not suffice, I am sure the instance of Florence and Pisa is enough. There the Florentines built fortresses in order to hold that city. They did not realize that when a city had always been an enemy of the Floren׳ tine state, had been free, and in rebellion had had liberty as a resource, they must, if they expected to hold her, use upon her the Roman method, that is, either make her an associate or demolish her. The value of the fortresses there is shown by the coming of King Charles; they surrendered to him either through the infidelity of their garrisons or through fear of a greater ill. Yet if they had not existed, the Florentines would not have founded their power to hold Pisa on them, and that king could not in that way have deprived the Floren׳ tines of the city. And the methods by which up to that time she had been kept would possibly have been enough to preserve her, and beyond doubt would not have made a worse showing than did the fortresses.

[Tarentum and Brescia as instances]

I conclude then, that in holding his hereditary city, a fortress hinders a prince. In holding cities that he conquers, fortresses are useless. I am sure the authority of the Romans is enough for me; in cities they wished to hold by force they tore down walls and did not build them. And if anyone against this opinion of mine brings forward in ancient times Tarentum and in modern ones Brescia, as places that through fortresses were recovered from rebellious subjects, I answer that for the recovery of Tarentum, Fabius Maximus was sent at the end of a year with the entire army, which would have been enough to recover her if there had been no fortress. And though Fabius did use that method, if the fortress had not been there he would have used some other that would have had the same effect.

And I do not know of what use a fortress is in restoring a city to you if her recovery demands a consular army with a Fabius Maximus as general. That the Romans would have regained the city in any case is seen from the instance of Capua, where there was no fortress; yet by virtue of their army they recaptured her.

But let us come to Brescia. I say that what happened in that rebellion seldom happens, namely that the fortress remaining in your power, after the city has rebelled, is connected with an army large and near at hand, like that of the French, because Monseigneur de Foix, the king's general, was at Bologna with the army when he heard of the loss of Brescia. Without wasting time, he marched off that moment, and arriving at Brescia in three days, by means of the fortress retook the city. Even the fortress of Brescia, therefore, to be of value needed a Monseigneur de Foix and a French army that in three days could relieve it. So this one instance, over against con-trary ones, is not enough, because in the wars of our times fortresses are often taken and retaken with the same fortune with which open country is retaken and taken, not merely in Lombardy, but in Ro-magna, in the Kingdom of Naples and in all parts of Italy.

[Good armies better than fortresses]

As to the building of fortresses to defend oneself against enemies from without, I say that they are not necessary to peoples and king-doms that have good armies, and to those that do not have good armies they are useless, for good armies without fortresses are enough for defense; fortresses without good armies cannot defend you. This is evident in the experience of those who have been held excellent both in affairs of government and in other things, such as the Ro-mans and the Spartans. For if the Romans did not build fortresses, the Spartans not merely refrained from them but did not allow any walls for their cities, because they intended that each man's valor—not any other defense—should protect them. This is the reason why a Spartan, asked by an Athenian if the walls of Athens seemed to him splendid, answered: "Yes, if they sheltered women."

[Fortresses useless to princes]

A prince who has good armies, then, will find fortresses on the shores and frontiers of his state useful—sometimes—in holding off the enemy a few days, until he is in order; but they are not essential.

But to a prince who does not have a good army, fortresses throughout his state or on his frontiers are harmful or useless. Harmful, because they are easily lost, and when they are lost they make war on you; or if they are actually so strong that the enemy cannot occupy them, they are left behind by the hostile army and are without profit. For good armies, when they do not meet very strong resistance, enter into hostile countries without hesitation over cities or over fortresses that they leave behind, as we see in ancient histories or as we see that Francesco Maria did, for in recent times, in order to attack Urbino, he left behind him ten hostile cities, without any hesitation.[4] A prince, then, who can form a good army can get on without building fortresses; one whose army is not good ought not to build them; he should, however, strengthen the city where he lives, and keep it supplied and its citizens friendly, so that he can resist hostile attack until either agreement or external aid frees him. All other plans are expensive in time of peace and useless in time of war.

[Roman wisdom]

And so he who considers all I have said must see that the Romans, as they were wise in all their other arrangements, so they were prudent in this decision about the Latins and the men of Privernum; not thinking of fortresses, with stronger and wiser methods they made sure of them.

4. *Francesco Maria della Rovere captured Urbino 6 Feb. 1517.*

CHAPTER 25. TO ATTACK A DISUNITED CITY, HOPING TO TAKE HER THROUGH HER DISUNION, IS FOOLISH

[Roman disunion]

There was such disunion in the Roman republic between the populace and the nobility that the Veientians, together with the Etruscans, imagined that through such disunion they could destroy the Roman state.[1] And when they raised an army and overran the country near Rome, the Senate sent against them Gaius Manlius and Marcus Fabius. When their army was near the Veientian army, the

1. *Livy 2. 44. For the narrative 2. 43–45. The name of the first general is better given as Cn. Manlius.*

Veientians did not cease, both with attacks and with insults, to injure and berate the Roman republic. So great was their rashness and insolence that the Romans united, instead of continuing dis-united; coming to combat, they broke and defeated the allies. We see, therefore, how much men deceive themselves, as we showed above, in taking up plans, and how many times they think to gain something, and they lose it. The Veientians expected by attacking the Romans when disunited to defeat them, but their attack caused Roman union and their own destruction. The disunion of republics usually results from idleness and peace; the cause of union is fear and war. Therefore, if the Veientians had been wise, the more disunited Rome was, the more they would have kept war away from her and sought to overcome her with the arts of peace.

[How to gain a disunited city]

The right method is to seek to gain the confidence of the dis-united city, and as long as her factions do not come to arms, to act as arbitrator between the parties. If they do come to arms, give sluggish support to the weaker party, both to keep them longer at war and to make them exhaust themselves, and that large forces may not arouse in both factions the fear that you plan to conquer them and become their prince. When this policy is well handled, it will almost always end as you have been expecting.

[Disunion in Pistoia, Siena, and Florence]

The city of Pistoia, as I said in another *Discourse* and for another purpose,[2] was subjected by the Florentine republic with no other art than this. Since the city was divided and the Florentines favored now one party, now the other, without getting the ill will of either, they brought her to such a pass that, wearied out by her harassed life, she came of her own accord to throw herself into the arms of Florence. The city of Siena has never changed her government with Florentine aid except when this aid has been weak and infrequent. Because when it has been frequent and strong, it has united that city in the defense of the government in power. I wish to add another instance to those given above. Filippo Visconti Duke of Milan many times began war against the Florentines, relying on their dissensions, and he always came out the loser. Hence he was forced to say, grieving

2. DISCOURSES 2. 21.

over his undertakings, that Florentine follies had made him spend uselessly two millions in gold.

So as I said above, the Veientians and the Tuscans were deceived by this opinion and at last were defeated in battle by the Romans. Similarly in the future anybody will be deceived who in a like way and for a like reason believes he can conquer a people.

CHAPTER 26. CONTEMPT AND INSULT ROUSE HATRED AGAINST THOSE WHO EMPLOY THEM, WITHOUT ANY PROFIT TO THEMSELVES

I believe it very prudent to abstain from menacing and insulting anybody with words, for neither of them takes any strength from the enemy. But menaces make him more cautious, insults make him hate you more and plan with greater zeal to harm you.

[*The Veientians pay the penalty of insolence*]

The Veientians, of whom I spoke in the chapter above, serve as an example, for to the injury of war against the Romans they added abuse in words. From this every prudent general will make his soldiers refrain, because such words inflame the enemy and egg him on to revenge, yet in no way impede him, as I said, in attack. Hence they are all weapons turned against you. Of this there once was a noteworthy instance in Asia, where Gabade, general of the Persians, encamped before Amida a long time; tired out by the tedium of the siege, he decided to leave. So when he did strike his camp, the garrison, having all come on the walls, in their pride of victory did not refrain from any sort of insult, but abused, scoffed at and insulted the enemy for their worthlessness and cowardice. Irritated by this, Gabade changed his plan, and when he returned to the siege, so great was his indignation at the insult that in a few days he took and sacked the town. And this same thing happened to the Veientians, for whom, as I have said, it was not enough to make war on the Romans, but they also affronted them with words and, going as far as the stockade of the camp to speak insults to them, irritated them much more with words than with arms, so that those soldiers who at first fought unwillingly forced the Consuls to join battle. Hence the Veientians, like the aforesaid, bore the penalty of their insolence.

[*Good leaders do not allow taunting*]

Good leaders of armies, then, and good rulers of republics employ all suitable measures against the use of insults and taunts either in their city or in their army, either among themselves or against an enemy, because, if used against an enemy, the troubles above mentioned result from them; among themselves they produce something worse, if not guarded against as prudent men always do guard against them.

[*The Romans forbade taunting jests*]

The Roman legions left at Capua plotted against the Capuans, as will be related in its place,[1] and this conspiracy produced a mutiny. When Valerius Corvinus settled this, among the articles put in the agreement, very heavy penalties were laid down for those who ever twitted a soldier with that mutiny. Tiberius Gracchus, having in the war with Hannibal been made leader of a certain number of slaves whom the Romans through lack of men had armed, very early decreed a capital penalty to anybody who twitted any of these men with slavery. So injurious a thing did the Romans esteem it, as has been said above, to taunt men and to twit them with any disgrace, for there is nothing that inflames the minds of men more or raises greater anger whether it is said in earnest or jokingly, "For rude jests, when too much founded on truth, leave a bitter memory."[2]

1. DISCOURSES 3. 6, *near the end.*
2. *Tacitus,* ANNALS 15. 68.

CHAPTER 27. FOR PRUDENT PRINCES AND REPUBLICS, TO CONQUER IS ALWAYS ENOUGH; GENERALLY, WHEN THAT IS NOT ENOUGH, LOSS RESULTS

[*False hopes lead to excessive demands*]

The use of disrespectful words to an enemy generally comes from haughtiness caused by victory or false hope of victory. This false hope makes men err not only in speech but also in action. Because such hope, when it enters men's breasts, makes them go beyond bounds and lose—generally—their opportunity to gain a good thing that is sure, through hoping to gain a better one that is unsure. And because this is a topic that deserves reflection, for men often deceive themselves about it, with injury to their states, I shall demonstrate it in detail with instances ancient and modern, since with arguments I cannot give such a clear demonstration.

[Carthage should have been satisfied with Cannae]

Hannibal, after defeating the Romans at Cannae, sent messengers to Carthage to announce his victory and ask assistance.[1] The Senate debated what was to be done. Hanno, an old and prudent Carthaginian citizen, advised them to use the victory wisely in making peace with the Romans, since, having conquered, they could do so with honorable conditions, and they could not expect to do so after a defeat; the Carthaginians should intend to show the Romans that they were strong enough to fight them, and after winning a victory they should strive not to lose it in the hope of a greater one. They did not adopt this plan, but nevertheless it was later recognized by the Carthaginian senate as indeed wise, after their chance was lost.

[The Tyrians should have accepted terms from Alexander]

When Alexander the Great had already taken all the East, the Republic of Tyre, noble in those times, and powerful because the city was surrounded by water, like that of the Venetians, observed Alexander's greatness; hence she sent him ambassadors saying that the Tyrians were willing to be his good servants and to give him the obedience he wished, but that they would not receive him or his people into their city. Alexander, angered because one city expected to close to him such gates as all the world had opened, rebuffed them and, not accepting their conditions, besieged the city. She was surrounded by water, and very well provided with food and other supplies necessary to defense, so that after four months Alexander realized that one city to its glory was taking from him more time than had been taken by many other conquests. Hence he determined to attempt an agreement and to yield them what they had asked. But the people of Tyre, who had grown haughty, not merely did not accept the agreement, but killed those who came to negotiate about it. Alexander, angered by this, set himself to the siege with such force that he took and demolished the city, and killed and enslaved the people.

1. *Livy* 23. 11–13.

[*Florentine overconfidence led to ruin*]

In 1512 a Spanish army came into Florentine territory to put the Medici back in Florence and to lay tribute on the city; they had been brought there by men inside the city, who had given them hope that as soon as they were in Florentine territory, the citizens would take arms in their favor. But after the Spanish entered the plain, and no one showed himself, and they were in need of food, they tried to make a truce. The people of Florence, made haughty by this, did not accept it. From this came the loss of Prato and the ruin of that government.

[*No offer of terms is so bad that it does not include some gain*]

Rulers who are attacked, then, cannot make a greater mistake, when the attack is made by men far exceeding them in power, than to refuse every agreement, especially when it is offered to them, be-cause there will never be an offer so bad that it will not in some way benefit him who accepts it, and contain something of victory for him. It should have been enough for the people of Tyre that Alexander would accept those conditions that he had first refused, and their victory was sufficient when, with weapons in their hands, they had made so great a man comply with their will. It should also have sufficed the Florentine people, because it was victory enough for them if the Spanish army yielded to some of their wishes and did not secure all of its own. That army's intention was, first, to change the government of Florence, second, to break off her alliance with France, third, to get money from Florence. If of these things the army gained two, the second and third, and to the people one was left, the preservation of their government, each party had in the agreement some honor and some satisfaction. The people should not have cared for the two things, if they were left alive. They should not have been willing, even though they looked for a greater and almost certain victory, to turn the outcome over in any way to the pleasure of Fortune, putting up their last stake, which no prudent man risks unless he must.

[*Hannibal's example*]

Hannibal, having left Italy, where he had won renown for six-teen years, on the summons of the Carthaginians to rescue his native city, found Hasdrubal and Syfax defeated; he found the kingdom of Numidia lost and Carthage confined to the space within her walls, with no resource left save himself and his army. Knowing that the city was his country's last stake, Hannibal did not wish to risk her until he had tried every other remedy; and he was not ashamed to ask for peace, judging that if his country had any remedy, it was in that and not in war. But when peace was then denied to him, he deter' mined not to refrain from fighting, even though he might lose, judging that it was still possible for him to win or, losing, to lose gloriously. And if Hannibal, who was so able and whose army was intact, sought peace rather than battle, when he saw that if it were lost his native land would become a slave, what should be done by a man less able and less experienced? But men make this blunder because they do not know how to put limits to their hopes. And when they rely on these and do not make an estimate of themselves, they fall.

CHAPTER 28. IT IS DANGEROUS FOR A REPUBLIC OR A PRINCE NOT TO AVENGE AN INJURY DONE TO THE PUB' LIC OR TO AN INDIVIDUAL

[The Romans did not punish the Fabii]

What anger makes men do can easily be learned from what happened to the Romans when they sent the three Fabii as ambas' sadors to the French who were attacking Tuscany and in particular Chiusi. The Romans sent these ambassadors because the people of Chiusi applied to Rome for aid against the French; in the name of the Roman people the three were to require the French to hold back from making war on the Tuscans. But being on the spot and better fitted to act than to speak, the ambassadors, seeing the French and the Tuscans in battle, put themselves at the front of the army to fight against the French. The result, since they were recognized, was that the French turned against the Romans all the anger they had felt against the Tuscans. After the French through ambassadors had complained to the Roman Senate about such an offense and asked that in satisfaction of the injury it should deliver up to them the aforesaid Fabii, their anger grew greater because not merely did

Rome not hand the Fabii over or in any way punish them, but when the elections came she made them Tribunes with consular power. Hence the French, seeing those honored who should have been punished, took it as all done to dishonor and humiliate themselves. Fired with scorn and rage, they marched against Rome and took it, except the Capitol. This defeat came upon the Romans merely as a result of their failure to observe justice, because, when their ambas-sadors had sinned "against the law of nations,"[1] and should have been punished, they were honored.

[*A prince must not injure an individual*]

So it must be remembered that every republic and every prince should take great care not to do such injury, not merely to a large body but even to an individual. Because if a man is greatly injured either by the state or by a single person, and is not avenged to his satisfaction, if he lives in a republic, he seeks, even with its ruin, to get his revenge. If he lives under a prince and has any nobility in himself, he is never quiet until in some way he has avenged himself on him, even though he sees therein his own injury.

[*Philip of Macedon's failure*]

To verify this, there is no finer or truer instance than that of Philip, King of Macedonia, Alexander's father. He had in his court Pausanias, a youth handsome and highborn; with him Attalus, one of the chief men close to Philip, fell in love. Having many times endeavored to get him to consent to him, and finding him averse to such things, Attalus determined to get by deception and force that which he saw he was not going to get in any other way. And giving a splendid banquet, to which Pausanias and many other highborn barons came, when each one was full of food and wine, he had Pausanias seized and put into bonds; then he not merely vented his lust by force, but also, for greater ignominy, had many others in the same way violate him. Of this injury Pausanias again and again complained to Philip; yet, after keeping him for a time in the hope that he would avenge him, Philip not merely did not avenge him, but put Attalus at the head of the government in one of the Greek provinces. Hence Pausanias, seeing his enemy honored and not punished, turned all his rage not against the one who had done him

1. *Livy 5. 36.*

the injury, but against Philip, who had not avenged him. And on the morning of a feast for the wedding of Philip's daughter, whom he had married to Alexander of Epirus, when Philip was going to the temple to celebrate it, Pausanias killed him between the two Alexanders, son-in-law and son.

This instance is much like that of the Romans, and noteworthy for whoever governs, for he ought never to esteem anyone so lightly as to believe that, when injury is piled on injury, an injured man will not decide on getting revenge, in spite of all danger and personal harm to himself.

CHAPTER 29. FORTUNE BLINDS THE INTEL-LECTS OF MEN WHEN SHE DOES NOT WISH THEM TO OPPOSE HER PLANS[1]

[The Heavens control human affairs]

If we observe carefully how human affairs go on, many times we see that things come up and events take place against which the Heavens do not wish any provision to be made. And if this I am going to speak of happened at Rome, where there was such great efficiency, so much religion, and such good organization, it is not strange that such things happen more often in cities or countries which lack the things aforesaid.

[The Heavens determined Roman history]

Because this instance is very noteworthy for showing Heaven's power over human affairs, Titus Livius explains it at length in very effective words, saying that since Heaven for some reason wished the Romans to know its power, it first caused the blunder of those Fabii who went as ambassadors to the French and by their actions stirred up the French to make war on Rome; then it arranged that nothing worthy of the Roman people should be done in Rome to put a stop to that war; before that, it had arranged for Camillus, who was their sole and only resource against such a great evil, to be sent in exile to Ardea. Then when the French came toward Rome, those who many times—to deal with attacks by the Volscians and other neigh-boring enemies—had set up a Dictator, on the coming of the French

1. Livy 5. 37.

did not establish one. Also in making their choice of soldiers, they did it feebly and without any exceptional effort; and they were so slow about taking arms that they were hardly in time to meet the French on the River Allia, ten miles distant from Rome. There the Tribunes pitched their camp, without any of their usual attention, not examining the place beforehand and not surrounding it with a ditch and a stockade, not using any resource human or divine. And in drawing up for the battle they made their order loose and feeble; as a result, neither the soldiers nor the leaders did anything worthy of Roman discipline. Then they fought without any bloodshed, for they fled before they were attacked; the larger part of them went off to Veii, the rest went back to Rome; these, without at all going into their houses, went into the Capitol, so that the Senate, without thought of defending Rome, did not even do so much as close the gates. Part of the people fled, part went with the soldiers to the Capitol. Still, in defending that, they used some methods that were not disorderly, for they did not burden it with unserviceable persons, they put there all the grain possible, so that they could endure a siege, and of the unserviceable throng of old men, women, and children, the greater part fled into the surrounding cities; the rest remained in Rome in the power of the French. Hence, he who has read the things done by that people for so many years before would not at all believe that it was the same people. When Titus Livius has spoken of all the aforesaid blunders, he concludes by saying: "To such an extent does Fortune blind men's intellects when she does not wish them to check her gathering might."[2] Nothing can be more true than this conclusion.

[Fortune and the Heavens]

Hence men who commonly live amid great troubles or successes deserve less praise or less blame, because most of the time we see that they have been pushed into a destructive or an elevated action by some great advantage that the Heavens have bestowed on them, giving them opportunity—or taking it from them—to work effec‑ tively. Skilfully Fortune does this, since she chooses a man, when she plans to bring to pass great things, who is of so much perception and so much ability that he recognizes the opportunities she puts before him. So in the same way when she intends to bring to pass

2. *See n. 1 above.*

great failures, she puts there men to promote such failure. And if somebody there is able to oppose her, she either kills him or deprives him of all means for doing anything good.

[Fortune caused Rome's greatness]

From this passage we easily see that Fortune, in order to make Rome stronger and bring her to the greatness she attained, judged that it was necessary to afflict her (as we shall discuss at length in the beginning of the following book) but did not wish entirely to ruin her. And for this reason she had Camillus exiled and not killed, had Rome captured but not the Capitol, arranged that the Romans in order to protect Rome should not plan anything good, and that later to defend the Capitol they should not fail to use any good measure. She arranged, in order that Rome might be taken, to have the greater part of the soldiers defeated at Allia run off to Veii. Thus she removed every way for defending the city of Rome. Yet in arranging this she prepared everything for its recapture, having brought a Roman army unharmed to Veii, and Camillus to Ardea, in order to be able to make a great muster, under a general not spotted with any ignominy through defeat and unharmed in reputation, for the recapture of their native city.

[Men can assist Fortune; they cannot thwart her]

We could bring up in support of what we have said some modern instances, but because we do not consider them necessary, since this is enough to satisfy anybody, we omit them. I assert, indeed, once more that it is very true, according to what we see in all the histories, that men are able to assist Fortune but not to thwart her. They can weave her designs but cannot destroy them. They ought, then, never to give up as beaten, because, since they do not know her purpose and she goes through crooked and unknown roads, they can always hope, and hoping are not to give up, in whatever fortune and whatever affliction they may be.

CHAPTER 30. REPUBLICS AND PRINCES TRULY POWERFUL DO NOT BUY FRIEND⁄ SHIP WITH MONEY BUT WITH THE MIGHT AND REPUTATION OF THEIR FORCES

[*Fortune aided the Romans at last*]

So the Romans were besieged in the Capitol, and though they looked for aid from Veii and from Camillus, yet being pressed by hunger they came to an understanding with the French to ransom themselves for a certain amount of gold. But when according to the agreement they were already weighing out the gold, Camillus came up with his army; this, says the historian, Fortune brought about "that the Romans might not live as bought with gold."[1] The event is noteworthy not merely in this matter but also in the course of this republic's history, in which it may be seen that they never gained cities with money, never made peace with money, but always by force of arms—something that I do not believe was ever true of any other republic.

[*If a state is powerful, its friendship is sought*]

And among the other signs by which a state's power is known is the way she lives with her neighbors. And when she conducts her⁄ self in such a manner that the neighbors, in order to have her as a friend, are her tributaries, that state gives a sure sign of power. But when the said neighbors, though inferior to her, get money from her, she gives an important sign of her weakness. Read all the Roman histories and you will see that the Massilians, the Aedui, the Rho⁄ dians, Hiero of Syracuse, Kings Eumenes and Massinissa, who all were near the boundaries of the Roman Empire, in order to have her friendship, competed in payment and tribute for her needs, not seeking from it any other return than to be defended.

[*States that hire friends are not strong*]

The opposite appears in weak states. And beginning with ours of Florence, in times past, when her reputation was greatest, there was not a lordling in the Romagna who did not have a subsidy from her. And besides she gave them to the Perugians, to the Castellani,

---

1. Livy 5. 49. *Fortune is less prominent in Livy than Machiavelli suggests.*

and to all her other neighbors. Yet if this city had been armed and
strong, everything would have gone in the opposite way, for many,
in order to have her protection, would have given money to her, and
would have sought not to sell their friendship but to buy hers. Nor
have the Florentines alone lived in such baseness, but also the Venetians and the King of France, who, with so great a kingdom, lives
as a tributary to the Swiss and to the King of England. This all
comes from his having disarmed his people and from having preferred—that king and the others named before—to enjoy an immediate profit, to be able to plunder the people, and to escape an imagined
rather than a real danger, instead of doing things that would give
them security and make their states happy for ever. This bad policy,
if sometimes it does produce some years of quiet, is in time a cause of
want, of damage, and of destruction that cannot be remedied. It
would take too long to tell how many times the Florentines, the
Venetians, and this kingdom have in their wars bought themselves
off, and how many times they have been subjected to insult—which
the Romans once only submitted to. It would take too long to tell
how many cities the Florentines and the Venetians have bought—
the folly of which appeared later, for what they acquire with gold
they cannot defend with steel. Yet the Romans kept to this noble
conduct and this policy as long as they were free, but when they
came under the emperors, and the emperors were wicked and loved
the shade more than the sun, they also bought themselves off, now
from the Parthians, now from the Germans, now from other peoples
nearby. This began the downfall of so great an empire.

[Strong states arm their own people]

Such troubles come, therefore, from having disarmed your people.
From this results another still greater, that the closer an enemy comes
to you, the weaker he finds you. For he who lives in the ways spoken
of above treats badly those subjects that are within his empire, and
treats well those on its boundaries, in order to have men well disposed for keeping the enemy at a distance. As a result of this, in
order to keep him more distant, he gives subsidies to those lords and
peoples who are near his boundaries. The result is that states of that
sort make some little resistance on their boundaries, but when an
enemy has passed them, they have no recourse. And they do not see
that such a way of proceeding is opposed to every good method.

The heart and the vital parts of a body should be kept armored, and not the extremities. For without the latter it lives, but when the former is injured, it dies; and these states keep their hearts unarmored and their hands and feet armored. What this error has done to Florence has been seen and is seen every day; and when an army passes her boundaries and comes within them close to her heart, she has no further resource. About the Venetians, a few years ago, the same thing was proved, and if their city had not been surrounded by the waters, we should have beheld her end. This has not been experienced so often in France, because that kingdom is so great that it has few enemies more powerful. Nevertheless, when the English attacked in 1513, the entire country trembled. And the King himself and everybody else realized that a single defeat might take away his kingdom and his government.

[Roman power founded on an armed people]

To the Romans the opposite would have happened, because the nearer an enemy approached to Rome, the stronger he found that city in resisting him. When Hannibal invaded Italy, after three defeats and after the deaths of so many generals and soldiers, they not merely held out against the enemy but won the war. It all was caused by having the heart well armored and taking less account of the extremities, because the foundation of her state was the Roman people, the Latin power, the associated cities in Italy, and the colonies, from which they drew so many soldiers that with these they were strong enough to fight and hold the world. That this is true is shown by the question Hanno the Carthaginian asked the messengers Hannibal sent after the defeat of Cannae. After they had enlarged on what Hannibal had done, Hanno asked if anybody had come from the Roman people to seek peace and if any city of the Latin nation and of the colonies had rebelled against the Romans, and when both questions were answered in the negative, Hanno replied: "This war is still as undecided as before."[2]

[Fortune shows her power when men are weak]

We see, therefore, both from this discussion and from what we have many times said elsewhere, how much in their way of proceeding present republics differ from ancient ones. We also see, for

2. *Livy* 23. 13.

this reason, every day miraculous losses and miraculous gains. Because, where men have little ability, Fortune shows her power much, and because she is variable, republics and states often vary, and vary they always will until some one arises who is so great a lover of antiquity that he will rule Fortune in such a way that she will not have cause to show in every revolution of the sun how much she can do.

CHAPTER 31. IT IS DANGEROUS TO BELIEVE BANISHED MEN

[*The mistake of Alexander of Epirus*]

It does not seem to me apart from the subject to consider in one of these *Discourses* how dangerous it is to believe those who have been driven from their native lands, since such matters must be dealt with every day by those who occupy places of authority. I do this especially since I can demonstrate it with a memorable example brought up by Titus Livius in his *History*,[1] though it is little related to his theme. When Alexander the Great crossed over into Asia with his army, Alexander of Epirus, his brother-in-law and uncle, came with soldiers into Italy, summoned by the banished Lucanians, who led him to expect that with their assistance he could take possession of that whole province. When therefore, by reason of their pledge and expectation, he came into Italy, they killed him, for their fellow citizens promised to take them back into their native city if they slew him.

[*Vain are the pledges of exiles*]

It should be observed, therefore, how vain are the pledges and promises of those who are excluded from their native city. For as to their loyalty, it must be reckoned that whenever through other means than yours they can enter again into their native city, they will leave you and ally themselves with others, notwithstanding any promises they have made. And as to vain promises and hopes, so violent is their desire to return home that they naturally believe many things that are false, and to these they artfully join many others. Hence, between what they believe and what they tell you they believe, they

1. Livy 8. 3.

fill you with such hope that, if you rely on it, you either enter into useless expense or go into an enterprise in which you are ruined.

[*Themistocles in exile*]

I hope the example of the aforesaid Alexander is enough, with the addition of Themistocles of Athens. The latter, when condemned as a rebel, fled into Asia to Darius, where he made such great promises, if the king would attack Greece, that Darius undertook the enterprise. When Themistocles later could not fulfil his promises, he took poison, either from shame or fear of punishment. And if Themistocles, a man of great ability, made such an error, we can estimate how much more they err in such matters who, having weaker minds, allow themselves to be more moved by their desires and passions. It is well then for a prince to be slow about getting into any undertaking on a banished man's information, because almost always he will at the end suffer shame or very heavy damage.

And because also only on rare occasions do men succeed in taking cities by fraud and by connections that they have inside them, it seems to me not inappropriate to discuss it in the next chapter, adding the many ways in which the Romans took them.

CHAPTER 32. IN HOW MANY WAYS THE ROMANS TOOK CITIES

[*The Romans did not use slow methods*]

Since all the Romans were experienced in war, they carried it on always with every advantage, both as to expense and as to everything that is needed in it. From this it came that they avoided taking towns by investment, because they believed the trouble and expense of this method much greater than the benefit they could get from the capture. Therefore they believed it better and more profitable to subjugate cities by any other method than by blockading them. Hence in so many wars and in so many years they carried out very few investments.

[*Methods of attack*]

The methods, then, by which they gained cities, were either direct attack or surrender. Direct attack was either by force and open violence, or by force mixed with fraud. The first method of open violence was assault, without battering the walls (which they called "to attack the city with a circle,"[1] because they surrounded the city with the whole army and attacked it on all sides); many times they were successful in taking a city, even though it was a very great one, by one assault, as when Scipio took New Carthage in Spain.[2] When such an assault failed, they set themselves to break the walls with rams and with their other machines of war; or they made a mine and through that entered into the city (in that way they took the city of Veii); or, to be on a level with those who defended the walls, they made towers of wood, or they made banks of earth resting against the walls from outside, in order to reach the height of the walls on them.

[Attack on all sides]

Against these assaults, the defenders of the city, in the first case, that of being attacked on all sides, were subject to more sudden danger and had more doubtful means of resistance; though they needed to have everywhere enough defenders, yet their soldiers were not so many that they could be adequate everywhere, or could be shifted to places in danger; or if they could be, they were not all of equal spirit to resist, and if the battle was yielded at one point they all were lost. For this reason, as I have said, this method many times had a fortunate outcome. But when it did not succeed at first, the Romans did not often try it again; it was dangerous because, being spread out through so much space, their army was everywhere too weak to resist a sally that those within might make, and also the soldiers were in disorder and scattered; but for once and as a surprise they would try that method.

[Methods of defense]

As to the breaking of the walls, the defenders thwarted it, as at the present time, with embankments. And to resist mines, they made a countermine, and thus combated the enemy, either with arms or with other devices. Among the latter was this: They filled tubs with feathers in which they put fire, and when they were burning they put

1. Livy 10. 43; 23. 44.
2. The attempt to take New Carthage at the first attack failed (Livy 26. 45); a later assault succeeded.

them in the mine, so that with their smoke and stench they impeded the entrance of the enemy. And if they were assailed with towers, they tried to destroy them with fire. And as to the mounds of earth, they broke the wall at the base, where the banks rested against it, and drew into the city the earth that those outside heaped up there; hence, since earth was put down outside and taken away inside, the bank did not increase.

[*Assault and blockade*]

These methods for capture cannot be tried at great length, but it is necessary either to give up the siege or to seek to win the war by other methods, as Scipio did when, after invading Africa, he assaulted Utica and did not succeed in taking it, for then he retired from the place and sought to defeat the Carthaginian armies.[3] Or investment can be tried, as at Veii, Capua, Carthage, Jerusalem, and like cities, which the Romans took by investment.

[*Stratagem and surprise*]

The conquest of cities by stealthy violence comes about as at Palaepolis, which the Romans took through secret dealings with those in the city. Many captures of this sort have been attempted by the Romans and others, but few of them have succeeded. The reason is that the slightest obstacle breaks the plot, and obstacles come easily. The conspiracy may be discovered before it is put into action; for such discovery is not difficult both through the disloyalty of those with whom the conspiracy is shared and through the difficulty of planning it, since arrangements must be made with enemies and with those to whom you are not allowed to speak, except under some pretext. But when the conspiracy is not discovered in the planning, there then rise a thousand difficulties in putting it into action. Because if you come before the time set, or if you come after it, everything is spoiled; if an accidental noise is raised, like the geese of the Capitol, if an accustomed routine is broken—the slightest error, the least mistake ruins the affair. To this must be added the shades of night, which cause great fear to those who work in these dangerous enterprises. And since most of the men who are taken into such enterprises are not expert in the layout of the city and of the places where they are led, they are upset, grow timid, are confused by the slightest

3. *Livy 29. 34-35; 30. 3-6.*

accident, and any deceptive appearance is enough to make them take
to flight. There has never been anybody more fortunate in these
tricky expeditions at night than Aratus of Sicyon, yet, however much
he was worth in these, in open operations by daylight he was to the
same extent a coward. It can be judged that this was rather the
result of an occult power in him than because night attacks ought
naturally to be more successful. Of these types, then, many are
planned, few are put to the test, and very few succeed.

[*The surrender of cities*]

As to gaining cities by surrender, either they are given up willingly or they are taken by force. Willingness comes either from some
external need that drives them to take refuge with you, as did Capua
with the Romans, or through a desire to be governed well, since they
are attracted by the good government that some prince furnishes those
who willingly put themselves into his arms, as did the Rhodians, the
Massilians, and other like cities that gave themselves to the Roman
people. As to forced surrender, either such force comes from a long
investment, as has been said above; or it comes from continual injury
by raids, pillaging, and other acts of injury; to escape these a city
gives up.

[*Victory in the field more profitable than siege*]

Of all the methods mentioned, the Romans used this last more
than any other. And they gave their attention for more than 450
years to wearing out their neighbors with defeats and with raids, and
by means of treaties getting ascendancy over them, as we have said in
other places.[4] And on such a method they always relied, though they
would try all of them, but in the others they found things either
dangerous or useless. For in an investment there are length of time
and expense; in an assault, risk and danger; in conspiracies, uncertainty. And they saw that by routing a hostile army they could
gain a kingdom in a day, but in taking a stubborn city by investment
they would use up many years.

4. DISCOURSES 2. 1, 4.

CHAPTER 33. THE ROMANS GAVE THE GENERALS OF THEIR ARMIES PLENARY POWER

I judge that anyone reading this *History* by Livy, to get profit from it, must consider all the ways in which the Roman People and Senate conducted themselves. Among the matters deserving consideration is the sort of authority with which they sent out their Consuls, Dictators, and other army leaders; their authority was very great, and the Senate reserved nothing except authority to start new wars and to make treaties. Everything else they handed over to the judgment and power of the Consul. When a war was determined on by the people and the Senate, against the Latins for instance, they left all the rest to the Consul's judgment; he could fight a battle or not fight one, and attack this city or the other, as he thought best.

[*The instance of Fabius*]

These things are confirmed by many instances, and especially by what happened in an expedition against the Tuscans. After Fabius the Consul had beaten them near Sutri, and then planned to march his army through the forest of Cimina and go into Tuscany, not merely did he not take counsel with the Senate but he did not give them any warning, though war would have to be made in a region new, risky and dangerous. This is testified to also by the decision made in opposition to this by the Senate, which, learning of Fabius' victory and fearing that he would resolve to march through the said forest into Tuscany, and judging it unwise to attempt that war and run that risk, sent two legates to Fabius to inform him that he was not to march into Tuscany. They arrived when he had already marched through and had won the victory; so instead of hinderers of the war they became announcers of his conquest and of the glory he had won.[1]

[*A general must be on the spot*]

He who will consider this method carefully will see that it was very prudently used; for if the Senate had decreed that in war a Consul should go along gradually, according to their directions, they

1. Livy 9. 35–36.

would have made him less watchful and slower, since he would have felt that the glory of the victory was not all his but was shared by the Senate, by whose advice he had been controlled. Besides this, the Senate would have taken the obligation of giving advice on a matter about which they would not be informed, for notwithstanding that all the men in it were very well trained in war, nonetheless, not being on the spot and not knowing countless particulars that one must know in order to advise well, they would have made countless mistakes in their advice. Because of this they wished the Consul to act for himself and to have all the glory; love of that they judged would be his rule and prescript for doing his best.

[Florentine and Venetian error]

This matter I note the more gladly because I see that the republics of the present times, such as the Venetian and the Florentine, understand it differently, and if their generals, overseers, and commissioners have to place one cannon, they wish to know it and to give advice. This method deserves the same praise as do their others, which, altogether, have brought them to the place they occupy at present.

BOOK THREE

CHAPTER 1. IF A RELIGION OR A REPUBLIC IS TO LIVE LONG, IT MUST OFTEN BE BROUGHT BACK TOWARD ITS BEGINNINGS

It is most certain that there is a limit for the existence of all things in the world; but they generally move through the entire course ordained for them by Heaven without getting their bodies into confusion but keeping them in the way ordained; this way either does not change or, if it does, the change is to their advantage, not to their harm. And because I am speaking of mixed bodies, such as republics and religions, I say that those changes are to their advantage that take them back toward their beginnings. And therefore those are best organized and have longest life that through their institutions can often renew themselves or that by some accident outside their organization come to such renewal. And it is clearer than light that if these bodies are not renewed they do not last. The way to renew them, as I have said, is to carry them back to their beginnings; because all the beginnings of religions and of republics and of kingdoms must possess some goodness by means of which they gain their first reputation and their first growth. Since in the process of time that goodness is corrupted, if something does not happen that takes it back to the right position, such corruption necessarily kills that body. The doctors of medicine say, speaking of the bodies of men, that "daily something is added that now and then needs cure."

[Republics]

This regress toward the beginning—as observed in republics—results from either external accident or internal prudence. As to the first, we see that Rome had to be captured by the French if she was going to be born again and that, being born again, she had to take on new life and new vigor and take up again the observance of religion and justice, which were getting corrupt. Livy's *History* makes this very intelligible, for he shows that in leading out the army against the French and in setting up the Tribunes with consular power, the Romans observed no religious ceremony.[1] So in the same

1. *Livy 5. 38.*

way not merely did they not punish the three Fabii who had fought the French "against the law of nations"[2] but they made them Tribunes. And one can easily suppose that they were taking less account of other good laws, laid down by Romulus and their other prudent princes, than was fitting and necessary for keeping their government free. Then came this blow from outside, in order that the city might renew all her basic institutions and the people might learn the necessity not merely of maintaining religion and justice, but also of esteeming good citizens and taking more account of their ability than of those comforts which, as a result of their deeds, the people themselves might lack. We see that this succeeded completely, because, as soon as they recaptured Rome, they renewed all the rites of their ancient religion; they punished those Fabii who had fought "against the law of nations"; and in addition they so much esteemed the ability and goodness of Camillus that the Senate and the others, abandoning all envy, put upon him the entire burden of the republic.

It is necessary, then, as I have said, that men who live together in any organization often examine themselves, either as a result of such external events or as a result of internal ones. As to the latter, the cause must be either a law, which often examines the record of the men who are in that body; or actually a good man who arises among them, who with his striking words and his vigorous actions produces the same result as the statute. This good effect, then, comes about in republics either by virtue of a man or by virtue of a law.

[Renovation by law]

As to the effect of law, the legal means that brought the Roman republic back toward its beginning were the Tribunes of the People, the Censors, and all the other laws that opposed the ambition and pride of the citizens. These legal means need to be brought to life by the wisdom of a citizen who courageously strives to enforce them against the power of those who violate them. Of such enforcement, before the capture of Rome by the French, there were notable instances in the death of the sons of Brutus, the death of the Ten Citizens, and that of Maelius the corn-merchant. After the capture of Rome came Manlius Capitolinus' death, the death of Manlius Torquatus' son, Papirius Cursor's prosecution of Fabius his Master of the Horse, and the accusations against the Scipios.

2. Livy 5. 36.

These things, because they were extreme and noteworthy, whenever one of them came up, made men draw back to their proper
stations; and as they became rarer, they also gave men more room for
growing wicked and acting in a more dangerous and lawless fashion.
For this reason, from one such enforcement of the law to the next,
there should be a lapse of not more than ten years, because, when that
time has gone by, men change their habits and break the laws; and
if something does not happen to bring the penalty back to their
memories and renew fear in their minds, so many offenders quickly
join together that they cannot be punished without danger. On this
matter, those who managed the government of Florence from 1434
to 1494 commonly said that every five years they needed to revise the
government. Otherwise they could hardly maintain it. By revising
the government they meant inspiring such terror and such fear in the
people as they had inspired on first taking charge, for at that time
they punished those who, according to that kind of government, had
done wrong. When the memory of such punishment disappears,
men take courage to attempt innovations and to speak evil; therefore
it is necessary to provide against them by moving the government
back toward its beginnings.

[Renovation by one man]

This movement of republics back toward their beginnings is
accomplished also by the mere excellence of one man, without reliance on any law that spurs people on to action; yet these men are of
such reputation and their example is so powerful that good men wish
to imitate them, and the wicked are ashamed to live a life contrary to
theirs. Those in Rome who especially produced these good results
were Horatius Cocles, Scaevola, Fabricius, the two Decii, Regulus
Attilius, and some others, who with their extraordinary and noble
examples produced in Rome almost the same effect as laws and customs. If such instances of enforcement as I mention above, together
with such individual examples, had appeared at least every ten years
in that city, their necessary result would have been that Rome would
never have become corrupt. But as soon as both of these became
rare, corruption increased, because after Marcus Regulus there is no
other such instance. Though there were two Catos, so great was the
distance from him to them and between them from one to the other,
and they were so solitary, that with their examples they could ac-

complish nothing good. Especially the last Cato, finding the city for the most part corrupt, could not with his example improve the citizens. Need I say more on republics?

[*Reform in religious bodies*]

In religious bodies these renewals are also necessary, as we see through the example of our religion, which, if Saint Francis and Saint Dominic had not brought it back toward its beginnings, would have entirely disappeared. They with their poverty and with the example of Christ's life brought it back into the minds of men when it had disappeared from them. The power of their new orders is the reason why the improbity of the prelates and the heads of our religion does not ruin it; for still living in poverty and having great influence with the people because of hearing confessions and preach-ing, they give them to understand that it is evil to speak evil of what is evil, and that it is good to live under the prelates' control and, if prelates make errors, to leave them to God for punishment. So the prelates do the worst they can, because they do not fear that punish-ment which they do not see and do not believe in. This renewal, then, has maintained and still maintains our religion.

[*Reform of kingdoms*]

Kingdoms also need to be renewed and to have their laws brought back toward their beginnings. We see what good results this plan produces in the kingdom of France, which lives under laws and under regulations more than any other kingdom. Of these laws and regulations the parliaments are the upholders, and especially that of Paris. They are renewed by it every time it prosecutes a prince of that kingdom and rules against the king in its decisions. Up to now it has held its own because it has been a firm enforcer of law against the nobility. But if at any time it fails to punish the nobility, and such cases multiply, without doubt either they will have to be corrected with great disturbance, or that kingdom will fall to pieces.

I conclude, therefore, that nothing is more necessary to a com-munity, whether it be religious group or kingdom or republic, than to give back to it such a reputation as it had in its beginning, and to strive that either good regulations or good men may produce this effect and that it will not need to be done by an external force. Because, though sometimes the latter may be the best remedy, as it was at Rome, it is so dangerous that it is not in any way to be desired.

[*The subject of the third book of the* Discourses]

To show everybody how the deeds of individuals increased Roman greatness, and how in that city they caused many good effects, I shall now narrate and discuss them. Within such boundaries this Third Book and the last part of this First Decade will conclude. Though the deeds of the kings were great and noteworthy, nonetheless, since history sets them forth at length, I shall omit them, speaking only of some things they did relating to their private benefit. I shall begin with Brutus, the father of Roman liberty.

CHAPTER 2. IT IS VERY WISE TO PRETEND MADNESS AT THE RIGHT TIME

Nobody was ever so prudent or looked upon as so wise because of any excellent action of his as Junius Brutus deserves to be considered for his pretended idiocy. Though Titus Livius does not make plain more than one cause that would have led him to such pretense—namely, to be able to live more securely and keep his inherited property—nonetheless, considering his way of proceeding, we can believe that he pretended this also in order to be noticed less, and to have more chance for overcoming the king and freeing his country whenever he might have an opportunity. That he contemplated this appears, first, in his interpretation of the oracle of Apollo, when he pretended to fall in order to kiss the earth, judging that as a result he would get the gods to favor his plans. Later, it appears when, standing beside the dead Lucretia, he, among her father and her husband and her other relatives, was the leader in drawing the knife from her wound and making those present take an oath never in the future to allow anybody to be king in Rome.[1] From his example all those discontented with a prince can learn something. They ought first to measure and weigh their forces, and if they are powerful enough to reveal themselves as his enemies and make war openly upon him, they ought to take this way as less dangerous and more honorable. But if they are such that their forces are not strong enough for making open war, they should use every effort to make

1. *Livy* 1. 56–59.

themselves his friends; to this end they should take all the roads they judge necessary, devoting themselves to his pastimes and finding pleasure in everything which they see pleases him. This intimacy, first, lets you live in security; then, without your being in any danger, it lets you enjoy the prince's good fortune along with him, and it furnishes you every opportunity for carrying out your intention. It is true that, with respect to princes, some say you should try to stand not so near them that their ruin will include you, nor so far away that when they are ruined you will not be in time to surmount their ruin. Such a middle course would be the best if you could take it, but because it is, I believe, impossible, you must choose between the two methods mentioned above, that is, either you must keep at a distance or you must bind yourself to them. Anyone who does otherwise, if he is a man whose position makes him noteworthy, lives in continual peril. It is not enough to say: "I do not care about anything, I do not desire either honors or profits, I wish to live in retirement and without trouble." Such excuses are heard but are not accepted. Men of rank cannot decide to sit quiet even when they decide truly and without any ambition, because they are not believed. Hence even when they do wish to be quiet, other people will not leave them in quiet. You must, then, play the fool like Brutus, and often you play the madman, praising, speaking, seeing, and doing things contrary to your purpose, to please the prince.

Since we have spoken of the prudence of this man in regaining the liberty of Rome, let us speak now of his severity in maintaining it.

CHAPTER 3. IN ORDER TO MAINTAIN NEWLY GAINED LIBERTY, BRUTUS' SONS MUST BE KILLED[1]

Not less necessary than useful was Brutus' severity in maintaining in Rome the liberty he had gained there. It is an instance striking among recorded events that the father should sit on the judgment seat and not merely condemn his sons to death but be present at their deaths. And those who read ancient history will always observe that after a change of government, either from republic into tyranny or from tyranny into republic, the enemies of present conditions must

1. *Livy* 2. 5.

suffer some striking prosecution. For he who seizes a tyranny and does not kill Brutus, and he who sets a state free and does not kill Brutus' sons, maintains himself but a little while. Because this is discussed at length above,[2] I refer to what I said then.

I shall bring up here just one instance, which in our days and in our native city is worthy of notice. This is Piero Soderini, who believed that with patience and goodness he could overcome the longing of Brutus' sons to get back under another government; but he deceived himself. And though, being prudent, he recognized the necessity I have mentioned, and though chance and the ambition of those who assailed him gave him opportunity to destroy them, none-theless he never made up his mind to do so. He hesitated because he believed that with patience and goodness he could extinguish evil factions, and with rewards dispose of some men's hostility. More-over, he thought (and many times assured his friends of it) that in order vigorously to attack his opponents and to crush his adversaries, he needed to seize extralegal authority and to use the laws to destroy equality among the citizens. Such action, even if he did not then apply it tyrannically, would so greatly alarm the people generally that after his death they never again would agree to set up a gonfa-lonier for life—a custom which he judged it well to strengthen and maintain.

This scruple was wise and good. Yet on the other hand, he should never have allowed an evil to continue for the sake of a good, when that evil could easily crush that good. And since his works and his intention would be judged by their outcome, he should have believed that if Fortune and life were with him he could convince everybody that what he did was for the preservation of his native city and not for his own ambition. He could also have regulated things in such a way that no successor of his could do for a wicked end what he had done for a good one. But he was deceived in his first opinion, since he did not know that malice is not mastered by time nor placated by any gift. Hence, not having the wisdom to be Brutus-like, he lost together with his native city his position and his reputation.

As it is hard to keep a free state safe, so it is hard to keep a king-dom safe, as will be shown in the next chapter.

2. *Bk. 1, chap. 16.*

CHAPTER 4. A PRINCE IS NOT SECURE IN A PRINCEDOM WHILE THOSE WHO HAVE BEEN DEPRIVED OF IT ARE ALIVE[1]

The death of Tarquinius Priscus, caused by Ancus' sons, and the death of Servius Tullius caused by Tarquinius Superbus, show how difficult it is, and how dangerous, to deprive a man of a king-dom and leave him alive, even though the usurper seeks to win his favor with benefits. We see that Tarquinius Priscus was deceived in his belief that because the Roman kingdom had been given to him by the people and confirmed by the Senate he possessed it lawfully, nor did he believe that the anger of Ancus' sons was so strong that they would not be satisfied with what satisfied all Rome. But Ser-vius Tullius deceived himself, since he believed he could win the favor of Tarquin's sons with new benefits.

Wherefore, as to the first, every prince can learn that he has no lasting security for his princedom as long as they are alive whom he has deprived of it. As to the second, every ruler can be reminded that never have new benefits erased old injuries; and so much the less in so far as the new benefit is less than the injury. Without doubt Servius Tullius was imprudent in believing that Tarquin's sons would patiently be the sons-in-law of him over whom they thought they ought to be king. For this appetite for being king is so strong that it enters the breasts not merely of those to whom the kingship belongs, but of those to whom it does not belong. So it was for the wife of young Tarquin, Servius' daughter, who, moved by this fury, against all paternal devotion urged on her husband against her father to take away his life and his kingdom—so much higher she valued being queen than being daughter of a king.

If, then, Tarquinius Priscus and Servius Tullius lost their king-dom through not knowing how to secure themselves against those from whom they had snatched it, Tarquinius Superbus lost it through not sticking to the methods of the ancient kings, as will be shown in the following chapter.

1. Livy 1. 35-48.

CHAPTER 5. WHAT CAUSES A KINGDOM TO BE LOST BY A KING WHO HAS IN- HERITED IT[1]

Tarquinius Superbus, having killed Servius Tullius, who left no heirs, came into secure possession of the kingdom, not needing to fear those things that had harmed his predecessors. Though his manner of taking the kingdom had been unlawful and hateful, nonetheless, if he had followed the old methods of the other kings, he would have been endured and would not have stirred up the Senate and the populace to take away his position. He was not, then, driven out because Sextus his son raped Lucretia, but because he broke the laws of the kingdom and governed tyrannically, for he took all authority away from the Senate and transferred it to himself; and such business as had been carried on in public places with the approval of the Roman Senate, he had carried on in his own palace, thus bringing on himself blame and envy. Hence in a short time he deprived Rome of all the liberty which under the other kings she had preserved. Nor was it enough for him to make the Fathers his enemies, for he roused the populace as well against him, making them labor at lowly tasks, very different from those in which his predecessors had employed them. So, by his unceasing acts of cruelty and pride, he had already prepared the spirits of all the Romans for rebellion, whenever they had an opportunity for it. If the catastrophe of Lucretia had not occurred, as soon as some other came about it would have produced the same result. For if Tarquin had lived like the other kings, and Sextus his son had committed that crime, Brutus and Collatinus would have appealed to Tarquin for vengeance against Sextus, and not to the Roman people.

Princes should know, then, that they begin to lose their positions at the hour when they begin to break the laws and those old ways and customs under which for a long time men have lived. After they are deprived of their positions, if they ever become so prudent as to realize with what ease princedoms are held by those who take a wise course, they will grieve much more for the loss they have suffered and condemn themselves to a greater penalty than any to which others might condemn them. It is much easier to be loved by the good than

1. *Livy* 1. 49–58.

by the wicked and to obey the laws than to try to dominate them. If princes wish to learn the method they must use in bringing this about, they do not have to endure other labor than to take for their mirror the lives of good princes, such as Timoleon of Corinth and Aratus of Sicyon. In their lives a modern prince can find so much security and so much satisfaction on the part of ruler and of ruled that he will desire to imitate them, since easily, for the reasons given, he can do it. For when men are well governed, they do not seek for nor wish any other liberty, as was true of the peoples governed by the two named above, who were compelled to be princes as long as they lived, though many times they attempted to retire to private life.

Because in this and the two preceding chapters I have spoken of the seditions stirred up against princes and of the conspiracies formed against their native cities by Brutus' sons, and of those formed against Tarquinius Priscus and Servius Tullius, I think it not apart from my subject to speak of them at length in the next chapter, since they are matters deserving the attention of princes and private persons.

CHAPTER 6. CONSPIRACIES

I have thought it improper to omit the discussion of conspiracies, since they are so dangerous to princes and to private persons, for we see that many more princes have lost their lives and their positions through them than through open war. Because power to make open war on a prince is granted to few; power to conspire against him is granted to everybody. On the other hand, private persons do not enter into any undertaking more dangerous and rash than a conspiracy, for in all its stages it is difficult and very dangerous. For this reason, many are attempted and very few have the outcome desired. In order, then, that princes may learn how to guard themselves against these dangers, and that private persons may be more cautious about entering into them—or rather that they may learn to be content to live under whatever rule Chance provides—I shall deal with conspiracies at length, not omitting anything important for the instruction of either sort of person. And certainly Cornelius Tacitus' axiom is golden, in which he says that men must honor past things and obey present things; they should wish for good princes, but should endure those of any sort. Certainly he who does otherwise generally ruins himself and his native city.

We must, then, in dealing with the subject, consider first against whom conspiracies are made. We find that they are made either against the conspirator's own city or against a prince. Of these two I intend to speak at present, because of those formed to give a city to enemies who besiege her, or that are in any way like them, we have said enough above.[1]

[*Conspiracies against princes*]

We shall speak, in this first part, of conspiracies against a prince, and shall first examine their causes. These are many, but one is by far the most important. That is to be hated by the people generally, because when a prince has roused general hatred against himself, we rightly suppose that he has especially injured some individuals who are eager to revenge themselves. This desire of theirs is increased by the general hostile feeling that they see roused against him. It is important, then, for a prince to avoid such private hatreds. How he must act to avoid them, since I have dealt with the matter elsewhere,[2] I shall not discuss here, because if he keeps himself from general hostility, simple individual offenses will raise less opposition against him. One reason is that he will rarely encounter men who will estimate one injury so high that they will put themselves in such great danger to avenge it. The other is that even if they have the spirit and the power to do it, they are held back by the universal good will that they see the prince possessing.

[*Private injuries*]

The injuries done by the prince affect property, life, or honor. Among injuries to life, threats are more dangerous than deeds; or rather, threats are very dangerous and there is no danger at all in deeds, because a dead man cannot be concerned with revenge. Those remaining alive usually leave concern about it to the dead.[3] But a man who is threatened and knows himself forced by necessity to act or to suffer becomes very dangerous to the prince, as in its place I shall explain with examples. Apart from this necessity, property and honor are the two things over which more than anything else men take offense. From injuries in these a prince ought to guard himself,

1. DISCOURSES 2. 32.
2. PRINCE 19.
3. *I follow the Florentine edition of 1531.*

because he cannot plunder a man so completely as not to leave him a dagger for revenging himself; a man cannot be so dishonored as not to retain a spirit determined on revenge. And of the kinds of honor that can be taken from men, that of women is the most important; after this comes shame to his own person. Such shame armed Pausa-nias against Philip of Macedon; in our times Luzio Belanti conspired against Pandolfo tyrant of Siena for no other reason than that the latter, after giving him as wife a daughter of his, then took her away, as we shall tell in its place. The chief cause for the Pazzi conspiracy against the Medici was Giovanni Bonromei's estate, taken from the Pazzi through a decision by the Medici.

[Conspiracies against tyrants]

Still another cause—a very great one—makes men conspire against a prince: this is the desire for liberating their native land which he has conquered. This cause moved Brutus and Cassius against Caesar; this has moved many others against Phalarises, Dionysiuses, and other conquerors of their native lands. From this passion no tyrant can protect himself except by laying down his tyranny. But because no one will do that, there are few tyrants who do not come to a bad end. This gave rise to that passage in Juvenal:

> To the son-in-law of Ceres few kings go down without slaughter and wounds, and by a dry death few tyrants (10. 112).

[One man against the prince]

The perils undergone in conspiracies, as I said above, are great and continue through their course, because in such affairs one runs risks in planning them, in carrying them out, and after they are carried out. Those who conspire are either one or many. When there is but one, we cannot speak of a conspiracy but of a firm determina-tion by one man to kill the prince. This single man escapes the first of the three dangers risked by conspirators. Before he carries out his plan, he is subject to no danger, since no other person possesses his secret; he therefore undergoes no danger that his intention will come to the prince's ear. A determination of this sort can enter into the mind of anyone of any rank, great, small, noble, not noble, close to or not close to the prince, because everybody is allowed at some time to speak to him; and he who is allowed to speak is allowed to carry out his intention. Pausanias, of whom I have spoken at other times, killed Philip of Macedon when he was going to the temple with a thousand armed men around him, and was between his son and his son-in-law; but Pausanias was a noble and intimate with the prince. A Spaniard, poor and of low rank, gave Ferdinand king of Spain a knife wound in the neck; the wound was not mortal, but evidently the man had spirit and opportunity to strike. A dervish, a Turkish priest, struck with a scimiter at Bajazet, father of the present Turk. He did not wound him, but still he had courage and opportunity to make the attempt. Of spirits of that sort many, I believe, resolve to do it because there is no pain or peril in resolving, but there are few who do it, and of those who do act, very few or none escape being killed in the attempt. For this reason you do not find anyone who plans sure death. But we drop these individual resolves and come to conspiracies among many.

[*Conspiracies by weak men*]

I say that, according to the histories, all conspiracies are made by men of rank or by those very intimate with the prince; others, if they are not actually mad, cannot conspire, because men without power and not intimate with the prince lack all the hopes and all the opportunities needed for the execution of a conspiracy. First, men without power cannot find supporters who will keep faith with them, because no one can concur in their intention with any of those hopes that make men enter into great dangers. Hence whenever they increase their numbers to two or three persons, they get themselves an accuser and are ruined. Even when they are so lucky as not to have any accuser, in the execution of their plan they are surrounded by such difficulties—not having easy access to the prince—that in executing the conspiracy they can by no possibility escape ruin. Hence if men of rank and those having easy access are overcome by such difficulties as I detail below, the difficulties of the weak must increase without end. Therefore (because in matters of life and property men are not wholly insane) when conspirators know they are weak, they are cautious. So when weak men dislike a prince, they spend their strength in cursing him and wait for those who have higher rank than theirs to revenge them. Indeed if any of low rank attempt such a thing, one may praise their intention and not their prudence.

[*Conspiracies by men of high rank*]

We see therefore that conspirators have all been men of rank or
intimates of the prince. Many of them have been influenced to
conspire rather by too many favors than by too many injuries, as was
Perennius against Commodus, Plautianus against Servius, Sejanus
against Tiberius. All these were established by their emperors in
such great riches, honor and rank that for the perfection of their
power they seemed to lack nothing else than the Empire; being
unwilling to lack that, they went to conspiring against the prince.
Their conspiracies all had the end befitting their ingratitude. Yet of
similar attempts in more recent times, that of Jacopo di Appiano
against Messer Piero Gambacorti the ruler of Pisa ended successfully,
for Jacopo, brought up and supported and made important by Piero,
then took away his position. Of the same sort was that of Coppola,
in our times, against King Ferdinand of Aragon. This Coppola,
having reached so high a position that he felt he lacked nothing
except the kingdom, lost his life in trying to get that too. Yet truly if
any conspiracy made against princes by men of rank could end
successfully, it should have been his, since it was made by another
king, so to speak, and by one having so excellent an opportunity for
carrying out his plan. But the lust for ruling that blinds such plotters
blinds them also in managing such an enterprise, because if they
knew how to carry out their wickedness with prudence, not to succeed would be impossible.

[*A prince should fear those he has benefited*]

A prince who attempts to guard himself against conspiracies,
then, is more afraid of the men to whom he has given too many
favors than of those to whom he has done too many injuries, because
the injured lack opportunity, the favored abound in it. Their intention is the same, because as great or greater is the desire to rule than
the desire for revenge. Princes should therefore give their friends only
such authority that there may be some interval between it and the
princedom and that there may be something desirable in the middle.
Otherwise it will be strange if they do not fare like the princes
mentioned above. But let us return to our outline.

[*Three dangers in conspiracy*]

Since I have said that conspirators must be men of rank having access to the prince, I may now consider what outcomes their under/ takings have had and see what has made them successful or unsuc/ cessful. As I said above, they offer dangers at three periods: before the deed, at its time, and after it. Few of them are successful because it is impossible, almost, to get through all these periods with good fortune.

[*Danger in preparation*]

First discussing the dangers before the deed, which are the most important, I say that conspirators must be very prudent and have great good luck if when they are planning a conspiracy it is not to be discovered. It can be discovered either through report or through suspicion. Report results from encountering disloyalty or impru/ dence in the men to whom you communicate it. Disloyalty is easily encountered, because you cannot communicate it except to men you trust, who for love of you will expose themselves to death, or to men who are dissatisfied with the prince. Of those to be trusted, you can find one or two, but if you wish to include more, you cannot find them. Further, their love for you must be indeed strong if the danger and their fear of punishment do not seem to them stronger. Still further, men deceive themselves, usually, about the love you judge a man feels for you, and you can never assure yourself of it without testing it; and to test it in this matter is very dangerous. And even though you have tested them in some other danger in which they have been faithful, you cannot from that fidelity measure this, because this danger far surpasses every other sort. If you measure their fidelity from their dissatisfaction with the prince, you easily deceive yourself, because as soon as you show any discontented man your intention, you give him means for becoming contented. His hatred must be great or your authority very great if it is to keep him faithful.

[*How conspiracies are revealed*]

Many conspiracies, therefore, are revealed and crushed in their first stages, and if one is kept secret by many men for a long time, everybody thinks it wonderful. Examples are that of Piso against

Nero and, in our times, that of the Pazzi against Lorenzo and
Giuliano de'Medici. These were known to more than fifty men, yet
went into effect before they were revealed. As to being revealed
through imprudence, this happens when a conspirator speaks without caution, so that a servant or a third person hears you, as in the case
of Brutus' sons, who, when planning the affair with the emissaries of
Tarquin, were overheard by a servant, who accused them.[4] Or you
may foolishly communicate it to a woman or a boy whom you love
or some similar foolish person; thus Dymnus, one of the conspirators
with Philotas against Alexander the Great, did when he communicated the conspiracy to Nicomachus, a boy he loved, who at once
told it to his brother Cebalinus, and Cebalinus to the King.

[Discovery by suspicion]

As to discovery by suspicion, an instance is the conspiracy of
Piso against Nero, in which Scaevinus, one of the conspirators, on
the day before he was to kill Nero, made his will, ordered Milichus
his freedman to see to the grinding of a dagger of his that was old and
rusty, freed all his slaves and gave them money, had bandages provided to bind wounds. By these indications becoming aware of the
matter, Milichus accused him to Nero. Scaevinus was taken, and
with him Natalis, another conspirator, for, on the day before, they
had been seen speaking together secretly and at length, and since
they did not agree about their conversation, they were forced to
confess the truth. Hence the conspiracy was discovered, with the
ruin of all the conspirators.

[Courage prevents revelation]

From such causes for the discovery of conspiracies it is impossible
for a plotter to guard himself so well that through malice or imprudence or carelessness he will not be discovered, whenever those
sharing his knowledge exceed the number of three or four. When
more than one of them are caught, discovery cannot be avoided,
because two will not agree in all they say. When only one of them is
caught, if he is a strong man, he can in the strength of his courage
keep silent about the conspirators. But necessarily the other conspirators must have no less courage than he, so that they stand firm
and do not reveal themselves by flight, because if a single man lacks

4. Livy 2. 4.

courage, whether the man who has been arrested or one of those who is free, he will reveal the conspiracy. Unusual is the instance told by Titus Livius of the conspiracy made against Hieronymus king of Syracuse: when Theodore, one of the conspirators, was arrested, with great fortitude he concealed all his associates and accused the King's friends; on the other hand, the conspirators so trusted Theodore's fortitude that none of them left Syracuse or gave any sign of fear.[5]

[*Precautions against discovery*]

You pass through all these perils, then, in managing a conspiracy before it comes to accomplishment. If you wish to escape them, you can find remedies. The first and surest remedy, or rather, to put it better, the only one, is not to give the conspirators time to accuse you, but to communicate the plan to them when you decide to carry it out—not before. Those who act in this way certainly escape the dangers of preparation, and generally the other dangers. Indeed all conspiracies so managed have ended successfully; any prudent man would have opportunity to conduct himself in this way. I think it enough to bring up two instances. Nelematus, unable to endure the tyranny of Aristotimus tyrant of Epirus, assembled in his house many relatives and friends whom he exhorted to liberate their country; some of them asked time to consider and to make arrangements. At once Nelematus had his servants lock the house and said to those he had invited: "Either you swear to put this into action now or I turn you all over to Aristotimus as prisoners." Moved by these words, they swore, and going without any loss of time, successfully they carried out Nelematus' plan. When a Magian by a trick had seized the kingdom of the Persians, Ortanes, one of the great men of the kingdom, learned of and uncovered the fraud. When he discussed it with six leading men of that state, saying that he was going to clear the kingdom from the tyranny of that Magian, some of them asked for time. Then Darius, one of the six summoned by Ortanes, rose and said: "Either we go now to carry out this deed, or I go to accuse you all." And so getting up together, without giving anybody time to repent, they executed their plans successfully.

Also like these two instances is the method the Etolians used in killing Nabis, the Spartan tyrant. They sent Alexamenus, one of their countrymen, with thirty horsemen and two hundred infantry,

5. *Livy* 24. 5.

to Nabis, under the pretense of sending him aid, and to Alexamenus alone they made known the secret; on the others they imposed, under pain of exile, the duty of obeying him in everything whatsoever. He went to Sparta and did not make his charge known until he was about to carry it out, so that he succeeded in killing Nabis. These men, then, in such ways escaped the dangers to which those who manage conspiracies are subject, and he who imitates them will always escape.

[Piso's conspiracy against Nero]

That anybody can do as they did, I shall show by the instance of Piso, mentioned above. He was a prominent and highly reputed man, intimate with Nero and greatly trusted by him. Nero often went into Piso's gardens to eat with him. Piso, then, was in a posi‑ tion to gain as his friends men of spirit and courage and whose dispositions were suited to conspiracy against the Emperor (a very easy thing for an important man). When Nero was in Piso's garden, Piso could tell his friends of his plan and encourage them with suitable words to do something they did not have time to refuse and which could not possibly fail to succeed. Likewise if the others are examined, few will be found that could not have been carried on in the same way. But on the average, men who do not understand the ways of the world often make great errors, and so much the greater in affairs offering so much that is unusual as do conspiracies.

[Avoiding evidence of conspiracy]

You should then never mention the conspiracy until you must and at the moment of action. If you do decide to tell it, tell it to one man only of whom you have had long experience or who is moved by the same causes as you are. To find one man of that sort is easier than to find more; for that reason the danger is less. Moreover, if even he deceives you, you have some possibility for protecting your‑ self, such as you do not have when many have conspired. I have heard a prudent man say that to one person only you can tell any‑ thing, because there is as much weight, if you do not let yourself be brought to writing with your own hand, in the *yes* of one as in the *no* of the other. But from writing one ought to guard oneself as from a shoal, because not a thing more easily convicts you than what is written with your own hand. Plautianus, wishing to have Severus the Emperor and his son Antoninus killed, entrusted the matter to Saturninus the Tribune. He, wishing to accuse Plautianus and not to obey him, and fearing that if it came to an accusation Plautianus rather than himself would be believed, asked for a note in his em' ployer's handwriting that would assure that commission. Plautianus, blinded by ambition, gave it to him. As a result, he was accused and convicted by the Tribune; yet without that note and certain other signs, Plautianus would have been the winner—with such boldness he denied it. There is, then, against the accusation of one man, some defense, when no piece of writing or other evidence convicts you; against that you must guard yourself.

In Piso's conspiracy there was a woman named Epicharis, who had in the past been a mistress of Nero's; she, judging that it would be advantageous to have among the conspirators a captain of some triremes that Nero kept for his guard, told him of the conspiracy but not of the conspirators. Then when that captain broke faith and accused her to Nero, so great was her boldness in denying that Nero, being puzzled, did not condemn her. There are, then, in telling the thing to one man only, two dangers: one, he may accuse you delib' erately; two, he may accuse you when he is overcome and compelled by torture, after he has been arrested as a result of some suspicion or some hint of guilt. Yet against both of these dangers there is some recourse: you can deny the first, giving as a reason the hatred the accuser has for you; you can deny the second, giving as a reason the force that compels him to tell the lies. It is, then, prudence not to tell the thing to anybody, but to act according to the instances written above; or if you do tell it, not to go beyond one person; in the last, though the danger is greater, yet it is much less than when you tell it to many.

[*Anticipating action against oneself*]

Very like the preceding situation is that in which necessity forces you to do to the prince what you know the prince intends to do to you—necessity so great as to give you no time, except for resolving to make yourself safe. This necessity almost always brings a conspiracy to the desired end; to prove it I think I need but two instances. Under the Emperor Commodus, Letus and Elettus were leaders of the Praetorian soldiers; they were among the Emperor's chief friends and intimates. Marcia was among his chief concubines or mistresses.

Because they sometimes reproved him for the ways with which he disgraced his person and his imperial office, he determined to have them killed. So he wrote down in a list Marcia, Letus, Elettus, and some others he intended should be killed the following night; that list he put under the pillow of his bed. When he had gone to wash himself, a boy of whom he was fond, while playing about the chamber and on the bed, happened to find the list. Going out with it in his hand, he met Marcia, who took it from him. When she had read it and understood its contents, at once she sent for Letus and Elettus; since all three realized their danger, they decided to forestall it; so without letting any time go by, that night they killed Commodus.

The Emperor Antoninus Caracalla was with his armies in Meso-potamia; his prefect was Macrinus, a man peaceful rather than soldierly. Now since princes who are not good always fear that somebody will do to them what they themselves think they deserve, Antoninus wrote to his friend Maternianus at Rome asking him to learn from the astrologers if anybody was aspiring to the Empire, and to let him know. Maternianus replied that Macrinus was aspiring to it. Since the letter came into Macrinus' hands before it came to the Emperor's, and from it he learned that before another letter came from Rome he must either kill Antoninus or die himself, he com-missioned Martial, a centurion whom he trusted (and moreover Antoninus had, a few days before, put his brother to death), to kill him. This he carried out successfully. You see, then, that a necessity which does not give time produces almost the same effect as the method, mentioned above, that Nelematus of Epirus took. You see also what I said almost at the beginning of this *Discourse*, that threats harm princes worse and are the cause of more effective conspiracies than injuries; from making threats a prince should guard himself, because prudence requires him either to befriend men or to make himself safe against them;[6] he should never bring them to a condition in which they are convinced that either they must die or the prince must die.

[Dangers in executing a conspiracy]

As to the dangers undergone in executing a conspiracy, they come either from varying the arrangements or from lack of courage in

6. *Make himself safe: as often in Machiavelli, deprive them of power to do injury, usually by violence. Security can also be gained through kindness (e.g.,* DISCOURSES 2. 24 *end).*

their executor or from a blunder he makes through imprudence or through not completing the thing, so that part of those remain alive whom he planned to kill. I say, then, that there is nothing that causes so much disturbance or hindrance to all men's actions as suddenly, without having time, to be obliged to change an arrangement and to shift from what was arranged before. If this change causes confusion anywhere, it does so in matters of war and in actions like those of which we speak. For in such deeds nothing is so necessary as that men resolve on carrying out the part assigned to them. If men have fixed their imaginations for many days on one method and one arrangement, and that suddenly changes, by no possibility can they avoid being completely upset and everything ruined. Hence they had much better carry a thing out according to the plan laid down, even though there is something unsuitable in it, than to enter into a thousand difficulties by trying to cancel the unfitness. This advice applies when there is no time for replanning; when there is time, a man can conduct himself as he wishes.

[*The Pazzi conspiracy against the Medici*]

The conspiracy of the Pazzi against Lorenzo and Giuliano de' Medici is well known. The plan fixed was that the Pazzi should give a breakfast for the Cardinal of San Giorgio and at that breakfast kill the Medici brothers. Certain men were assigned to kill them, others to take the Palace[7] and others to run through the city and summon the people to liberty. It happened that when the Pazzi, the Medici and the Cardinal were in the cathedral church of Florence at a solemn office, news came that Giuliano would not breakfast with them that morning. This caused the conspirators to assemble, and what they were going to do in the house of the Medici they determined to do in the church. This disturbed the whole plan, because Giovambatista da Montesecco would not join in the murder, saying he would not do it in the church. Hence they had to substitute new agents in every action; these, not having time to settle their courage, made such mistakes that in carrying out their plan they were overpowered.

7. *The Palace of the Signory, the City Hall, as it were, of Florence, now called the Palazzo Vecchio.*

[Failure in courage]

The courage of one who carries out a plot fails either through reverence or through the agent's personal cowardice. So great are the majesty and reverence accompanying a monarch's presence that they easily soften or frighten one deputed to act. To Marius, when he was taken by the people of Minturnum, a slave was sent to put him to death; but terrified by the presence of Marius and by the memory of his name, the slave became cowardly and lost all power to kill him. And if this capacity is to be found in a man who is bound and a prisoner and overwhelmed by bad fortune, we easily suppose it much greater in a prince who is at liberty, with the majesty of his insignia, of his splendor and of his retinue. Such splendor can terrify you or actually, when joined with a pleasant greeting, mollify you. Certain persons plotted against Sitalces King of Thrace; they set the day for carrying it out; they came together at the place assigned, where they found the prince; none of them made a move to harm him. After leaving without having attempted any-thing and without knowing what had impeded them, they accused one another. They fell into the same mistake several times, so that when the plot was discovered they suffered punishment for the evil they could have done and did not have the will to do. Against Alphonso Duke of Ferrara two of his brothers plotted, using as their instrument Giannes, a priest and singer of the Duke. At their re-quest, he many times brought the Duke among them, so that they had it in their power to kill him. Nonetheless, never did either of them dare do it. Hence when they were found out, they suffered the penalty of their cowardice and imprudence. This inaction could not have resulted from anything except that his presence must have frightened them or some kindness of the prince made them humble.

[Bewildered assassins]

In such attempts, confusion and mistake come from imprudence or from lack of courage, because these two things bewilder you and make you, when you are carried away by that perplexity of brain, say and do what you should not. That men are thus bewildered and confused, Titus Livius cannot show better than when he tells of Alexamenus the Aetolian, when he planned to kill Nabis the Spar-tan, whom we have mentioned above. When the time for action came and he revealed to his followers what was to be done, "he himself settled his courage, bewildered by the thought of so great an act," as Titus Livius says (35. 35). Indeed it is impossible for any man, even though of firm courage and wonted to killing men and to the use of steel, not to be bewildered. Hence men experienced in such affairs should be chosen and no others trusted, though held very courageous. About courage in important matters no one with' out experience can promise himself certainty. It can happen, then, that perplexity will make your weapons fall from your hands or make you say something that will have the same result. Lucilla, Commodus' sister, planned that Quintianus should kill the Emperor. Waiting at the entrance to the amphitheatre and meeting Commodus with a naked dagger, Quintianus shouted: "This the Senate sends you." These words caused his arrest before he could bring down his arm to strike. Messer Antonio da Volterra, chosen to kill Lorenzo de'Medici, as I said above,[8] coming toward him said: "Ah traitor!" These words were the salvation of Lorenzo and the ruin of that conspiracy.

[*Conspiracy against two princes*]

A conspiracy can fail of execution, for the reasons given, when directed against one ruler, and can easily fail of execution when directed against two. Indeed the latter is so difficult that success is almost impossible, because to carry out parallel assassinations at the same time in different places is almost impossible, yet two such deeds cannot be done at different times, if the first is not to ruin the second. Hence if conspiring against one prince is an uncertain thing, danger' ous and imprudent, to conspire against two is altogether vain and foolish. And if I did not respect the historian, I should never believe what Herodian says of Plautianus possible, namely, that he charged Saturninus a centurion that he alone should kill Severus and Anto' ninus, who lived in different places, because the story is so far from reasonable that any support other than this authority would not make me believe it. Certain Athenian young men plotted against Diocles and Hippias, tyrants of Athens. They killed Diocles, but

8. *Antonio da Volterra is not named earlier, or later, in the* DISCOURSES. *See* HISTORY OF FLORENCE *8. 5, 6. Did Machiavelli shift material from the manuscript of the* DISCOURSES *to that of the* HISTORY? *Was the* HISTORY *in manuscript when this* DISCOURSE *was written?*

Hippias, who escaped, avenged him. Chion and Leonidas, citizens of Heraclea and disciples of Plato, conspired against Clearchus and Satirus, tyrants. They killed Clearchus, but Satirus, who was left alive, avenged him. The Pazzi, whom I use many times as an example, succeeded in killing only Giuliano. Hence everybody ought to abstain from such conspiracies against several rulers because they do no good either to oneself or to one's country or to anybody. On the contrary those who remain become more unbearable and harsher, as is known to Florence, Athens and Heraclea, which I have earlier mentioned. It is true that Pelopidas' conspiracy to liberate Thebes, his native land, confronted all these difficulties (nevertheless it had a most successful end), because Pelopidas conspired not merely against two tyrants but against ten; not merely was he not intimate with the tyrants, so that his entry to them was not easy, but he was an outlaw. Nonetheless he was able to come into Thebes, to kill the tyrants and to liberate his native city. He did it all with the aid of one Charon, adviser to the tyrants, through whom he had an easy entry for his action. Nobody nonetheless should take him as an example because, just as it was an impossible attempt and marvelous in its success, so it was and now is thought by the historians who praise it a thing rare and almost unparalleled.

[The false suspicions of conspirators]

Such an action can be interrupted by a false suspicion or by an unforeseen accident that arises in the course of execution. That morning when Brutus and the other conspirators intended to kill Caesar, it happened that he spoke at length with Gnaeus Popilius Laenas, one of the conspirators. The others, seeing this long conversation, feared that the said Popilius would reveal the conspiracy to Caesar; hence they were going to try to kill Caesar there, without waiting until he was in the Senate. They would have done it if, when the conversation ended, they had not seen that Caesar made no unusual motion; then they were reassured. These false suspicions are to be considered and to be prudently respected, and so much the more as they are easy to form, because if your conscience is not clear you easily believe you are spoken of; you can hear a word, spoken for another purpose, that disturbs your courage and makes you believe it spoken about your affair. The result is that you yourself reveal the conspiracy by flight, or upset the deed by hastening it at the wrong time. This comes about so much the more easily when many are aware of the plot.

[Accidents may reveal conspiracies]

Accidents, because they are unexpected, I can present only by examples, to make men cautious in accord with them. Luzio Belanti of Siena, whom I mentioned above,[9] in his anger against Pandolfo, who took away from him the daughter that earlier he had given him as his wife, determined to kill the ruler. Luzio chose his time as follows. As Pandolfo went almost every day to visit one of his sick relatives, he passed Giulio's[10] dwelling. The latter, noting this, planned to have his fellow conspirators in his house to kill Pandolfo as he passed. When they were placed with their weapons in the entrance, he stationed one man at a window to give a signal when Pandolfo in passing was near the door. It happened that as Pandolfo approached, and after the signal was given, he met a friend who stopped him, while some of his companions kept on going; these men, hearing and understanding[11] the noise of arms, discovered the ambush. So Pandolfo was saved and Giulio and his companions had to flee from Siena. The chance of that meeting impeded their action and made Giulio's attempt fail. For such chances, because they are rare, no remedy can be provided. It is, however, very necessary to consider all the possibilities and to provide against them.

[Dangers after an assassination]

Nothing now remains to discuss except the dangers that a conspirator runs after the deed is done. There is but one, namely, that someone is left to avenge the dead prince. Those left can be brothers or sons or other adherents, who would succeed to the princedom. Either through your negligence or through the causes mentioned above, persons can be left who will execute this vengeance. So it happened to Giovanni Andrea da Lampognano who, with other conspirators, killed the Duke of Milan; since the Duke's son and two brothers were left, they stood ready to avenge his death. Truly in such cases conspirators are excusable, because there is no remedy.

9. *In the present chapter.*
10. *The same as Luzio, just above.*
11. *Not a literal rendering.*

But when revengers are left alive through their imprudence or their negligence, then they do not deserve excuse. In Forlì conspirators killed Count Girolamo their ruler and captured his wife and small children. These conspirators knew they were not secure if they were not masters of the fortress, but the castellan was unwilling to surrender it. Then Madonna Caterina (for so the Countess was called) promised that if the conspirators would let her enter the fortress, she would have it surrendered to them; they might keep her children as hostages. With that promise, they let her enter. As soon as she was inside, she reproached them from the wall with the death of her husband, threatening them with every kind of revenge. And to show that she did not care about her children, she uncovered to them her genital members, saying she still had means for producing more children. So, unprovided with a plan and realizing too late their mistake, with lifelong exile they paid the penalty for their imprudence.

[Dangers from the angry people]

Of all the dangers that can appear after the deed, there is none more certain or more to be feared than when the people love the prince you have killed; for this, conspirators have no remedy, because they can never make themselves safe from the people. Caesar is an instance; since the Roman populace loved him, it avenged him, for by driving the conspirators from Rome, it became the cause why all of them, at various times and places, were killed.

[Conspiracies against republics]

Conspiracies against their own cities are less dangerous for conspirators than those against princes, because in preparing them the dangers are fewer; in carrying them out the dangers are the same; after their execution there is no danger. In preparing them there are not many dangers because a citizen can fit himself for power without showing his determination or design to anybody and, if his plans are not interrupted, can complete his enterprise successfully. If some law does interrupt him, he can bide his time and try some other way. This applies to a republic where there is some corruption, because in one not corrupt, where no evil has begun, such thoughts cannot enter a citizen's mind. Citizens can, then, strive for the princedom by many means and in many ways without undergoing any danger of opposition, both because republics are slower than a prince, are less suspicious and therefore less cautious, and because they have more regard for their important citizens; therefore the latter are rasher and bolder in acting against them. Everybody has read about the conspiracy of Catiline as narrated by Sallust, and knows that when the conspiracy was discovered, Catiline not merely remained in Rome but went into the Senate and spoke insultingly to the Senate and to the Consul—so great was the regard that city had for its citizens. And when he had gone from Rome and was already with his army, Lentulus and those others would not have been arrested except that letters in their handwriting declared their guilt plainly. Hanno, a very great citizen in Carthage, aspiring to the tyranny, planned at the marriage of one of his daughters to poison all the Senate and then to make himself prince. When this plan was learned, the Senate did not make any other provision than a law that limited the expense of banquets and weddings—so great was their regard for his rank and abilities.

[Dangers in carrying out a conspiracy against a republic]

It is true, however, that in carrying out a conspiracy against your own country, the difficulties and the dangers are greater because it rarely happens that your own forces are enough for conspiring against so many, and not everybody is leader of an army, as was Caesar or Agathocles or Cleomenes, and the like, who have at one stroke and with their own forces conquered their native countries. For to such as these the way is very easy and very secure; but the others, who do not have such additions to their forces, have to do things either with deception and ingenuity or with foreign forces. As to deception and ingenuity, when Pisistratus the Athenian had conquered the Megarians, and through this gained favor with the people, he went out one morning, wounded, saying that the nobility had injured him through envy, and asked that he be allowed to have armed men to guard him. By means of this authority he easily rose to such greatness that he became tyrant of Athens. Pandolfo Petrucci returned, with other exiles, to Siena, and into his charge was given the guard of the Public Square, as a base thing that others refused. Nonetheless those armed men, at an opportune time, gave him such reputation that in a short time he became prince. Many others have employed other schemes and other means, and in the course of time and without danger have succeeded. Those who with their own forces or with foreign armies have plotted to conquer their native lands have had varied success, according to Fortune. Catiline, mentioned above, was ruined at it. Hanno, of whom we have spoken above, when poison did not succeed for him, armed many thousands of persons who were his partisans, and they and he were killed. Some leading citizens of Thebes, in order to make themselves tyrants, called to their aid a Spartan army and seized the tyranny of that city. Hence, if you examine all the plots formed against native cities, you will find none or but few that were crushed when they were being prepared, but all of them have either succeeded or been ruined in the carrying-out. When they have been carried out, they then are not subject to dangers other than those to which by nature the princedom is subject, be-cause when a man becomes a tyrant, he is liable to the natural and ordinary dangers which tyranny brings upon him, for which he has no other remedies than those discussed above.

[Assassination by poison]

This is all I think of to write about conspiracies. If I have discussed those carried out with steel and not with poison, I have done so because they are all subject to the same laws. Those with poison are in truth more dangerous through being more uncertain, because opportunity for them is not open to everybody; hence they must be delegated to those who do have opportunity, and this neces-sity for delegating brings danger. Then for many reasons a drink of poison may not be deadly, as when conspirators poisoned Com-modus; he vomited the poison, so they were obliged to make sure of his death by strangling him.

[How to thwart a conspiracy]

A prince, then, does not have a greater enemy than the conspira-cy, for when a conspiracy against him is carried out, it either kills or disgraces him: if it succeeds, he dies; if he discovers it and executes the conspirators, he is always believed to have invented the charge to satisfy his avarice and cruelty against the property and lives of the men executed. I do not wish, however, to fail in offering this caution to all princes and republics conspired against: when a conspiracy is revealed to them, they should postpone any attempt at vengeance, while they cautiously seek a clear understanding of its nature and measure well the conditions of the conspirators and their own; when they find the conspiracy great and powerful, they should never make it public until they are ready with sufficient forces to crush it. If they do otherwise, they will make public their own ruin. Hence they ought with every device to pretend not to know it, because conspira- tors, on seeing themselves discovered, being driven by necessity, act without hesitation. The Romans are an instance.[12] When they left two legions of soldiers to guard the people of Capua against the Samnites, as we said elsewhere, the leaders of those legions conspired to subjugate the people of Capua. When their plan was learned at Rome, Rutilius, the new Consul, was charged to take measures against it. In order to put the conspirators to sleep, he spread a report that the Senate had renewed the assignment of the Capuan legions. These soldiers, believing it and supposing they had time to carry out their plan, did not try to hurry the matter up, but kept quiet until they saw that the Consul was separating one legion from the other. This made them suspicious and caused them to reveal them- selves and put their plan into practice. There cannot be a better instance than this on either side, because it shows how slow men are in things in which they think they have time, and how rapid they are when necessity drives them. Princes and republics that for their own advantage wish to defer revealing conspiracies cannot use better means than artfully to offer in the immediate future an opportunity to the conspirators. They will wait for it, supposing they have plenty of time, and thus will give the prince or the republic time to punish them. He who does otherwise hastens his own ruin, as did the Duke of Athens and Guglielmo de' Pazzi. The Duke, when tyrant of Florence, learning that there was a conspiracy against him, without examining further, arrested one of the conspirators. This made the others at once seize their weapons and take away his position. Guglielmo, Florentine commissioner in Valdichiana in 1501, having heard that there was a conspiracy to take Arezzo from the Florentines in favor of the Vitelli, at once went into that city; without considering the conspirators' forces or his own, and without providing himself with any force, on the advice of the bishop his son, arrested one of the conspirators. After that arrest, the others at once took up arms and snatched away the city from the Florentines; and Guglielmo was no longer a commissioner but a prisoner. Yet when conspiracies are weak, they can be and should be crushed without regard.

12. *Livy* 7. 38–41.

[*Unwise procedure in time of conspiracy*]

Further, two methods that have been used, almost opposite to each other, are in no way to be imitated. The Duke of Athens, named above, tried one of them when in order to show that he believed he had the good will of the Florentine citizens, he put to death a man who revealed a plot to him. Dion of Syracuse tried the other, when to test the intention of a man he suspected, he allowed Callippus, whom he trusted, to pretend a conspiracy against him. Both of these came out badly. The first took away courage from accusers and gave it to anybody who wished to plot. The other made easy the road to Dion's death, or rather he was the real head of the conspiracy against himself. So indeed it came out, because Callippus, enabled to conspire against him without caution, con-spired so well that he took from him his position and his life.

CHAPTER 7. WHY CHANGES FROM FREEDOM TO SLAVERY AND FROM SLAVERY TO FREEDOM ARE SOMETIMES WITHOUT BLOOD-SHED, SOMETIMES ABOUND IN IT

Some will wonder perhaps why, of the many changes made from free government to tyranny, and the opposite, some are made with bloodshed, some without it. As we learn from history, in such shifts sometimes countless men are killed; yet sometimes no one is injured, for in the change Rome made from kings to consuls, no one was driven away except the Tarquins, without injury to anybody else. That depends on the following: any government that is changed came into existence with violence or not. Since when it originates with violence, it must originate with injury to many, of necessity on its fall the injured try to revenge themselves; from this desire for revenge come bloodshed and deaths. But if that government was established by the common consent of a large group that has made it great, there is no reason, if then the said large group falls, for injuring anyone else than its leader. And of this kind was the government of Rome and the expulsion of the Tarquins. And so too was the government of the Medici in Florence, for at their fall in 1494 none other than they was injured. So such changes do not turn out very dangerous. On the other hand, exceedingly dangerous are those made by men who have to revenge themselves, and they have always been of a sort to terrify him who only reads of them. Because histories are full of instances of these, I am going to omit them.

CHAPTER 8. HE WHO WISHES TO CHANGE THE GOVERNMENT OF A STATE MUST CONSIDER ITS MATTER[1]

[*Spurius Cassius tries to buy Roman liberty*]

I explained above that a wicked citizen cannot damage a state that is not corrupt—a conclusion that is strengthened, in addition to the reasons I gave,[2] by the examples of Spurius Cassius and Manlius Capitolinus. This Spurius was an ambitious man, eager to seize unlawful authority in Rome and to gain the plebeians' good will by doing them many favors, as by dividing among them the fields the Romans took from the Hernici. Yet the Fathers, discovering his ambition, so far brought it under suspicion that when he spoke to the people offering them the money derived from the grain the state imported from Sicily, they wholly refused it, believing that Spurius was trying to give them the price of their liberty. But if the people had been corrupt, they would not have refused that price, but would have opened to him the road to tyranny that they closed.

[*The subversive designs of Manlius Capitolinus*]

A more important instance of this is Manlius Capitolinus, who reveals how much excellence of mind and of body, how many good deeds done for the advantage of a man's country are later canceled by a vicious longing to rule. This longing, as it seems, was caused by his envy of the honors given to Camillus; his mind became so blinded that, not thinking on the city's mode of life, not examining its matter, which was not yet fit to receive a bad form, he set out to raise rebellion in Rome against the Senate and against his country's laws. The incident reveals the perfection of that city and the goodness of its material, because in his case none of the nobility, though very fierce defenders of one another, did anything to support him; none of his relatives undertook any action in his behalf; yet for others who were

1. *Matter, that of which it is made, as opposed to its form.*
2. DISCOURSES 3. 6.

accused they were in the habit of appearing unkempt, clad in black, full of sadness, to gain pity for the accused; but in Manlius' behalf not one of them was seen. The Tribunes of the plebeians, who usually gave their support in matters that seemingly would result to the people's advantage—and the more any actions opposed the wishes of the nobles, the more the Tribunes pushed them ahead—in this case united with the nobles, to put down a common plague. The populace of Rome, very eager for their own advantage and loving what worked against the nobility, might have given much support to Manlius. Nevertheless, when the Tribunes laid a charge against him and gave over his case to the judgment of the populace, that populace, changed from defender into judge, without any hesitation condemned him to death.

[All classes united in defense of liberty]

So I do not believe that Livy's *History* gives any instance better suited to show the goodness of all classes in that republic, for we see that no one in Rome attempted to defend a citizen abounding in every sort of ability and who publicly and privately had done a great many praiseworthy deeds. In all the people love of country was more powerful than any other consideration, and they thought much more on present perils for which he was responsible than on past deserts—so much so that with his death they set themselves free. So Titus Livius says: "Such was the end of a man who, if he had not been born in a free state, would have been worthy of remembrance" (6. 20). In this two things are to be considered: one, that in a corrupt city men have to seek glory in other ways than they do in a city still living in accord with law; the other (which is almost the same as the first), that men in their conduct, and so much the more in their great actions, ought to think of the times and adapt themselves to them.

[Harmony with the times]

Those who because of a bad choice or natural inclination are out of harmony with the times, generally live in misfortune and their actions have a bad outcome; it is the opposite with those who are in harmony with the times. Without doubt, then, according to the words of the historian earlier quoted, if Manlius had been born in the times of Marius and of Sulla, when the material was already corrupt and he could have imprinted on it the form of his ambition, he

would have had the same career and the same end as Marius and
Sulla and the others who after them strove to gain tyrannical power.
So likewise, if Sulla and Marius had lived in Manlius' times, in their
first undertakings they would have been crushed. A man can indeed
with his schemes and his bad measures begin corrupting the people
of a city, but one man's life cannot be long enough to corrupt them so
much that he himself will be able to get advantage from it. Even if
he could do so as to length of time, he could not on account of the
way men conduct themselves, for they are impatient and unable to
defer long any passion of theirs. Besides, they deceive themselves in
their affairs, and especially in those that they much desire; hence,
either because of impatience or because they deceive themselves, they
enter into an undertaking contrary to the times and come out badly.

[Only in corrupt times can liberty be overthrown]

Of necessity, therefore, a man wishing to get authority in a republic and to imprint a bad form on it, must come to it when its matter
is already injured by time, having been little by little, from generation
to generation, brought to evil. And a republic necessarily gets to
that place, as is explained above,[3] when it is not often reinvigorated
by good examples, or is not by new laws brought back to its first
condition. Manlius, then, would have been an unusual man and
worthy of remembrance if he had been born in a city already corrupt.
Therefore citizens in a republic who make some move either in the
direction of freedom or in the direction of tyranny should consider
the material on which they must work, and determine from that the
difficulty of their undertakings. For it is as difficult and dangerous to
try to set free a people that wishes to live in servitude as it is to try to
bring into servitude a people that wishes to live free. Since I said
above that men in their activities should consider the qualities of the
times and proceed according to them, I shall speak of the topic at
length in the following chapter.

3. Ibid. 3. 1.

CHAPTER 9. HE WHO EXPECTS ALWAYS TO HAVE GOOD FORTUNE MUST CHANGE WITH THE TIMES

Many times I have observed that the cause of the bad and of the good fortune of men is the way in which their method of working fits the times, since in their actions some men proceed with haste, some with heed and caution. Because in both of these methods men cross the proper boundaries, since they cannot follow the true road, in both of them they make errors. Yet a man succeeds in erring less and in having prosperous fortune if time fits his ways, for you always act as Nature inclines you.[1]

[*The times of Fabius fitted his nature*]

Everybody knows that with his army Fabius Maximus proceeded heedfully and cautiously, far from all impetuosity and all Roman boldness, and good fortune caused his method to fit well with the times. Hannibal, a young man and with a youthful fortune, had come into Italy and had already defeated the Romans twice, so that the republic was almost bereft of her good soldiers and was frightened. Hence no better fortune could come to her than to have a general who by slow movement and caution would impose delay on the enemy. Likewise Fabius could not have met with times more suited to his ways—the result was that he became famous. That Fabius so acted through nature and not through choice is plain, because when Scipio wished to cross into Africa with his armies to end the war, Fabius was much opposed to it, being unable to give up his habits and his customary conduct. So, if it had been left to him, Hannibal would still be in Italy, for he was a man who did not understand that times changed methods of warfare. If Fabius had been king of Rome, he could easily have lost that war, because he would not have known how to vary his policy as times varied; but he was born in a republic where there were different citizens and different opinions; hence, just as Rome had Fabius, who was the best in times requiring that the war be endured, so later she had Scipio, in times fit for winning it.

1. *An instance of Machiavelli's frequent shift from the third person to the second.*

[*A republic can employ diversity of temperaments*]

Thence it comes that a republic, being able to adapt herself, by means of the diversity among her body of citizens, to a diversity of temporal conditions better than a prince can, is of greater duration than a princedom and has good fortune longer. Because a man accustomed to acting in one way never changes, as I have said. So of necessity when the times as they change get out of harmony with that way of his, he falls.

[*Piero Soderini*]

Piero Soderini, already mentioned, acted in all his affairs with kindness and patience. Prosperity came to him and to his native city while the times were in harmony with his way of acting, but when afterward times came in which he needed to break off his patience and humility, he could not do it. Hence, along with his city, he fell. Pope Julius II, throughout his pontificate, proceeded with haste and vehemence, and because the times fitted him well, his enterprises succeeded—all of them. But if times requiring a different plan had come, of necessity he would have fallen, because he would not have changed either his method or his rule of action.

[*Republics shift slowly*]

We are unable to change for two reasons: one, that we cannot counteract that to which Nature inclines us; the other, that when with one way of doing a man has prospered greatly, he cannot be persuaded that he can profit by doing otherwise. That is why Fortune varies for the same man; she varies the times, but he does not vary his ways. This also brings about the ruin of cities, because republics do not vary their methods with the times, as we explained at length above, but they are slower, since it is more trouble for them to vary, because variation must result from times that agitate the entire state. To make the state vary, one man alone who varies his own mode of action is not enough.[2]

Because we have mentioned Fabius Maximus, who kept Hannibal delaying, I shall in the following chapter discuss whether a general wishing in any case to fight a battle with the enemy, can be hindered by them from doing so.

2. See DISCOURSES 1. 59. *A prince of vigorous character can make an immediate change, but in a republic a man of such character must first bring many of the less vigorous over to his views.*

CHAPTER 10. A GENERAL CANNOT ESCAPE
BATTLE WHEN HIS OPPONENT IS DETER-
MINED TO FIGHT IN ANY CASE

[The value of ancient example in warfare]

"Gneus Sulpitius the Dictator dragged out the war against the
Gauls, being unwilling to commit himself to Fortune against an
enemy whom time and a foreign land were daily making weaker"
(Livy 7. 12). When an error persists, in which all men or the greater
part deceive themselves, I hold that to censure it is frequently not a
bad idea. Therefore, though already I have several times shown how
much our actions in great affairs are unlike those of ancient days,
nonetheless I think that to repeat it at present is not superfluous.
Because if at any point we deviate from ancient customs, we deviate
especially in military actions, in which at present we do not practice
any of the things that the ancients greatly valued. We are in this bad
condition because republics and princes have given this duty to
others, and to avoid danger have drawn away from military activity.
If we do sometimes see a king in our times going to war in person,
we are not therefore to believe that he is fostering other customs that
deserve further praise. Indeed when they do undertake this activity,
they undertake it for display and not for any other praiseworthy
reason. Yet by sometimes visiting their armies and keeping in their
own power the title of commander, they make smaller mistakes than
republics do, especially those in Italy. These, trusting in someone
else and not understanding in any way what pertains to war, yet on
the other hand undertaking to decide about it, in order that they may
appear to be in control, make in such decisions a thousand mistakes.
Though I have discussed some of them elsewhere, I wish at present
not to be silent about a very important one.

[The dangers of refusing battle]

When these lazy princes or effeminate republics send out one of
their generals, the wisest command they think they can give him is
that he shall by no means come to battle, but rather, above everything
else, shall refrain from combat. Yet though they believe that in this
they imitate the prudence of Fabius Maximus who, by deferring
combat, saved their state for the Romans, they do not understand

that in most instances their command is worthless or damaging. We have to accept this conclusion: a general who decides to remain in the field cannot escape battle whenever his adversary intends to engage in it no matter what. So orders not to fight amount to saying: "Fight the battle when the enemy wishes to, not when you do." Because if you decide to remain in the field and not to fight a battle, you have no other sure protection than to put yourself fifty miles at least away from the enemy, and then to keep good scouts, so that if he comes toward you, you will have time to remove. Another plan in such a case is to shut yourself up in a city. Either of these plans is very injurious. With the first, your country is left as a spoil for the enemy; therefore a brave prince will prefer to tempt the fortune of combat rather than to lengthen the war with such damage to his subjects. With the second plan, your loss is evident, because it is likely that if you retire with an army into a city, you will find yourself besieged and in a short time will suffer hunger and will surrender. Hence, to avoid battle by these two ways is very damaging. The method Fabius Maximus used, of remaining in strong places, is good when you have so effective an army that the enemy will not have the courage to attack you in the midst of your advantages. Nor can it be said that Fabius avoided battle, but rather that he wished to enter it to his own advantage. Indeed if Hannibal had marched to attack him, Fabius would have waited for him and fought a battle with him, but Hannibal never dared to fight on Fabius' terms. So battle was avoided as much by Hannibal as by Fabius. But if one of them had decided to fight without respect to conditions, the other would have had only one of three remedies: the two mentioned above, or to run away.

[*Philip of Macedonia as an example*]

That what I say is true is evident from a thousand instances, and especially in the war that the Romans carried on with Philip of Macedonia, Perseus' father. Philip, assailed by the Romans, determined not to come to combat, and in order not to do so, decided at first to act as did Fabius Maximus in Italy; he put himself with his army on the summit of a mountain, well fortified, thinking that the Romans would not have courage to attack him. But going there and fighting with him, they drove him from that mountain; not being able to resist, he fled with the greater part of his people. What kept him from being destroyed entirely was the difficulty of the country, which prevented the Romans from following him. Philip then, not wishing to engage in battle and being encamped with his army near the Romans, was obliged to flee. Having learned from this experience that, not wishing to fight, it was not enough for him to remain on the mountain tops, and not wishing to shut himself up in cities, he determined to take the other method, that of remaining many miles distant from the Roman army. Hence, if the Romans were in one province, he went to the other, and so always he went in where the Romans went out. And seeing at last that in lengthening the war in this way his condition grew worse and his subjects were burdened now by himself, now by the enemy, he determined to tempt the fortune of combat, and so came to a formal battle with the Romans.

[Circumstances determine the wisdom of combat]

It is, then, useful not to fight when conditions are as they were for Fabius' army and, as I have just said, for that of Gneus Sulpitius, that is, when you have an army so good that the enemy does not dare attack you in your fortresses, and when the enemy is in your country without having set up a good base, so that he suffers from a scarcity of food. In that situation the plan is useful, for the reasons that Titus Livius gives: "He refused to commit himself to Fortune against an enemy whom time and a foreign land were daily making weaker." But in every other situation, by no possibility can you avoid battle, except with dishonor and peril to yourself. For to flee as Philip did is like being defeated, and with more shame, in so far as there has been less proof of your vigor. Though he succeeded in saving him/self, another would not have succeeded who was not aided by the country as he was. That Hannibal was not a master of war, nobody would ever say. Yet when he was opposed to Scipio in Africa, if he had seen any advantage in prolonging the war, he would have done it, and perhaps, since he was a good general and had a good army, he could have done it, as Fabius did in Italy. But since he did not, we must believe that some important reason moved him. So then, a prince who has an army assembled, and sees that for lack of money or of friends he cannot keep such an army a long time, is altogether mad if he does not tempt Fortune before his army begins to go to pieces, because if he waits, he certainly loses; if he makes the attempt, he may conquer.

[*Reputation*]

There is yet another thing to be pondered here. This is that a general wishes to gain renown even when he loses, and there is more renown in being overcome by force than by some other obstacle that makes you lose. So Hannibal would have been moved by this necessity. And on the other side (if Hannibal had deferred the battle, and Scipio had not had courage to attack him in strong places) Scipio, who had already overcome Syphax and gained so many cities in Africa, would not have allowed Hannibal to remain there as securely and easily as in Italy. This was not the situation of Hannibal when he was opposed to Fabius, nor of the French who were opposed to Sulpitius.

[*An invader cannot avoid battle*]

Still less can a general avoid battle when with his army he is attacking a foreign country because, if he intends to enter the land of the enemy, he must fight when the enemy comes against him. If he is besieging a city, he is so much the more obligated to battle. In our times that was the situation of Duke Charles of Burgundy who, when besieging Morat, a Swiss city, was attacked and defeated by the Swiss. Likewise the French army besieging Novara was defeated by the Swiss.

CHAPTER 11. HE WHO HAS TO STRIVE WITH MANY, EVEN WHEN HE IS INFERIOR, IF ONLY HE CAN REPEL THEIR FIRST ATTACKS, WINS

[*How the Roman Tribunes were managed*]

The power of the Tribunes of the People in the city of Rome was great, and it was necessary, as we have many times explained, because otherwise there would have been nothing to check the ambition of the nobility, which would have corrupted that republic much earlier than it actually did become corrupt. Nonetheless, because in everything, as we have said elsewhere, is hidden some evil of its own that brings forth new emergencies, there must be new laws to provide against such evil. Therefore, when the power of the Tribunes became overweening and dangerous to the nobility and to all Rome, trouble would have resulted, dangerous to Roman liberty, if Appius Clau-dius had not shown how to defend it against the Tribunes' ambition. His device was that they find among the Tribunes one who was timid or who could be bribed or who loved the common good; that Tribune they would induce to oppose any plan of the others to put into effect some decision against the will of the Senate. This device was an important moderator of their great authority and many times was useful to Rome.[1]

[A single united state will defeat powerful allied enemies]

This makes me observe that when many powers allied against one power are together much stronger than he, nevertheless more can be hoped from the power who is alone and less strong than from the many others, even though they are very strong. Because, putting aside all the things through which one alone is stronger than many (which are countless), it will always happen that by using a little cleverness the one will disunite the many and weaken that strong body. I do not need to bring up ancient examples, though there are many; I am sure there are enough modern ones in our time.

[Examples of the defeat of many by one]

In 1483 all Italy formed a league against the Venetians; they, entirely defeated and no longer able to keep their army in the field, bribed Lord Lodovico, who ruled Milan. Through such bribery, they made an agreement by which they not merely got back the cities they had lost but took possession of part of the Ferrarese terri-tory. So those who lost in the war were victors in the peace. A few years ago, all the world made a league against France. Nevertheless, before the war ended, Spain broke away from the confederates and made a truce with her; hence the other confederates were obliged soon after to make a truce for themselves. Without doubt, then, when a war is undertaken by many against one, we should always reckon that the one will be the winner, if he is strong enough to repel the first attacks and delay until the right time comes.

[Concessions must be made early]

If the one ruler is not strong enough to delay, he is subject to a thousand dangers, as were the Venetians in 1508; if they had managed

1. Livy 6. 37–42.

to delay the French army and had had time to gain over to their side some of those leagued against them, they would have escaped that ruin. (Yet since they did not have armies efficient enough to delay the enemy, and therefore did not have time to detach any of them, they fell.) We see, indeed, that the Pope, when he had his possessions again, became their friend; so did Spain; and very gladly, if they could have done so, those two princes would have saved supremacy in Lombardy for the Venetians in opposition to the French king, in order to keep him from becoming so great in Italy. The Venetians, then, could have given up part in order to save the rest. To have done so early enough to make it appear not a necessity would have been a very wise plan. Yet after the beginning it was contemptible and perhaps of little value. Before the war began, however, few of the Venetian citizens could see their danger, very few could see the remedy, and nobody advised it.

To return to the first part of this *Discourse*, I conclude that just as the Roman Senate had a medicine for the health of the country against the ambition of the Tribunes, because they were many, so any prince who is attacked by many will have a medicine against them, whenever he knows how to use with prudence measures suited for disuniting them.

CHAPTER 12. A PRUDENT GENERAL LAYS EVERY NECESSITY FOR FIGHTING ON HIS OWN SOLDIERS AND TAKES IT AWAY FROM THOSE OF THE ENEMY

[*The power of necessity*]

At other times we have indicated how useful to human actions necessity is and to what renown it has brought them, and that some moral philosophers have written that the hands and the tongue of man, two most noble instruments for making him noble, would not have worked perfectly or brought human actions to the height they have reached if they had not been urged on by necessity.

[*Necessity makes soldiers obstinate*]

Since, then, the ancient leaders of armies knew the power of such necessity and the extent to which it made their soldiers' spirits stubborn in fighting, they used every effort to have it impel their soldiers. And on the other hand they applied all their skill to freeing their enemies from it, and therefore many times opened to the enemy a road that they could have closed, and to their own soldiers closed a road that they could have left open. He then who wishes that a city be stubbornly defended, or that an army in the field should contend stubbornly, ought above everything to impose such necessity on the hearts of those who are going to fight. Therefore a prudent general who must attempt the capture of a city, measures the ease or difficulty of capturing it by learning and considering what necessity impels its inhabitants to defend themselves, and if he finds that great necessity impels them to defense, he judges capture difficult; otherwise he judges it easy.

[Hatred causes bitter warfare]

For this reason cities after rebellion are reconquered with more difficulty than at their first conquest; at the outset, not having cause to fear punishment because they have given no offense, they easily yield; but when later they have rebelled, being aware that they have given offense, and as a result fearing punishment, they become diffi-cult to conquer. This stubbornness also is produced by the natural hate neighboring princes and neighboring republics feel for each other. Such hate results from ambition to rule and jealousy of neigh-bors' power, especially among republics, as in Tuscany; this strife and rivalry always have made and always will make difficult the conquest of one by the other. Moreover, he who well considers the neighbors of the city of Florence and the neighbors of the city of Venice will not wonder, as many do, that in her wars Florence has spent more and gained less than Venice. The whole reason is that the cities near Venice were not so obstinate in defense as those near Florence. All the cities in the neighborhood of Venice were used to living under a prince and not in freedom. Those in the habit of serving often show little concern about changing their masters; in-deed they are many times eager to do so. Thus Venice, though she had neighbors more powerful than those of Florence, yet finding those cities less stubborn, overcame them more quickly than Florence could—surrounded by nothing but free cities.

[*Fine promises deceive the multitude*]

It is wise, then—to return to the early part of this *Discourse*—for a general when attacking a town to make every effort to remove from its defenders such necessity and consequently such stubbornness, promising pardon if they fear punishment, and if they fear for their liberty, showing them that he is acting not against the common good but against a few ambitious men in the city. This plan has many times made easier movements against cities and their capture. And though such pretenses are easily discerned, especially by prudent men, yet they often deceive the people, who, longing for immediate peace, close their eyes to all the traps hidden under such big promises. And in this way countless cities have become slaves, as did Florence in recent times. So it happened to Crassus and his army. Though he understood the empty promises of the Parthians, made to deprive his soldiers of any necessity for defending themselves, nevertheless he could not keep his men firm, since they were blinded by the offers of peace their enemies made, as can be read in detail in his *Life*.

[*Necessary war*]

I instance, too, the Samnites, who, through the ambition of some of them, contrary to the terms of the treaty, raided and plundered the fields of the Roman allies, and then sent ambassadors to Rome to ask for peace, offering to restore the property that had been taken and to give over as prisoners those who had caused the disorders and the plundering, but they were refused by the Romans. And on their return into Samnium without hope of agreement, Claudius Pontius, then general of the Samnite army, showed in a noteworthy speech that the Romans intended war in any case, and though on their part the Samnites wished peace, necessity made them go ahead with war. His words were: "A war has justice for those to whom it is necessary, and arms are sacred to those who save in arms have no hope" (Livy 9. 1). On such necessity he and his soldiers founded their hope of victory.

[*The power of necessity in Roman war*]

In order not to have to return later to this matter, I shall bring up such Roman instances as are most worthy of note. When Gaius Manlius with his army was opposing the Veientians, part of the

Veientian army got inside his stockade; whereupon Manlius with a regiment hurried to the rescue, and so that the Veientians could not escape, he occupied all the exits of the camp. Then the Veientians, seeing they were closed in, fought with such rage that they killed Manlius and would have overcome all the rest of the Romans if the prudence of a Tribune there had not opened to them a way for getting out. Here we observe that as long as necessity forced the Veientians to fight, they fought most savagely, but when they saw the way open, they thought more about fleeing than about fighting.

The Volsci and the Aequi with their armies had entered Roman territory. The Consuls were sent against them. As a result, in carrying on the combat, the army of the Volscians, of which Vetius Messius was head, was suddenly shut in between its stockades, which were occupied by the Romans, and the other Roman army. Seeing that he must either die or make his way with steel, he said to his soldiers: "Come with me, not wall or ditch but armed men oppose armed men; you are equal in courage; in the last and chief weapon, necessity, you are superior" (Livy 4. 28). So this necessity is called by Titus Livius "the last and chief weapon." Camillus, the most prudent of all the Roman generals, being already inside the city of the Veientians with his army, in order to make its capture easier by taking from the enemy the last necessity for defending them-selves, gave orders, in such a way that the Veientians heard him, that nobody should harm those who were without weapons. So, since weapons were thrown down, that city was taken almost without blood.[1] This method was afterwards used by many generals.

1. Livy 5. 21.

CHAPTER 13. IS A GOOD GENERAL WITH A WEAK ARMY OR A GOOD ARMY WITH A WEAK GENERAL MORE TO BE TRUSTED?

[Generals need soldiers; soldiers need generals]

Coriolanus, when an exile from Rome, fled to the Volsci, whence, having raised an army to avenge himself on his fellow citizens, he marched on Rome. He then left the city, more through respect for his mother than on account of the Roman forces. On this passage, Titus Livius says it teaches that the Roman republic succeeded through the valor rather of the generals than of the soldiers, if a reader considers that in the past the Volsci had been conquered and that later they were conquerors only when Coriolanus was their general.[1] And though Livy is of this opinion, nonetheless many places in his *History* indicate that the excellence of the soldiers without a general accomplished marvelous feats and that they showed better discipline and more spirit after the deaths of the Consuls than before, as did the Roman army in Spain under the Scipios. This army, after the deaths of the two generals, through its valor not merely saved itself but overcame the enemy and retained that province for the republic. Thus going through the whole, we find many instances in which the ability of the soldiers alone has won the battle, and many others in which the ability of the generals alone produced the same effect. Hence we decide that the first has need of the second, and the second of the first.

[A leader without an army, an army without a leader]

So it is well to consider, first, which is more to be feared: a good army badly led, or a good general supported by a bad army. In Caesar's opinion, either one should be valued low. For when he went into Spain against Afranius and Petraeus, who had an excellent army, he said that he valued them low, "since he went against an army without a leader," showing the weakness of the generals. On the contrary, when he went into Thessaly against Pompey, he said: "I go against a leader without an army."

[Armies train generals; generals train armies]

Another thing to be considered is whether it is easier for a good general to make a good army, or for a good army to make a good general. On that, I say that such a doubt seems settled, because many good men will more easily find or teach one man until he becomes good, than one will many. Lucullus, when he was sent against Mithridates, was wholly inexperienced in war; nevertheless that good army, where there were many excellent leaders, quickly made him a good general. The Romans, lacking men, armed many slaves and assigned them for drill to Sempronius Gracchus, who in a short time made a good army. Pelopidas and Epaminondas, as we say elsewhere, after getting Thebes their native city out of slavery to

---

1. *Livy* 2. 40.

the Spartans, in a short time made the Theban farmers into excellent soldiers who could not merely repel the Spartan warriors but could defeat them. So soldiers and general stand on a level, because one good thing finds another. Nevertheless a good army without a good leader is likely to become overbearing and dangerous, as did the Macedonian army after Alexander's death, and as did the veteran soldiers in the Roman Civil Wars. Hence I believe that more confidence can be put in a general who has time to instruct his men and opportunity to arm them than can be put in an arrogant army with a head whom it has riotously selected. Therefore I double the glory and renown of generals who not merely have defeated the enemy but, before they came to combat, have been obliged to instruct their armies and make them good. Such generals have shown double capacity—so rare that if such a task were given to many commanders they would as a result have much less honor and reputation than at present.

CHAPTER 14. THE EFFECTS OF NEW DEVICES THAT APPEAR AND NEW WORDS THAT ARE HEARD IN THE MIDST OF A BATTLE

The great importance in conflicts and battles of a new event, caused by something seen or heard for the first time, is shown in many places, and especially by this instance in the battle the Romans fought with the Volsci: Quintius, seeing one of the wings of his army yielding, in a loud voice ordered the men to stand firm because the other wing of the army was victorious. Having with these words given courage to his men and caused terror to the enemy, he won.[1] Now if the effects of such words on a trained army are great, on a confused and badly trained one they are very great, because the whole army is moved by the same wind.

[A Perugian instance]

I wish to bring up a striking instance in our times. A few years ago the city of Perugia was divided into two parties, the Oddi and Baglioni. The Baglioni were in power; the Oddi were exiles. By means of their friends, the Oddi got together an army and assembled

1. *Livy* 2. 64.

in some villages of theirs near Perugia; then with the aid of their party they one night entered that city, and without being discovered went on to seize the public square. Because at all the street corners that city has chains that keep it barred off, the soldiers of the Oddi had at their front a man who was breaking the locks with an iron hammer, to let the cavalry pass. When only the one opening into the public square was left to break, and the shout "To arms!" had already been raised, the man breaking the locks was so impeded by the crowd behind him that he could not raise his arms enough to strike; hence, in order to do so, he said: "Move back." When one rank after another passed along the word "Back," it made the rear-most run away, and in turn the others, with such speed that they defeated themselves. Thus the plan of the Oddi came to nothing, because of so slight an unforeseen event.

[How an army differs from a crowd]

This affair suggests that regulations in an army are needed not so much to enable it to fight in good order as to prevent the slightest unforeseen event from throwing you into disorder. Crowds of people are useless in war for no other reason than that every noise, every word, every confusion, upsets them and makes them flee. Therefore a good general, among his other rules, indicates those who are to take the word from him and pass it on, and he accustoms his soldiers not to trust any others, and his officers not to say anything except what he orders, because when this matter is not well observed, it often causes the greatest confusion.

[Examples of puzzling devices in battle]

As to seeing new things, every general should make an effort to have something appear, when the armies are engaged, that gives courage to his men and takes it away from their enemies, because among the events that give you victory, this is very effective. As proof of this, one can bring up Caius Sulpitius, the Roman Dictator. Coming to battle with the French, he armed all the plunderers and worthless people of the army, made them mount the mules and other beasts of burden, with such arms and ensigns that they seemed cavalry, put them under these ensigns behind a hill and ordered them at a given signal, just when the combat was hottest, to leave their hiding place and come into the enemy's view. This device so arranged and carried out caused such terror to the French that they lost the day. Therefore a good general ought to do two things: one is to try to confuse the enemy with some of these new devices; the other is to be so well prepared that if such devices are used by the enemy, the general can expose them and make them come to nothing. So the King of India did to Semiramis: she, seeing that the King had a large number of elephants, in an attempt to frighten him and show him that she also had plenty, made many elephants from the hides of buffalos and cows and, putting them on camels, sent them ahead. But since the King penetrated the trick, he made that scheme of hers not merely useless to her but harmful. When Mamercus the Dictator was opposing the Fidenates, the latter, to frighten the Roman army, ordered that in the heat of the action a number of soldiers with flames on their spears should come out of Fidenae, so that the Romans, surprised by the novelty of the sight, would disorder their military formation.

[Devices may turn against their inventer]

On this I comment that when such devices have more of truth than of fiction, they can be staged before men, because if they have enough of the convincing, their flimsiness cannot very soon be found out. But when they have more of the fictitious than of the true, they should not be used or, if they are used, should be kept at a distance, in such a way that they cannot quickly be discovered, as Caius Sulpitius did the mule riders. Because if they are flimsy, they are quickly found out when they come close, so that they cause you loss and not gain, as the elephants did to Semiramis and the flames to the Fidenates. At the beginning the flames disturbed the Roman army a little; yet the Dictator came up and called out to them that they should not disgrace themselves by running away from smoke like bees and that they should turn back against them; then he shouted: "With their flames destroy Fidenae, which you have not been able to please with your favors" (Livy 4. 33). Thus that device became useless to the Fidenates and they lost the combat.

CHAPTER 15. ONE GENERAL AND NOT MANY SHOULD BE PUT IN COMMAND OF AN ARMY; HOW SEVERAL COMMAND⁄ERS DO HARM

When the Fidenates rebelled and killed the colony the Romans had sent to Fidenae, the Romans, to deal with this outrage, set up four Tribunes with consular power. One of these they left to guard Rome, and three they sent against the Fidenates and the Veientians. The three, holding different views and disunited, got from the cam⁄paign dishonor but not injury; as to the dishonor, the Tribunes caused it; if they received no injury, the efficiency of the soldiers caused it. Hence the Romans, seeing this confusion, resorted to choosing a Dictator, so that one man would reorder what three had disordered. This teaches that to have several commanders in an army or in a city that is to be defended, is unprofitable. Titus Livius could not say that more clearly than with these words: "Three Tribunes with consular power teach that plural control in war is very ineffective; since each general held to his own plans and they were all different, the enemy had a good opportunity" (Livy 4. 31).

[*A Florentine instance*]

Though this example is sufficient to prove the trouble made in war by too many commanders, I wish for greater clarity to bring up some others both modern and ancient. In 1500, after Louis XII the King of France recaptured Milan, he sent his soldiers to Pisa to restore her to the Florentines, who sent there as commissioners Gio⁄vambatista Ridolfi and Luca di Antonio degli Albizzi. And because Giovambatista was a man of reputation and older, Luca left the complete control of everything to him. Though he did not show his ambition by opposing him, he showed it by remaining silent and by neglecting and belittling everything, in such a way that he did not aid the actions of the army with deeds or with counsel, as if he had been a man of no importance. But then the very opposite appeared. Giovambatista, as the result of some accident, had to return to Flor⁄ence, whereupon Luca, left alone, showed how strong he was in courage, industry, and counsel, though all of these were lost while his companion was there.[1]

I wish again to bring up, in confirmation of this, words of Titus Livius, who tells that when the Romans sent Quintius and Agrippa his colleague against the Aequi, Agrippa wished the entire adminis-tration of the war to be in the hands of Quintius. Livy comments: "It is most beneficial in the administration of great things that the chief authority should be in one man" (3. 70). This is contrary to what these republics and princes of ours do today by putting into their offices, in order to administer them better, more than one com-missioner and more than one head; this makes confusion beyond reckoning. If we seek causes for the ruin of the Italian and French armies in our times, this will be found the strongest. Certainly we can conclude that it is better to send on an expedition one normally prudent man only rather than two very able men as associates with equal authority.

1. *Machiavelli was secretary to these commissioners.*

CHAPTER 16. IN DIFFICULT TIMES TRUE ABILITY IS SOUGHT FOR; IN EASY TIMES ABLE MEN DO NOT HOLD OFFICE, BUT THOSE WHO THROUGH RICHES OR FAMILY ARE MOST POPULAR

[Nicias as an example]

It always has been and always will be true that in republics great and exceptional men are neglected in times of peace; at such times envy of the reputation their ability gives them raises in many citizens a desire to be not merely their equals but their superiors. On this there is a good passage in Thucydides the Greek historian, showing that when the Athenian republic had the advantage in the Pelopon-nesian War and had bridled the pride of Sparta and almost subjugated all the rest of Greece, she became so proud that she planned to conquer Sicily. This undertaking was debated in Athens. Alcibia-des and some other citizens advised the attempt, in their concern not with the public good but with their own reputation, since they planned to be in charge of such an expedition. But Nicias, the man of highest reputation in Athens, spoke against it. In addressing the people, the chief argument he brought forward to give them faith in him was this: when he advised that war should not be made, he advised something not to his own advantage, because he knew that, when Athens was at peace, countless citizens were eager to be advanced ahead of him, but if they made war, he knew that no citizen would be superior or equal to him.

[*In quiet times republics neglect capable men*]

We see, then, that republics show this defect: they pay slight attention to capable men in quiet times. This condition makes such men feel injured in two ways: first, they fail to attain their proper rank; second, they are obliged to have as associates and superiors men who are unworthy and of less ability than themselves. This abuse in republics has produced much turmoil, because those citizens who see themselves undeservedly rejected, and know that they can be neglected only in times that are easy and not perilous, make an effort to disturb them by stirring up new wars to the damage of the republic. When I consider possible remedies, I find two: the first is to keep the citizens poor, so that, when without goodness and wisdom, they cannot corrupt themselves or others with riches; the second is to arrange that such republics will continually make war, and therefore always will need citizens of high repute, like the Romans in their early days. Because that city always kept armies in the field, she always needed able men. Hence she could not take a position from one who deserved it and give it to one who did not deserve it. If sometimes Rome did so, at once she got into such great confusion and peril that she quickly returned into the true way.

But other republics, which are not organized like her and which make war only when driven by necessity, cannot protect themselves from such an abuse. On the contrary, they will always run into it, and disturbances will always result when a citizen such as I have described, neglected but able, is inclined to revenge, and has some reputation and following in the city. The city of Rome for a time did protect herself, but she also, when she had overcome Carthage and Antiochus (as I have said elsewhere)[1] and no longer feared her wars, assumed that she could entrust her armies to whomever she wished, not paying so much attention to efficiency as to those other qualities that give favor with the people. We see that many times

1. DISCOURSES 2. 1.

Paulus Emilius was defeated for the consulship and that he was not made Consul until the Macedonian war broke out. Since this was judged a dangerous war, it was committed to him with the approval of the entire city.

[Antonio Giacomini]

In our city of Florence, when after 1494 there were many wars and all the Florentine citizens made a wretched showing, the city by chance came upon a man who demonstrated how they ought to manage armies. This was Antonio Giacomini. And as long as dangerous wars were to be carried on, all the ambition of the other citizens disappeared, and in the choice of commissioner and head of the armies he had no competitor. But when a war was to be carried on in which there was no fear and much honor and rank, he had many competitors; thus when they chose three commissioners to besiege Pisa, he was left out. And though it does not plainly appear that evil for the republic resulted from not sending Antonio there, yet it can easily be conjectured because, since the Pisans had nothing further to defend themselves with or to live on, if Antonio had been there, they would have been so much more strictly blockaded that they would have surrendered to the Florentines.[2] But since they were assailed by commanders who did not know how to blockade them or to assault them, they kept going so long that the city of Florence bought them, when she could have had them by force. It is to be expected that such a slight would be very powerful with Antonio, and he needed to be patient and good indeed not to attempt to revenge himself, either with the ruin of the city, if he could, or with harm to some individual citizens. From this a republic ought to guard herself, as will be explained in the following chapter.

2. *In his* DISCOURSE TO THE MAGISTRACY OF THE TEN ON THE AFFAIRS OF PISA, *Machiavelli deals at length with the ways in which a Florentine army blockading the city could cut off her supplies. He touches also on direct assault.*

CHAPTER 17. A MAN SHOULD NOT BE INJURED AND THEN ASSIGNED TO IMPORTANT ADMINISTRATION AND CONTROL[1]

A republic should be very careful not to put any important business under the charge of a man to whom someone has done a notable injury. Claudius Nero left the army with which he was facing Hannibal and with part of it went into the Marches to join the other Consul, in order to attack Hasdrubal before he could unite with Hannibal. Earlier when Claudius was opposing Hasdrubal in Spain, he shut his enemy into a place where he was obliged either to fight at a disadvantage or to die of hunger. Hasdrubal then so astutely diverted Claudius with certain suggestions for truce as to free himself and deprive Claudius of that chance for victory. This affair, when known at Rome, brought Claudius blame from the Senate and the people, and he was vilified all through the city, not without much dishonor and outrage. Then being later made Consul and sent against Hannibal, he adopted the aforementioned plan, which was so perilous that Rome was full of fear and excitement until news came of Hasdrubal's defeat.

When Claudius was later asked why he adopted so dangerous a plan, on which without extreme necessity he had as it were staked the liberty of Rome, he answered that he had done it because he knew that if he succeeded he would reacquire such glory as he lost in Spain; if he did not succeed, and this plan of his had an opposite end, he knew that he would revenge himself on that city and those citizens who had so ungratefully and imprudently injured him. If passions of that sort for such injuries were so powerful in a Roman citizen, in those times when Rome was still uncorrupted, we can imagine how powerful they would be in a citizen of some other city that is not such as she was then. And because no certain remedy can be given for such troubles that rise in republics, it follows that an everlasting republic cannot be established; in a thousand unexpected ways her ruin is caused.

1. *Livy* 26. 17; 27. 34, 44.

CHAPTER 18. NOTHING IS MORE MERITORI-
OUS IN A GENERAL THAN TO FORESEE
THE ENEMY'S PLANS

[Instances of failure to know what an enemy is doing]

Epaminondas the Theban was accustomed to say that nothing
was more necessary and more useful to a general than to learn the
decisions and plans of the enemy. Because such knowledge is difficult to get, a commander merits so much the more praise when he
works in such a way that he conjectures them. It is not so difficult
to understand the purposes of the enemy as it sometimes is to understand his actions, and not his actions done at a distance so much as
those in the present and nearby. For many times it happens that
when a battle lasts until night, the victor believes he has lost, and the
loser believes he has won. Such mistakes cause decisions opposed to
the well-being of the man who makes them. That was true of Brutus
and Cassius, who through such a mistake lost the war, because when
Brutus won on his wing, Cassius, who lost on his, believed the
whole army defeated, and in that error, despairing of safety, killed
himself. In our times, in the battle fought in Lombardy at Santa
Cecilia by Francis King of France against the Swiss,[1] when night
came on, such of the Swiss as remained in order believed that they
had conquered, since they did not know about those who were
defeated and killed. This mistake kept them from saving themselves,
since they waited to fight again in the morning, with such great
disadvantage. And they also caused the army of the Pope and of
Spain to accept their mistake and through that mistake almost to
ruin itself, for on the false news of the victory, it crossed the Po, and
if it had marched too far would have been captured by the French,
who were victorious.

This same mistake was made in the Roman armies and in those
of the Aequi. In that instance, when the Consul Sempronius with
his army was opposing the enemy and battle was joined, the struggle
lasted until evening, with various fortune on either side; and when
night came, since both armies were half defeated, neither of them
returned to its camp; on the contrary, each retired into the nearest
hills, where they thought they were more secure. The Roman army

1. *Usually known as the battle of Marignano. See also* DISCOURSES 2. 18, 22.

was divided into two parts; one of these went with the Consul, the other with a certain Tempanius, a centurion, through whose valor that day the Roman army had not been defeated entirely. When morning came, the Roman Consul, without learning anything further of his enemies, moved toward Rome. The Aequian army likewise withdrew, for each believed the enemy had won and there-fore each retired without feeling any concern about leaving its camp as booty. When Tempanius, who was with the remainder of the Roman army, was also retiring, he learned from some wounded Aequi that their generals had gone, abandoning their camp. There-fore, upon this news he entered the Roman camp and saved it, then sacked the Aequian camp and returned to Rome victorious. This victory, it is clear, rested merely on which first learned of the enemy's confusion. Here we observe that often two armies opposed to each other may be in the same disorder and suffer the same necessities; and then that one is victor which first understands the other's necessity.

[A comic Florentine instance]

I wish to give a local and modern instance of this. In 1498, when the Florentines had a large army in Pisan territory and pressed that city hard, the Venetians, who had undertaken her protection, not seeing any other way to save her, determined to divert the war by attacking Florentine territory from another side. Raising a powerful army, they came through the Val di Lamona, occupied the village of Marradi, and besieged the castle of Castiglione on the hill above. The Florentines, learning of this, determined to rescue Marradi and not to weaken the forces they had in the territory of Pisa. And having raised new infantry and organized new cavalry, they sent them in that direction. Their leaders were Jacopo IV d'Appiano, lord of Piombino, and Count Rinuccio da Marciano. When these soldiers, then, were led to the top of the hill above Marradi, the enemy raised the siege of Castiglione and retired completely into the village. After these two armies had confronted each other for some days, both of them suffered much for food and for every other necessary. And neither one having courage to attack the other, and neither knowing the troubles of the other, on the same evening they decided—both of them—to strike camp the following morning and retreat, the Venetian army toward Bersighella and Faenza, the Florentine toward Casaglia and the Mugello. Then when morning came and both of the armies were sending off their baggage, by chance a woman left the village of Marradi and came toward the Florentine army, since she felt safe through her age and her poverty, wishing to see some of her relatives who were in that army. Learning from her that the Venetian army was leaving, the leaders of the Florentine troops were made brave by the news and, changing their plan, moved toward the enemy as if they had dislodged them. Then they wrote to Florence that they had driven them back and won the war. This victory resulted from nothing else than their hearing earlier than their enemies that the hostile army was going away. This information, if it had come first to the other side, would have been used in the same way against our forces.

CHAPTER 19. WHETHER IN CONTROL-LING A MULTITUDE INDULGENCE IS MORE NECESSARY THAN PUNISHMENT[1]

The Roman state was disturbed by the hostilities of the nobles and the people; nevertheless, when war was upon them, they sent out in command of their armies Quintius and Appius Claudius. Appius, being cruel and rough in commanding, was not obeyed by his men, so that he fled from his province almost defeated. Quintius, being kind and of a humane temperament, won the obedience of his soldiers and bore off the victory. This indicates that it is better, in ruling a multitude, to be humane rather than proud, merciful rather than cruel. Nevertheless, Cornelius Tacitus, with whom many other writers agree, in one of his aphorisms makes the opposite decision, saying: "In controlling a multitude, punishment is more effective than indulgence."

[*A prince should avoid hatred by subjects*]

Considering how these opinions can both hold true, I say: Either you have to control men who normally are your companions or men who are always your inferiors. When they are your companions, it is not possible simply to use punishment or that severity of which Cornelius speaks, and because the Roman people had in Rome equal authority with the nobility, anyone who became their leader for a limited time could not use cruelty and roughness in managing

1. *Livy* 2. 55–60.

them. And many times better results were gained by the Roman generals who made themselves loved by their armies and who man﹣ aged them with indulgence than by those who made themselves extraordinarily feared, unless indeed they were gifted with unusual ability, as was Manlius Torquatus. But he who commands subjects such as Cornelius speaks of, if they are not to become overweening and, because of your excessive tolerance, to kick you, needs to put attention rather on punishment than on indulgence. But this too he ought to moderate in such a way as to avoid hate, because to be hated is not for any prince's advantage. The way to avoid hate is to let your subjects' property alone, because no prince desires their blood except when compelled, if greed is not hidden under his desire; and such compulsion seldom comes. But desire for blood, when greed is mixed with it, appears continually, and there is never a lack of cause or desire for bloodshed, as I explain in another tractate where I discuss this matter at length.[2] Quintius, then, deserved more praise than Appius, and the opinion of Cornelius, within its limits, and not under the conditions dealt with by Appius, deserves to be approved.

And because I have spoken of punishment and of indulgence, I think it not superfluous to show that a striking act of kindness was more effective with the Falisci than were arms.

2. PRINCE 17. *Yet how could Machiavelli call a small part of a short chapter long?*

CHAPTER 20. AN INSTANCE OF KINDNESS WAS MORE EFFECTIVE WITH THE FALISCI THAN ALL THE ROMAN POWER[1]

When Camillus had surrounded with his army a city of the Falisci and laid siege to it, the teacher of a school for the highest﹣born youths of that city planned to get the favor of Camillus and of the Roman people. With the excuse of exercise, going with his pupils out of the city, he led them all to Camillus' camp and into his presence, and offering the boys, told him that for their sake the city would give herself into his hands. Not merely did Camillus not accept his offer, but stripping that schoolmaster naked, binding his hands behind him, and putting a stick into the hands of each of the boys, he had them drive their teacher, with many blows, back to the

1. *Livy* 5. 27.

city. When this affair was known to those citizens, the kindness and honor of Camillus pleased them so much that without attempting to defend themselves longer, they decided to surrender. This true instance shows that sometimes a kind and benevolent act has much more effect on the minds of men than a fierce and violent action, and that often provinces and cities not opened by arms, implements of war, and every sort of human effort have been opened by an instance of kindness and compassion, of chastity or of liberality.

[Fabricius, Scipio, Cyrus]

In history there are many instances of this besides the one given. We see that Roman arms could not drive Pyrrhus from Italy, but that the liberality of Fabricius did drive him out, when he showed the King the offer to poison him made to the Romans by one of his intimates. We also see that Scipio Africanus did not get so much reputation in Spain from the capture of New Carthage as from that famous instance of chastity, when he returned the wife, young, beautiful, and untouched, to her husband. The report of that act gained him the friendship of all Spain.[2] We see further how much the people desire this quality in great men and how much authors praise it, both those who narrate the lives of princes and those who present the rules by which they ought to live.[3] Among these Xenophon takes great pains to show how many honors, how many victories, how much good reputation Cyrus attained by being kind and pleasant and by not giving in his conduct any instance of pride or cruelty or lust or the other vices that spot men's lives.

Yet since on the other hand Hannibal gained great fame and great victories with opposite methods, I shall discuss in the next chapter the reasons for it.

2. Livy 26. 46–50.
3. Writers de regimine principum (on the conduct of princes); cf. PRINCE 15.

CHAPTER 21. WHY HANNIBAL, WHOSE PROCEDURE WAS UNLIKE SCIPIO'S, PRO⁄DUCED IN ITALY EFFECTS SIMILAR TO THOSE OF SCIPIO IN SPAIN[1]

I judge that some will marvel on seeing that some generals, in spite of their very different practice, have nevertheless produced re⁄sults like those of men whose practice was that described above. Hence victories apparently do not result from the aforementioned causes. On the contrary, the methods just discussed seem not to bring you more power or better fortune, since opposite methods can bring fame and reputation. So in order not to get away from the men mentioned above and to explain better what I am trying to bring out, I say that Scipio, entering Spain, with that kindness and compassion of his quickly made that province his friend and made himself worshiped and loved by the people. On the other hand, Hannibal, entering Italy, with methods just the opposite—that is, with cruelty, violence, plunder, and every sort of perfidy—produced the same effects as Scipio did in Spain, for to Hannibal all the cities of Italy went over, all the peoples followed him.

[Fear more effective than love]

Reflecting on what caused this, we see many reasons for it. The first is that men are so eager for changes that most of the time there is as much desire for change among those who are well off as among those who are badly off, because, as I have said—and it is true—men are bored in good times and complain in bad ones. This desire, then, causes gates to open to any man who makes himself leader of a revolution in a province. If he is a foreigner, people hasten to follow him; if he is a native, they join him, strengthening him and aiding him. Hence, however he proceeds, he makes great gains in those places. Besides this, men are driven chiefly by two things: love and fear. Therefore a leader can command who makes himself loved, just as he can who makes himself feared; but most of the time the leader who makes himself feared is better followed and better obeyed than he who makes himself loved.

1. Livy 21. 4, 21, 43–44; 27. 20; 39. 51.

[Extraordinary ability is the secret]

It therefore matters little which of these two roads a general travels, if only he is an able man and his ability gives him renown among the people. When his ability is great, as was that of Hannibal and Scipio, it cancels all errors that result from his making himself too much loved or too much feared. From either one of the two courses can come difficulties great enough to overthrow a prince: he who is too eager to be loved gets despised; he who too much endeavors to be feared, if he exceeds the norm ever so little, gets hated. He cannot keep exactly the middle way, because our nature does not allow it, but he must with extraordinary ability atone for any excess, as did Hannibal and Scipio. Nonetheless, we see that both of them were damaged by their ways of acting, and at the same time were raised higher.

[Scipio's humanity]

The height to which both of them were raised has been mentioned. The damage to Scipio was that his soldiers in Spain rebelled against him, along with part of his friends. This came from nothing else than not fearing him, because men are so restless that if the smallest door is opened to their ambition, they at once forget all the love for a prince that his humanity has caused them to feel, as did the soldiers and friends mentioned above. They went so far that Scipio, to cure this ill, was forced to use some of the cruelty he had avoided.

[Hannibal's cruelty]

As to Hannibal, there is no special instance in which his well-known cruelty and bad faith injured him, but we can well suppose that Naples and many other towns that remained loyal to the Roman people so remained for fear of those qualities. We are well aware that his pitiless conduct made him more hateful to the Roman people than any other enemy that republic ever had. Hence, whereas when Pyrrhus was in Italy with his army, they revealed to him the man who planned to poison him, Hannibal they never forgave, though he was disarmed and exiled, until at last they caused his death. To Hannibal, then, through the common belief that he was pitiless and a breaker of his word and cruel, there came this disadvantage. But on the other hand he gained a very great advantage, admired by all the historians, namely that in his army, though it was made up of various sorts of men, there never was any internal strife, either among the soldiers or against himself. This cannot be explained except by the terror caused by his personal traits; this was so great that, combined with the renown his ability gave him, it kept his soldiers united and quiet.

[*Ability rather than method is what counts*]

I conclude then, that it does not much matter which method a general practices, if only he is able enough to impart a good flavor to either way of behaving. As I have said, in either one there is defect and peril, if extraordinary ability does not correct it. So if Hannibal and Scipio, one with praiseworthy actions, the other with detestable ones, produced the same result, I think I should not fail to discuss also two Roman citizens who with different methods, both praiseworthy, attained equal glory.

CHAPTER 22. THE HARSHNESS OF MANLIUS TORQUATUS AND THE KINDNESS OF VALERIUS CORVINUS GAINED FOR EACH ONE THE SAME GLORY

Living in Rome at the same time were two excellent generals, Manlius Torquatus and Valerius Corvinus; these men were equal in ability, equal in victories and in fame, and each of them, as to the enemy, gained his standing with equal ability. But as to the armies and as to their dealings with the soldiers, they proceeded diversely, for Manlius with every sort of severity, without allowing his soldiers any break in their fatigue or labor, kept them under orders. Valerius, on the other hand, in every way and manner kind and full of familiar intimacy, treated them pleasantly. We see that in order to have the obedience of the soldiers, one killed his son, and the other never harmed anybody. Nonetheless, with such diverse conduct each one obtained the same result, both against enemies and to the advantage of the republic and of himself. For no soldier ever refused combat or rebelled or was in any way out of harmony with their wishes, though the orders of Manlius were so harsh that all other orders that went beyond measure were called Manlian orders.[1]

1. *Livy* 8. 7.

[Harshness versus kindness]

In this situation one is to consider four things. First, what drove Manlius to act so harshly? Second, why did Valerius act so humanely? Third, why did these diverse methods produce the same result? Finally, which is the better and, when imitated, more profitable? Anybody who considers well Manlius' nature from the first mention of him by Titus Livius sees that he was a very strong man, devoted to his father and his native city and very respectful to his superiors. These facts are to be learned from the death of that Frenchman you know of, from his defense of his father against the Tribune, and from his words to the Consul before he entered the combat with the Frenchman: "Without your command I shall never fight against an enemy, not if I see victory certain" (Livy 7. 10). When a man of that sort comes to commanding rank, he reckons on finding all men like himself, and his strong spirit makes him command strong things; that same spirit, after they are commanded, expects them to be carried out. It is a true rule that when you give harsh orders, you must be harsh in having them carried out; otherwise your expectation will be deceived. This teaches that if you expect to be obeyed, you must know how to command. Men who know that compare their capacities with those of the men who are to obey. When they see that such capacities correspond, then they give commands; when they see lack of that correspondence, they refrain from it. Therefore a prudent man was wont to say that if a state is to be held with force, he who uses force must correspond in strength with him who is subject to it. When such correspondence exists, we can believe that such use of force can continue; but when he who is subject to force is stronger than he who is using force, we must fear that any day such use of force will end.

[The stern commander]

But returning to our subject, I say that a man who commands hard things must be hard, and he who is hard and commands hard things cannot then let them be carried out with gentleness. He who lacks this hardness of spirit should guard himself from giving extraordinary orders, and in ordinary ones he can use kindness; for ordinary punishments are not charged to the prince but to the laws and the regulations. We should, then, believe that Manlius was forced to proceed so severely by those extraordinary commands to which his nature inclined him. These are useful in a state because they bring back its laws to their beginning and to their ancient vigor. If a state were fortunate enough, as we said above,² to have frequently a leader who with his example would renovate its laws, and would not merely stop it from running to ruin but would pull it backward, it would be everlasting. So Manlius was one of those who with harsh orders kept up military discipline in Rome, being impelled first by his nature, then by his desire that what his natural inclination had made him arrange should be carried out.

[*The kind commander*]

On the other side, Valerius could act kindly, since it was enough for him that the things usual in the Roman army should be carried out. This tendency, because it was good, was enough to bring him honor. To act according to it was not difficult and did not force Valerius to punish transgressors, both because there were none of them and because any there might be would, as I said, charge their punishment to the laws and not to the cruelty of the commander. Hence Valerius was able to represent as coming from himself every kind action through which he gained favor with the soldiers and satisfied them.

[*Success demands unusual ability*]

The result was that, both having the same authority, they brought about the same effects, though working in opposite ways. Those who try to imitate them may fall into those bad habits causing contempt and hatred that I mention above in treating Scipio and Hannibal³—something you can avoid if you have unusual ability, but not otherwise.

[*Is sternness or kindness better?*]

It now remains to consider which of these two methods of procedure is most praiseworthy. I believe this debatable, because writers praise both methods. Nonetheless, those who write on how a prince ought to conduct himself⁴ side with Valerius rather than with Man-

2. DISCOURSES 3. 1.
3. DISCOURSES 3. 21. *See also* THE PRINCE, *chap.* 17.
4. *Works* de regimine principum *or on the conduct of princes. For Machiavelli's relation*

lius; and Xenophon, mentioned above,[5] giving many instances of Cyrus' kindness, is in close agreement with what Titus Livius says of Valerius. When he was Consul against the Samnites, and the day came when he had to fight, he spoke to his soldiers with the kindness he always practiced. On a kind speech of his Livy com- ments: "Never was a leader more friendly with the soldier, since among the soldiers of lowest rank he carried on all his duties un- grudgingly. In military sports also, when equals entered contests of swiftness or strength, he won or lost with the same courteous ex- pression; nor was anybody repulsed who offered himself as an equal; friendly in his deeds according to circumstances; in his words by no means less mindful of the liberty of others than of his own dignity; and (than which nothing is more popular) he carried on the magis- tracies with the same methods by which he gained them" (7. 33). In the same way Titus Livius speaks of Manlius with respect, showing that his severity in the death of his son made the army so obedient to the Consul as to cause the victory the Roman people won over the Latins. He goes so far in praising him that, after such a victory, having described all the course of the fight and shown all the perils the Roman people encountered in it and their difficulties in winning, he draws this conclusion: the efficiency of Manlius alone gave that victory to the Romans. And making a comparison of the forces of the two armies, he declares that the side would have conquered which had Manlius as Consul.[6] Hence, considering all that the historians say about the two Romans, I find a decision between kindness and harshness difficult.

[Harshness safer for the state]

Nevertheless, in order not to leave this matter unsettled, I say that for a citizen who lives under the laws of a republic, I believe Manlius' procedure more praiseworthy and less dangerous, because his way is wholly for the benefit of the state and does not in any respect regard private ambition, since by his way a leader cannot gain partisans, for he shows himself always harsh to everybody and loves solely the common good. By so acting he gains no special

to them see Gilbert, MACHIAVELLI's "PRINCE" AND ITS FORERUNNERS (Duke Univ. Press, 1938).

5. DISCOURSES 3. 20. See also THE PRINCE, chap. 14.

6. Livy 8. 10.

friends, such as those we call partisans, as I put it above. Hence, no way of proceeding can be more useful than this or more desirable in a city, because it does not lack public advantage, and there cannot be in it any suspicion of private power. But in Valerius' conduct we see the contrary, because if indeed with respect to the public it produces the same results, nonetheless a good deal of fear is caused through the special good will he gains with the soldiers, lest in a long period of power it produce bad results, opposed to freedom. If Publicola produced none of these ill effects,[7] the reason was that the spirits of the Romans were not yet corrupt, and he was not long and continuously in command.

[*Kindness wiser for a prince but dangerous to a citizen*]

But if we have to consider a prince, as Xenophon did, we would wholly take the side of Valerius and abandon Manlius; for a prince ought to seek in his soldiers and in his subjects obedience and love. Obedience results from his being an observer of established institutions and being looked upon as able; love results from affability, kindness, pity, and from Valerius' other qualities, which Xenophon says Cyrus also possessed. For a prince to be in high favor as an individual and to have the army as his partisan harmonizes with all the other demands of his position. But that a citizen should have the army as his partisan—this does not at all fit with the demand that he live under the laws and obey the magistrates. It appears in the ancient records of the Venetian republic that once when the galleys returned to Venice, some difference arose between the galley men and the people, with rioting and the use of arms, and the affair could not be quieted by the force of the officers or by respect for the citizens or fear of the magistrates. Then suddenly before the sailors came a gentleman who the year before had been their commander, for love of whom they departed and gave up the strife. This obedience created such suspicion in the Senate that a little later the Venetians, through either prison or death, secured themselves against him. I conclude, therefore, that the procedure of Valerius is useful in a prince but harmful in a citizen, not merely to his country but to himself: to her because such methods prepare the way for tyranny; to him because his city, having suspicious fears of his conduct, is

7. For his ambition, see bk. 1, chap. 28; Livy 2. 2, 6–7. *P. Valerius Publicola lived more than a century earlier than Valerius Corvinus.*

driven to secure herself against him to his injury. On the contrary, I affirm that Manlius' conduct is damaging to a prince but profitable to a citizen, and especially so to his country. It also seldom causes injury, unless indeed the hate your severity brings upon you is increased by the suspicion which, as a result of your high reputation, your other virtues bring upon you, as I shall show below in Camillus' case.

CHAPTER 23. WHY CAMILLUS WAS DRIVEN OUT OF ROME

We have decided above that by proceeding like Valerius a man injures his country and himself, and by proceeding like Manlius he benefits his country and sometimes injures himself. This is well established through the instance of Camillus, who in his conduct resembled Manlius rather than Valerius. Hence Titus Livius, speaking of him, says that "the soldiers hated and marveled at his efficiency" (5. 26). What made him considered marvelous was his care, his prudence, his great courage, his excellent method in administering and commanding armies. What made him hated was that his severity in punishing the soldiers exceeded his liberality in rewarding them. Titus Livius brings up these causes for this hatred. First, he added to the public funds the money coming from the sale of the Veientian property, instead of dividing it with the spoil. Second, in his triumph he had his triumphal chariot drawn by four white horses. About this they said that through pride he wished to equal himself to the Sun God. Third, he vowed to give to Apollo the tenth part of the Veientian plunder. If he were to fulfil his vow, he had to take the plunder from the hands of the soldiers who had already seized it.[1]

Here we see well and easily what makes a prince hateful to the people. The most important of these is depriving them of something profitable. This is very important, because when a man is deprived of things that bring profit, he never forgets them, but every slight necessity makes you remember them;[2] and because necessities come every day, you remember them every day. The other thing causing hatred is to appear proud and puffed up; the people, especially the

1. Livy 5. 23.
2. *Machiavelli shifts person, as often in* THE PRINCE.

free, hate nothing worse. Even though that pride and that display cause them no trouble, yet they hate him who indulges in them. From such pride a prince ought to guard himself as from a shoal, because to bring hatred on himself without any return is in every way rash and imprudent.

CHAPTER 24. THE PROLONGATION OF THE HIGHEST MILITARY AUTHORITY MADE ROME A SLAVE

On considering well the course of the Roman republic, we see two causes for that republic's dissolution: first, the struggles provoked by the Agrarian Laws; second, the prolongation of supreme commands. If these things had been well understood from the beginning and the proper remedies applied to them, free government would have lasted longer and perhaps been more peaceful. Though the prolongation of supreme command apparently never caused rioting in Rome, nevertheless it is evident how much a city is injured by the authority that citizens obtain through such decrees. If the other citizens whose magistracy was extended had been wise and good, as was Lucius Quintius, the city would not have been subject to this ill. His goodness appears in a notable instance. An agreement for a truce had been made between the people and the Senate, and the people had prolonged for a year the authority of the Tribunes, judging them strong enough to resist the ambition of the nobles. Then the Senate, in competition with the people and in order not to seem weaker than they, wished to prolong the consulate of Lucius Quintius. But he entirely rejected such a decree, saying that it was necessary to seek to get rid of bad examples, not to increase them with another worse example; so he urged the choice of new Consuls.[1] Such goodness and prudence, if possessed by all the Roman citizens, would not have let them introduce that habit of prolonging the magistracies, and from that they would not have come to the prolongation of supreme commands—a thing that in time ruined the republic.

1. *Livy* 3. 21.

[The dangers of prolonged command]

The first whose command was extended was Publius Philo.[2] When, as he was beseiging the city of Palaepolis, the end of his consulate came, the Senate judged that he had victory in hand; they therefore did not send his successor but made him Proconsul, so that he was the first Proconsul. This practice, though begun by the Senate for public good, in time made Rome a slave, because the farther the Romans went abroad with their armies, the more necessary they thought this extension of command and the more they used it. It resulted in two ills. One was that a smaller number of men had experience in command; therefore reputation became restricted to a few. The other was that when a citizen was for a long time commander of an army, he gained its support and made it his partisan, for that army in time forgot the Senate and considered him its head. In this way Sulla and Marius found soldiers who, in opposition to the public good, would follow them. In this way Caesar could conquer his country. If the Romans had never prolonged the magistracies and the commands, they might not have come so quickly to great power, for their conquests might have been later, but they would have come later still to slavery.

2. Livy 8. 26.

CHAPTER 25. THE POVERTY OF CINCINNATUS AND OF MANY ROMAN CITIZENS

[Poverty and freedom]

We have argued elsewhere that the most useful thing a free state can bring about is to keep its citizens poor.[1] Though it does not appear what arrangement produced this effect in Rome, especially since the Agrarian Law met so much opposition, nevertheless experience reveals that, four hundred years after Rome had been built, her people were still in the utmost poverty. I cannot believe that any condition was stronger in producing this effect than the knowledge that poverty did not close your road to whatever rank and whatever honor, and that men went to seek Ability whatever house she lived in. Such a state of society evidently gave less desirability to riches.

1. DISCOURSES 1. 37, and the Index under poverty.

To give an instance, when Minutius, the Consul, with his army was besieged by the Aequi, terror filled Rome lest that army should be lost, so they decided to appoint a Dictator—their last resource in any hard situation. They chose Lucius Quintius Cincinnatus, who then was at his little farm, which he worked with his own hands. Titus Livius relates this affair in golden words: "It is worth listening to by those who contemn all human things in comparison with riches, and who find no place for great honor and for ability, unless wealth flows in abundance" (3. 26). Cincinnatus was plowing his little farm, which did not exceed four *jugera* in extent, when the Senatorial legate came from Rome to announce his election as Dic- tator and to show him the present peril of the Roman republic. Putting on his toga, he went to Rome, got together an army, and set out to free Minutius. Having defeated and pillaged the enemy and freed the Consul, he did not allow the besieged army to share in the plunder, speaking these words: "I do not allow you to share in the plunder of those whose plunder you were to be" (Livy 3. 29). And he deprived Minutius of the consulate and made him legate, saying to him: "Remain in this rank until you learn to be Consul" (*ibid*). As his Master of the Horse, he had appointed Lucius Tarquinius, who because of poverty served on foot. This makes plain, as I have said, that in Rome poverty was honored, and that a good and able man, such as Cincinnatus, thought four *jugera* of land enough to support him.

[*Poverty honors cities*]

Important citizens were also poor in the time of Marcus Regulus, because when he was in Africa with the army, he asked leave from the Senate to return to take care of his farm, which his laborers were spoiling. In this narrative two things are noteworthy. One is pover- ty; with it Roman citizens were contented; to get honor from war was enough for them, and all the gain they left to the public. If Regulus had expected to enrich himself from the war, any damage to his fields would have given him little anxiety. The other noteworthy thing is to observe the noble minds of those citizens. When they were put at the head of an army, the greatness of their spirits raised them above every prince; they took no account of kings or of repub- lics; they were confused or terrified by nothing whatever; yet on returning to private stations, they became economical, humble, careful of their little properties, obedient to the magistrates, respectful to their elders, so that it seems impossible that one and the same spirit could undergo such change. This poverty lasted, too, even to the times of Paulus Emilius, which were almost the last happy times of that republic;[2] until then, a citizen who with his triumph enriched Rome nevertheless remained poor himself. Poverty was still so much respected that Paulus, honoring a man who had conducted himself well in war, gave a son-in-law of his a silver cup, which was the first silver there was in his house. I could show with a long speech that poverty produces much better fruits than riches, and that one has honored the cities, the provinces, the religions, and the other has overthrown them, if the writings of other men had not many times made the subject splendid.

2. *About 186* B.C. *Rome after this date seemed to Machiavelli not admirable.*

CHAPTER 26. HOW A STATE FALLS BECAUSE OF WOMEN

[Roman instances]

In the city of Ardea contention arose between the patricians and the plebeians over a marriage, for when a rich woman was ready to marry, a plebeian and a noble both asked for her; and since she had no father, her guardians wished to join her to the plebeian, her mother to the noble. This caused so much strife that it came to arms; all the nobility armed themselves to help the noble, and all the plebeians to help the plebeian. So when the plebeians were overcome, they left Ardea and sent to the Volsci for aid; the nobles sent to Rome. The Volsci were first; reaching Ardea, they encamped. The Romans came next and shut up the Volsci between the city and themselves, compelling them, overcome with hunger, to surrender at discretion. Then the Romans, entering Ardea and killing all the leaders of the disturbance, settled the affairs of that city.[1]

[Aristotle's opinion exemplified]

In this passage several things are to be noted. First, it appears that women have caused much destruction, have done great harm to those who govern cities, and have occasioned many divisions in

1. *Livy* 4. 9.

them; for, as we see in this *History* of ours,² the outrage to Lucrece took their position from the Tarquins. That other outrage, to Virginia, deprived the Ten of their authority. So Aristotle gives among the first causes for the falls of tyrants some injury in a matter of women, either by whoring them, or raping them, or by breaking off marriages, as we have indicated in detail in the chapter where we discuss conspiracies.³ I say, then, that absolute princes and governors of republics are to take no small account of this matter, but ought to consider the evils that can result from such an event, and find a remedy so early that the remedy will not bring injury and disgrace to their state or their republic. The Ardeans may be a warning; by letting that competition grow among their citizens, they came to division among themselves; in attempting to reunite, they sent for outside help—which is one of the chief startingpoints for imminent slavery.

But let us pass to another notable thing, the method of uniting cities, of which we shall speak in the next chapter.

2. *Livy's* HISTORY *1. 58; 3. 44 ff.*
3. *Chap. 6 of the present book.*

CHAPTER 27. HOW TO ACT IN UNITING A DIVIDED CITY; THERE IS NO TRUTH IN THE OPINION THAT IN ORDER TO HOLD CITIES A RULER MUST KEEP THEM DIVIDED

[Fomenters of sedition must be killed]

From the example of the Roman Consuls who reconciled the people of Ardea we learn the method of consolidating a divided city. This is no other—nor can the disease be otherwise cured—than by killing the leaders of the disorders. For it is necessary to take one of three ways: either to kill them, as the Consuls did; or to remove them from the city; or to make them make peace, with the agreement that they will not attack one another. Of these three ways, this last is most harmful, least certain and most ineffective. For where much blood has run or there have been other similar injuries, a peace made by force cannot last, when every day enemies look each other in the face. For them to keep from injuring one another is difficult, since every day, because of their intercourse, new causes of complaint rise among them.

[*A foolish theory applied to Pistoia*]

Of this we cannot give a better instance than the city of Pistoia. That city was divided fifteen years ago, as she still is, into Panciatichi and Cancellieri; but then she was under arms and today she has laid them down. After many disputes, the parties came to bloodshed, to the ruin of houses, to the plundering of property and to every other sort of hostility. The Florentines, who tried to quiet them, always used the third method; and always greater disturbances and greater discords resulted. Hence, tired out, they came to the second method, that of removing the party leaders; some of them they put in prison, others they kept within limits in various places,¹ so that the agree-ment made could stand, and it has stood until this day. Yet without doubt the safest method would have been the first. But because such decisive actions have in them something great and noble, a weak republic cannot carry them out; they are so alien to her spirit that she scarcely brings herself to the second remedy.

[*Modern ignorance and weakness*]

So these are the errors I spoke of in the beginning, that the princes of our time make when they have to decide about great affairs.² As a consequence they should be glad to hear how rulers in antiquity who had to decide about such matters conducted themselves. But men's feebleness in our day, caused by their feeble education and their slight knowledge of affairs, makes them judge ancient punishments partly inhumane, partly impossible. They have modern notions, far remote from the truth, like that which the wise men of our city were in the habit of uttering, a while ago: Pistoia must be held with parties and Pisa with fortresses. So they do not perceive how profitless both of these policies are.

1. *That is, they were exiled to places which they were forbidden to leave.*
2. *See the Preface to the* DISCOURSES. *The word* princes *here includes all persons with governmental authority, though it also hints that Machiavelli when composing was not intent on republics alone.*

[*The evils of disunion in cities*]

I shall omit fortresses because I speak of them at length above,[3] and I shall discuss the harm that comes from keeping the cities you control divided. First, you cannot keep the friendship of both parties in such a divided city, whether you who govern be prince or republic. For Nature decrees that men take sides in any division, and that one thing shall please them better than another. Hence, to keep part of a subject city discontented causes you to lose her in the first war that comes up, because to protect a city that has enemies without and within is impossible. If a republic governs her, there is no finer way to make your own citizens corrupt and to cause divisions in your own city than to control a divided city,[4] for each party seeks to get favors and each makes friends for itself with various sorts of bribery. Thus such division produces two very great difficulties. First, you never make the parties your friends, through inability to govern them well, since the government is often changed, being now with one, now with the other party. Second, such concern with parties necessarily divides your own state. Blondus, speaking of the Florentines and Pistolese, assures us of it, saying: "While the Florentines schemed to reunite Pistoia, they divided themselves."[5] Hence we easily imagine the evil that results from such division.

[*Weak rulers try to divide and rule*]

In 1502, when we lost Arezzo and all the Val di Tevere and Valdichiana, taken from us by the Vitelli and by Duke Valentino, a Monseigneur de Lant was sent by the King of France to restore to the Florentines all the cities they had lost. Finding in every town men who, on visiting him, said they were of the party of the Marzocco,[6] Lant greatly blamed this division, saying that if in France one of the King's subjects should say he was of the King's party, he would be punished, because such a remark would mean nothing else

3. DISCOURSES 2. 24; THE PRINCE 20. *Lack of reference to* THE PRINCE *hints that Chapter 20 was not composed when this* DISCOURSE *was written. Since, however, the events just mentioned took place in Pistoia fifteen years before, they indicate composition of this* DISCOURSE *in 1516. Machiavelli was in Pistoia as Florentine commissioner in 1501. Relevant letters appear in his diplomatic correspondence.*

4. *An instance of Machiavelli's use of the impersonal you.*

5. HISTORY, *decade 2, bk. 9.*

6. *Marzocco: the lion symbolizing Florence. Various letters on Arezzo appear in Machiavelli's official correspondence.*

than that persons unfriendly to the King lived in that city. That King expects all his cities to be his friends, united and without parties. All these methods and ways diverse from the truth come from the weakness of rulers; when they cannot hold their states through force and personal ability, they turn to such schemes. These sometimes are of some use in quiet times, but when adversity and hard times come, they show that they are deceptive.

CHAPTER 28. ATTENTION SHOULD BE GIVEN TO CITIZENS' DEEDS, BECAUSE OFTEN UNDER A WORK OF MERCY THE BEGINNING OF TYRANNY IS HIDDEN

[*An improper attempt to gain popularity*]

When the city of Rome was afflicted with hunger, and the public stores were not enough to stop it, a certain Spurius Melius, very rich according to those times, got the idea of laying in privately a stock of grain and at his own expense feeding the plebeians. Because of this, such a crowd of people became his partisans that the Senate, considering the trouble that his liberality could produce, in order to suppress it before it got more power, set up a Dictator over him and had him put to death.[1] Here we observe that many times works that seem good, and that cannot reasonably be condemned, become culpable and are very dangerous to a state, if they are not at an early hour corrected.

[*Personal ambition should aid republics*]

To discuss popularity in more detail, I say that a republic without citizens of reputation cannot last and cannot in any way be governed well. On the other hand, reputation gained by citizens is the cause of tyranny in republics. If reputation is to be regulated, there must be such an arrangement that citizens will get repute from popularity that aids and does not injure the city and her liberty. Therefore we should examine the methods by which they get reputation. These in fact are two, public and private. The public methods are when a person advising well and acting better, for the common good, gains reputation. To this honor, the way should be opened to citizens, and

1. *Livy* 4. 13-16.

for their advice and their actions rewards should be set up, with which they will be honored and satisfied. When reputations obtained in such ways are genuine and simple, they never are perilous. But when they are gained in private ways—the other method mentioned above—they are very dangerous and altogether injurious. The private ways are the conferring of benefits on various private persons by lending them money, marrying off their daughters, protecting them from the magistrates, and doing them similar private favors. These make men partisans of their benefactors and give the man they follow courage to think he can corrupt the public and violate the laws.

[*Honors for public service*]

A well-ordered republic, therefore, opens the ways, as has been said, to those who seek support by public ways, and closes them to those who seek it by private ways, as Rome did. As a reward for men who worked well for the public, she established the triumphs and all the other honors she gave to her citizens. But for the overthrow of those who with various excuses sought by private ways to make themselves great, she established accusations; when these were not enough, and the people were blinded by a false appearance of good, she established the Dictator, who with his kingly arm made those return within bounds who had gone outside them, as she did in punishing Spurius Melius. One such case that goes unpunished is enough to ruin a republic, because when she has such an example, she is with difficulty brought back into the right way.

CHAPTER 29. THE SINS OF THE PEOPLE ARE CAUSED BY THEIR PRINCES

[*The ruler's example*]

By no means should princes complain about any sin committed by the people they have in charge, because such sins of necessity come either from a prince's negligence or from his being spotted with like faults. Anyone examining the people who in our days have been supposed prolific in robberies and like sins sees that those sins originated entirely with those who ruled them, who were of like nature. The Romagna, before Pope Alexander VI destroyed the lords who

ruled that district, exemplified the most wicked ways of living, because from the slightest cause the most serious slaughter and rapine
would result. This came from the wickedness of those princes, not
from the wicked nature of their subjects, as the rulers said it did. The
princes, because they were poor and wished to live as though they
were rich, were constrained to resort to a great amount of plundering
and to carry it on in various ways. One of their dishonorable methods was to make laws forbidding certain actions; then they were the
first who gave reason for non-observance of those laws, nor did they
ever punish those not observing them except when they saw that
many of their subjects had become liable to penalties. Then they
turned to punishment, not in zeal for the law that had been made,
but in their eagerness to collect the penalty. From this resulted many
evils, and above all, this, that the people were made poor and were
not restrained. And those who were made poor strove, at the cost of
those who were less strong than they, to enrich themselves. From
this resulted all those ills mentioned above, the cause of which was
the prince.

The truth of this is shown by Titus Livius. He narrates that the
Roman ambassadors carrying the gift from the Veientian spoil to
Apollo were captured by the pirates of Lipari in Sicily and taken to
that city. When Timasitheus their prince learned what gift this was,
where it was going and who sent it, he conducted himself, though
born at Lipari, like a Roman, showing the people how sacrilegious
it was to seize such a gift; so with the general consent he let the
ambassadors go with all their goods. The words of the historian are
these: "With religion Timasitheus filled the multitude, which is
always like the ruler" (5. 28). And Lorenzo de' Medici, in confirmation of this idea, says: "What the ruler does, afterward the many do,
because on the ruler all eyes are turned."[1]

1. *Lorenzo the Magnificent*, LA RAPPRESENTAZIONE DI SAN GIOVANNI E PAOLO,
OPERE *(Bari, 1914)* 2. 100.

CHAPTER 30. IF A CITIZEN IN A REPUB-
LIC WISHES TO MAKE SOME GOOD USE
OF HIS INFLUENCE, FIRST HE MUST
GET RID OF ENVY; AND HOW, WHEN
THE ENEMY ARE COMING, THE DEFENSE
OF A CITY SHOULD BE ORGANIZED

[*The ability of Camillus did not excite envy*]

The Roman Senate, learning that all Tuscany had made a new
levy in order to attack Rome, and that the Latins and the Hernicians,
who had in the past been friends of the Roman people, had allied
themselves with the Volscians, long-standing enemies of Rome,
judged that this war would be perilous. Since Camillus was Tribune with consular power, he decided that they could get on without
creating a Dictator if the other Tribunes, his colleagues, were willing
to concede him supreme power. This the other Tribunes did
willingly, for, as Titus Livius says: "They did not think that
anything they yielded to his authority was taken away from their own
authority" (6. 6). So Camillus, taking this obedience literally, commanded that three armies should be enrolled. Of the first, he himself
was to be head, in order to attack the Tuscans. Of the second, he
chose as leader Quintius Servilius, with orders to remain close to
Rome, to oppose the Latins and the Hernicians, if they should move.
Of the third, he put Lucius Quintius in command; this he enrolled
in order to keep the city guarded and the gates and the assembly
defended in any emergency. Besides this, he arranged that Horatius,
one of his colleagues, should provide the arms and the grain and the
other things demanded by times of war. He also put Cornelius his
colleague in charge of the Senate and the public council, in order
that he might be able to advise about the actions that every day
would have to be attended to. Thus, for the safety of their city, the
Tribunes in those times were ready to command and to obey.

[*Envy yields to goodness*]

This passage shows what can be done by a good and wise man,
and how much good he can bring about, and how much he can
benefit his country when, by means of his goodness and ability, he
has extinguished envy, for envy many times prevents men from

working well, since it does not permit them to have the authority necessary in things of importance. For extinguishing such envy there are two ways: either through some emergency difficult and hard to deal with, in which each man, seeing himself perishing, lays aside all ambition and gladly runs to obey one he thinks can by means of his ability rescue him. Thus it happened to Camillus, who—having given so many proofs that he was a superior man, and having been three times Dictator, and having always managed that office to the public advantage and not to his own profit—had given men reason not to fear his greatness; and because he was so great and had such a reputation, they did not think it disgraceful to be sub- ordinate to him (and for that reason Titus Livius wisely says those words quoted above: "They did not think" etc.).[1]

[A reformer must use violence against the envious]

In a second way envy is got rid of, when either through violence or in the natural course of events those die who have been your competitors while you have been coming to such reputation and to such greatness, for as long as they see that you have a higher reputa- tion than they, they never acquiesce and keep quiet. And when they are men used to living in a corrupt city, where education has not produced any goodness in them, they cannot because of any emer- gency reverse themselves; but to gain their desire and to satisfy their perversity of mind, they are content to see the ruin of their country. For subduing this envy there is no other method than the death of those affected with it. When Fortune is so propitious to an able man that the envious die naturally, without contention he becomes famous, since without obstacle and without offense he can show his ability. But when he does not have this good fortune, he has to plan in every way to get the envious out of his path, and before he does anything, he has to adopt methods for overcoming this difficulty. He who reads the Bible intelligently sees that if Moses was to put his laws and regulations into effect, he was forced to kill countless men who, moved by nothing else than envy, were opposed to his plans.

1. *This ends the first method for getting rid of envy. The second should begin* or, *to cor- respond with the* either, *above, but the construction is characteristically changed.*

[Savonarola and Soderini]

This necessity was well recognized by Frate Girolamo Savona-rola. It was also recognized by Piero Soderini, the Gonfalonier of Florence. The first (namely the Frate) could not overcome envy because he did not have power enough and because he was not well understood by his followers who did have power. Nevertheless this envy did not continue through his ignorance, for his sermons are full of accusations against "the wise men of the world," and of invectives against them; so he called those who envied him and opposed his measures. The second, Piero Soderini, believed that with time, with goodness, with his fortune, and by benefiting others, he could ex-tinguish envy, for he was so young and had so much support as the result of his policy that he believed he could overcome any number who opposed him through envy, without any dissension, violence, and tumult. He did not know that Time waits for no one, goodness is not enough, Fortune varies, and Malice receives no gift that placates her. Hence both of them fell; and their ruin was caused by not knowing how or not being able to overcome envy.

[Confusion prevents defense]

The other notable thing is the system Camillus arranged, both inside and outside Rome, for the safety of the city. And truly not without cause good historians, such as this one of ours, give certain events in detail and clearly, in order that those who come later may learn how in similar emergencies they can defend themselves. So this passage teaches that there is no more perilous or more useless defense than one made in confusion and without system. This is shown by the third army Camillus enrolled in order to leave it in Rome as a garrison for the city. For then as now many would judge that measure superfluous, since the Romans were ordinarily armed and warlike, and therefore would not need to be further enrolled; to have them take arms when necessity demanded would be enough. But Camillus—like the wise man he was—judged differently, be-cause he never permitted a multitude to take arms except with a fixed order and in a fixed way. Therefore, according to this instance, a man who is in charge of a city's garrison ought to avoid, as though it were a shoal, letting men take arms in confusion. He ought beforehand to enroll and select those he wishes to arm; and to indicate whom they are to obey, where they are to meet, where they are to go; and to command all those not enrolled to remain in their houses, to guard them. Those who keep such order in a city that is attacked can easily defend themselves; he who does otherwise will not imitate Camillus and will not defend her.

CHAPTER 31. STRONG REPUBLICS AND SUPERIOR MEN KEEP THE SAME SPIRIT AND THE SAME DIGNITY IN ALL FORTUNES[1]

Among the splendid things that our historian makes Camillus say and do, in order to show what an excellent man is, he puts in his mouth these words: "As for me, the dictatorship did not exalt my spirits nor exile depress them" (Livy 6. 7). From this we learn that great men are always in every sort of fortune just the same; if that varies, now raising them, now putting them down, they do not vary, but always keep their courage firm and so closely united with their way of life that we easily see that Fortune does not have power over a single one of them. Quite different is the conduct of weak men, because they grow vain and are made drunk with good fortune, assigning all their prosperity to an ability which they have not displayed at any time. As a result, they become unbearable and hateful to all around them. From this situation, then, issues some sudden change in their lot, and when they look that in the face, they fall at once into the other defect and become despicable and abject. Consequently princes of that sort, when in adversity, think more about running away than about defending themselves, since, having used good fortune badly, they are unprepared for any defense.

[*The Romans were superior to Fortune*]

This virtue and this vice, which I say exist in individuals, also exist in republics; instances are furnished by the Romans and the Venetians. As to the first, no bad luck ever made them despondent nor did any good fortune ever make them overweening, as plainly appears after their defeat at Cannae and after their victory over Antiochus. By reason of this defeat, though it was very serious through being their third, they did not become low-spirited but sent out armies; they did not consent to pay ransom for their prisoners,

1. *Livy* 37. 45.

contrary to their laws; they did not send to Hannibal or to Carthage to ask for peace. More than that, putting behind them all such cringing ways, they thought always about war, arming their old men and their slaves for lack of soldiers. When Hanno learned of this situation, as I said above, he showed the Carthaginian senate how little reckoning they must make of the defeat at Cannae.[2] So we see that difficult times did not frighten them or make them humble. On the other hand, prosperous times did not make them overweening. For example, when Antiochus sent ambassadors to Scipio to ask a truce, before they came to battle and before Antiochus was defeated, Scipio gave him as terms of peace that he should retire into Syria and leave the rest to the decision of the Roman people. Antiochus, after refusing this truce, coming to battle, and being defeated, again sent ambassadors to Scipio, with authority to accept all the terms laid down by the conqueror. Yet Scipio did not require other conditions than those he offered before he won, adding these words: "The Romans, if they are defeated, are not depressed in spirit, nor, if they conquer, do they grow arrogant."

[*The Venetians were subject to Fortune*]

The exact opposite of this was done by the Venetians. In good fortune, believing they had gained it with a courage and a wisdom they did not have,[3] they grew to such arrogance that they called the King of France the son of San Marco; they did not respect the Church; they did not find Italy large enough for them, and they imagined that they were going to form a monarchy like the Roman. Then, when good luck abandoned them and they received a semidefeat at Vailà from the King of France, not merely did they lose all their territory by rebellion, but they gave a good part of it to the Pope and to the King of Spain in abjectness and despondency of spirit. They so debased themselves that they sent ambassadors to the Emperor to make themselves his tributaries, and wrote letters to the Pope full of abjectness and humility to move him to compassion. To such discouragement they came in four days and after a semidefeat; because, after their army had fought, in retiring about half of it got into combat and was defeated. Yet afterward one of their supervisors

2. *Livy* 23. 12.

3. *A condensed expression. They thought they had gained their territory with courage and wisdom, but they did not possess those qualities.*

who escaped got to Verona with more than twenty-five thousand soldiers, foot and horse together. In such circumstances, if at Venice and in their institutions there had been any sort of courage and wisdom, they would easily have been able to reorganize and again to show their faces to Fortune, and to be ready to win or lose more gloriously or to have a more honorable peace. But the meanness of their spirits, caused by the nature of their institutions—not good in matters of war—made them lose at the same time their territory and their courage. So it will always happen to whoever conducts himself as they did. For such arrogance in good fortune and cowardice in bad fortune results from your method of acting and from the education with which you have been brought up. This, when it is empty and weak, renders you like itself. When your education has been quite different, it renders you too of another kind, and since it makes you know the world better, it makes you rejoice less at anything pleasant and feel less discouragement at anything harmful. Moreover what I say of one man alone can be said also of many living in the same republic, who attain to such excellence as its government permits.

[Good laws and good arms]

And though elsewhere[4] I have said that the foundation of all states is good military organization, and that where this does not exist there cannot be good laws or anything else good, I think repetition not superfluous, because at every point in reading Livy's *History* this certainty appears. An army evidently cannot be good if it is not trained, and it cannot be trained if it is not made up of your subjects. Because a country is not always at war and cannot be, she must therefore train her army in times of peace, and she cannot apply this training to others than subjects, on account of the expense.

[Camillus as an instance]

As we said above, Camillus had led his army against the Tuscans, and when his soldiers saw the size of the hostile army, they were all frightened, since they believed themselves too inferior to

4. Cf. THE PRINCE 12; DISCOURSES 1. 4, 21. Machiavelli uses the same formula (altra volta) in referring to a passage within the DISCOURSES (3. 34). It is not, then, necessary to suppose this a reference to THE PRINCE. If it is not, can this passage be earlier than THE PRINCE? See also ART OF WAR, preface; HISTORY OF FLORENCE 2. 5.

resist the enemy's attack. When his army's bad state of mind came to Camillus' ear, he showed himself in public and, going through the army talking to various soldiers, got that notion out of their heads; so at last, without making any different arrangement in the army, he said: "What anybody has learned or is in the habit of doing, let him do" (Livy 6. 7). He who considers well this method and the words he used in animating them to go against the enemy, will observe that he could not have said any such things or done them to an army that had not first been organized and trained both in peace and in war. A general cannot trust soldiers who have not learned to do anything, and he cannot believe they will do anything good. Even if they were commanded by a new Hannibal, they would ruin him, be-cause while a battle is going on a general cannot be everywhere; hence if he has not first arranged that in every place he has men who possess his spirit and even his methods and way of acting, he will inevitably be ruined.

[*Courage and preparation master Fortune*]

If, then, a city is armed and organized like Rome, and every day her citizens, both individually and in public, have occasion to test their ability and the power of Fortune, always in whatever weather they will have the same spirit and keep the same dignity. But when they are unarmed and rely merely on the rapid motions of Fortune and not on their own strength and wisdom, they will vary as she varies, and will always conduct themselves as the Venetians have done.

CHAPTER 32. METHODS FOR IMPEDING A TREATY

[*How to forestall reconciliation*]

Two colonies, Circeii and Velitrae, hoping to be defended by the Latins, rebelled against the Roman people. When the Latins were defeated and the colonists deprived of hope in them, many of their citizens advised that ambassadors be sent to Rome to ask con-sideration from the Senate.[1] This plan was upset by the authors of the rebellion, who feared that the entire penalty would come down on their own heads, for in order to get rid of all discussion of peace,

1. *Livy* 6. 21.

they stirred up the populace to take arms and raid Roman territory. Certainly when anybody wishes either a people or a prince entirely to give up any disposition to treaty, no means is surer or more lasting than to have them carry out some serious villainy against the one with whom you do not wish the treaty to be made, because always fear of that punishment which they think they deserve for the evil they have done, will keep such a treaty beyond consideration.

[Outrages not to be pardoned]

After the first war between the Carthaginians and the Romans, the soldiers in Sicily and Sardinia, whom the Carthaginians had employed for that war, when peace was made went into Africa. There, not being satisfied with their pay, they turned their arms against the Carthaginians. Selecting from among themselves two leaders, Matho and Spendius, they captured many Carthaginian cities and sacked many. The Carthaginians, in order to test first every other means than battle, sent to them as ambassador, Hasdrubal, a citizen who they thought would have some influence among them, since he had formerly been their general. When he arrived, Spendius and Matho, wishing to force all the soldiers never in the future to hope for peace with the Carthaginians, and thereby to force them into war, persuaded them that they had better kill him, along with all the other Carthaginian citizens who were their prisoners. Hence they not merely killed them but first tortured them with a thousand torments, adding to this wickedness an edict that all Carthaginians taken in the future would be slain in like manner. This decision and its execu‑ tion made that army cruel and stubborn against the Carthaginians.

CHAPTER 33. IN ORDER TO WIN A BATTLE, TO MAKE AN ARMY CONFIDENT BOTH IN ITSELF AND IN ITS GENERAL IS NECESSARY

[The competent general; religion]

An army that is to win a battle must be made so confident as to believe it will win in any case. It becomes confident when well armed and organized and when each man knows the others; such confidence and organization cannot appear except in soldiers who are born and live together. The general must be so esteemed that the men trust his prudence; and they always will trust it if they see him prepared, attentive, and courageous, maintaining well and reputably the dignity of his rank. And he always will maintain his dignity if he punishes offenses and does not make the soldiers labor without result, keeps his promises to them, presents them with an easy road to victory, and conceals or makes light of things that at a distance appear dangerous. These things, well carried out, give an army strong reasons for trusting him, and trusting, to conquer. The Roman practice was that their armies should gain this confidence from religion. For this reason, with auguries and auspices they chose Consuls, carried on the conscription, marched away with the army, and came to battle. So without doing some of these things, a good and wise general would never undertake any action, reckoning that he could lose easily if his soldiers did not first learn that the gods were on their side; and if any Consul or other general of theirs had fought contrary to the auspices, they would have punished him, as they punished Claudius Pulcher.

[*Religion in a republic*]

Though this matter appears in all the Roman histories, yet it is proved more surely by the words that Livy puts in the mouth of Appius Claudius. On complaining to the plebeians of the arrogance of the Tribunes of the People, and showing that they were allowing the auspices and other things pertaining to religion to become debased, he spoke as follows: "Those who wish may mock at religious ceremonies, saying: 'What does it matter whether chickens eat, whether they come out of their coop slowly, whether a bird chirps?' These are little things, but by not despising these little things, our fathers made this republic great" (Livy 6. 41). Indeed in these little things is that force for holding the soldiers united and confident which is the first cause of every victory.

[*Valor indispensable*]

Nevertheless to these things valor must be joined; otherwise they are useless. The Praenestians, having their army in the field against the Romans, encamped on the River Allia, where the Romans were defeated by the French. This they did to give confidence to their soldiers and to terrify the Romans because of the fortune of the place. And though this plan of theirs was commendable, for the reasons I

have presented above, nonetheless the outcome of the affair showed
that true valor does not fear every little accident. This the historian
says very well with words put in the mouth of the Dictator, who
spoke to his Master of the Horse as follows: "You see that they,
trusting to Fortune, have posted themselves on the Allia. But you,
trusting in arms and courage, are to attack their center" (Livy 6. 29).
For true valor, good organization, security derived from so many
victories, cannot be destroyed by things of little importance, nor does
an empty thing frighten them or something exceptional disturb them.
This was plainly shown at the time when the two Manlii were
Consuls against the Volsci: after they had rashly sent part of the
army to find plunder, it happened that at the same time both those
who had gone and those who had stayed behind were attacked; from
this danger not the prudence of the Consuls but the valor of the
soldiers themselves delivered them. On the incident Titus Livius
speaks these words: "The soldiers, even without a leader, by their
firm valor gained safety" (6. 30).

[Skilful use of mystery]

I do not intend to omit a method used by Fabius to make his
army confident when for the first time he led it into Tuscany,
reckoning such assurance the more necessary on account of his
having taken it into a new land, against new enemies: namely,
speaking to the soldiers before the combat, he said, after mentioning
many reasons through which they could hope for victory, that he
could in addition tell them certain things that were good, and from
which they would see that victory was certain, if it were not dangerous to make them public. This method, when it is wisely used,
deserves to be imitated.

CHAPTER 34. WHAT SORT OF REPUTATION OR REPORT OR OPINION MAKES THE PEOPLE SIDE WITH A CITIZEN; AND WHETHER THEY ASSIGN OFFICES WITH GREATER DISCRETION THAN A PRINCE

[Piety gains popularity]

We tell above how Titus Manlius, who later was called Torquatus, saved his father, Lucius Manlius, from a charge made against

him by Marcus Pomponius, Tribune of the People.[1] Though his method of rescue was somewhat violent and improper, nonetheless his piety toward his father was so pleasing to the people generally that not merely did they not blame him, but when they had to choose the Tribunes for the legions, they put Titus Manlius in the second place. Because of this success, I believe it well to consider the method used by the people in judging men in their assignment of offices, and to ask whether, from what we see, all that has been decided above is true, namely, that the people are better assigners than a prince.[2]

[*How to gain reputation in a republic*]

I declare, then, that the populace in its assignment follows what public report and reputation says of someone—when it does not, from his known actions, learn something different—or it follows its inference or opinion about him. These two things either are derived from the fathers of such men—because, since they have been great and powerful in the city, everyone believes that their sons must be like them, until through their deeds the people understand the con-trary—or the ways of the man we speak of causes them. The best ways such a man can follow are to associate with serious men of good habits, who are looked upon as prudent by everybody (and because there can be no better evidence about a man than his habitual associates, he who has virtuous associates deservedly gains a good name, for he must be in some way like them). Or assuredly[3] this general reputation can be gained through some extraordinary and noteworthy action, even though private, that has ended honorably. Of the three things that originate a good reputation, none furnishes a better reputation than this last. The first kind, from relatives and fathers, is so untrustworthy that men are cautious about it and in a short time it vanishes, if the worth of the man himself who is to be judged does not match it. The second, in which you are estimated from your habits, is better than the first, but is much inferior to the third, because so long as you yourself give no indications of ability, your reputation is founded on belief, very easily destroyed. But the third one, since its origin and basis are fact and your deeds, gives you

1. *Livy* 7. 5. *See* DISCOURSES 1. 11.

2. DISCOURSES 1. 58.

3. *The reader expects the alternative* And to; *but Machiavelli changes the construction to* Or assuredly.

as it originates such a great name that afterward you must actually do many things contradicting it before you can annul it. Men born in a republic should, then, follow this formula, and early in life strive to become prominent through some unusual action. Many Romans in their youth did this either by proposing a law for the common benefit, or by bringing a charge against some powerful citizen as a transgressor of the laws, or by doing something else noteworthy and strange which would make them talked about.

[*A prince should follow the examples of Manlius and Scipio*]

Not merely are such actions essential as a start in giving a man a reputation but they are also essential for preserving and increasing it. To do so, he must produce new wonders, as through his whole life Titus Manlius did, because after defending his father so valiantly and extraordinarily, and by that deed getting his first reputation, in a few years he fought with that Frenchman and, killing him, took from him the collar of gold that gave him the name of Torquatus. This was not enough, for later, by then middle-aged, he put his son to death for fighting without permission even though he overcame the enemy.[4] These three actions, then, gave Manlius a greater name and through all ages made him more famous than did any triumph or any victory, though he was distinguished for these as much as any Roman. The reason is that in his victories he had many like him; in these individual acts he had very few or none. Scipio the Elder did not gain so much glory from all his triumphs as from two early deeds: while still a youth, he protected his father on the Ticino; after the defeat of Cannae, with unsheathed sword he valiantly made many Roman youths swear that they would not abandon Italy, as they had already decided among themselves to do. These two actions were the beginning of his reputation and became steps to his triumphs in Spain and in Africa. His reputation was further increased when he sent back the daughter to her father and the wife to her husband in Spain.[5] Such a course of conduct is essential not only to citizens who hope to gain fame in order to secure positions in their republic, but is also essential for princes who are to keep up their reputations in their princedoms, because nothing makes them so much esteemed

4. *Livy* 7. 10; 8. 7.
5. *Livy* 21. 46; 22. 53; 26. 50.

as to display extraordinary ability in some rare action or saying, in keeping with the common good, that shows the lord as high-minded or liberal or just, and gets to be a sort of proverb among his subjects.[6]

[*The people judge merit better than do princes*]

But to return to the place where we began this *Discourse*, I say that the people, when they first give an office to a citizen, if they base themselves on those three causes mentioned above, do not have a poor basis. Afterward, when many examples of a man's good conduct make him better known, the people have a firmer basis, so that in such a case they hardly ever are deceived. I speak only of those positions that are given to men in the beginning, before they are understood through solid experience, or when they pass from one activity to another unlike it. In this, both as to false opinion and as to improper influence, the people always make fewer mistakes than princes do. Yet it can happen that the people will be deceived about a man's reputation, standing, and deeds, thinking them greater than they actually are. That, however will not happen to a prince, because he will be informed and warned by those who advise him. So in order that the people too will not lack such advisers, good organizers of republics ordain that when the highest offices of the city (where it would be dangerous to put inadequate men) are to be filled, if popular opinion seems directed toward an inadequate choice, every citizen has the right (and it is to be considered an honor) to announce in the public assembly the shortcomings of the candidate; then the people, not lacking knowledge of him, can decide better. That this was the custom at Rome is proved by the speech of Fabius Maximus, made to the people in the second Punic War, when in the election of Consuls the votes were moving toward the choice of Titus Ottacilius; Fabius, judging him incompetent to manage the consulate in those times, spoke against him, showing his incompetency; thus he deprived Titus of that office and turned the people's choice to one who better deserved it. In the choice of magistrates, then, the people judge men according to the indications they think most reliable; when they can be advised like princes, they err less than princes. Any citizen who wishes popular support should gain it early, with some noteworthy action, as did Titus Manlius.

6. *This paragraph seems like an early study for* THE PRINCE *21.*

CHAPTER 35. THE DANGERS ENCOUN-
TERED IN ACTING AS LEADER IN ADVISING
SOMETHING; THE MORE UNUSUAL IT
IS, THE GREATER THE DANGERS

[Dangers to a prince's adviser]

The dangers of acting as leader in something new that is important
to many, and the difficulty of managing and completing such a
thing, and of keeping it going when completed, are matters too time
consuming and too lofty for discussion. Hence, saving them for a
more fitting place, I shall speak only of those dangers which citizens,
or a prince's advisers, undergo in taking the lead in a serious and
important decision, when all the advice on the matter will be charged
to them. Such advising is dangerous because, since men judge
things by their results, all the evil produced by an undertaking is
charged to the man who advised it; if good results, he is indeed commended; but by a great deal the reward does not weigh as much
as the harm.

[Turkish and Roman instances]

The present Sultan Selim, called the Grand Turk, after preparing (as some say who come from his lands) for a campaign against
Syria and Egypt, was encouraged by one of his bashaws whom he
kept on the frontiers of Persia to go against the Sophy. Influenced
by this advice, he went on that campaign with a numerous army;
and coming to a very level region, where there are many deserts and
few streams, and meeting the difficulties that long ago caused the
ruin of many Roman armies, he was so afflicted by them that, though
victor in the war, he lost there a large number of his soldiers. Hence,
enraged against the author of the advice, he killed him. We also
read that many citizens have given encouragement to some undertaking and, because it turned out badly, have been sent into exile.
Certain Roman citizens made themselves leaders in the choice in
Rome of a plebeian Consul. It happened that the first who went out
with the armies was defeated; from this those advisers would have
suffered harm, if there had not been great strength in the party in
whose behalf that decision was made.[1]

1. Livy 6. 42; 7. 1.

[*Give advice modestly*]

It is, then, something very certain that those who advise a republic and those who advise a prince are put in the following straits: if they do not, without reservation, advise things that they believe useful, either for the city or for the prince, they fail in their duty; if they do advise them, they put themselves in danger of life and position, since all men blindly judge good and bad advice by its outcome. After considering how they can avoid both this reproach and this danger, I see no other way than for an adviser to be moderate and not to seize upon any of the plans brought forward as his own undertaking, and to speak his opinion without passion, and without passion modestly to defend it, so that the city or the prince who follows it does so voluntarily, and does not seem to enter upon it as pushed by your urgency. When you act thus, it is not reasonable that a prince or a people should wish you ill because of your advice, since they have adopted it without opposing the wishes of many other advisers. The danger arises whenever many oppose you, for if your plan results badly, they unite to ruin you. And if by such moderation you miss the glory gained by being alone against many in urging something that results happily, your course still has two advantages. One is that it lacks danger. The other is that if you advise a thing modestly, and through opposition your advice is not taken, yet from other people's advice some calamity results, you obtain the utmost glory. And though you cannot enjoy glory resulting from the distress either of your city or your prince, nevertheless it has some value for you.

[*The duty of giving advice*]

Other advice I believe I cannot give on this matter, because to advise men to be silent and not to speak their opinions would be to make them useless to their republic or their prince and would not shield themselves from danger, since in a short time they would become suspected. And it could even happen to them as to the friends of Perseus, King of the Macedonians: after he was defeated by Paulus Aemilius and was fleeing with a few friends, it chanced as they were discussing past events that one of them told Perseus of many errors that had caused his ruin. Turning to him, Perseus said: "Traitor, so you have put off telling me until now when I have no further remedy!" And with these words, he killed him with his own hands. And so that man suffered punishment for having kept silent when he should have spoken and for having spoken when he should have kept silent; he did not escape the danger by not giving the ad/vice. So I believe it is best to keep and observe the limits given above.

CHAPTER 36. WHY THE FRENCH HAVE BEEN AND STILL ARE CONSIDERED TO BE MORE THAN MEN WHEN BATTLES BEGIN, AND LATER TO BE LESS THAN WOMEN[1]

The savage valor of that Frenchman at the River Anio, who challenged any Roman to fight with him, and then the combat fought between him and Titus Manlius,[2] reminds me of what Titus Livius says many times, namely, that the French at the beginning of a combat are more than men, and as the fighting goes on and on they become less than women. On considering the reason for this, many conclude that such is the nature of the French, which I believe is true. But it is not therefore true that this nature of theirs, which makes them valorous at the beginning, cannot be so controlled by art as to keep them fiery to the end.

[Armies are of three kinds. (1) Ardor with discipline]

To prove this, I say armies are of three kinds. The first possesses ardor with discipline, because from discipline come ardor and effi/ciency. Such was the Roman army, for all their histories show that in their army there was good discipline, produced by long/continued military training. In any well disciplined army nobody carries on any activity except according to rule. We see that in the Roman army, which, since it conquered the world, should be a model for all other armies, the soldiers did not eat, they did not sleep, they did not trade,[3] they did not perform any action either military or domestic without the Consul's order. Armies that do otherwise are not real armies, and if they accomplish some things, they do it by ardor and impetuosity, but not by efficiency. Yet when efficiency is disciplined,

1. Livy 10. 28.
2. Livy 7. 10.
3. My copy of the Giunta edition of 1531 reads mercantava. The word probably refers to buying food.

it uses its ardor in the right way and at the right time, and no emergency daunts it or takes away its courage, because good discipline fed with the expectation of victory preserves courage and ardor. And this expectation never fails as long as discipline is unshaken.

[(2) Ardor without discipline]

The opposite happens in armies that possess ardor but not discipline, such as those of the French. In combat they usually failed if they did not win by their first charge. After that, because the ardor in which they trusted was not supported by disciplined efficiency, so that they had nothing but ardor on which to rely, they failed when their ardor grew cold. The Romans on the contrary, fearing dangers less because of their good discipline, and having no doubt of victory, fought firmly and stubbornly with the same courage and the same efficiency in the end as in the beginning. More than that, stimulated by arms, they grew all the time more fiery.

[(3) Armies without either ardor or discipline]

The third type of army possesses neither natural ardor nor acquired discipline, such as are the Italian armies of our times, which are wholly useless; if they do not encounter an army that through some accident runs away, they never win. Without bringing up other instances, we can see every day that they give evidence of having no efficiency. So because by means of the testimony of Titus Livius, everybody may learn what good military discipline is and what bad discipline is, I bring up Papinius Cursor, for when he was about to punish Fabius, Master of the Horse, he said: "Nobody would have any respect for men or for gods; the commands of the generals, the auspices would not be attended to; without leave of absence the scattered soldiers would wander about in friendly regions and in hostile ones; forgetful of their oath, on their own authority, when they pleased they would give themselves their discharge; they would leave the standards deserted; they would not come together on command nor could they be found, day or night; in a bad or in a good place, with or without the orders of the general, they would fight; and they would pay no attention to signals or orders; like a gang of thieves, they would form a blind and chance-directed army, rather than one devoted and oath-bound" (Livy 8. 34). So this passage easily lets us see, then, whether the soldiery of our days is blind and chance-directed or oath-bound and devoted, and how much it lacks any resemblance to what can be called an army, and how far it is from being fiery and disciplined like the Roman, or fiery only, like the French.

CHAPTER 37. IF LITTLE COMBATS BEFORE BATTLE ARE NECESSARY; AND HOW TO FIND OUT ABOUT A NEW ENEMY AND YET AVOID THESE LITTLE COMBATS

[Bad is always mingled with good; aid from Fortune]

As we have said elsewhere, in the actions of men—besides the other difficulties in trying to bring something to perfection—in connection with good there seems always to be something bad, which so easily grows up along with the good that to avoid bad while striving for good seems impossible. This is apparent in everything men do. Therefore to achieve something good is difficult unless Fortune, aiding you, with her power overcomes this usual and natural difficulty. I have been reminded of this by the combat of Manlius and the Frenchman, of which Titus Livius says: "This combat had great influence on the outcome of the entire war, because the Gallic army, in terror, retired into the country of Tibur and then into Campania" (7. 11). Hence I believe, on one side, that a good general should avoid, completely, doing even any slight thing that can have a bad effect on his army. Because to begin a fight in which all your forces are not used but all your fortune is risked is altogether rash, as I said above when I condemned the guarding of passes.[1]

[Slight combats as tests]

On the other hand, I believe that wise generals, when about to encounter a new enemy of high reputation, have their soldiers test such an enemy with slight combats before they come to battle in order that by understanding and dealing with him they may get rid of the fear excited by his fame and reputation. A general's ability in this is very important, because necessity almost forces you on, since you seem to go to obvious defeat unless first, with small tests, you

1. DISCOURSES 1. 23.

have succeeded in removing from your soldiers' minds all fear caused
by the enemy's reputation.

Valerius Corvinus was sent by the Romans with their armies
against the Samnites, new enemies, for in the past never had either
side tested the other's arms. On this Titus Livius writes that Valerius
had the Romans fight some slight actions with the Samnites, "lest a
new war and a new enemy frighten them" (7. 32). Nevertheless
there is very great danger, if your soldiers are beaten in such combats,
that their fear and discouragement will increase, and the results will
be contrary to your intention, that is, you will frighten them, though
you planned to assure them. Indeed this is one of those places in
which good and bad are so close together that you easily get one
when you think you are getting the other.

[It is injurious to lose what one has planned to defend]

On this I say that a good general watches very diligently that
nothing occurs through which some accident can take away the
courage of his army. That which can take away its courage is to lose
early; therefore the good general guards himself from little combats
or allows them only with very great advantage and with sure hope of
victory. You ought not to attempt to hold passes where you cannot
assemble your entire army. You ought not to garrison cities unless
they are such that if you lose them their loss will necessarily result in
your ruin. And those you do garrison should be so managed, both
as to their garrisons and as to your army, that if there is an attempt to
capture them, you will be able to make use of all your forces. The
others you ought to leave undefended, because whenever you lose a
thing you have abandoned, if your army is still afoot, you do not lose
your reputation in the war or your hope of winning it. But when
you lose a thing you have planned to defend and that everybody
expects you to defend, then come the harm and the loss, and, like the
French, you have almost lost the war through something of slight
importance. Philip of Macedon, father of Perseus, a soldierly man
and of great importance in his times, when attacked by the Romans
judged that many of his towns could not be garrisoned; hence he
abandoned them and laid them waste.[2] This was the act of a man
who, being prudent, judged it more damaging to lose his reputation
through inability to defend what he set out to defend than, by leaving

2. Livy 32. 13.

it in the power of the enemy, to lose it as something abandoned. The Romans, when after the defeat of Cannae their affairs were in a bad state, refused assistance to many of their dependents and subjects, allowing them to defend themselves as best they could.[3] Such decisions are much better than to undertake their defense and then not to defend them, because by failure a state loses friends and forces, by refusal it loses friends only.

[Testing combats to be fought at an advantage]

But returning to the little combats, I say that if a general is actually forced by the newness of the enemy to engage in some combats, he ought to engage in them with such great advantage that he will not be in any danger of losing them; or indeed he may do as Marius did (which is the better plan) when he was moving against the Cimbri, very fierce peoples, who came to plunder Italy. Since their coming caused great consternation through their fierceness and their numbers and through their having already beaten a Roman army, Marius judged that before he came to battle he needed to do something to make his army lay aside the terror roused by their fear of the enemy. Hence like a very prudent general, more than once he put his army in a place where the Cimbri with their army were going to pass. Thus he enabled his soldiers, within the fortifications of their camp, to observe that enemy and accustom their eyes to the sight of them, so that seeing a disorderly multitude, laden with baggage, with ineffective weapons and part of them without armor, they would reassure themselves and become eager for combat. That plan, as Marius adopted it wisely, so others should imitate it diligently, in order not to run into the dangers I speak of above and not to be like the French, "who, frightened by a thing of little importance, moved to the region of Tibur and into Campania."

And because we have brought up Valerius Corvinus in this *Discourse*, I wish through his words to show in the following chapter what a general ought to be.

3. Livy 23. 5.

CHAPTER 38. THE QUALITIES OF A GENERAL WHOM HIS ARMY CAN TRUST

[How a general should act]

As we said above, Valerius Corvinus was serving with his army against the Samnites, new enemies of the Roman people. So, in order to reassure his soldiers and make them understand the enemy, he had his men start some slight combats. And since this was not enough for him, he addressed them before the battle; in his speech he showed with complete effectiveness how low an estimate they ought to put on such enemies, urging in support the soldiers' ability and his own. We can learn from the words Livy gives him what a general must be if his army is to trust him. He spoke thus: "Then also you should consider under whose leadership and control the battle is to be entered, whether you are to listen to him merely as a splendid spellbinder, ardent only in words, ignorant of military affairs, or whether he knows how to handle weapons, to march ahead of the standards, and to show activity in the thickest press of battle. My deeds, not my words, soldiers, I wish you to follow; to ask from me not merely instruction but even example, for I with this right hand have won three consulates and the greatest glory" (Livy 7. 32). These words, well considered, teach everybody how he should act if he is to hold the rank of general. And he who is of another sort will in time find that such rank, if through Fortune or ambition he reaches it, will take reputation away but will not give it, because offices do not renown men; men renown offices.

[The training of a new army]

At the beginning of this *Discourse* I should also indicate that if great generals have employed unusual means to stiffen the courage of a veteran army when it was to confront a new foe, ingenuity is the more necessary to the commander of a new army that has never looked an enemy in the face. Because if an unwonted enemy rouses terror in an old army, so much the more must every enemy rouse it in a new army. Yet many times good generals have prudently over-come this difficulty, as did Gracchus the Roman and Epaminondas the Theban, whom we have mentioned in other places; with new armies they overthrew armies of veterans thoroughly trained. The method of these generals was for a few months to train their men in mock battles and accustom them to obedience and discipline. After that, with the utmost confidence they employed them in actual com- bat. No military man, then, need despair of making good armies if he does not lack men. Indeed any prince who abounds in men and lacks soldiers should complain not of the worthlessness of his men but only of his own sloth and imprudence.

CHAPTER 39. A GENERAL SHOULD UNDER- STAND TOPOGRAPHY

[*Hunting like war*]

Among the things necessary to a commander of armies is the understanding of positions and countries, because without this knowl- edge both universal and particular, a commander cannot properly carry out anything. Indeed though all branches of knowledge re- quire experience if they are to be perfectly understood, this one demands experience to the utmost. This experience or this under- standing of particulars is gained more by means of continual hunting than through any other activity. Hence the ancient writers say that the heroes who ruled the world in their time were brought up in the forests and in hunting, because hunting teaches us, in addition to this knowledge, countless things necessary in war. So Xenophon in his *Life of Cyrus* shows that when Cyrus was about to attack the King of Armenia, in explaining that campaign he reminded his followers that this was just another of those hunts in which they had many times been with him. He reminded the men he sent into ambush on the mountains that they were like those who went to stretch nets on the summits, and the men he sent to ride through the plain that they were like those who went to drive the animal from its lair in order that when pursued it would run into the nets.

[*The hunter learns topography*]

This I say to show that hunting expeditions, as Xenophon makes plain, are images of war; therefore to men of rank such activity is honorable and necessary. Nor can this knowledge of different re- gions be gained in any convenient way except through hunting, because hunting makes him who engages in it know in detail the lay of the land where he hunts. And as soon as a man has made himself thoroughly familiar with one district only, he then easily learns all new regions, because every region and every part of one have some similarity with others, in such a way that from the knowledge of one it is easy to pass to the knowledge of another. But only with difficulty or rather never, except after a long time, can a man not thoroughly experienced in one district understand another.

[A general's eye for topography]

He who has such experience knows at a glance how that plain lies, how that mountain rises, how far that valley extends, and all such things of which he has in the past gained solid understanding. That this is true Titus Livius shows us by the example of Publius Decius, when he was Tribune of the Soldiers in the army that Cornelius the Consul led against the Samnites. When the Consul had got into a valley where the army of the Romans could be shut in by the Samnites and appeared to be in great danger, Publius said to him: "Do you see, Aulus Cornelius, that summit above the enemy? It is the castle of our hope and safety, if (since the blind Samnites have neglected it) without delay we take it" (7. 34). Before giving these words by Decius, Titus Livius says: "Publius Decius, Tribune of the Soldiers, saw one hill rising very abruptly, hanging over the camp of the enemy, difficult of access to a column with baggage, not at all hard for light-armed men" (7. 34). So after the Consul had sent Publius to its summit with three thousand soldiers, and he had saved the Roman army and was planning, when night came, to leave and save also himself and his soldiers, Titus Livius has him say: "Go with me, while there is some light left, to find out where the enemy has put guards, so our exit will be clear.' Clad in a soldier's cloak so that the enemy would not notice that the leader was moving about, he examined everything" (7. 34). He who considers this entire passage, then, sees that for a general to know the nature of various regions is very useful and necessary. If Decius had not known and understood them, he could not have judged what advan-tages the occupation of that hill would bring to the Roman army, nor could he have made certain, from a distance, whether that hill was accessible or not, and when he had got on it and wished to leave it to return to the Consul, with the enemy around him, he could not from a distance have distinguished the roads by which he could get away and the places guarded by the enemy. Hence we necessarily conclude that Decius was perfect in such knowledge. This enabled him by occupying that hill to save the Roman army. So he knew how, when he was attacked, to find the way for saving himself and those who were with him.

CHAPTER 40. TO USE FRAUD IN CARRYING ON WAR DESERVES FAME

Although to use fraud in all one's actions is detestable, neverthe-less in carrying on war it is praiseworthy and brings fame; he who conquers the enemy by fraud is praised as much as he who conquers them by force. This appears from the judgment given on it by those who write the lives of great men, for they praise Hannibal and the others who have been extraordinary in actions of that sort. Since everybody has read plenty of examples, I shall not give any. I shall say only that I do not believe fraud deserves fame when it makes you break promises you have given and pacts you have made, because such fraud, though it sometimes wins for you position and kingly power, as was explained above,[1] will never win you glory. I am speaking of fraud used against an enemy who does not trust you, such as appears especially in the conduct of war. Of this kind was Hannibal's when at the Lake of Perugia he pretended flight in order to surround the Consul and the Roman army, and when, in order to get out of Fabius Maximus' power, he set on fire the horns of his cattle.[2]

Similar to these frauds was that used by Pontius, general of the Samnites, to shut up the Roman army in the Caudine Forks. Having concealed his army in the mountains, he sent some of his soldiers in shepherd's clothing with a large herd to the plain.[3] These, being taken by the Romans and asked where the Samnite army was, agreed, according to Pontius' instructions, in saying that it was at the siege of Nocera. Believing this, the Consuls shut themselves up among the Caudine precipices, and after they had gone in, they were soon besieged there by the Samnites. This victory, gained by

1. DISCOURSES 2. 13. Cf. THE PRINCE 8. Is THE PRINCE later than this DIS-COURSE?
2. Livy 22. 4, 17.
3. Livy 9. 2.

fraud, would have been very glorious for Pontius if he had heeded his father's counsel that the Romans should be either generously preserved or all killed, but the middle course should not be taken, for it "neither provides friends nor takes away enemies" (Livy 9. 3). This course is always ruinous in matters of state, as I explain above.[4]

4. DISCOURSES 2. 23.

CHAPTER 41. ONE'S COUNTRY SHOULD BE DEFENDED WHETHER WITH DISGRACE OR WITH GLORY; SHE IS PROPERLY DEFENDED IN ANY WAY WHATSOEVER

As I said above, the Consul and the Roman army were besieged by the Samnites. When the latter proposed to the Romans disgraceful conditions (namely, to send them under the yoke and let them go back to Rome unarmed), the Consuls were as though dazed, and all the army was in desperation. Then Lucius Lentulus, the Roman legate, said that he believed that no expedient whatever for saving their country was to be rejected; since the life of Rome consisted in the life of that army, he thought it should be saved at all events. One's country is properly defended in whatever way she is defended, whether with disgrace or with glory. If that army were saved, Rome would have time to cancel the disgrace; if it were not saved, even if it should die gloriously, Rome and her liberty were lost.[1] So his advice was followed.

This idea deserves to be noted and acted upon by any citizen who has occasion to advise his country, because when it is absolutely a question of the safety of one's country, there must be no consideration of just or unjust, of merciful or cruel, of praiseworthy or disgraceful; instead, setting aside every scruple, one must follow to the utmost any plan that will save her life and keep her liberty.

This theory determines the words and actions of the French when they defend the majesty of their king and the power of their kingdom, for they hear no speech more impatiently than one which says: "Such a decision is shameful for the king." They say that their king cannot be disgraced by any policy of his, whether in good or in adverse fortune, because if he loses, if he wins, they say it is entirely a kings' affair.

1. *Livy 9. 4.*

CHAPTER 42. PROMISES MADE UNDER COM-PULSION SHOULD NOT BE KEPT

After the Consuls, with their disarmed soldiery and with the disgrace they had received, returned to Rome, the first who said in the Senate that the peace made at Caudium ought not to be kept was the Consul Spurius Postumius who said that the Roman people were not obligated, but that nevertheless he himself and the others who had made the peace were obligated; and therefore the people, if it wished to be free from every obligation, must give into the hands of the Samnites as prisoners himself and all the others who made the agreement. With such firmness he stuck to this belief that the Senate accepted it, and sending him and the others as prisoners to Samnium, declared to the Samnites that the treaty was not valid. In this instance Fortune was so favorable to Postumius that the Samnites did not hold him; when he had returned to Rome, Postumius was more renowned among the Romans after losing than Pontius was among the Samnites for winning.[1]

Here two things are to be noted. One is that fame can be gained in any action whatever. In victory it normally is gained; in defeat it can be gained either by showing that such loss has not come about through your fault or by doing immediately some prudent and courageous action that cancels it. The other is that it is not disgraceful not to keep promises that you are forced to make. Forced promises in public matters, when the force is removed, will always be broken, without disgrace for him who breaks them. Of this we read examples in all the histories, and every day in the present times we see them.

[When princes do not keep promises]

And not merely are forced promises not kept among princes when the force is removed, but also all other promises are not kept when their causes are removed. Whether this is praiseworthy conduct or not, and if such methods should be used by a prince or not, we debate at length in our tractate *On the Prince*;[2] therefore at present we shall say nothing on it.

1. Livy 9. 8–12.
2. THE PRINCE 18. *Machiavelli here uses the Latin title* DE PRINCIPE; *for a variant see 2.1, above.*

CHAPTER 43. THAT MEN BORN IN ANY REGION SHOW IN ALL TIMES ALMOST THE SAME NATURES

[*The world the same*]

Prudent men are in the habit of saying—and not by chance or without basis—that he who wishes to see what is to come should observe what has already happened, because all the affairs of the world, in every age, have their individual counterparts in ancient times.[1] The reason for this is that since they are carried on by men, who have and always have had the same passions, of necessity the same results appear. It is true that human activity is at one time more efficacious in this region than in that, and more in that than in this, according to the nature of the training from which the people acquire their manner of life. Future things are also easily known from past ones if a nation has for a long time kept the same habits, being either continuously avaricious or continuously unreliable, or having some other similar vice or virtue.

[*The qualities of the French and the Germans*]

He who reads of early events in our city of Florence and considers as well those of recent times will find the German and the French people full of avarice, pride, cruelty and treachery, because all four of these things at different times have greatly injured our city. As to treachery, everybody knows how many times Florence gave money to King Charles VIII, and he promised to hand over to her the fortresses of Pisa, yet he never did hand them over. In this affair that King showed his treachery and his great avarice. But let us pass over these recent things. Everybody knows what happened in the war the Florentine people fought against the Visconti, dukes of Milan. When the Florentines were deprived of other possibilities, they planned to bring the Emperor into Italy, so that with his influence and his forces he would attack Lombardy. The Emperor promised to come with many soldiers and to carry on war against the Visconti and to protect Florence from their power, if the Florentines would give him a hundred thousand ducats when he started and a hundred thousand more when he was in Italy. To these conditions

1. *Cf. the preface to* CLIZIA.

the Florentines agreed. Yet though they paid him the first sum and then the second, when he had reached Verona he turned back without doing anything, pretending that they had impeded him by not carrying out their agreements with him. Hence, if Florence had not been forced by necessity or conquered by passion, and had read or learned the ancient habits of the barbarians, she would not have been deceived by them at this and many other times, for they have always been of one sort and have under all conditions and with everybody shown the same habits.

[The qualities of the ancient French]

So they did in ancient times to the Tuscans. These, oppressed by the Romans and many times put to flight and defeated by them, seeing that with their own forces they could not sustain the Roman attack, agreed to give the French who lived in Italy on this side of the Alps a sum of money, on their promise to unite their armies with the Tuscan armies and march against the Romans. What resulted was that the French, after getting the money, would then not take arms, saying that they accepted it with the condition not that they would fight the Tuscans' enemies but that they would abstain from plundering their territory. Thus the Tuscans, through the avarice and treachery of the French, were deprived at once of their money and of the aid they hoped for.[2]

Thus it appears from this instance of the ancient Tuscans and from that of the Florentines that the French have always used the same methods. From this it easily can be inferred how much princes can trust them.

2. Livy 10. 10.

CHAPTER 44. BY VIOLENCE AND AUDACITY WE MANY TIMES GAIN WHAT WITH ORDINARY METHODS WE NEVER WOULD GAIN

[Do not allow time for consideration]

When the Samnites were attacked by the Roman army and were not strong enough to keep their army in the field facing the Romans, they determined to leave all their cities in Samnium guarded and to move their entire army into Tuscany, which was at truce with the Romans, to see if through such a movement they could by the presence of their army induce the Tuscans to take up arms again, though they had refused this to the Samnite ambassadors. In the speech the Samnites made to the Tuscans, especially in showing for what reasons they had taken up arms, they used a striking expression, namely that "they had rebelled because peace is harder for slaves than war is for the free" (Livy 10. 16). Thus, partly with persuasions, partly through the presence of their army, they induced the Tuscans to take up arms again. From this I infer that when a wise prince hopes to obtain something from another, he does not, if the opportunity allows, give the other prince time for consideration, but manages to make him see the necessity for quick decision; that is, the other prince sees that refusing or putting off will cause sudden and dangerous anger.

[*Pope Julius' impetuosity*]

This method was well used in our times by Pope Julius against the French, and by Monsieur de Foix, general for the King of France, against the Marquis of Mantua. Pope Julius, planning to drive the Bentivogli from Bologna, judged that for his purpose he needed French forces and the Venetians must remain neutral. Having made trial of both and got uncertain and shifty replies, he determined, by giving them no time, to make them come to his view. So leaving Rome with all the soldiers he could gather, he went toward Bologna, and sent to the Venetians to tell them to remain neutral and to the King of France to send him forces. Hence both of them, limited by lack of time and seeing that they would cause the Pope evident anger if they delayed or refused, yielded to his wishes. The King sent aid and the Venetians remained neutral.

[*De Foix's promptness*]

Monsieur de Foix, when in Bologna with his army, hearing of the rebellion at Brescia, decided to recapture the place. He had two roads, one through the King's territory, long and slow; the other, short, through Mantuan territory. And not merely did he have to pass through the territory of that marquis, but of necessity he would go into certain narrow places between swamps and lakes, of which that region is full, which with fortresses and other means were locked and guarded against him. Hence, deciding to go by the shorter road, de Foix, in order to overcome every difficulty and not to give the Marquis time for thought, at once moved his army by that road and requested the Marquis to send him the keys of the passage. The Marquis, overcome by this rapid decision, sent him the keys; yet he never would have sent them if Foix had conducted himself more timidly, since the Marquis was in league with the Pope and the Venetians, and one of his sons was in the Pope's power—things that gave him many honorable excuses for refusal. But when assailed by that rapid determination, he yielded, for the reasons mentioned above. So the Tuscans yielded to the Samnites, on account of the presence of the army, taking up those arms they had at other times refused to employ.

CHAPTER 45. WHETHER IN BATTLES THE BETTER PLAN IS TO RECEIVE THE ENEMY'S ATTACK AND, HAVING RECEIV- ED IT, TO CHARGE HIM, OR AT THE BE- GINNING TO ATTACK HIM WITH FURY

Decius and Fabius, the Roman Consuls, with two armies were confronting the armies of the Samnites and the Tuscans; since they came to combat and to battle at the same time, we can learn from such an action which of the two different ways of proceeding used by the two Consuls is better.[1] Decius with great vehemence attacked the enemy with all his power. Fabius merely resisted them, judging the delayed attack more useful and reserving his vehemence to the last, when the enemy had lost their first ardor for fighting and, as we say, their wind. From the outcome of the affair, we see that Fabius was much more successful with his plan than was Decius. The latter was disordered in the first assaults in such a way that, seeing his division in flight rather than otherwise, in order to gain in death the glory he had not attained by victory, in imitation of his father he sacrificed himself for the Roman legions. Learning this, Fabius— that he might not gain less honor while living than his colleague had gained by dying—pushed forward all the forces he had reserved for such a necessity, and thereby won a most complete victory. From

1. Livy 10. 28, 29.

this we see that Fabius' way of proceeding is safer and more to be imitated.

CHAPTER 46. WHY AT ANY ONE TIME THE HABITS OF A FAMILY IN A CITY ARE UNIFORM

It seems that not merely one city has certain methods and customs different from those of another, and produces men who are either more vigorous or more effeminate, but that in the same city such differences exist between one family and another. This is true in all cities, and in the city of Rome we read of many instances: the Manlii were hard and stubborn, the Publicoli were kind and loved the people, the Appii were ambitious and hostile to the plebeians; and similarly many other families had their qualities distinct from the others. These differences cannot come solely from their blood, because that will vary with diverse marriages; it must come from the different training in one family and in another. It is very important that a boy of tender years hears praise or blame of a certain thing, because it will of necessity make an impression according to which he will govern his conduct in all periods of his life. If this were not so, it would have been impossible for all the Appii to have the same ambition and to be disturbed by the same passions, as Titus Livius notes of many of them.[1] The last instance is that when one of them was Censor, and at the end of eighteen months his colleague, as the law directed, laid the magistracy down, Appius would not consent to lay it down, saying he could hold it five years, according to the law first enacted on the Censors. Though over this affair many assemblies were held, and many disturbances raised, nonetheless there never was such a solution that he consented to lay it down, though he was opposing the will of the people and of the greater part of the Senate. Anybody who reads the speech he made against Publius Sempronius, Tribune of the People, will observe all the Appian haughtiness, and all the goodness and kindness practiced by countless citizens in order to obey the laws and conform to the authority of their country.

1. *Livy 2. 21, 23, 56, 58; 3. 32–58; 5. 2; 9. 33, 34.*

CHAPTER 47. A GOOD CITIZEN FOR LOVE OF HIS NATIVE CITY WILL FORGET PRIVATE INJURIES

Marcus the Consul was with the army opposed to the Samnites; when he was wounded in battle, and his soldiers therefore were in some danger, the Senate decided that it must send Papirius Cursor there as Dictator, to make up for the disability of the Consul. It was necessary that the Dictator be named by Fabius, who was Consul with the armies in Tuscany. Fearing that he would not be willing to name Papirius, who was his enemy, the Senators sent two ambassadors to beg that, laying aside his private hatred, he would for the benefit of the state consent to name him. Fabius did so, moved by love for his native city, though with silence and in many other ways he indicated that such a nomination was hard for him to bear.[1] He may be an example to all who wish to be considered good citizens.

1. Livy 9. 38.

CHAPTER 48. WHEN AN ENEMY SEEMS TO BE MAKING A GREAT MISTAKE, WE SHOULD BELIEVE IT HIDES A TRICK

When Fulvius was left as Legate with the Roman army in Tuscany, since the Consul had gone to Rome for some ceremonies, the Tuscans, to see if they could catch him by a stratagem, put an ambush near the Roman camp and sent some soldiers in the dress of shepherds, with large flocks, who were to come into the view of the Roman army. So disguised, they approached the stockade of the camp. The Legate, puzzled by their presumption, which he thought unreasonable, managed to discover their deception. Thus the Tuscan plan was ruined.[1] It is fitting to observe here that the general of an army should put no faith in a mistake the enemy make openly; it always hides some stratagem, since it is unreasonable for men to be so incautious. But often the desire for victory so blinds men's perceptions that they see nothing except what appears to their advantage.

The French, after defeating the Romans at the Allia, when they reached Rome and found the gates open and without guards, waited

1. Livy 10. 3, 4.

all that day and that night without going in; they feared a stratagem and could not believe there was in Roman hearts such cowardice and imprudence that they would abandon their native city.[2]

[*A Florentine instance*]

When in 1508 the Florentines were besieging Pisa, they held as prisoner Alfonso del Mutolo, a Pisan citizen. He promised that if he were free he would deliver to the Florentines one of the gates of Pisa. He was freed. Then, to carry the business along, he came many times to speak with the appointees of the Florentine commissioners, coming not secretly but openly and accompanied by Pisans, whom he left waiting while he talked with the Florentines. He did this in such a way that his treacherous purpose could be inferred, because it was unreasonable, if his dealings were honest, that he would carry them on openly. But their wish to take Pisa so blinded the Florentines that, going according to his arrangements to the Lucca Gate, to their disgrace they left there many of their leaders and other soldiers, as a result of the said Alfonso's simulated treachery.

2. *Livy* 5. 39.

CHAPTER 49. A REPUBLIC, IF SHE IS TO BE KEPT FREE, REQUIRES NEW ACTS OF FORESIGHT EVERY DAY; AND FOR WHAT GOOD QUALITIES QUINTUS FABIUS WAS CALLED MAXIMUS

[*Rome's severity in punishment*]

It must be, as I have said before, that every day in a large city emergencies will occur that have need of a physician, and in proportion as they are more important, a wiser physician is needed. If ever in any city there were such emergencies, they occurred in Rome—strange and unexpected ones. Such was the emergency when it seemed that all the Roman wives had conspired against their husbands to kill them—there were so many who did poison them and so many who had prepared poison for doing so. Such was also the conspiracy of the Bacchanals, discovered in the time of the Macedonian war, in which actually thousands of men and women were concerned. If it had not been discovered it would have been dangerous to the city, or if the Romans had not been accustomed to punish large numbers of those who did wrong. If countless other indica-tions did not show the greatness of that republic and the power of her deeds, the punishments she inflicted on wrong-doers would show them. She did not hesitate to punish with death a whole legion at once, and an entire city, and to banish eight or ten thousand men under penalties so strange that they could not be carried out by one man alone, much less by so many. For example, those soldiers who fought unsuccessfully at Cannae she banished to Sicily, requiring them to find lodgings outside the cities and to eat standing up.[1]

[Decimation as a military punishment]

Of all her actions the most terrible was the decimation of an army, in which by lot one out of every ten men in a whole army was put to death. It is not possible, chastising a multitude, to find a punishment more terrifying than this. When a multitude commits a crime in which the one responsible is not evident, all cannot be pun-ished because there are too many. To punish part of them and leave part unpunished would wrong those who are punished, and the unpunished would have courage to do wrong another time. But if the tenth part are killed by lot, when all deserve it, he who is pun-ished grieves for his fate; he who is not punished fears that another time the lot will fall on him, and is careful not to do wrong.

The poisoners and the Bacchanals, then, were punished as their crimes deserved. Though in a republic these sicknesses produce bad effects, they are not fatal, because there is almost always time to cure them. But there is not time in those sicknesses that have to do with the government. If they are not cured by a prudent man, they ruin the city.

[Quintus Fabius Maximus]

In Rome, through the liberality practiced by the Romans in giving citizenship to foreigners, so many children were born in new families that soon such numbers of them obtained the right to vote that the administration was growing uncertain and moving away from the policies and men formerly important. When Quintus Fabius, who was Censor, realized this, he put all those new families—

1. Livy 8. 18; 39. 41; 23. 25.

the cause of the difficulty—into four tribes, so that, shut into a small space, they could not infect all Rome. This matter was clearly under stood by Fabius, who applied to it, without any revolution, a good remedy, so well received by that commonwealth that he deserved to be called great.[2]

2. Livy 9. 46.

www.ingramcontent.com/pod-product-compliance
Lightning Source LLC
Chambersburg PA
CBHW030854270326
41929CB00008B/420